Summer Stock!

Also by Martha S. LoMonaco:

Every Week, a Broadway Revue: The Tamiment Playhouse, 1921–1960 (1992)

Summer Stock!

An American Theatrical Phenomenon

Martha Schmoyer LoMonaco

Foreword
by
Marian Seldes

palgrave
macmillan

SUMMER STOCK!
© Martha Schmoyer LoMonaco, 2004

First published 2004 by
PALGRAVE MACMILLAN™
175 Fifth Avenue, New York, N.Y. 10010 and
Houndmills, Basingstoke, Hampshire, England RG21 6XS
Companies and representatives throughout the world

PALGRAVE MACMILLAN is the global academic imprint of the Palgrave Macmillan division of St. Martin's Press, LLC and of Palgrave Macmillan Ltd. Macmillan® is a registered trademark in the United States, United Kingdom and other countries. Palgrave is a registered trademark in the European Union and other countries.

ISBN 1–4039–6542–0 hardback

Library of Congress Cataloging-in-Publication Data
LoMonaco, Martha Schmoyer.
    Summer stock! : an American theatrical phenomenon / by Martha Schmoyer LoMonaco.
        p. cm.
    Includes bibliographical references and index.
    ISBN 1–4039–6542–0
    1. Summer theater—United States—History—20th century. I. Title.

PN2269.L66 2004
792.02′24—dc22   2003063242

A catalogue record for this book is available from the British Library.

Design by Newgen Imaging Systems (P) Ltd., Chennai, India.

First edition: June 2004
10 9 8 7 6 5 4 3 2 1

Printed in the United States of America.

Dedication

This book is dedicated to everyone who ever worked in American summer stock theatre. Some of us went on to professional careers in the theatre as producers, performers, directors, designers, stage managers, technicians, front-of-house personnel, administrators, and educators, while others used the skills gained in the rough-and-tumble world of summer stock in a myriad of professions. Many of us worked at summer stock theatres that are not mentioned in this book, not even in the appendix, which enumerates as many theatres for which I had information. I suspect that in addition to the 800 theatres listed, there were hundreds more that survived only a season or two, which I unintentionally have neglected. The fact is that summer stock theatre was, for much of the twentieth century, the most prevalent and vibrant theatre in the United States. With the possible exception of the short-lived Federal Theatre Project of the late 1930s, which was part of Franklin Delano Roosevelt's Works Progress Administration, summer stock, in the aggregate, was truly America's national theatre.

I hope you find this history fulfilling and compelling, and true to your personal experiences. No doubt, you will share many of these memories, since the challenges and joys of producing one-a-week stock steadily for three or four months are very similar from theatre to theatre. Cherish both your memories and the importance of this history. Summer stock is our common legacy to the American theatre.

MARTHA SCHMOYER LOMONACO
March 2004

Contents

Acknowledgements

Virtually everyone I know has a summer stock story. Part of that, of course, is that I work in theatre and live in the northeastern United States, the traditional locus of summer stock theatres. Yet, even those people who aren't theatre professionals have a personal tale—some actually performed while others ushered (one friend even wore costumes while ushering that related to the theme of the show!), painted scenery, lent properties, hung posters in shop windows, and made a point of seeing the shows. Their memories are fond and often frolicsome, and all have helped me, in many significant ways, to shape this book.

The impetus for this book came out of my research for my earlier book on the history of Pennsylvania's Tamiment Playhouse, which was a significant summer theatre (but not summer stock) that produced original weekly revues, some of which became the basis for television's legendary program, *Your Show of Shows*. So many of the people I interviewed also had worked in summer stock, and they bemoaned the fact that its history had yet to be recorded. To all of you, here it is—finally—with my best wishes.

The research for this book extended over ten years and entailed on-site visits to many theatres, where I toured everything from backstage to scene shop to business office; oral history interviews with theatre personnel, past and present; lots of digging in formal and informal archives; visits to the surrounding area to better understand the environment in which the theatre thrived; and seeing as many summer stock productions as possible. Although all of these visits were delightful and proved extremely beneficial for my understanding of summer stock, many are not recorded in this book, other than in the acknowledgements and list of interviewees, which follows the bibliography. I heartily thank everyone, not only those people I formally interviewed, but also the many people who spent hours talking to me and taking me through their theatres, and who helped to make my visit as comfortable and congenial as possible. I regret that I was unable to tell all of your stories here. Finally, the *New York Times* graciously published an author's query in the Sunday Book Review section, which elicited well over a hundred responses. My thanks to all of you who took the time to write and share your summer stock memories that have been immeasurably helpful.

There were also many archivists and librarians who not only assisted with my every need, but also remembered what I was working on and would make suggestions for further research. I especially salute the staff of the Billy Rose Theatre Collection at the New York Public Library for the Performing Arts at Lincoln Center, who have cheerfully dealt with me for years, particularly Donald Fowle, who invariably had yet another helpful suggestion every time I walked in the door. I am also deeply appreciative to Maryann Chach and the staff at the Shubert Archive; Ben Brewster and the staff at the Wisconsin Center for Film and Theater Research at the University of Wisconsin-Madison; Geraldine Duclow at the Free Library of Philadelphia; Margaret Adams, former archivist for the Cape Playhouse Archives; Polly Pierce of the Stockbridge Public Library, Stockbridge, Massachusetts; Barbara Rumsey of the Boothbay Region Historical Society, Boothbay Harbor, Maine; Warner Lord at the Charlotte L. Evarts Memorial Archives, Madison Town Hall, Madison, Connecticut; Jim Crabtree at the Peterborough Historical Society, Peterborough, New Hampshire; and the staffs of the Harvard Theatre Collection, Yale School of Drama Library, Library of Congress, and DiMenna-Nyselius Library at Fairfield University.

Another important resource for this study is the Actors' Equity Association Archive in the Performing Arts Collections of the Robert F. Wagner Labor Archives at New York University. Since I was the archivist for this collection in the 1980s, it was particularly satisfying to make extensive use of these papers years later as a researcher. I would like to thank my processing archivist, Jean Tepsic, without whom the collection would never have been finished, as well as the many graduate students from NYU's archival program in the Department of History who assisted us in cleaning and organizing the papers. I also would like to acknowledge the tremendous help and guidance of the late Debra E. Bernhardt, who, as the indefatigable Director of the Wagner Archives, made sure that this collection would be preserved for posterity.

Thanks are extended to the Faculty Research Committee and Humanities Institute, both at Fairfield University, for their support of my research and travel as well as awarding me the sabbatical leave that allowed me to complete this manuscript. Thanks also go to George Mayer, who put aside copies of the entire run of *Blueprint for Summer Theatre* at the NYPL for the Performing Arts book sale, knowing that I'd want to buy them; Helaine Feldman, Associate Editor of *Equity News*, for keeping me apprised of important current issues; Jay Buss, a Fairfield colleague who recommended several volumes of American economic history; Dr. Mary Douglas Dirks, for valuable research assistance; Richard Babcock, whose expertise on historic barns was invaluable; Jason Rubin, who made sure that I didn't miss the Totem Pole Playhouse; John Frick, who made sure that I got to the Stockbridge Public Library; and Brooks McNamara, who instilled a love of American popular entertainments and taught me how to write its history. I also want to thank my editor, Michael Flamini, his assistant, Matthew Ashford, the associate production manager, Sonia Wilson, and the rest of the staff at Palgrave Macmillan for their enthusiastic support of my work. Finally, I would like to thank my parents, Roy and Gertrude Schmoyer, for taking me to see summer stock as a child, where I first fell in love with this wonderful form of theatre.

I cannot thank Don B. Wilmeth enough for his decade-long encouragement and research assistance with this study. He also edited much of the manuscript and made many incisive suggestions for improvements.

This book would not have happened without the love, support, computer expertise, and ruthless editorial advice of my husband, Karl G. Ruling. As he finished reading the much-revised last chapter of this book, he burst into tears, perhaps because it was finally over but more likely (I hope) because he really liked it. Thank you, Karl, for everything you are and for all that you have given—and continue to give—me.

List of Illustrations

Foreword

Martha LoMonaco's endearing dedication of this book to those of us who worked in stock companies means a great deal to me. This cornucopia of remembrance and detail is indeed a phenomenon in American theatre history, and it touches me to relive so much of my early theatre life in these pages. From the time I graduated from The Neighborhood Players in 1947, the stock companies became my school. My first engagement was at the Cambridge Summer Theatre, and I continued working in summer and winter stock through 2000. I did not expect to recognize so many parts of my early career in these pages, but as I read—and reread—this fascinating book, the memories of certain theatres, actors and actresses, and directors sprang to vivid life.

To think that a young actress had the opportunity to work with Elissa Landi, Libby Holman, Lillian Harvey, Blanche Yurka, Dame May Whitty, Bert Lahr (who got me my first Equity card), Victor Jory, Neil Hamilton, Buddy Ebsen, Judy Holliday, and twice with Edward Everett Horton and Ruth Chatterton and Christopher Plummer in plays ranging from *The Importance of Being Earnest* to *The Little Foxes* to *Springtime for Henry* and *Lady in the Dark*. Many of the engagements were in plays that had been successful in New York; others were tryouts of new plays. In 1994, Edward Albee's *Three Tall Women* had its American premiere at the Three River Arts Repertory in Woodstock, New York.

Dear reader, dear audience, I know that you will be as entranced as I am with this book.

Dear Martha, thank you.

MARIAN SELDES
January 2004

Preface

The term "summer stock" refers to a particular type of summertime entertainment that evolved in the northeastern United States during the 1920s and 1930s. It is an umbrella term for those independent theatres with a resident company presenting a number of different plays in weekly or biweekly repertory, either in a permanent house or on tour, between the months of June and September. The theatres were established in attractive rural environments near the new resorts developed for middle- and working-class clientele who, thanks to advances in corporate management and federal legislation, now enjoyed annual paid vacations. Wherever city dwellers fled to escape the summer heat at sylvan lakes, beaches, and mountainsides, a summer stock theatre was likely to appear to provide nightly entertainment.

During the early years of the twentieth century, Americans witnessed the fruits of their own cultural maturation as creative artists. Prior to this time, the American theatre and allied arts were largely an imitation of British and European models. Little had been created that truly represented the American character until Eugene O'Neill's first plays premiered in the late 1910s at Provincetown's Wharf Theatre on Cape Cod, Massachusetts. Although the Wharf was more properly an outgrowth of the "little theatre" or "art theatre" movement pioneered by devoted amateurs, the fact that it operated at a beach resort in the summer months provided strong encouragement to entrepreneurs eager to start their own theatres. These ventures became so successful, both artistically and financially, that hundreds sprang up during the next 40 years, frequently by converting a nearby barn or other spacious building into a rustic but workable theatre. They ranged widely in artistic quality and intent, but all fulfilled the dual purpose of providing much-needed work for theatre artists and low-cost entertainment for vacationers. They also brought legitimate theatre to remote areas, thus affording many local residents an opportunity to see professional productions for the first time. Hence, summer stock, as America's first truly regional theatre, had a major effect on the cultural, economic, and sociological development of the United States.

Summer stock was, and continues to be, a vital force in the American theatre industry. From the 1930s through the early 1960s, summer stock was the leading employer of theatre professionals in the United States. More actors, directors, designers, and technicians worked in legitimate theatre during the summer months than at any other time of the year. It also has provided a place for young theatre artists to garner their first professional credentials and to learn their craft. It is still true that most theatre professionals, including this author, have worked at some time during their careers in summer stock.

The best of the stock houses became vital cultural centers for their communities, popular with permanent residents and tourists alike. These theatres exposed hundreds of thousands of people with little access to live professional theatre to new American plays and performance styles and, occasionally, to important European work. They also proved a boon to the local economy because playgoers would patronize area restaurants, hotels, and merchants. Many stock theatres became tourist destinations in themselves and thus brought pride and prosperity to the towns that supported them. Although the heyday of stock ended in the 1960s, those venues with strong community bases have carried on, reinventing themselves as necessary to continue to attract audiences in the twenty-first century.

Despite summer stock's importance to American theatre and society in the twentieth century, it has been largely ignored by historians. It suffers from the same negative image that, until recent years, impeded the serious study of other popular entertainments, such as burlesque, vaudeville, and circus, which were nonliterary, commercial amusements designed for mass consumption. For most of its history, summer stock, like all popular entertainments, was produced by professional showpeople for profit. It also, like the rest, specialized in light, nonintellectual shows that would delight rather than challenge audiences. Hence it has been viewed as little more than fluff, unworthy of consideration as serious art.

Summer stock, however, has always operated as legitimate theatre, offering fully scripted plays. This fact alone should have distinguished it from other popular entertainments, which are performance rather than textually based. Yet, since a typical stock season featured revivals of recent Broadway hits, not-so-recent Broadway hits, and what are commonly termed "old chestnuts"—hit shows of the distant past—it was accorded the same respect as a second-run movie house. Add to this that many of these shows were laugh-out-loud comedies, melodramatic murder mysteries, and, in later years, frothy musicals, all of which were mounted quickly without benefit of new interpretation, and the entire form quickly became negligible to a chronicler of culture. Historians, however, finally have accorded serious examination to nonscripted entertainments, such as minstrel shows and dime museums, as wholly American fabrications that reflected unique facets of our national character. Certainly, summer stock also was distinctively American and, therefore, worthy of historical documentation.

A final important point is that summer stock theatres were in rural, frequently remote, locales, far from urban centers. The term "regional," which bears a pejorative connotation, is still employed to lump together all professional, resident, repertory theatres outside of New York City. Although these theatres may do excellent work, they frequently are most valued for productions they send to Broadway. Very few summer stock theatres introduced future Broadway hits, and even those that did, like Lakewood's premiere of *Life With Father*, which still holds the record as Broadway's longest running nonmusical show, were conveniently forgotten.

In addition to the tendency to dismiss summer stock as rural populist fodder, there is another reason that its history has yet to be recorded. Because summer stock was not properly a movement but simply a broad term for all theatres operating during the summer months on the model of nineteenth-century stock companies, it is an amorphous and unwieldy topic. As Samuel Marx commented in a 1939 survey of summer stock theatres, it's hard to make generalizations about them "because every summer theatre is an entity, having no connection with any other summer theatre."[1] Although in later years when many theatres formed associations to co-produce and tour shows on a prescribed circuit, each summer venue was still a unique operation that reflected the personalities and interests of its producing artists and supporting community. Hence, finding the common threads that link their individual histories is a daunting task.

This is not to say, however, that a comprehensive history has not been attempted and that at least one major cultural institution found it a topic worthy of funding. In 1969, the Rockefeller Foundation awarded a $12,900 grant to Day Tuttle, a seasoned summer stock manager and sometime Broadway producer, to write "a history of the golden age of summer theatre in the United States," a period that it defined as the late 1920s through World War II. "We think the summer theatre represents a part of our history that ought to be captured through the eyes of a man who was a leading character in that field during that period," a spokesman explained to the *New York Times*.[2] Unfortunately, Tuttle never finished the manuscript. Although a few chapters are extant, they are anecdotal and largely nostalgic reminiscences that exhibit little evidence of historical research.

Another researcher, seeking a master's degree at the Florida State University School of Theatre, completed a thesis titled "The Development of the

Summer Stock Movement in America: 1890–1941." Although the student, Rebecca Garrison Wong, relied heavily on articles in *Theatre Arts Monthly* and *Variety* as primary research, her work is a noble attempt to begin to tell the story. A fellow graduate student of mine at New York University briefly contemplated writing his doctoral dissertation on summer stock until he did a bit of research. "I decided that I wanted to actually finish my degree during this century," he declared, clearly daunted by the enormity of the task.

Although, other than Wong's thesis, there are no attempts at comprehensive histories, there are several published monographs on select theatres. Most were commissioned by the theatres themselves to commemorate a notable anniversary year, but others are academic theses and dissertations. Two books devoted to individual theatres are of particular interest. Norris Houghton's *But Not Forgotten* chronicles the history of the short-lived University Players Guild, which trained a sizable number of theatre luminaries including Josh Logan, Henry Fonda, Jimmy Stewart, and Houghton himself. Charlotte Harmon, who founded and produced the Chapel Playhouse, a summer stock theatre in Guilford, Connecticut, wrote a chatty memoir commemorating the experience, *Broadway in a Barn*. Co-written with Rosemary Taylor, it is mostly filled with gossip about the famous actors who starred in her productions, but it does provide insight into the daily mayhem involved in running one of the star-circuit houses of the 1940s and '50s.

Many theatrical memoirs, penned by celebrated actors, producers, and directors, devote several pages, if not whole chapters, to summer stock experiences. Notable among these are Lawrence Langner's *The Magic Curtain*, Richard Aldrich's *Gertrude Lawrence as Mrs. A*, Dorothy Stickney's *Openings and Closings*, and Harold J. Kennedy's *No Pickle, No Performance*. The business aspects of summer stock, along with a short history of the form, are recorded in Stephen Langley's very useful *Theatre Management and Production in America*. Langley is also responsible for the summer stock entry in the *Cambridge Guide to American Theatre*, co-edited by Don B. Wilmeth and Tice L. Miller. All of these sources are listed in the bibliography, and many are quoted throughout this book.

I embarked on this project as an outgrowth of my first book, *Every Week, A Broadway Revue: The Tamiment Playhouse, 1921–1960* (Greenwood, 1992), a study of the history and significance of the Tamiment Playhouse, which was, arguably, America's most influential summer theatre. It was not, however, a summer stock theatre because it focused on the development of original work in the form of short sketches, dance, and musical pieces, presented in weekly revues. Many of the artists who worked at Tamiment, and whom I interviewed for my book, had also worked in summer stock, and all lamented the fact that its history had yet to be told. This book will, I hope, fill this considerable gap in the history of American theatre, American studies, culture studies, and travel and leisure studies of the mid-twentieth century. It also should prove useful to writers of regional and local history; current arts and entertainment professionals, amateurs, and enthusiasts; sociologists; community planners and outreach personnel who are interested in how summer theatres affect the economic, social, and cultural life of their communities; and people interested in the creative process—how art happens— particularly with what, traditionally in summer stock, has been limited time, resources, and money.

What really compelled me to write this book, however, is to tell the story of the extraordinary people I have interviewed and researched who made summer stock their life's work. Although these people were well known within the theatre industry during stock's heyday, most are now forgotten or are, at best, remembered only by ardent fans who fondly recall magical evenings in their theatres. This book is an attempt to immortalize these stalwart theatre professionals, most of whom were truly larger-than-life characters, who had the courage and stamina to take an old barn, church, or carriage house in a small rural town and turn it into a successful theatre. It was at their theatres that most twentieth-century Americans saw the latest Broadway hits and were introduced to the excitement of live performance. In an era after the demise of touring road companies and before the proliferation of the regional theatre movement of the 1960s, summer stock was the popular regional American theatre. Without these indefatigable souls, it never would have happened.

Introduction

Summer Stock: An All-American Tradition

Rehearsals for a new musical, "Falling in Love," by writer/director/choreographer and dancer extraordinaire, Joe D. Ross, have been going on daily in the old barn, newly rechristened the Falbury Barn Theatre. Chickens and roosters scamper amid dancers hoofin' in the hay, cows nod benevolently and occasionally wander upstage during the love scene, a hay wagon is appropriated as a rehearsal prop stand-in for a swan boat, and the leading man conks his head on a lantern suspended from a crossbeam. When not rehearsing, the city-slicker actors bumble their way through farmhand chores including gathering (and breaking) eggs, slopping hogs, and (unsuccessfully) milking cows, all to the disdain of the local farmers and the hilarity of their comrades-in-arms.

After the company quits for the evening, the farm's starry-eyed proprietor, Jane, walks out on the dramatically darkened stage, bathed in pools of softly colored light. Joe emerges from the shadows to catch her trying out a few dance steps; they laugh and romance is in the air. They speak of the magic of theatre. "But wait till opening night when the people come in," Joe exclaims. "Even the air gets exciting. You can feel them out there. You can't see them but you can feel them—it's like electricity." "You really love this, don't you?" Jane asks earnestly. "What, show business?" Joe rejoins. "There's nothing else in the world. If I couldn't be up here, I'd work backstage or sell tickets." Joe leads her stage right where he picks up a tube from the make-up table. "Now, close your eyes," he gently commands. "Take a whiff of that. You like it? Sure you do. It's greasepaint." Jane laughingly agrees. Joe warns "Go easy, it's very potent stuff. You smell it once too often, it gets way down inside of you. You can wipe it off your face, all right, but you'll never get it out of your blood."

The production is beset by problems, despite the non-stop fun and excitement of summer stock. Both of the show's stars take off, unannounced, for what they think will be greater glories in New York. "This is not theatre, just a little barnyard entertainment," the male lead sniffs. By opening night, however, the old barn miraculously has transformed into a sophisticated theatre and Jane has become Joe's leading lady, on and offstage. The show is a hit, the right couples have finally gotten together, and everyone, we're sure, will live happily ever after. And, for many Americans, this was the glamour of *Summer Stock*, immortalized on screen by Judy Garland, Gene Kelly, and Metro-Goldwyn-Mayer.[1]

Hollywood glorified something it called summer stock, which, in turn, became the real thing for the moviegoing public. Even those filmgoers who frequented summer stock theatres were probably happy to accept the Hollywood version of their summertime recreation. Hollywood's idyllic notions were formed largely by popular journalism, which, even from stock's humble beginnings in the 1920s, painted an entertaining and romantic portrait of this new form of theatre. This list of euphemisms and amusing descriptives, gleaned from newspaper and magazine articles published from the 1920s through the 1950s, provides an insightful glance into the dichotomous marriage of theatre and farm. Venues were called barn, barnyard, and stable theatres, and straw hats, bucolic mimehouses, dramadens, alfalfa acting cells, and white pants playshops. Producers and directors were known as barnyard Belascos, fresh air entrepreneurs, and rural Reinhardts; the theatre companies collectively were barnstormers. Summer stock was variously known as the straw hat; hayseed; cowbarn; silo; and citronella circuit; the rural rialto; the poison ivy belt; the rustic trail; drama in the dell or in the barn belt; countrified culture; and St. Genesius Over the Cowshed, a reference to the patron saint of actors in a decidedly new locale. Farm, farmyard, and farmer jokes abounded, most capitalizing on a dichotomy between the plain, commonsense farm folks and the fast-talking city slickers who put on the shows. Most were similar to this pundit's take on the farmer's eagerness to turn over his barn to playmakers: "It was only later that he realized that his cows made the same noise—and gave milk besides. The only things milked in the cowbarns were the curtain-calls."[2]

The real summer stock is a far more complex and less glamorous enterprise than Hollywood cared to portray. Yet, there is a degree of truth in the film's romantic notions of finding fame and fortune in the honest, unspoiled countryside that is miles, both geographically and psychologically, from the competitive, industrialized city. By the 1920s, when summer stock theatres were, quite literally, displacing cows and hay in old barns, theatre in America had become a tough, highly competitive industry. Aspiring actors, directors, designers, and producers, eager for a career, had little choice but to go to New York and audition or submit a résumé to one of the large syndicates that controlled commercial theatre nationwide. The dream of starting their own theatre, where they would make all the artistic and financial decisions, plus enjoy a scenic, healthful, vacation-like environment, had considerable appeal. The fact that many of these new entrepreneurs were so successful legitimized the enduring romance; from the late 1930s through the early 1960s, summer stock was the largest employer of actors and other theatre personnel in the United States. Young hopefuls could mount theatre in a barn and find success—perhaps not of the caliber of Garland and Kelly, but they could make a living in the profession they loved.

Although the term "summer stock" has been loosely employed to refer to all summertime entertainments, technically speaking it refers to the resident troupe of actors and other stage personnel presenting a number of different plays in weekly or biweekly repertory, either in a permanent house or on tour, between the months of June and September. These theatre companies were founded predominantly in rural sections of the northeastern United States, from Maine to Virginia and as far west as Pennsylvania, to service vacationers at the newly developed middle- and working-class resorts of the 1920s and 1930s. Wherever city dwellers fled to the countryside to escape the heat, chances were a summer stock theatre would soon appear.

The company owned "stock" scenery, props, and costumes that would be used and reused throughout the summer season in an attempt to keep production costs low. Between six and eight actors were engaged for their specialty "lines"—leading, character, and juvenile players of both sexes being the most common—and were cast according to type in each production. Small roles were assumed by company apprentices and interns, who also built and painted scenery, managed costumes and properties, and did just about everything else the theatre required in exchange for room and board and the honor of working with theatre professionals. Many apprentices, in fact, paid for the privilege of working with the company, which frequently would provide formal classes in acting and stagecraft to enhance their educational experience.

Most theatres played one-a-week stock, offering a different play every week throughout a summer season of 8 to as many as 14 or 15 weeks. Many of the plays were revivals of recent Broadway hits that had name recognition for audiences. Most companies presented comedies, romances, mysteries, and thrillers—so-called light entertainment, although the occasional serious drama would also appear. Some theatres also premiered new plays, particularly in the early years of stock (1920s–1930s), in the hopes of transferring a new hit property to Broadway. Still others were self-described "serious" theatres that offered significant dramas from the world repertoire, including works by Shakespeare, Shaw, Ibsen, and Strindberg.

Summer stock was essentially a reincarnation of the nineteenth-century stock companies prevalent in both the United States and England. Sadly, the history of summer stock paralleled that of its precursors all too closely by following the same pattern from resident stock to star system to combination company (known here as "star package" or "package tour") to eventual demise, but within the abbreviated span of a few decades. Since summer stock was dependent on the rapidly developing—and fluctuating—tourist market, it enjoyed even less stability than its predecessors. The heyday of summer stock, consequently, was quite short, lasting only from the 1920s through the 1960s. Although there were precursors and a significant number of survivors—summer stock, in the broader sense of summertime theatrical entertainments, is thriving into the twenty-first century—the golden age of summer stock effectively ended as Americans sought more exotic vacation destinations in the 1960s and the price of keeping theatres open became increasingly prohibitive.

Although theatrical stock originated and flourished in England, summer stock is a uniquely American phenomenon that combined an independent artistic spirit with capitalist incentives. Although there is summer entertainment all over the world, where performers and audiences alike take advantage of the good weather to enjoy outdoor venues, there was and is nothing else like American summer stock. Even in Britain, which has had a solid stock tradition both in London and regionally for several centuries, a separate summer stock tradition has never developed.

A confluence of events and conditions in the early decades of the twentieth century contributed to summer stock's development. First and foremost was the growth of hundreds of resorts and vacationlands, particularly in the northeastern United States, to service middle- and working-class Americans who were now enjoying annual paid vacations. A second, related rationale was the "back-to-nature" movement, which had begun in the mid-nineteenth century as a philosophical excuse for the idle rich to take a country holiday. Its vigorous renewal in the early twentieth century as an answer to the malaise of city workers helped both the new resorts and their adjunct theatres to grow. Third, the new performance venues afforded opportunities to young theatre artists eager to develop their craft and get professional experience in front of paying audiences. They also were happy to have work, since the concurrent effects of the Great Depression and the burgeoning film industry reduced the number of available jobs in live theatre.

A fourth factor in the development of summer stock was the influence of the "little theatre" movement of the 1910s. Intellectually minded amateurs, disgusted by the prurience, commercialism, and frippery of much of what appeared on the American stage, founded their own small theatres, which were inspired by the new European art houses featuring the work of serious modern playwrights. Perhaps the most famous of these was the Provincetown Playhouse, but quite a few less famous but equally fervent art theatres sprang up in remote locales. These will be discussed in more detail in chapter 1.

Finally, the rural locales where summer stock thrived guaranteed minimal competition from the new mediated entertainments of film, radio, and, later, television, which were drawing the audiences and revenues away from live theatre. There were no cinemas in the hinterlands and vacationers, even if they had radios—and later television—simply preferred to go out. What better place to go than the local rustic barn that offered entertainment, culture, and nature in one charming package?

Summer stock never would have developed without the tremendous boom in travel and leisure for the middle and working classes in the first decades of the twentieth century. "Leisure was primarily a by-product of industrialism," according to sociologist Foster Dulles. "The reduction in the hours of work had taken place almost automatically as the application of mechanical power enabled society to satisfy its normal needs in progressively less working time."[3] By the 1920s, the typical workweek was 48 hours with a half-day's work on Saturdays and, for increasing numbers of employees, a week or two of paid vacation. Economic hardships occasioned by the Great Depression gradually reduced the average workweek in an attempt to distribute jobs more equitably throughout the populace. As a result, in 1937 Congress enacted the Fair Labor Standards Act to normalize a 40-hour week. Interestingly, the Depression also spurred a dramatic increase in the number of companies that offered employees paid vacations. However, as historian Cindy Aron points out, the apparent corporate beneficence was motivated mostly by the hope of increased profits in a climate of growing union strength and government regulation. While experts argued that rested workers were more efficient, lawmakers were considering legislation that, in emulation of countries around the world, would mandate annual vacations with pay. "The decision to extend vacations to industrial workers," Aron contends, "came primarily from businesses hoping simultaneously to increase the bottom line while forestalling union organizing."[4] These actions, however, resulted in both free time and discretionary income to be enjoyed by the working classes. Dulles describes how "working men and working women—factory operatives, plumbers, waitresses, bank clerks, farm-hands, stenographers, storekeepers, subway guards, mill-hands, garment workers, office boys, truck-drivers—found countless pleasures and amusements readily available that had once been restricted to the privileged few."[5]

The resorts and vacationlands that eventually would embrace most American workers and concurrently spawn the development of summer stock theatres began appearing in the decades following the Civil War. Initially, however, these were designed to accommodate the new middle classes. The growth of large corporations, mass retailers, and an expanding government bureaucracy propelled a demand for educated white-collar workers who joined the ranks of lawyers, physicians, and small business owners. Although salaries within this group varied widely—the professionals were earning substantially more than the government clerks—all shared the belief that an inherent privilege of being middle class included the possibility of a summer holiday. Furthermore, their employers, barraged with medical and sociological warnings about the dangers of overwork for "brain workers," seemed to agree that at least one week's paid vacation was a necessity.[6] Consequently, resorts were built to accommodate these vacationers. Aron quotes an 1889 issue of *Century Magazine*: "'Summer hotels are everywhere. They form an almost continuous line along the coast of New England and the Middle States. One mountain region after another has succumbed to their invasion.'"[7] In the twentieth century, the more prosperous among the middle class, who had long been accustomed to taking annual holidays, began to build or buy modest cottages or bungalows so "their families could enjoy domestic rather than hotel life along lakeside or seashore."[8] These bungalow colonies, filled with educated, cultured vacationers who regularly attended the theatre at home, proved the greatest lure for the new summer stock ventures.

Since theatre box offices sell tickets to all, however, one cannot dismiss the importance of the new vacationlands created for the lower-middle and working classes, who could not afford their own summer homes. Hotels, motels, and serviced campgrounds were built to suit every budget, mode of transportation (motels and campgrounds were particularly geared toward travelers with cars), and length of stay, and these proliferated in the same congenial locales that housed the more privileged vacationers. Since most summer stock theatres featured light entertainments that changed weekly, they equally attracted the long- and short-stay vacationers. In addition, the theatres normally would do their change-over between shows on Monday or Tuesday, thus affording most people the possibility of seeing two different productions in one week.

These new opportunities for travel and leisure coupled with the back-to-nature movement, propelled the new vacationers to rural areas far removed from the hustle and bustle of city life. Historian Peter Schmitt traces this movement from its intellectual and Romantic roots among the eighteenth- and nineteenth-century aristocracy to its reinvention as an Arcadian ideal by the urban middle class of the early twentieth century. "Ordinary city dwellers longed for contact with the natural world," he avers, "and looked upon fields and forests as inspirational resources for their urban life."[9] Schmitt cites volumes of popular literature produced from the late 1890s onward that encouraged urban folk to adopt the "ideal life . . . which combines something of the social and intellectual advantages and physical comforts of the city with the inspiration and peaceful joys of the country."[10] Richard Hofstadter, in his influential study of turn-of-the-century America, *The Age of Reform*, terms this phenomenon "the agrarian myth" in which Americans paid "a kind of homage . . . to the fancied innocence of their origins." "The more commercial this society became," Hofstadter contends, "the more reason it found to cling in imagination to the noncommercial agrarian values."[11]

The "nature lovers," as they were unabashedly known, became more plentiful as both they and American industry prospered and as their devotion earned high-ranking endorsements. Schmitt cites a number of influential sources, all of which attest to the extremely high profile of this movement. For example, President Calvin Coolidge held a National Conference on Outdoor Recreation in 1924, during which he told delegates from 128 organizations "that the right to outdoor life was as important as the right to work." Coolidge's imminent successor, Herbert Hoover, in addressing the 1926 conference, declared that "the spiritual uplift, the good will, cheerfulness, and optimism that accompanies every expedition to the outdoors is the peculiar spirit that our people need in troublous times of suspicion and doubt." It had become not only the American's privilege but his duty to seek outdoor recreation, and what Henry S. Canby termed the "note of woods longing" became central to American thought.[12] Additionally, the increased production of automobiles, which grew from four thousand in 1900 to four million by 1923, aided mobility to sites previously deemed inaccessible.[13]

Accordingly, wealthier Americans would purchase abandoned farms and turn them into bourgeois equivalents of English country estates; the middle classes built their bungalow colonies; and the less well-heeled would take a one- or two-week summer holiday at a rented cottage or boarding house adjoining a scenic beach, mountain lake or idyllic wood. According to a 1930 census, there were 6,200 boarding-house farms, most of which were in New England and the Middle Atlantic states, and cottage colonies were sprouting up in all the new resort areas.[14] Historian Earl Pomeroy describes this new summer world: "The normal routine of summer set in, of afternoons on beaches and porches, of hikes to the wild berry patches, of occasional fishing and clamming expeditions, of country church-bazaars and whist-parties, of watching at the nearest dock or railroad station for weekend visitors and for fathers and grandfathers come from the city for a week or two."[15]

Most of the new summer stock entrepreneurs not only were aware of this movement but, as city workers themselves, were equally anxious for an excuse to enjoy the great outdoors. Although old barns were pragmatic choices for theatre conversions because of their large expanses, sturdy structure, and easy availability, producers quickly discovered that the rustic barn, particularly one that looked and even smelled as if the farmer had removed the last of the hay just yesterday, was also the right kind of environment to fulfill the city dwellers' longing for nature.

Significantly, theatre served not only as a postdinner destination but also as a welcome means of cultural edification to round out the holiday experience. Americans historically have suffered deep ambivalence about taking a vacation. On the one hand, they enthusiastically sought the right to take time off with pay; on the other, they feared the consequences of too much leisure and recreation. Hence, many felt the need to justify their holidays by planning a full range of activities designed to exercise and strengthen minds and bodies. This was particularly true during the Depression when people with paid vacation time felt guilty in the face of the economic hardships experienced by less fortunate Americans.[16] Hence, the artistic and cultural benefits of summer stock theatres helped assuage the vacationers' unease while enhancing the attraction of the local resorts. It was clearly a win-win situation for all concerned.

The possibility of opening and operating a summer stock theatre was attractive to the many young—and not-so-young—artists aspiring to careers in the professional theatre which, at this time, was almost exclusively based in New York City's Broadway theatre district. In the early twentieth century, virtually all professional theatre in the United States originated either on Broadway or via a touring company with a New York–based producer. Since the demise of the resident stock companies, which had all but vanished by the early 1900s, there were few paid positions outside of New York and, except in the new amateur and university-based companies, precious few opportunities to gain much-needed experience. Even within New York at this time, Broadway was it. The alternative theatre movements, which created independent producing theatres off and off-off Broadway in the 1950s and 1960s, were still decades away. There were plenty of competing entertainments which came and went with the popular tastes—vaudeville, burlesque, revue, extravaganzas, spectaculars, and the like—but what *Variety*, the principal theatrical trade paper, termed "legitimate" theatre was actually a relatively small market with an even smaller group of people running it.

The summer stock houses had the additional advantage of operating during the very season when the theatre world went dark. Broadway, as well as the regional touring houses, largely shut down in summer in emulation of the great European theatres, which traditionally suspended production for two or three months. The decision to close was equally influenced by the weather, since cities all over the United States tend to experience oppressive heat waves, particularly in July and August, and theatres were not air-conditioned prior to the 1950s. Professional theatres, especially those boasting the new technologies in lighting and other stage equipment, can get quite hot under normal circumstances; high outside temperatures can cause them to become virtual saunas. Hit plays would go on a two- or three-month hiatus, only to re-open again in the fall, usually with the same cast.

As summer stock developed and became financially successful, the New York theatre world invaded the cool country barns quickly. Theatre stars who before had taken their summers off were now traveling the stock houses on lucrative guest star contracts. Likewise, many New York theatre producers, seeing that ready money was to be made in the rural tourist trade, quickly set up shop in rustic barns. Ironically, the summer stock theatres that originally were havens for tyro talents and others who were shut out or ignored by the system were taken over by the establishment theatre. That story will be explored in greater depth in subsequent chapters.

The new mediated entertainments—motion pictures, particularly the "talkies" introduced in 1927, radio, and, after World War II, television—also had a profound effect on the theatre industry and, by extension, the development of summer stock. These enticing amusements, which allowed ordinary folks to patronize glamorous movie palaces at very reasonable rates or, more conveniently, enjoy radio and television programs in the comfort of their own homes, induced the theatre's greatest competition for audiences to date. Stephen Langley reports that the average cost of a movie ticket in 1920 was 50 cents, as opposed to $2 to see live theatre.[17] Although the most deleterious effects of the new media were suffered by popular entertainments such as revues, vaudeville, and burlesque (all of which were emulated in both form and content by radio and television), legitimate theatres still felt the pinch. Langley estimates that "between 1900 and 1932, the number of theatres presenting live entertainment decreased from about five thousand to as few as one hundred, thirty-two of which were located in New York City."[18] Hence, there were even more young hopefuls flocking to summer stock seeking both work and experience than ever before. Luckily, summer stock audiences, at least in the years before World War II, were not lured away by the new entertainments because most resorts were miles from the nearest cinema.

Although there were no movie theatres in rural areas, the film industry did have a critical effect on the transformation of many summer stock theatres via the popular "star system," which began in the mid-1930s, and, later, the even more injurious "star package" tours. Initially, the guest stars lured to summer stock were New York–based actors who were on enforced holidays when the city theatres where they were appearing closed for July and August. Business-minded summer stock managers, however, soon discovered that Hollywood movie stars, who were known to a much wider public than most stage actors, could be enticed to their theatres with lucrative contracts. They suspected, and were proven correct, that audiences would be willing to pay high ticket prices to see their favorite movie stars in the flesh. In addition, the fame and prestige afforded their theatres via the highly publicized guest stars' appearances, saved them countless advertising dollars. Many popular movie actors, however, had no formal theatre training and proved to hold little of their cinematic allure on stage. Eventually, audiences tired of seeing mediocre performances and of subsidizing their exorbitant fees. The star invasion of summer stock will be explored in detail in chapter 6.

Finally, the effects, both negative and positive, of the Great Depression on the development of summer stock must be considered. At its height in the early 1930s, the Depression generated 25 percent unemployment nationwide. Hence, competition for professional theatre jobs became all the more fierce, and many turned to the new summer stock houses as possible avenues for employment. Interestingly, the development of new venues did not seem inhibited by the Depression, which in fact proved to be a period of rapid expansion in the summer stock industry. Dulles cites studies that "conservatively estimated . . . that the American people were spending something like eight per cent of their entire income on recreation—a total of $4 billion" in 1935. About half of this money was spent on vacation travel, principally via the now ubiquitous automobiles, while the rest went for commercial amusements and recreational products. Although Dulles credits motion pictures as being, by far, the most popular amusement, he ranks legitimate theatres as number two.[19] Consequently, the summer stock theatres were in the right place at the right time to reap maximum benefits during what, for others, was an economically unstable era.

The number of summer stock theatres grew exponentially between the 1920s and 1950s. In the 1920s, there were fewer than 30 theatres. By 1936, the first year that the Actors' Equity Association began writing contracts specifically for summer stock theatres and keeping detailed records, there were 120 companies, about 50 of which were union operations. The number grew steadily each year, although well over 50 percent of the theatres were dark during World War II, largely because of gas rationing, which prohibited summer travel. Summer stock made a powerful comeback following the war, however. In 1948, there were 130 Equity companies alone; that number grew to 152 by 1950. It is safe to estimate that in addition to the union operations there were at least 100 non-Equity stock theatres. Hence, during the 1950s, there were approximately 250 to 300 stock houses operating principally in the northeastern United States each summer.

Summer stock evolved or, depending on your perspective, devolved as time went on from a seat-of-the-pants endeavor that focused on performance to a solid business industry that focused on profit. It is important to remember that summer stock of the golden era always was a commercial venture, since it flourished before the era of not-for-profit theatre companies, but the original impetus for both producers and artists was to make a living, not a killing. Producers were interested in keeping their theatres in business from year to year while artists desired a fiscally stable operation to which they could return annually. Profits, of course, were welcomed, but they were not the overriding goal.

The establishment theatre, however, viewed success and growth differently. Summer stock was deemed to be successful and, by extension, a professional operation only when it made a profit. Artistic quality was important only inasmuch as it might affect box office sales. Although theatre critics, as well as the serious-minded artists still working in summer stock, frequently lamented the proportional decrease in artistic integrity in favor of increased profits, operational decisions were guided principally by the marketplace.

Professionalism in the American theatre prior to the early 1950s meant commercial theatre; the notion of a not-for-profit professional theatre in a capitalist society was not only strange but viewed with deep suspicion. Equally suspicious was the idea of arts subsidy, particularly in the wake of the ill-fated but noble experiment of the Federal Theatre Project (FTP) during the 1930s. The FTP, run to great success by the indomitable Hallie Flanagan, was part of President Franklin Delano Roosevelt's innovative Works Progress Administration (WPA), developed to aid unemployed workers during the Depression. The FTP brought quality theatre to virtually every state of the nation and thus exposed people, many for the first time, to the magic of live performance. Although, from the perspective of the serious theatre community, the FTP was wildly successful and became the closest thing the United States has ever had to a truly national theatre, it, along with the rest of the WPA projects, fell prey to communist-baiting in Congress. By 1939, on the eve of World War II, the FTP was effectively ended amid fear that communist sympathizers were operating in what were widely viewed as socialist programs. Government subsidy of the arts would not be renewed until the creation of the National Endowment for the Arts in 1965. The arts did receive substantial support from private organizations beginning in the mid-1950s, most notably from the Ford Foundation under the spirited leadership of W. MacNeil Lowry, but by then summer stock theatres were on the wane. The new regional theatres—resident repertory theatres outside of New York, several of which grew out of old summer stock ventures—were the chief recipients of this funding.

Since summer stock, unwittingly or not, followed in the footsteps of its nineteenth-century progenitor, it is not surprising that in the profit-mad business climate following the Great Depression, these new stock companies fell prey to the same failings as the old. Consequently, the emphasis turned to who was in the play rather than to what the play was or whether it spoke to the audience. The main distinction between the nineteenth- and twentieth-century parades of stars invading the resident stock theatres were their nationalities. In the nineteenth century, many of the star attractions were European imports. In twentieth-century summer stock, the stars were Americans who largely were known to their audiences via Hollywood films.

Summer stock needs to be distinguished from the more generic term "summer theatre," which describes all entertainments, usually in rural areas and frequently held outdoors, that occur during the summer months. During summer stock's golden age from the 1920s through the 1960s, the principal summertime competition included outdoor dramas, such as the Roanoke Island, North Carolina production *The Lost Colony* (presented annually since 1937), which were designed as historical or quasi-historical celebrations of a local character or event and were marketed largely as tourist attractions; adult summer camps, which frequently had their own resident theatres, such as Tamiment in Pennsylvania's Pocono Mountains and Green Mansions in New York's Adirondack Mountains; civic musical theatres like the St. Louis Municipal Outdoor Theatre (known as MUNY) and the Kansas City Starlight Theatre, which featured large-scale productions of opera, operettas, and musical comedies before thousands of people under the stars; Borscht Belt theatres active in New York's Catskill Mountains, which more frequently presented revues or stand-up comedy in favor of legitimate dramas; and

Chautauquas, the touring tent shows that combined vaudeville with dramatic sketches, lectures, and other types of cultural programming. The Chautauqua circuits, which were the major form of summer entertainment throughout the country in the first two decades of the twentieth century, were dwindling at the time that summer stock was beginning. A few of the tents did remain, however, and there were—and are—still active programs at their home base on Lake Chautauqua in upstate New York near the Ohio border. In later years, and after the decline of summer stock in the 1960s, many additional forms of summer entertainments arose, including the various theatrical and variety shows offered at major theme and amusement parks; Renaissance fairs, which hire professional actors to dress in period costume and enact various plays, games, and events typical of the early seventeenth century; summer Shakespeare festivals, many of which perform outdoors and run the gamut from relatively humble, single-production operations to major performing arts centers with multiple stages and a repertory of eight or more productions; summer dinner theatres, usually housed in tents or held outdoors, which began as a result of the widely popular dinner theatre circuits founded in the 1960s; and summer arts festivals, many of which are held in major U.S. cities such as New York, Chicago, and Los Angeles, and which generally offer theatre and other live entertainments such as dance, music concerts, and mixed-media performances. All of these were, and continue to be, important entertainments that have generated significant numbers of jobs and revenue during the summer months. The most widely known have been profiled in historic monographs and other publications that are listed in the bibliography at the end of this book.

Although the golden age of summer stock could be characterized as a movement, it is doubtful whether a true movement ever existed other than in the minds of theatre historians. Summer stock may have looked like a movement because it was a great opportunity to found new theatres that was exploited by many within a relatively short time span. Hence, in the sense of a movement as a trend or tendency, it could be so considered. More realistically, however, summer stock was a natural development of practical-minded theatre people who viewed the new resorts as an obvious place to set up shop. As Foster Dulles proclaims in his *History of Recreation*: "The people of no other country and no other age had ever had anything like the leisure, the discretionary income, or the recreational choices of the American people in the mid-twentieth-century. It was overwhelming."[20] Since, as he asserts, "the American people had learned to play," what better playground than in an idyllic summer theatre? Hence, summer stock was born.

1

Of Entertainment and Art: The Parallel Roads to Summer Stock

Summer stock theatres developed to fulfill the dual needs for art and entertainment at the new vacationlands of the 1920s. The founders of these playhouses were not inventing a whole new form of theatre but one that had progressed logically from its immediate forebears. There were, on the one hand, two early summer enterprises that were turn-of-the-century reincarnations of nineteenth-century resident stock companies moved from an urban to rural milieu. There also was the more recent influence of the art or little theatre movement, which, although begun in the first decade of the 1900s, was still flourishing in the 1920s. Some of these enterprises were established in rural oases and often incorporated natural settings as backdrops for their dramatic presentations. It is significant that all these theatres were independently owned and operated at a time when nationwide monopolies virtually controlled the American stage. These early examples of quality theatre, surviving outside of the stranglehold of New York producers, showed later summer stock entrepreneurs that they could launch their new theatres with confidence.

Another important influence, affiliated with the little theatre movement, was the growth of theatre arts programs in universities. Inclusion in the academy legitimatized the study and production of serious theatre and generated a whole new group of trained professionals, who were eager to test their skills in theatres where they could maintain artistic and financial control.

Independent stock companies had been the most prevalent form of legitimate theatre throughout the United States until the 1870s. These companies rented or owned their own theatres, or toured a standard circuit of cities and towns, or did both, usually by premiering a new show at their home base and then taking it on tour. All shared basic characteristics: a resident company of actors and other stage personnel, a cache of stock scenery, properties, and costumes, and a sizable repertory of classic and contemporary plays that allowed for weekly, semiweekly, or even nightly changes of bill. Actors were hired to play particular types of roles, known in the trade as "lines," in any and all pieces that demanded that kind of character. The most common lines were leading man and woman, juvenile and ingénue leads, low comedians, heavies to play the villains, and character actors. Hence, an actor hired as the heavy, for instance, would play roles such as Iago in *Othello* and Simon Legree in *Uncle Tom's Cabin*. In the best of circumstances, versatile performers enjoyed a panoply of wonderful acting opportunities. In the worst, as one critic commented, "each claimed as of right the part which came nearest to his or her specialty; and each played all his or her parts in exactly the same way."[1] In most instances, however, the resident actors were adored by faithful fans, who came to the theatre each week to cheer their idols in a new or favorite role. It is significant that in small towns and cities across America before the era of film, radio, and television, the local stock company provided the only regular amusement available.

The demise of the independent stock company paralleled the growth of railroads spanning the country, which, in turn, revolutionized commercial theatre. The era of theatre as big business, with New York City as its base of operation, began in the 1870s. Train travel provided a cost-effective means of moving whole production companies from one town to the next for engagements at the local theatre. Hence, a new kind of entertainment, known as the combination company, was developed quickly by business-minded producers who were principally interested in making money rather than art. Extensive tours of these combination companies—theatrical packages of a single show that featured one or more stars, a supporting cast, and often all the technical and scenic elements to maintain a consistent quality of production—heralded the beginning of "the road" and the end of resident stock. As John Frick notes in the *Cambridge History of American Theatre*, during the 1870s alone, "the number of first-class stock companies declined precipitously from fifty in 1872 to eight in 1880, whereas the number of traveling combinations rose from five in 1872 to nearly a hundred just four years later."[2] Since many of the stock companies had been presenting a standard repertoire of plays with largely the same cast, costumes, and scenery for decades, audiences eagerly embraced the change. At the same time that the combinations were proliferating, there were a wide variety of popular entertainments that competed for audience dollars. Minstrel and Wild West shows, circus, revues, light opera and other early musical theatre, and, in particular, variety and vaudeville shows were alluring diversions that helped to empty seats in the old stock houses.

Less than a century later, theatre history would repeat itself in the rise and fall of summer stock as resident stock succumbed to package tours (the new name for the old combination companies) and live performance itself was threatened by the most successful of all popular entertainments—television. In the late nineteenth century, however, the idea of establishing stock theatres in rural locales for a limited summer season, far away from competing entertainments, was appealing and quite successful. This was particularly true in the 1890s for two remote theatres, one in Colorado and the other in Maine, which share the honors as the first summer stock theatres in America. Neither, however, was founded principally as a theatre; both developed as added attractions to amusement park resorts at the end of a trolley line. Both have long, distinguished histories of production, attracted noted stars to their stages and audiences, and were commercial operations that ultimately became the preeminent attractions in their respective parks. Both found success in out-of-the-way locales where visitors could add theatregoing to a day's holiday in the country. Most of their audiences arrived via trolley where they could purchase half-price tickets for the show on their way to the theatre. The trolley owners, assured of business long into the evening, were happy to oblige.

Historians have long recognized the analogous development of American trolleys and amusement parks; it is now evident that this history further encompasses the beginnings of summer theatre. In the years following the Civil War, trolley companies promoted the growth of public pleasure gardens, which offered walking paths amid tranquil scenery, wide open spaces to play sports, and simple amusements like swings and carousels, by extending their rail lines to the park entrance, a plan that served a number of people very well. City folk, who had little opportunity to enjoy the great outdoors and no means of conveyance, now had easy, convenient access; the trolleys were attracting a new clientele and expanded hours of service; and park owners, now enjoying many more customers, could readily increase their offerings.[3] Historians further credit Chicago's Columbian Exposition of 1893 for promoting the amusement park boon of the late nineteenth century but, in Denver, Colorado, the park and its attendant theatre predated the Chicago fair.

Elitch's Gardens

The first summer theatre in America opened in 1890 at the end of the trolley line, six miles from downtown Denver. Elitch's Gardens was created by John and Mary Elitch, who had purchased 16 acres of farmland on Berkeley Lake in 1887. Although the farm was intended to supply produce for their successful Denver restaurant, in 1889 they decided to convert it into a pleasure garden suitable for picnics, boating, and country outings. Denver, which had been founded 28 years earlier in 1859, had not yet developed any parks, and the public was clamoring for a local greenway where they could relax and enjoy fine weather. The success of their first season propelled the Elitches to exploit the commercial potential of the gardens, which clearly could provide patrons far more than wide open space. Their scheme was aided by Denver officials, who authorized the construction of a rapid transit trolley to bring city dwellers to the park. New attractions for the 1890 season included a small zoo, athletic fields, refreshment stands, an open-air cafe, and a theatre. The theatre, a 12-sided building with a canopied roof at the end of a winding path through the gardens, had two open sides through which visitors could enter, a design feature intended to better integrate the theatre into the open-air park.[4] According to Mary Elitch, when the theatre was crowded, audience members could stand under the trees outside and still get good views of the stage.[5]

John Elitch was a sometime actor and stock company owner with numerous professional contacts who were willing to help him with the new theatre. Perhaps because of the failure of his old stock company and the current rage for popular entertainments, he and two actor friends opted to begin with vaudeville. Certainly the theatre's architecture, with its nearly circular shape, open sides, small orchestra pit, modest stage (30 by 20 feet), and canvas roof, was more suitable to vaudeville and other variety shows than to stage plays.[6] Elitch's first season, which commenced May 1 and ran through October 19, featured standard vaudeville programs, with a change of bill every Sunday. A typical show included comedy sketches, acrobats, jugglers, singers and dancers, animal acts, female impersonators, and novelty acts, all guaranteed to be first-rate family entertainment. Throughout its history, Elitch's was dedicated to offering shows that were "wholly acceptable to ladies and children" and were devoid of anything of a "vulgar nature."[7] During the opening day speeches, Denver's mayor heralded the Elitches for establishing a resort "where mothers and children can come to spend a quiet day free from household cares and worryings" and "where the working man and his family can come on Sundays."[8]

Audiences arrived at the theatre via the Berkeley Motor Rapid Transit Line, known as "the motor," which linked downtown Denver with the Gardens. Although Mary Elitch would describe it as "a rattling old steam train," it was a boon to city dwellers in 1890 when their only other options were to hire a carriage at considerable expense or walk.[9] In later years, Elitch's provided parking space for patrons with automobiles, but in the early years, the theatre remained viable thanks to the trolley service.

In March 1891, while on tour with a new minstrel company co-run by Elitch and his business partners from the Gardens, John Elitch died suddenly at the age of 41. *The New York Dramatic Mirror*, one of the principal theatrical newspapers in the country, reported the loss in its April 4 edition, thus signifying the importance Elitch's had already gained as a major new performing venue in just one season. A consortium of Denver businessmen purchased the Gardens and established a corporation, the Elitch Gardens Amusement Company, which managed both the park and the theatre from 1891 through 1893.[10] Prior to the May 1891 opening, the theatre building acquired a permanent roof and fully enclosed sides, thus becoming a more versatile space suitable for other forms of entertainment. In the 1893 season, the company hired New York-based actor-manager Frank Norcross to present its first season of summer stock.[11] Unfortunately, the financial panic of 1893 hurt attendance, and in mid-August, Elitch's closed and was placed in a receivership. The following March, Mary Elitch purchased the property and began her 21-year reign as "the lady of the Gardens," as christened by Denver theatre critic Frank W. White. Although she continued to maintain the high quality of the pleasure gardens and other amenities at the park, she principally focused on making the theatre a successful, if not renowned, enterprise.

Between 1894 and 1899, Mary Elitch experimented with different types of entertainment to determine what best appealed to popular tastes. She employed several different stock companies, variously presenting melodramas, comedies, or light dramas; a light opera company; and vaudeville acts. Sometimes all were combined in the same season. The engagement of Walter Clarke Bellows to direct a resident stock company in 1899, however, transformed Elitch's permanently. Bellows was a proponent of the "David Belasco school of realism" and thus modeled both the choice of play and style of production on the popular Broadway director's work.[12] He held auditions in New York City and hired actors with Broadway credits as well as experience in the new genre of realism that dominated American legitimate theatre at the turn of the century. Bellows established Elitch's as a traditional nineteenth-century style stock company, and, because this was a summer theatre located in an amusement park, it inadvertently set certain standards that would become typical of the summer stock theatres two decades later.

Bellows hired a resident company of 10 to 16 actors who would appear in most, if not all, the productions, and thus become familiar to and even beloved of regular theatregoers. As usual in stock situations, some actors would leave midseason for better offers or join the company after completing engagements elsewhere. Bellows also engaged star performers periodically to bolster the theatre's image in the local and national press and to increase revenues at the box office.[13]

The season, which normally ran between 11 and 14 weeks, would feature the occasional offering of a Shakespearean or other classic play and a steady diet of recent as well as older Broadway successes, all carefully selected to adhere to Mary Elitch's policy of presenting only wholesome, family entertainment. Management was especially pleased when it could acquire the rights to produce a recent Broadway hit relatively quickly, thus keeping a close tie to the New York theatre world. David Belasco's *Under Two Flags*, for instance, was presented at Elitch's just five months after its Broadway opening in 1901.[14] Production values also garnered increased attention under the new stock system. In accordance with his taste for Belasco-style realism, Bellows ordered sets designed individually for each production, a rarity in stock theatres, and Elitch supported him via generous scenic budgets of about $1000 per show. The theatre did own at least ten complete sets by the 1898 season, however, many of which were modified and repainted as necessary.[15]

Elitch's Gardens was notable as an independent theatre in an era when virtually every legitimate house in the country was controlled by the Theatrical Syndicate or, later, its principal rival, the Shubert Brothers. The syndicate was a group of powerful businessmen who, in the late 1890s, consolidated the combination companies, which had propelled the end of independent stock, under one all-inclusive producing organization that controlled everything from casting to ticket sales. Organized as a typical turn-of-the-century business trust (John D. Rockefeller's Standard Oil Co. was the most notorious example), the syndicate controlled first-class theatrical production throughout the United States by 1903. Its domination was broken in the second decade of the century by the Shubert Brothers, which became an even more ruthless and powerful monopoly. Denver's other principal theatres, most of which were center-city roadhouses that usually were dark in summer, all were under syndicate control, which means they presented only those shows featuring affiliated playwrights and performers. Hence, Elitch had the privilege of introducing Denver to some of the finest actors of the period, including Sarah Bernhardt, Minnie Maddern Fiske, and David Warfield, as well as to the plays of David Belasco, all of whom, as outspoken opponents of the syndicate, were barred from its theatres.

As Elitch's staunch independence differentiated it from other western U.S. theatres, it also helped serve as a forerunner to the autonomous group of small producing theatres that, as a means of circumventing the New York theatre monopoly, would become summer stock. Other characteristics of this theatre also helped lay the groundwork for the new wave of summer ventures. The Gardens was a locally owned and managed company with Mary Elitch in permanent residence. She personally oversaw all aspects of the productions and would make changes as necessary in response to audience expectations and desires. The long period of experimentation with differing types of entertainment in the 1890s, in fact, grew from her attempt to satisfy popular tastes.[16] She also acknowledged Denver-area thespians by supplementing the professional casts and crews with local talent whenever scripts called for more small roles, crowd scenes, and technical support than the resident company could fulfill.

Elitch's enjoyed excellent actor-audience relations. Many stock actors became audience favorites and were invited to social engagements in town, although, as the *Denver Post* lamented, few invitations were accepted because of the "unusually strenuous schedule at the gardens."[17] Summer stock, which generally mounted a new show every week, was always an exhausting venture; companies would hold morning and afternoon rehearsals for next week's show while giving between 8 and 11 performances a week of the current offering. As one actress put it, "You were forgetting one show, playing another, and memorizing the next, all at the same time."[18] Denver socialites patronized the theatre, and even had their own unofficial "society night" on Mondays, when they would don splendid garb and arrive at the Gardens as much to see as to be seen.[19] All of these elements figured prominently in the development of summer stock.

Another parallel, particularly in the early years of stock, lay in Elitch's propensity to produce the classics as well as new scripts. Both are notoriously difficult to perform well within a single week's rehearsal time, and the design and technical staff is taxed to the limit with the added demands of conceiving and building new sets, costumes, and properties in the same constricted time frame. Although the theatre did not produce either type of show often— perhaps once a season at best—it felt obligated, as a theatre dedicated to serving all factions of the local community, to include both time-honored texts and forays into new American playwrighting, an art form which was developing in earnest in the first decades of the twentieth century.

Finally, stock companies, particularly those offering full and varied repertoires, have always been excellent training grounds for young theatre professionals. Within a short period of time, actors, designers, technicians, and other personnel are presented with numerous challenges and opportunities that must be quickly realized in production. Although this system can, and has, resulted in mediocre work, it also can stimulate remarkable feats of artistry and lively invention. It also provides a theatre education like no other for young artists in search of experience in a wide range of play genres and production styles. Since one of the common hazards of playing stock is burnout over a long theatre season, thus producing dull or shoddy work, the summer stocks had the advantage of a short season. Although the work at Elitch's was considered "strenuous," it was over in 11 to 14 weeks. Hence, performances could remain fresh and production values high.

Elitch's Gardens ran successive stock seasons between 1899 and 1915, when Mary Elitch was forced to sell the property. Under subsequent owners, however, the Gardens continued to present stock more or less continuously until 1991. The story of the 1915 financial collapse is interesting because in certain respects it, too, is analogous to the history of the later stock ventures. A combination of rising production costs, escalating competition, and bad weather was deemed the principal culprit, although the increased ownership of automobiles, which allowed people to find recreation wherever they wished rather than necessarily at the park, and the proliferation of movies are also cited as concerns.[20] The latter two stem from Elitch's location on the fringes of a major U.S. city, a problem that many of the remotely located summer stock theatres never shared because automobiles were necessary to their survival (many stock houses closed during World War II because gas rationing prohibited audiences from coming), and movie theatres were rarely found in the hinterlands. Bad weather, however, will always wreak havoc with any business dependent on tourist dollars in resort locales. Although summer theatres enjoyed great business on the occasional rainy day, continued inclement weather quickly emptied resorts and their resident theatres.

Rising costs, which often lead to make cuts that result in substandard productions, are a problem shared by all theatres, as is the challenge of increasing competition. By 1912, Elitch's had three rival summer stock operations competing for audiences that, no longer dependent on public transportation to access entertainment, were enjoying freedom of choice. Although the theatre periodically suffered financial difficulties, it ultimately managed to survive for more than one hundred years. In 1991, the old Elitch property was sold and the name purchased by the Six Flags Corporation, which opened a new Elitch Gardens Amusement Park, without a summer stock theatre, in another section of Denver in 1994.

Lakewood Theatre

While Elitch's Gardens was prospering at the end of one trolley line in the West, the Lakewood Theatre, 5 miles north of Skowhegan, Maine, was flourishing at the end of another. The only operational difference between the two houses was that Lakewood actually owned the trolley, as well as a water ferry, to usher patrons to and from the performances. In fact, Skowhegan's Somerset Traction Company, which owned the trolley and a resort that included a lakeshore hotel, bandstand, two bowling alleys, a cafe, tree-lined walkways and a children's playground, opened the theatre in 1898 to increase ticket sales for the trolley line.[21] Like Elitch's, the theatre presented touring vaudeville companies in its first few seasons and also underwent several changes of management. With the arrival of Herbert L. Swett in 1901, the Lakewood Theatre began to develop into a prominent summer theatre which fully earned its epithet, "Broadway in Maine."

Despite local legend, Swett did not actually bring the first summer stock company to Lakewood; he assumed his duties as the new resort manager several weeks after the company had completed its inaugural season. The first four seasons of stock, 1901–1904, featured Boston-based actors and directors who offered weekly changes of bill for 9 to as many as 14 weeks each summer. To keep royalty payments low, the plays chosen were mostly revivals of nineteenth-century Broadway classics by Bronson Howard, William Gillette, and Steele MacKaye, and other populist fare, including William Pratt's long-run hit temperance play, *Ten Nights in a Bar-Room*. Since admission was only 10 cents (5 cents for those who paid the round-trip trolley fare of 25 cents), the theatre had minimal operating funds and couldn't afford to pay high royalty fees for new Broadway hits. From 1905 to 1907, Swett contracted with the Joseph J. Flynn agency to provide weekly vaudeville programs along with several special screenings of motion pictures, which, as the hot new medium, were a source of wonder and fascination to the general public. In 1908, resident stock returned to Lakewood, and, except for the occasional week of vaudeville and movies, it would become the mainstay of the theatre season for the next 70 years.[22]

The first 15 years of Swett's management at Lakewood were, by his own admission, "too many years" when "nothing much happened."[23] He had been hired with little professional business experience shortly after graduating from Bowdoin College. He also knew nothing about theatre, so was content to hire people who did to manage that aspect of the resort. By all accounts, the resort was fairly run-down when he came to Lakewood in 1901, and he effected few improvements until the late 1910s. The theatre building was erected in 1882 as a spiritualist meeting hall, was converted two years later into an ice-skating rink, and, in 1898, was made into a theatre for the inaugural season of vaudeville. Although little is known about this first theatre, information from the 1917 renovation suggests that there was a simple platform stage with a proscenium arch and removable seats so the theatre could double as a dance hall. Initially, the theatre was open-air, but a permanent peaked roof was added sometime in the first few years. This roof proved inadequate for scenic changes, according to a 1918 playbill, so a rectangular roof 40 feet above the stage floor was added during the renovation. The expanded stage measured 40 feet deep by 60 feet wide, and the new roof, equipped with a fly system, could handle more sophisticated scenic equipment.[24] The opening program of the refurbished theatre boasted that "the company can play anything on Lakewood's stage that can be produced in the largest New York theatres, except the mammoth Hippodrome."[25] By this time, however, Swett finally had decided to turn Lakewood into a "theatrical resort colony" and was making positive moves in all aspects of the operation, from artistry through audience.[26] What is remarkable is that, unlike Mary Elitch, Swett was able to make Lakewood survive for so long on what were clearly mediocre entertainment and meager facilities.

Swett's concept of a theatre resort coincided with his desire to raise the quality of performance at Lakewood. After the necessary upgrade to the theatre building, Swett actively pursued New York-based actors with Broadway credits. Although he couldn't pay high salaries, he could offer actors a working vacation in the Maine woods. He experimented with this concept in 1916 when he hired James Beall to create the Lakewood Musical Comedy Company, consisting of all Broadway performers. Beall persuaded actors to take the low-paying jobs in Maine with the promise of a built-in summer vacation. According to the opening playbill, the same company would have cost $1,600 per week in New York while Swett's weekly payroll was just over $300.[27] Although musical stock was never revived, Swett used the same premise to lure other notable performers and writers to Lakewood in subsequent seasons. Always the businessman with a keen eye to profit, he paid paltry salaries but ensured that accommodations and food were more than adequate and gave the players plenty of free time to enjoy the resort amenities of swimming, boating, tennis, and golf. Dorothy Stickney, who spent seven summers at Lakewood in the 1920s, remembers her time there fondly, although she admits that "no one went there for the money." "We were all paid exactly the same," she declares, "thirty dollars a week and our room and board." However, since there was little to spend money on, no one cared. "Nothing could possibly have fulfilled my wants and wishes as Lakewood did," since she had "a chance to spend the summer in an idyllic spot" and "more importantly, watch fine actors work and learn as much as I could from them."[28]

The quality of the acting company, which had been growing steadily since 1916, was well established by 1925 with the arrival of Howard Lindsay as theatre director. Lindsay was a successful Broadway actor and director who often managed to do both simultaneously, such as in the 1921 hit comedy *Dulcy* by George S. Kaufman and Marc Connelly. At Lakewood, he specialized in producing recent New York successes, frequently ones he had directed or with members of the original company repeating their Broadway roles, and trying out new plays that either were pre-booked for Broadway engagements or were new scripts in development. Two examples of shows arriving "direct from Broadway" were *The Nervous Wreck* (1925), which featured Lakewood favorites Dorothy Stickney and Albert Hackett, and *The Boomerang* (1926), directed by and starring the popular actor Arthur Byron, whom Lindsay had engaged for the full summer season. Between 1926 and 1929, Lindsay premiered 15 new plays at Lakewood, most of which went on to Broadway productions. These include several plays co-authored by Lindsay and Bert Robinson, *Tommy Helps Himself* (produced as *Tommy* in New York in the 1926–27 season) and *Your Uncle Dudley* (1928); Sophie Treadwell's 1927 play *Bound*, produced at Lakewood under the title *Better to Marry*; and *Hoosiers Abroad* by Booth Tarkington and starring Elliot Nugent, which was scheduled to open on Broadway in the fall following its July 1927 Lakewood premiere.[29]

By the end of Lindsay's tenure in 1930, Lakewood had established itself as a valuable tryout center where New York producers eagerly tested new properties. According to a *Boston Sunday Globe* feature article, "Broadway Shows in Maine Woods," there was a strict process for the consideration of new plays. To begin, the producer needed to guarantee that the play would open on Broadway in the autumn. Lindsay would then read the script, and if he liked it he would give it to the rest of the Lakewood Company to read. Only if everyone approved would the play be included in the upcoming season.[30] The new play policy continued to flourish under Lindsay's successor, Melville Burke, who came to Lakewood after 4 years of directing productions at Elitch's Gardens. Herbert Swett also was an avid proponent of these premieres, which had been important factors in putting his theatre on the map of important regional houses. In a 1936 playbill, Swett explained that he felt "a sense of duty" both to "give the patron something new" and "to contribute as much as possible to the discovery and establishment of new manuscripts." He added that premieres gave members of the acting company wonderful opportunities to originate roles and perhaps repeat them in New York.[31]

Swett also attracted new plays because he offered playwrights a summer retreat where they could write and revise their work. Several noted writers, including Owen Davis, who late in his distinguished career made Lakewood his permanent home, and Clifford Odets, who escaped to Lakewood in 1939 to work on *Silent Partner*, were joined by at least five or six lesser-knowns each summer. Famous actors such as Cornelia Otis Skinner and Walter Hampden also would rent Lakewood bungalows for extended holidays, punctuated by occasional guest appearances on stage. This clustering of New York literati and name performers gained Lakewood a reputation as an artists' colony where they could "work just as hard as they ever did on Broadway and at the same time get enough Maine woods background to make their work and play a happy combination."[32]

The most famous of the Lakewood premieres was *Life with Father* by Howard Lindsay and Russel Crouse, which still holds the record as the longest-running nonmusical play in Broadway history. Unfortunately, Swett missed his opportunity to reap considerable financial gain from the show. He had been offered a 10 percent share in the Broadway production in exchange for providing room, board, and partial transportation costs for company members who had been brought to Lakewood especially for the premiere. Always the cautious businessman, Swett declined, assuming that the likelihood of the play's becoming a commercial hit was remote.[33] According to historian John Oblak, the playhouse publicity organ and local press also failed to grasp the potential of this new play, which was based on a best-selling novel by Clarence Day. They were more interested in the return to the Lakewood stage of co-stars Howard Lindsay and Dorothy Stickney, who had married following the 1927 summer season, than they were in Lindsay's play. This quickly changed after the New York press reviewed the Lakewood production and pronounced the show to be one of the most promising plays of the coming Broadway season.[34]

Swett's theatrical resort colony succeeded financially because, in addition to quality theatre, it provided equally attractive accommodations, dining, and recreational opportunities for paying guests. By 1925, the resort offered 40 sophisticated bungalows replete with full baths, fireplaces, screened-in porches, and maid and bell boy service. In order to keep the theatre filled for every performance, Swett preferred that guests stay only one night so that other theatre patrons might be likewise accommodated the following evening.[35] An added attraction for visitors was the ability to mingle freely with the stars at the restaurant, snack bar, and recreational facilities, which were enjoyed by all. Swett's transformation of Lakewood from a pleasure grove for day-trippers to a full-service resort propelled the closing of the trolley service in 1927, since the fashionable clientele now arrived in their own automobiles. Lakewood continued as a one-of-a-kind summer stock resort colony until the 1940s, when it succumbed, as did so many other theatres, to the lure of combination companies and the gradual demise of stock.

Elitch's Gardens and Lakewood Theatre are significant historically for several reasons. They were important forerunners of the summer stock phenomenon, which proved that nineteenth-century style stock companies could be successful as limited-season ventures within a summer resort milieu. Both theatres were so well established, with national reputations for consistently fine performances, that they not only flourished through the golden age of stock but also managed to outlast many of their later competitors. Their success as privately owned and operated theatres in an age when most theatres were beholden to one of the major monopolies demonstrated that one could operate independently of the syndicates and realize a profit. The theatres also provided a critical link between the centuries, maintaining the vital traditions of nineteenth-century legitimate theatre while embracing new plays and modes of production in the twentieth.

Despite the occasional presentation of a classic play, neither Elitch's nor Lakewood could be described as an art theatre. Nor did either theatre seem to be influenced by the enthusiasm for art or little theatres that swept dramatic circles in the first few decades of the twentieth century. This is because both were fundamentally commercial ventures providing entertainment to boost the popularity of their resorts. Although Lakewood did produce Norman Bel Geddes's radical adaptation of *Hamlet* during its 1929 season, this was not its normal bill of fare. The art theatres had a different agenda; their mission was not commercial. Rather, they existed to introduce America to the serious new theatre of Europe and to engender a like-minded emphasis on the development of new plays and modes of production in this country.

The Little Theatre Movement

The little theatre movement flourished in the first decades of the twentieth century thanks to amateur enthusiasts of drama. Although some of their

ventures grew into semiprofessional and professional houses and the beginnings of the regional and off-off Broadway theatre, many continued to flourish
as amateur endeavors and evolved into what we now know as American
community theatre. A few even developed at, or consciously chose, scenic
resort locales and operated as summer enterprises. Wherever and however
they were founded, all shared similar visions and goals. All were weary, if not
disgusted, by the superficiality, tawdry spectacle, prurience, and blatant commercialism of turn-of-the-century American theatre. The founders were well-
read, well-traveled people who were entranced by the serious experimental
dramas and new modes of staging promulgated by European independent
theatres, such as Otto Brahm's Freie Bühne, André Antoine's Théâtre Libre,
and J. T. Grein's Independent Theatre. They eagerly read and produced the
work of Ibsen, Strindberg, Chekhov, Shaw, and other modernist playwrights,
and found inspiration in the theoretical writings of Edward Gordon Craig,
Adolphe Appia, and Richard Wagner for scenographic alternatives to realism
and naturalism. Influences from the allied arts—dance, painting and sculpture, music, and fiction—were also incorporated into their new dramatic
visions as these formerly separate art forms, in the spirit of Wagner and
Craig, began to merge into a unified, organic art. The examination of social
issues, as well as myth, symbolism, fantasy, poetic visions, and sensuality,
marked these theatres as experimental, adventuresome, and thoroughly anti-
commercial. As early as 1914, Sheldon Cheney was heralding the little theatres for fostering "the true progress of dramatic art in America."[36] They
"have advanced far beyond the professional playhouses because their ideal
lies in the realm of dramatic art rather than of commercial success," he avers,
"and their methods are experimental rather than traditional and set."
Although, by 1914, these theatres had not yet introduced new American
playwrights and had not "freed the American theatre from the inartistic
faults of setting and staging and acting that have all but strangled to death
whatever other drama was brought to it," Cheney still gives them "most of
the credit for whatever advance has been made toward either ideal."[37]

    The epithet "little theatre" was inspired by one of the more famous of these
ventures, Maurice Browne's Little Theatre in Chicago, founded in 1912.
Although the theatre existed a mere five years, its influence in promoting literary and poetic drama was profound. Cheney considers it a prototypical art
theatre, both in Browne's ability to "whip into shape from amateur material
an organization which stands to-day as one of the most vital expressions of
the new dramatic spirit in America" and to boldly present challenging and
obscure plays. In its first season alone, Browne produced Euripides's *The*

Trojan Women, Strindberg's *Creditors* and *The Stronger*, William Butler Yeats's *On Baile Strand* and *The Shadowy Waters*, and Schnitzler's *Anatol*.[38] Browne's theatre served as a major inspiration in the development of two of America's most important producing organizations, the Washington Square and Provincetown Players, both described in greater detail below. Other like-minded ventures, such as The Hull-House Theatre, also in Chicago, were more interested in presenting social realism and plays with a decidedly political message. The Hull-House Players, founded in 1897 as an outgrowth of the social rehabilitation work of Hull-House founders Jane Addams and Ellen Gates Starr, in fact, constituted one of the first art theatre collectives. Addams believed in the transformative power of drama to help her constituents achieve richer lives. By so doing, she hoped that through hard work and increasing production experience, they would create theatre that was as artistically notable as it was socially beneficial.

According to Constance D'Arcy Mackay, who wrote the first history of the little theatre movement, there were 63 such ventures scattered across the United States by 1917.[39] Although the names of the most famous are mentioned in historical footnotes (in addition to those listed above, others included Mrs. Lyman Gale's Boston Toy Theatre, Sam Hume's Arts and Crafts Theatre in Detroit, and Raymond O'Neil's Cleveland Play House, which Frederic McConnell transformed into a professional regional theatre in 1921), many were fledgling operations in small towns that truly were for the edification of the local populace. One such organization, the Huguenot Players of New Rochelle, New York, identified itself as being "affiliated with the Little Theatre Movement" and published a sophisticated pamphlet that put forth its mission and ideology and asked for community support. The booklet begins with an 8-page history of Western theatre that leaps from Shakespeare's Globe Theatre to the Huguenot Players' own humble enterprise:

> From the time of Shakespeare until within a few years the theatre has been for the people, but not of the people. The dramatic urge, latent in every human being, was forced to find its outlet in watching the acting of others. In protest against this situation there has been a movement of late to establish in various communities the Little Theatre, the theatre of the people, for the people, by the people. Here the creative instinct and the art of expression may be fostered and the interest of the community focused upon its own talent, thereby increasing civic pride. Here the playwright, the scene-painter, the costume designer, the musician, the dancer and the actor may together create that which is beautiful and worth while.[40]

Following a lengthy outline detailing the specifics of their plan, they ask the reader for support. "Such a community theatre the Huguenot Players of New Rochelle aim to establish . . . . May we count on you?"[41]

The Washington Square Players

At the same time that art theatres were springing up all over the country, there was a similar impetus among New York City's intelligentsia. A sub-group of Greenwich Village's Liberal Club, an association of writers, artists, political figures, businesspeople, and newspaper reporters and publishers who regularly came together at their club, known as the "Meeting Place for Those Interested in New Ideas," decided to form a drama group to produce plays. Shortly after their debut, a second group of Liberal Club members, spearheaded by Lawrence Langner and other enthusiastic amateurs who were unimpressed with the initial efforts of the club's "dramatic branch," formed the Washington Square Players in 1914. Langner, who was both a patent attorney and theatre aficionado, joined with two up-and-coming playwright-directors, Edward Goodman and Philip Moeller, to write the group's manifesto professing their belief "in the future of the theatre in America." The writers decried "the present condition of the American drama" and expressed profound admiration for the current Broadway season of Harley Granville Barker's company, which was "delighting New York audiences" with "the culmination of a growth of some years in the development of new methods of acting and production." The Players pledged "hard work and perseverance coupled with ability and the absence of purely commercial considerations" for their enterprise, which asserted the policy of producing only plays that "have artistic merit." They would give American plays preference but also wanted to include in their repertory "the works of well-known European authors which have been ignored by the commercial managers."[42]

The group presented three seasons of mostly one-act plays, which were the staple of the art theatre repertoires, featuring, pursuant to their manifesto, the works of new American authors as well as significant plays from Europe. The troupe was well received both by the New York press and general public and would have carried on had it not been for the American intervention in World War I. The Washington Square Players disbanded in 1917 but reformed in 1919 at Langner's instigation as the Theatre Guild, which became one of the most important theatrical producing organizations of the twentieth century.

The Provincetown Players

At the same time that the Washington Square Players were formally presenting their work in New York City, another group of Liberal Club members was informally presenting theirs in Provincetown, Massachusetts. The Provincetown Players did not actually acquire that name until after their second summer season on Cape Cod, at which point they officially organized, wrote a constitution, elected officers, and repaired to New York City to their first MacDougal Street theatre. Although they retained the Provincetown moniker, they never returned to the seaside wharf where, as a group of keen amateurs with varied talents, they premiered plays by Susan Glaspell, George Cram "Jig" Cook, John Reed, Neith Boyce, Hutchins Hapgood, and, in their second season, Eugene O'Neill. It is the actors' association with O'Neill that has secured their place in history as the first theatre to produce and actively promote his work, and it is for this reason, too, that they may be the most well-known summer theatre. Although their influence on later summer stock is undeniable, they never could be considered a part of that group. Rather, the Provincetown Players are a classic example of an art theatre that, because the members all had summer cottages in Provincetown, began presenting plays at an idyllic seaside resort. The minute they decided to seriously form a producing theatre, they moved to New York City.

It was those summers of 1915 and 1916 in Provincetown, however, that are a fascinating sidebar in the history of American summer theatre; they also, outside of O'Neill's two premieres during the second season, tend to be largely ignored by theatre historians. The Provincetown Players may have been theatrical amateurs, but they represented a rich and varied array of writers, artists, and political activists, all of whom were disillusioned with the war in Europe and what they viewed, in the words of Hutchins Hapgood, as the "poison" inherent in a society where "the thought and emotion of the day was anaemic and rudderless." It was their desire to "be free of the poison of self and the poison of the world" which ultimately led them to founding a theatrical group.[43] Hapgood explains further:

> So these few persons at Provincetown...were inspired with a desire to be truthful to their simple human lives, to ignore, if possible, the big tumult and machine and get hold of some simple convictions which would stand the test of their own experience. They felt the need of rejecting everything, even the Systems of Rejection, and of living as intimately and truthfully as they could; and, if possible, they wanted to express the simple truth of their lives and experience by writing, staging, and acting their own plays.[44]

"These few persons at Provincetown" were brought together by the "infectious enthusiasm and dedication to spontaneous group creativity" engendered by Jig Cook.[45] Cook was an author, an aesthete, and a visionary who dreamed of creating a Platonic community in emulation of the Hellenic age. His notion of collective creation, gleaned from European art theatres such as Ireland's Abbey Theatre and the Moscow Art Theatre as well as the work of his friend Maurice Browne, in which everyone takes turns at writing, directing, acting, designing, producing, and doing whatever else needs to be done to mount a production, was central to the life of the Provincetown Players and is widely considered to be the prototype for later theatre companies (the Living Theatre and San Francisco Mime Troupe, for instance) that organized on this model. This same model became the standard operating practice at many summer stock theatres, in which all company members, of necessity, pitched in and helped with everything, regardless of their special expertise.

Cook co-founded the Provincetown group with his third wife, Susan Glaspell, a successful novelist and writer of short fiction. They were joined by the political activist and reporter John Reed, who is best known for his Communist Party activities, both in America and in Russia, and his burial in the Kremlin wall; Mary Heaton Vorse, the popular novelist and labor activist whose fishhouse at the end of Lewis Wharf dock served as the group's first official playhouse; the former Columbia philosophy professor Max Eastman, who was editor of the revolutionary magazine *The Masses*; Eastman's wife, Ida Rauh, an artist and actor affiliated with the Washington Square Players (as were other members of the Provincetown group); Hutchins Hapgood, the anarchist and sociologist who shared Cook's vision of a utopian society; Hapgood's wife, Neith Boyce, who was a published fiction writer; and John Reed's Harvard roommate, Robert Edmond Jones, who, according to legend, created the acting troupe's first set by making scenery from sofa cushions in Hapgood and Boyce's living room.[46] The fact that the group presented its first evening of theatre in a private home attests to its humble beginnings.

The popularity of that first evening of one-acts, which featured the premieres of Glaspell and Cook's *Suppressed Desires*, a satire of Freudian psychoanalysis, and Neith Boyce's *Constancy*, a thinly veiled exposé of John Reed's stormy love affair with Mabel Dodge (another member of the group), prompted a second performance in Boyce's home followed by yet another in the new makeshift theatre on Mary Heaton Vorse's fish wharf. The impromptu season closed with the premieres of two new plays at the wharf, Cook's *Change Your Style* about the feud between objective and nonobjective art and starring painter Charles Demuth, and a politically charged offering by novelist Wilbur Daniel Steele called *Contemporaries*, based on the true story of activist Frank Tannenbaum's arrest the previous winter for leading a group of homeless men into a church for shelter.[47] The group closed the first season said Glaspell, "without knowing they were the Provincetown Players."[48]

The 1916 season was much better organized and outfitted, since the Wharf Theatre had undergone a decent cleaning and a bit of renovation, including the installation of electricity, in the intervening months. The troupe presented seven bills of one-acts between July and September, including two premieres by Eugene O'Neill. The opening performance of the first, *Bound East for Cardiff*, was memorialized by Susan Glaspell a decade later:

> I may see it through memories too emotional, but it seems to me I have never sat before a more moving production than our *Bound East For Cardiff* when Eugene O'Neill was produced for the first time on any stage. Jig was Yank. As he lay in his bunk dying, he talked of life as one who knew he must leave it.
>
> The sea has been good to Eugene O'Neill. It was there for his opening. There was a fog, just as the script had demanded, fog bell in the harbor. The tide was in, and it washed under us and around, spraying through the holes in the floor, giving us the rhythm and the flavor of the sea while the big dying sailor talked to his friend Drisc of the life he had always wanted deep in the land, where you'd never see a ship or smell the sea.
>
> It is not merely figurative language to say the old wharf shook with applause.[49]

A second O'Neill one-act, *Thirst*, was given at the end of the summer, by which time it was apparent to all that O'Neill was a serious talent whose work deserved a much wider audience. The troupe had a second strong playwright in Susan Glaspell, whose dramatic talents, like those of many others, were stimulated by Jig Cook. Although the Cook/Glaspell collaboration *Suppressed Desires* had launched the theatre the previous summer, both were novice playwrights at that time. Glaspell's second play, *Trifles*, now one of her most well known, was written because Cook announced a new play by her for the third bill of 1916.[50] When she protested that she didn't know how to write a play, he responded, "Nonsense. You've got a stage, haven't you?"[51] Confronted with having to produce a script very quickly, Glaspell took Cook's advice and drew inspiration from their ramshackle theatre in the sea: "So I went out on the wharf, sat alone on one of our wooden benches without a back, and looked a long time at that bare little stage. After a time the stage became a kitchen.... Then the door at the back opened, and people all bundled up came in.... Whenever I got stuck, I would run across the street to the old wharf, sit in that leaning little theatre under which the sea sounded, until the play was ready to continue."[52]

The importance of this rural playhouse, precariously perched on a dock with the sea pounding beneath, as a source of inspiration and rejuvenation to the theatre troupe, along with Cook's zealous leadership, were critical to the growth of the Provincetown Players, who were sufficiently buoyed by the success of the 1916 summer season to try their fortune in New York. These same two elements—the unpretentious stage in a natural environment, far removed from Times Square and any vestige of the theatre industry, and the figure of a charismatic guru who functioned as organizer, teacher, scholar, psychiatrist, spiritual leader, and motivator—were equally central to the development of summer stock theatres. Add to these Cook's concept of collective creation, where gifted individuals come together to form "a laboratory of human emotions" and willingly take on whatever tasks need accomplishment, and you have the foundation for summer stock.[53] The only other necessity is the joint determination to forge ahead, scraping together whatever is needed but, ultimately, to just do it. This quality is perhaps the one most popularly associated with summer stock via the late 1930s series of "Andy Hardy" films co-starring Mickey Rooney and Judy Garland in which they ostensibly cried, "Hey, kids, let's put on a show!"[54] Although one may not associate that unabashed, youthful exuberance with the serious-minded sophisticates of the Provincetown Players, Mary Heaton Vorse's memory of the group's beginnings is not far afield:

> No group of people ever had less sense of having a mission than did the Provincetown Players. This theater which began so modestly with no aim except the amusement of its own members altered the course of the history of the theater in America.... From the first the leadership was with Jig Cook, without whom there could never have been any Provincetown Players. The plays touched off a fire in him since for years he had been thinking of the theater as a community expression—the old dream of people working together and creating together.[55]

Vorse goes on to describe the beginnings of the Wharf Theatre and, how like a children's playhouse, it came together:

> [The first two plays] were so amusing, there was such a breath of life in the performance, that we wanted to do more. Our wharf, with the fishhouse on the end, was conveniently at hand to serve as a theater.... We dragged out the boats and nets which still stood there. We all made contributions to buy lumber for seats and fittings. We made the seats of planks put on sawhorses and kegs. We ransacked our houses for costumes and painted our own scenery. Our first curtain was a green rep curtain my mother had made for me for "theatricals" in our attic in Amherst. Out of these odds and ends we made a theater ...[56]

Theatre in Academe

The ferment to create theatre art was further abetted by what could be considered the most logical of places—the university. Yet, here, too, as in the nation at large, the notion of theatre as a serious art form worthy of scholarly inquiry was a new phenomenon. Although dramatic literature had been a standard component of university curricula, to study Shakespeare or Sophocles as a performing art rather than as an armchair literary exercise was a radical concept at the turn of the century. Even more astonishing was the idea that the making of theatre could or should be taught in the academy. These innovations were largely introduced through the pioneering work of Professor George Pierce Baker at Harvard. In 1905, he began offering English 47, a course in playwrighting, which employed the then unheard of pedagogy of reading plays aloud in class (done by Baker solus) followed by student and professorial critique. He soon was offering advanced courses and, in 1912, founded the famous 47 Workshop to further the development of the best of his class plays via full productions. As one former student, critic John Mason Brown, later described it:

> He was sparing, almost stingy, with praise. His thanks for something he liked or appreciated was a slight pat on the back, a hastily muttered "That's fine." That was all. But it was by means of these few words, which were as treasured by those who earned them as if they were public testimonials, that he reared the astonishing organization which flourished at Harvard; that he persuaded men and women, who received no pay and little credit for it, to sit up night after night to slave on his stage crews; that he got his actors, in spite of the courses they might be taking and the fact that the 47 Workshop counted for nothing as an undergraduate activity, to feel duty-bound to come promptly to all rehearsals; that he mesmerized designers into competing for the privilege of setting one of his productions; and that he built up and held together that loyal Cambridge audience (he has done the same thing in New Haven) which felt itself honored to be allowed to sit in at the performances of what were usually very bad plays.[57]

Baker's influence on the shaping of American theatre is extraordinary. Not only do his former students, both from Harvard and later Yale, where he founded the department of drama in 1925, read like a who's who of the twentieth-century stage, but his efforts helped legitimize theatre, both in society and in academe, as a serious art. His particular influence on the development of American playwrighting and production, with a separate and distinct identity from its European forebears, is undeniable: he trained

Eugene O'Neill, Robert Edmond Jones, and Kenneth Macgowan, who together assumed the directorship of the Provincetown Players after Cook's departure, as well as Sidney Howard, Philip Barry, Percy Mackaye, George Abbott, Winthrop Ames, Theresa Helburn, Lee Simonson, and Donald Oenslager, to cite just a few of his most famous protégés. His work also encouraged other universities to institute similar programs. Sheldon Cheney, in his 1914 book, *The New Movement in Theatre*, cites significant theatrical activities at the University of California at Berkeley, the University of Minnesota, the University of Wisconsin at Madison, Dartmouth College, Stanford University, and Wellesley College, among others. Cheney declared that "what the American theatre most needs to-day is *freedom*," and he celebrates these institutions for exercising their right to experiment freely, eschewing traditional forms and conventional thought:

> The revivals of widely varying sorts of play, showing how this master or that achieved dramatic beauty; the experiments in setting, demonstrating how independent true drama is of the gaudy trappings and distracting naturalistic details of the usual modern background; the refreshing absence of artificiality, with the physical charm of unspoiled faces and youthful figures; the teamwork acting, without stars; the student playwrights who know no better than to break all the traditional rules of form—these things are of the very essence of progress in the American theatre.[58]

The first two decades of the twentieth century were critical in the development of theatre as an independent American art which, while continually drawing inspiration from Europe, was striking out boldly on its own. Both the art and university theatres were plumbing the richness of Western drama and theatre practice while confidently moving toward creating something new. Equally significant was the refusal of these blossoming artists to blithely succumb to the power of the established theatre industry, which was working hard to maintain its autocracy of the American stage. Elitch's Gardens and the Lakewood Playhouse, as commercial establishments dependent on box office revenue, may not have focused as intently on artistic innovation, but they certainly declared their right to operate independently, with full freedom to decide both repertory and production style. All of these factors—and their cross-pollination—were vital in establishing an atmosphere that was ripe for the development of a new group of theatres.

2

The Pioneers

The pioneers of American summer stock theatre were an eclectic group of theatre impresarios whose philosophies and methodologies had little in common. They did, however, share certain characteristics. Most were young, generally in their twenties, university-educated men from socially prominent families who could afford to provide the seed money—or more—to open a new theatre. There also were a few female founder/producers, who, like their male counterparts, were from socially and financially privileged backgrounds. They tended, however, to be established society matrons with wealthy husbands who lent both money and prestige to the operation. Regardless of sex, an education, a good family name, and a ready supply of cash were essential to all fledgling producers, who promoted their education and social standing in their advertising, a fact that, given the nature of their intended audiences, is not surprising. To gain support in rural New England, where the populace traditionally had shunned public entertainments and entertainers on religious and moral principles, entrepreneurs needed to prove their worth. Presumably, people of high social standing could be trusted to provide decent, morally uplifting diversions, and to comport themselves properly in public.

This profile is quite a contrast to the Judy/Mickey mythology of the young nobodies with talent, good looks, and loads of energy but no money or status, who would become the icons of summer stock. Although Judy and Mickey prototypes would eventually work in stock, particularly as interns and apprentices, they certainly were not the proprietors. Moreover, during the formative years in the 1920s, they did not have the resources, nor the models, from which to build this new American theatre.

This chapter will describe five pioneering companies founded in the 1920s. The first two, albeit short-lived, were inventive, resourceful enterprises that influenced the development of later theatres and nurtured the talents of people who would become famous for their stage work. The last three are major summer stock venues that continue to operate into the twenty-first century. Collectively, these 5 theatres create a composite portrait of the beginnings of summer stock.

The Jitney Players

The earliest theatre of prominence, the Jitney Players, was an anomaly because it is the only company in the history of summer stock to have no permanent theatre building. Instead, the group toured in a custom-designed truck complete with a three-tiered stage, lighting equipment, curtains, and storage for the twin tents that doubled as dressing rooms and sleeping quarters. In the spirit of English strolling players, they presented a summer stock season of one-night stands in New England from 1923 through 1928. From 1929 through 1939, they traveled throughout the United States and Canada, playing winter as well as summer stock. The troupe's home base, however, was in Madison, Connecticut, a town that proudly claims to be the birthplace of summer stock because it boasts both the first converted barn theatre (see chapter 3) as well as the Jitney Players, who traditionally opened and closed each season there.

The Jitney Players was the brainchild of 22-year-old Horace Bushnell Cheney III, known as "Bush," who conceived the idea of an itinerant summer stock company and designed the truck to suit all its needs. His dual inspirations were the university and little theatres; Cheney had studied drama at Yale (from which he graduated in 1921) and decided that audiences were in need of quality theatre outside of New York City. As his wife and partner, Alice Keating, remembered, "outside of New York there was no theatre to speak of." She and Cheney felt that "somebody should do something about this unfair state of things" and thus founded the Players.[1]

Their name and initial reputation were provided courtesy of a *New York Times* reporter, George MacAdam, who appeared at the Cheneys' "Little Red House" on the Boston Post Road in Madison shortly before the troupe gave its inaugural performance in July 1923. His article, "The Strolling Player Returns by Jitney," which appeared in the *Sunday Times Book Review and Magazine*, provided superb publicity that generated more press as well as numerous bookings that summer. The Cheneys immediately adopted the name the Jitney Players.[2] MacAdam's article details the elite backgrounds of the group's members based on information which, he claims, came from their own publicity materials. "The Jitney Players are upon a rung so high up that it's really a perch," he avers, since "socially they can look down, a long way down, upon the mass of humanity."[3] Cheney was the great-grandson of the founder of Cheney Brothers, a silk manufacturing firm, which, as the eldest son, he would inherit from his father, Horace B. Cheney. Keating was the daughter of Francis Keating, a prominent citizen of Buffalo, New York, and a professional actress, whose most noted role was the Ophelia she understudied and played opposite John Barrymore's Hamlet. All other company members are identified by their prominent parents, education, and notable stage experience, which, since most were fresh out of college, was largely in university productions. The men were graduates of Yale, Harvard, Princeton, and Williams, while the women were educated mostly in Paris and London. Because of the company members' prominent biographies, MacAdam predicts, "the eye of the constable will not be hard and beady. Wherever they pitch their tents and set up their stage, they will be welcomed as guests."[4]

The repertory expanded from a series of one-acts in the Players' first season to almost 70 full-length and one-act plays by the company's dissolution in 1939. Included were new plays and adaptations of stories written by company members, such as Ethel Barrymore Colt's version of Washington Irving's *Rip Van Winkle;* contemporary plays by Maxwell Anderson, S. N. Behrman, Noël Coward, Bernard Shaw, and William Butler Yeats, among others; little-known nineteenth-century classics by W. S. Gilbert and J. R. Planché; and major classics by Molière, Oliver Goldsmith, and Richard Brinsley Sheridan that seldom were produced in America. Regardless of the bill, all performances began with a greeting to the audience and the delivery of the following prologue, written by company member Hardwicke Nevin:

> We players come to you to entertain;
> The serious mood, the learned argument,
> The labored phrase, the borrowed discontent,
> The art which lives indoors we do not feign.
> What lies beyond a brook, a hill, a plain,
> It is not in our nature to invent;
> Our art is simply where we pitch our tent,
> We follow avenues of sun and rain.
>
> The open road has given us our parts;
> Forest, field and hill have filled our hearts
> Till in our acts were woven sun and wind,
> The night, the stars, the clouds, the color blue;
> So, if your feet can't follow, let your mind
> Go down this open road we proffer you.

A fascinating aspect of the Jitney Players was their traveling stage, which was built according to Cheney's specifications on the body of an old Ford truck by a maker of circus wagons.[5] It could be set up in little more than an hour and broken down in less. After the truck was parked in position and adequately braced to provide a level playing space, the back was opened and the tents, costumes, properties, and lighting equipment unloaded. The sides of the truck unfolded to create a playing space 16 feet wide by 14 feet deep that was supported by a steel framework on hinged legs. Four telescoping stanchions, which extended to ten and a half feet each, supported the canvas roof, which opened like an umbrella. Lighting equipment was hung overhead, and drapes were attached to the sides, back, and across the front to create both a proscenium arch and act curtain, which drew left to right. A cyclorama was hung upstage at a 45-degree angle that simultaneously served as a sky backdrop, a guy for the roof, and a shelter for the Ford engine in case of rain.[6]

The tailgate of the truck opened into a flight of stairs to the stage. When scripts demanded multiple locales, the troupe could use three playing areas—a wooden platform measuring 10 feet long by 4 feet wide that rested on the ground at the foot of the steps and was considered a forestage, the main stage which extended from the back of the truck, and a tiny third stage perched on the roof over the truck's cab, which MacAdam describes as "the size of three old-fashioned cracker boxes placed in a row."[7] Entrances and exits could occur either from the wings or via the two auxiliary tents placed on either side of the stage, which doubled as male and female dressing rooms and sleeping quarters. In 1925, a third tent, similar to a circus big top, was added to protect the audiences in bad weather.

The company traveled in two cars, later adding two auxiliary trucks, which accompanied the stage truck on tour and also stored luggage, costumes, 300 red folding chairs for the audience, a tiny red piano, and a Delco generator to power the lights. The lighting, which was fairly sophisticated for a mobile operation in the early 1920s, consisted of colored lights run on dimmers.[8] One of the added trucks was exclusively for lighting equipment including the generator, requisite cables, and additional audience lighting once the big top was incorporated.[9]

Cheney formed his company along the lines of Maurice Browne's and Jig Cook's notion of collective creation: everyone did anything and everything necessary to put on the show. Stagehands were employed because they also could play the violin, and actors had to act, sing, dance, and perform acrobatics. Everybody had to know how to stake out tents, put up a camp cot so that it would stay up, fold blankets into a compact roll, drive a car, battle insistent mosquitoes, meet society matrons and country storekeepers with equal poise, and preserve a presentable appearance throughout a "clothes-in-a-suitcase-and-not-much-time-for-pressing" summer.[10] Richard Aldrich, who would later produce the major summer stocks on Cape Cod, began his summer theatre career as the Jitney's business manager in the mid-1920s. He remembers that everyone received a standard weekly salary for performing her or his multifarious duties and got a bath only "when our tour brought us near the locker room of a country club."[11]

Over its 17-year history, the troupe had 149 members who played more than a thousand performances in 36 states. The extensive tours during the first six summer seasons, when the troupe frequented village greens, college campuses, and baronial estates throughout New England and occasionally to New Jersey, Long Island, and other parts of New York State, introduced quality theatre, presented by an upstanding and charming group of young people, to the rural Northeast. Aldrich credits the organization for "sowing the seeds that would sprout in summer stock theatres" since nearly everywhere they played, a summer theatre sprang up. "We were a sort of Johnny Appleseed of the movement," he claimed, no doubt proudly because without his managerial prowess, the Jitney Players, who were better skilled at making art than at handling finances, might have disbanded within their first few seasons.[12] Although it is impossible to assess the group's immediate influence on the development of future theatres, two repercussions are certain. First, the Jitney Players helped to mollify any hostility or lingering skepticism about the morality of plays and players in many communities, thus paving the way for a positive reception to future resident theatres. Second, the company chose prime locations to set up its outdoor theatre, and the natural beauty of the surroundings enhanced the romance of the playgoing environment. It was not surprising that future entrepreneurs would choose the same locales to build their theatres. Although most summer stock theatres performed indoors, the surrounding scenery, which frequently served as theatre lobby and entr'acte cafe and bar, were deemed equally important to the success of the evening's entertainment.

The University Players Guild

The Jitney Players may also have helped to inspire another elite, university-trained company, named appropriately the University Players Guild (UPG). Although the UPG opted for a permanent home, the two companies were remarkably similar both in their emphasis on prior university training and in their belief in collective creation. The UPG, however, took both ideas several steps beyond the Jitney Players, and, although it didn't emphasize its society connections as blatantly, the UPG's leaders actually had more money and status than the Jitney Players, along with the benefit of several major theatrical supporters to promote it.

The UPG's history is eloquently chronicled in *But Not Forgotten: The Adventure of the University Players* (New York: William Sloane, 1951), by former member Norris Houghton, whose subsequent career included the founding of New York's famed Phoenix Theatre (1953–64). Houghton describes the company's genesis in December 1927 when the co-founders, Charles Leatherbee and Bretaigne Windust, were introduced at a fashionable New York salon hosted by mutual family friends. Both were sophisticated, well-traveled young men who were college juniors, Leatherbee at Harvard and Windust at Princeton, and campus leaders in dramatic activities. In the spring, they, along with other enthusiastic recruits, met in Leatherbee's rooms at Harvard to solidify plans to open a theatre that summer on Upper Cape Cod in Falmouth, Massachusetts. Windust, Leatherbee, and two others each contributed $100 as seed money, and Leatherbee assured them that any additional expenses could be charged and repaid later, since his "family's credit was good in Falmouth." They found a suitable venue at a movie-house known as the Elizabeth Theatre, at which the proprietor agreed to let them perform on Monday and Tuesday nights during July and August if they would "split their gross intake, giving him fifty-five percent." As Houghton comments, this transaction typified the troupe's "flair for bad bargaining which marked their entire collective career." Undaunted, they set about making all the necessary arrangements for their "great adventure."[13]

The importance of Leatherbee's family connections should not be underestimated in establishing the UPG as a serious producing theatre. Even though the company eschewed monetary gifts, the family's in-kind contributions were considerable. Leatherbee's father allowed the group to use his old yacht as the men's dormitory while his mother, by then married to the son of the president of Czechoslovakia, invited four company members to reside at Charlie's "camp" on her nearby estate, Whitecrest. The camp was a large one-room building with full bathroom that also had a sizable screened-in porch, larger than the stage at the Elizabeth Theatre, that was used for rehearsals. In addition, she hosted the full company at a lavish dinner party every Wednesday night, which assured them of at least one good meal a week. These parties also provided the opportunity to mingle with many of her important friends, several of whom, including Winthrop Ames, Eva Le Gallienne, and Robert Edmond Jones, had allowed their prestigious names to be used as endorsements in the troupe's publicity materials. In yet another grand act of generosity, Leatherbee's grandfather provided the $20,000 loan used to build their new theatre prior to the second season. Although the troupe used box office earnings to repay the sum in its entirety within three years, it is doubtful whether they could have built a playhouse, or even opened a second season, without the family's support.[14]

The first season was a great success that earned the company $20,000 in box office revenues, which, after paying the cinema owner his overly generous share and production expenses, left a profit of $1,200. They had performed mostly light comedies and the first of many murder mysteries, which became the troupe's favorite genre. In the belief that they needed to prove their ability to play serious drama, the second bill of the season was Eugene O'Neill's *Beyond the Horizon*. Although the local critics praised their inventive, well-executed set (the UPG's elaborate sets quickly became a company hallmark as well as virtual assurance that the troupe would never become rich since they poured their earnings into complex scenery), the reviews also expressed the hope that this would be the only tragedic offering of the summer. Despite the high-brow nature of their audience, which largely consisted of wealthy summer beach residents, retired professionals who now made the Cape their year-round home, and the scientists of the nearby Woods Hole Marine Biology Laboratory,[15] the shows that packed the 900-seat house were what would be characterized as the light fare typical of summer stock. A. A. Milne's slight but affable drawing-room comedy, *The Dover Road*, George Kelly's *The Torchbearers*, a farce comedy about amateur theatricals, Sam Benelli's sardonic comedy *The Jest*, popularized by John and Lionel Barrymore, and the season's blockbuster, the aforementioned murder mystery, *In The Next Room*, collectively won the approbation of critics and audiences and proved to the company that its original play list, featuring a season well balanced among classics, serious dramas, and comedies, could be discarded in favor of froth, fun, and folly. Houghton admits "that this theatre of ours always faced the pressures of commercialism and took pleasure in meeting them" and was most interested in "presenting good plays well done" although no one could determine exactly what constituted a good play nor what "well done" actually meant.[16] The UPG wasn't an art theatre nor did it pretend to be, although if it "could improve the public's taste and temper (and in time it did), well and good."[17] Paramount to its philosophy and, no doubt, a key to its success was the importance of achieving excellence in all aspects of production. "We abhorred sloppiness," Houghton said of company members, and "thanks to the standards set up by our directors we became perfectionists in our craft."[18]

A second hallmark of the UPG was its structure as a theatre collective. The company enjoyed a communal lifestyle in which members lived, ate, and spent every waking hour in each other's company and engaged in the kind of collective creation advocated by Jig Cook in Provincetown. Everyone, quite literally, did everything. At many theatres, this spirit was borne out by actors' helping to paint the set and stagehands' willingly distributing publicity materials. The UPG took it much further, with a member serving as lead actor one week, director the next, usher the third, and set designer the fourth. No one was ever featured or billed as the star in the company's five-year existence, despite the growing fame of some members such as Margaret Sullavan, who alternated Broadway engagements with UPG productions. Although this egalitarian approach is now typical of educational theatre programs that require diversified training, here it was embraced by the members themselves, who were eager to continue developing their skills but in a professionally recognized environment. Consequently, people emerged with a great deal of practical experience, which translated into impressive resumes. As Houghton asks, what 23-year-old job seeker can walk into a manager's office, as Joshua Logan did in 1932, and honestly say he had directed 16 professional productions, as well as acted in, designed, and stage managed a host of others? Or, as Henry Fonda did, claim to have played more than 40 parts, and found time to direct a few plays as well?[19]

Another distinction of the company was its adherence to admitting only university-educated members. They need not have taken degrees—it's important to remember that much of the company, including Leatherbee and Windust, were still in college when the troupe formed—but they had to have spent some time as full-time college students. It was an argument over this point during the third summer that instigated the only serious threat to the company's continuance, with Windust in favor of maintaining the policy and Leatherbee, along with other members, supporting its suspension. Despite the fact that this rule excluded several excellent prospects, Houghton contends that "the university part" of the players "must not be minimized" for "these youngsters had a perspective on life that was grounded in their educational background and that had been strengthened through their association with each other."[20] UPG playbills always had the university affiliation listed in parentheses behind the member's name although, as Houghton points out, there was never a reference key. The (H) for Harvard and (P) for Princeton may have been pretty obvious given the founders, but a (C) could have meant Columbia, Cornell, Colgate, or many other schools, and as time went on, the Players happily accepted talent from many less prestigious institutions.

The second season opened in June 1929, at the company's newly completed playhouse at Old Silver Beach in the far western section of Falmouth. The theatre was built in only 20 days, ostensibly because both Leatherbee and Windust were busy graduating from college rather than supervising construction. Although exterior photographs suggest it was a modest, unadorned structure, Houghton, who joined the UPG as an experienced stage technician, claims that inside it was one of the best-equipped summer theatres he had ever seen. The proscenium was 30 feet wide, and the stage depth could expand to 60 feet by lifting a fire curtain that constituted the upstage wall and extending the playing space into the scene shop. The stage floor was completely trapped, allowing for any sections to be removed at will, and a full counterweight system accommodated flying scenery. The theatre owned state-of-the-art lighting equipment and had a well-outfitted scene shop to provide the fine scenography that characterized UPG productions. Across the theatre lobby was a large room with ocean views on three sides that served as the "tea room" (the theatre was built during Prohibition) and nightclub. In addition to a weekly change of bill, the company offered dinner, dancing to the accompaniment of a resident orchestra, and late-night cabaret, where company members like Josh Logan and Henry Fonda would perform stand-up comedy routines worked out between rehearsals. These enticements would become standard fare at summer stock theatres to generate extra income. The after-theatre cabarets also became very popular with performers who were as intent on developing their nightclub acts as they were on honing their dramatic skills.

The company directorship became a triumvirate in the UPG's fourth season when Windust and Leatherbee asked Josh Logan to join them. Logan had been with the company from the start but had not particularly distinguished himself other than as the "big, fat freshman" writer from Princeton who was called upon to handle comic roles and play the life of the party on and off stage. He had grown in ability as the years progressed and established himself as a playwright and also as a director and producer, experiences that would lead in later years to the creation of *South Pacific, Mister Roberts*, and other notable achievements. Windust also enjoyed a noteworthy directing career on stage, film, and television that was highlighted by his work with Alfred Lunt and Lynn Fontanne in *Idiot's Delight* (1936) as well as the original productions of *Life with Father* (which premiered at Maine's Lakewood Theatre in 1939) and *Arsenic and Old Lace* (1941). Leatherbee, who died of pneumonia in 1935, was, according to Houghton, not the most talented of theatre men, but was vital to the company's existence. A spiritual descendant of Jig Cook,

Leatherbee was the first of many inspirational gurus who were the driving force behind summer stock ventures. Houghton's description marks Leatherbee as typical of the breed:

> Charles Leatherbee was an idealist. He was a man of courage. He made you want to follow him. Just as he persuaded me to set my sights towards his goal and make it mine, so he persuaded everyone in the company. He was a tower of strength to the fainthearted. He made you want to do more than you were aware you could, and he made you able to do so. As I look back upon him, it strikes me that he had no great talent for acting or directing; the scenic effects he loved to fashion were not always so faultless as they might have been. His judgment about plays was not infallible. But he had a talent for people and a talent for living. If the story of the University Players had a single hero it would have to have been he. There would have been no company without him.[21]

(Chapter 4 is devoted to profiling these dynamic individuals like Leatherbee without whom summer stock would never have happened.)

The triumvirate envisioned the UPG as a place that provided solid theatre experience to university-educated people whose résumés had suffered by their spending their late teens and twenties in college rather than on Broadway. UPG productions also gave New York producers the opportunity to see the work of college people, who, according to Houghton, were quite scarce around Times Square because of a long-standing industry bias against "overly educated people." Thanks to the well-placed contacts of Charles Leatherbee's family, producers did see UPG productions and were sufficiently impressed to offer company members Broadway jobs. Winthrop Ames who, along with Eva Le Gallienne and Robert Edmond Jones, had leant support to the troupe while it was still a paper enterprise, not only saw performances but also attended rehearsals, offered recommendations for improvement, and even unearthed a custom-built trick desk for *In the Next Room*, which Ames had premiered years earlier in New York, and sent it to the Cape for use in the UPG production. He also hired away one of the UPG's best actresses, Eleanor Phelps, for his Broadway revival of *The Merchant of Venice* starring George Arliss. The following summer, Theresa Helburn, a producer with the Theatre Guild, hired both Leatherbee and Windust as stage managers for its fall season. Two years later, Cheryl Crawford, who then served as the Theatre Guild's casting director, offered a similar post to Houghton, who turned it down in order to join the UPG on its next great adventure, propelled by the visit of yet another producer. Leonard McLaughlin of the Maryland Theatre in Baltimore came to see the company's work in August 1931 and promptly offered it the use of his theatre for a winter repertory season.

Although the company had yearned to move into winter stock, the Baltimore season was ill-fated for a number of reasons, not the least of which was its timing during the height of the Depression in the winter of 1931–32. The non-union UPG also was engaged to play in a union house, an unfortunate circumstance that delayed the opening and caused much ill will with the local theatre community. This, combined with a difficult selection of plays, gives credence to Houghton's assessment that the UPG's leaders had a "flair for bad bargaining" and were not the most astute of businessmen.[22] Nevertheless, company members survived the experience and returned to Old Silver Beach for what would be their final summer season.

The company's last hurrah came during the fall of 1932 via its Broadway debut in a new play, *Carry Nation*, based on the life of the prohibitionist, which had failed to draw enthusiasm either on Cape Cod or in Baltimore in its pre-Broadway tryouts. The company was bankrupted by the New York engagement and, since it was the middle of winter, was unable to return to its unheated beachside theatre. Despondent and demoralized, the company simply broke up. It is noteworthy that rather than fall back on Leatherbee's considerable resources, company members chose to throw in the towel.

Despite the failure of the UPG as a theatre company after five hard-working years, it actually achieved its original objective of promoting college talent; most members were offered good jobs fairly quickly after the company's demise. The Broadway stage and Hollywood film industry gained the expertise of directors Joshua Logan, Bretaigne Windust, and Norris Houghton as well as a brace of performers, notably Henry Fonda, Jimmy Stewart, Mildred Natwick, Charlie Arnt, Myron McCormick, and Margaret Sullavan.

The UPG and the Group Theatre

Houghton relates an interesting story in *But Not Forgotten* that clearly delineates a typical summer stock theatre operation from what could be deemed serious theatre art. Playing a two-week engagement across town in Baltimore from the UPG, by this time known simply as the University Players, was another young theatre collective, the Group Theatre, run by a directorial triumvirate consisting of Harold Clurman, Cheryl Crawford, and Lee Strasberg. The Group, which concentrated on developing new American plays of social significance and who modeled its acting style on the theories of Constantin Stanislavsky, was as far removed socially, politically, and philosophically from the UPG as possible. When the companies met at social engagements, each drew shallow opinions of the other: "We thought them overly earnest and humorless; they thought us light-minded dilettante youngsters," Houghton said, adding that "both were right and both were wrong."[23] With benefit of historic hindsight, however, we can see that the comparisons and contrasts of these troupes offer a rich insight into the development of twentieth-century American theatre. Despite their essential differences, both companies believed in collective creation and were structurally modeled on prominent foreign companies which had, in turn, influenced the American art theatre movement of the 1910s. Both established summer theatres as a means of developing themselves and their craft although, unlike the UPG, the Group focused on intensive acting study and experimentation rather than on public performance. Both were committed to producing "good plays well done," although they had different ideas as to what that meant, and to showing the Broadway establishment that they had something worthy to offer. Most significant, both generated a long list of major talents who took their appropriate places on the two spectra of the American performing arts, what can be loosely categorized as grand entertainment and serious art. Both genres occupied the same spheres in the 1930s through 1950s and managed to co-exist successfully and peacefully. The Broadway stage, for instance, featured both Josh Logan's *Mister Roberts* (co-written and directed by Logan and starring Henry Fonda) and several Group-produced plays by Clifford Odets, including *Awake and Sing!* and *Golden Boy*. Broadway and Hollywood embraced Bretaigne Windust's directing prowess and a host of aforementioned UPG actors at the same time that the Group's actor-turned-director Elia Kazan became famous for his work with Group-trained "Method" actors. These collaborations launched some of the most important plays of the American theatre, such as Miller's *Death of a Salesman* and Williams's *A Streetcar Named Desire*, which were subsequently made into films. Both companies and the parallel paths they chose are honorable, necessary, and vital to the totality of American performing arts.

The Jitney Players and University Players Guild were important, albeit short-lived, ventures that proved that Elitch's Gardens and the Lakewood Playhouse were not anomalies. Summer stock theatre could attract audiences, produce quality work, serve as a training ground for young performers, and, to a greater or lesser extent, survive on box office receipts. Three other 1920s theatres that were also complex hybrids of artistic and commercial influences and were equally reflective of the individualism and dynamism of their respective leaders were founded at about the same time. These ventures, however, firmly took root and, despite significant changes along the way, have survived into the twenty-first century. It is these three—the Manhattan Theatre Colony (later known as the Ogunquit Playhouse), the Berkshire Playhouse, and the Cape Playhouse—which because of their early establishment and continuing prominence, are most representative of the summer stock pioneers.

Mariarden and the Manhattan Theatre Colony

The history of the Manhattan Theatre Colony properly begins at Mariarden, an outdoor stage and summer school of drama and dance just outside Peterborough, New Hampshire. Mariarden was founded by Marie Glass Buress Currier, a retired actress who had married well and could afford to purchase and redevelop the former Four Winds Farm into an outdoor performing arts center. She parlayed her own and her husband's contacts to build an impressive board of directors, which included Margaret Anglin, Jane Cowl, Ina Clair, Theresa Helburn, and Kenneth Macgowan. She also managed to lure Ruth St. Denis and Ted Shawn, whose company then included the young Martha Graham, to Mariarden to set up an Eastern Denishawn School of Dancing during the 1923 season. Currier had the good fortune to enroll talented young students such as Bette Davis, the Bennett sisters (Joan, Constance, and Barbara), and Walter Pidgeon, whose abilities helped to attract audiences to the public performances as well as future students to the school.

The school's hefty tuition fee—$400 for an eight-week summer session—was considerable even for the prosperous economy of the early 1920s, thus restricting potential students to the monied class. Some, like Bette Davis, however, were awarded full-tuition scholarships for their apparent promise and potential.[24] Currier's establishment of the school in conjunction with a professional performing company set a precedent for the summer stock movement in which school tuitions largely underwrote theatre production costs.

Mariarden also may have been the prototype for the rural performing arts complex, so prevalent throughout the United States in the late twentieth century. In these, lush, expansive grounds serve as the backdrop for a number of producing theatres, featuring an array of performing arts and artists, an affiliated school often with housing on the premises, a professional lecture series, and tourist amenities such as restaurants and gift shops. Although another outdoor cultural enclave, Chautauqua, in upper New York State, was founded much earlier in 1874, Chautauqua's focus was on religious edification, whereas Mariarden was devoted solely to the arts. It grew to 40 buildings spread out over 150 acres, which included cabins for students and guest artists, a refectory to provide all meals on site, a natural swimming pool, and nearby sporting facilities for golf, tennis, and horseback riding.

Mariarden had three spaces used for performances, rehearsals, and class sessions. There was a small, enclosed theatre as well as a barn studio space used for play and dance rehearsals, but the main attraction was what is described in school brochures as an outdoor Shakespearean stage created at the bottom of a natural amphitheatre. Possibly designed by Kenneth Macgowan and built in Boston and trucked to Peterborough to be reassembled on site, the stage appears, from extant photographs, to be a permanent perspective set featuring a symmetrically arranged series of buildings and entryways on a staired platform leading to an arched doorway at upstage center. Two-thirds of the doorway was open to the elements, revealing forest and sky, while the lower third, delineating the back wall of the stage, was a fence of vertical logs. The fence, which helped to define the performance space, presumably also allowed for actors to cross over from stage right to stage left behind the theatre and out of the audience's view. The theatre design reflects a hybrid of ideas gleaned from historical sources in its combination of an outdoor fixed stage of the type used for medieval passion plays on the European continent and Serlian perspective scenery dating from the Italian Renaissance. This unusual permanent stage appears to have accommodated any scenic environment required for classical theatre, as well as to have provided a wide open platform for dance performances, hence sparing Mariarden the considerable expense of creating sets on a production-by-production basis.

The school's curriculum is described only in vague, very florid terms in the published brochure. In the summer of 1923, it offered an eight-week program consisting of modules in "Interpretative Dancing and Rhythmic Movement," drama, and makeup, but there is little indication of what each entailed. The profile of the dance class serves more to confuse than to elucidate: "The high school or college student who has spent the academic year in indoor classrooms needs the advantages of open-air classes in dancing of this type to best fit her to return refreshed by the joy of perfect body control obtained through the combined harmony of music of the great musicians allied with the dance which the experienced and careful dancing instructors work out at Mariarden."[25] Perhaps the brochure went to press prior to Currier's signing of Denishawn and is deliberately inexplicit; certainly Denishawn's own brochure for the summer curricula is exacting in its detail and includes classes in ballet technique, music visualization, plastiques and Delsarte, Oriental dances, ensemble dances, and practical stage fundamentals. Ted Shawn also offered a special class for professional and advanced students in Native Spanish Dances and Technique gleaned from his two-month residency in

Spain, while Ruth St. Denis gave a one-week course for teachers in which they learned to choreograph and stage a ballet based on the myth of Cupid and Psyche that was designed expressly for young dance students. In addition to providing dance instruction to Mariarden students, Denishawn concurrently offered its professional course as well as the normal course for teachers of dancing in 12-week programs that were run simultaneously at its school in New York City.[26]

There is no separate pamphlet to better explain Mariarden's theatre program, which seems to have been based on the premise that students would learn by association with theatre professionals who constituted "the nucleus of a stock company," supplemented, in the smaller roles, by the students themselves. "These professionals will act with and thereby instruct the pupils in plays according to their talents," Currier declares, and would also eradicate any "peculiarities of diction" they encountered. Students were required to attend daily rehearsals, where they were to learn "many of the bewildering stage traditions which are never written down. This was the plan of the old stock companies," she contends, "and we feel that this is the only satisfactory way for you as a student of the stage to ascertain whether you have those qualities which will fit you for the life of the theatre."[27]

Denishawn did not return to Mariarden the following summer, citing in its 1924 brochure the difficult commute for instructors between "a city school and a country school," an understandable decision since the journey took at least eight hours one way. Currier carried on for several more seasons but in 1927 chose to rent the theatre to Walter Hartwig, who was looking for a suitable place to establish his own summer school and performing ensemble, the Manhattan Theatre Camp. Hartwig had roots in the commercial theatre—he had worked as general manager for Daniel Frohman—but in the 1920s he became a leading proponent of the little theatre movement when he founded and ran the international little theatre tournaments held in New York City. In October 1924, he organized the Manhattan Little Theatre Club, which was incorporated in the state of New York as a stock corporation "for the purposes to encourage and cultivate a taste for music, literature and the arts, and to erect, maintain, purchase or rent one or more buildings for that purpose." The terms of the incorporation were extremely broad, allowing the group considerable leeway in its choice of program and location: "The operatic or dramatic representations, concerts, and other entertainments might be given in New York, Boston, or any other cities or towns in the U.S. and elsewhere." It also stipulated that the group would acquire costumes, scenery, properties, musical libraries, and other material for use in presenting plays or operas.[28]

It is speculative as to whether the Manhattan Theatre Camp was an outgrowth of the Little Theatre Club, but certainly the camp was established in its spirit and Hartwig served as its guiding light. Unlike Currier's indeterminate operation of several years earlier, Hartwig set up a comprehensive training program worthy of a university theatre department, plus a professional stock company, which used Mariarden as its base for touring New England. Students declared a concentration in stagecraft, acting and directing, or playwrighting, to which they would devote three hours' intensive work per day. They also were required to take classes in history of the drama, voice control, body control, stage lighting, costuming, makeup, theatrical publicity, and dramatic criticism, as well as in all three specialty areas designated above. The course brochure contained substantial information on the content and objectives of each class, akin to a condensed version of a university class syllabus. The faculty was quite prestigious: author and drama critic Walter Prichard Eaton taught history; Alexander Wyckoff of Carnegie Institute of Technology taught stagecraft; Dagmar Perkins, a leading vocal coach and president of the National Association for American Speech, taught voice; John Anderson, of the *New York Evening Post*, taught dramatic criticism; and Hartwig himself taught acting and directing. Special lectures in theatre business management, play agents and their practices, and traditions of the American theatre were offered by other notables such as producer Brock Pemberton and educator Barrett H. Clark.[29]

Hartwig's eight-week course was designed for advanced students, preferably those who were already working in the profession but were interested in gaining a broader background in the allied arts. He explained that it would help "the actor who wants to direct; the designer who wants to learn the secrets of scenic construction and lighting; and the playwright who wants to see manuscripts turned into complete productions." He also encouraged dramatic instructors as well as people preparing for stage careers to consider taking the course. Along with the excellent education provided, a selling point of the school for Hartwig, as it was for Currier, was its charming location and excellent facilities. In addition to Mariarden's immediate attractions, Hartwig notes that the MacDowell Colony, an artists' retreat created in 1907 in memory of the composer Edward MacDowell, was right next door, as was the town of Peterborough itself, long noted as a summer arts colony and one that would develop further in the next few years with the founding of the Peterborough Players. Peterborough would become most famous, however, thanks to resident Thornton Wilder's 1938 Pulitzer Prize—winning play, *Our Town*, for which the fictitious setting of Grovers Corners, New Hampshire, serves as a thinly disguised portrait of the town at the turn of the century.

The Manhattan Theatre Camp returned to Mariarden for the following two summers, where it continued to offer high-quality dramatic instruction as well as two fully staged productions per season. There is little record of the latter, except the indication in the course brochure that "one standard poetic play and one new modern comedy" would be produced, and a 1928 broadside announcing the summer's poetic offering, the medieval mystery play *Adam*. The anonymous twelfth-century text was translated into modern English by Edward Noble Stone, and its sizable dramatis personae provided an opportunity for a joint production of the professional and student companies. From the looks of the broadside, it probably was a true ensemble effort: the acting company was listed in a uniform typeface with only a small separation of professionals and students. Hartwig directed the production, and other faculty designed scenic effects, lighting, costumes, and stage movement. There is a note indicating that the show would travel to Washington, D.C., under the auspices of the Episcopal Actors' Guild of America for presentation before the General Convention of the Episcopal Church in October. It is also noteworthy that among the listed patrons was Marie Glass Buress Currier, who no doubt took an active interest in Hartwig's operation.[30]

After the 1929 season, Hartwig moved his camp, now named the Manhattan Theatre Colony, to Bristol, Connecticut, where, in addition to the same quality and range of theatre education established at Mariarden, he offered an eight-week professional stock season. The Bristol locale afforded him two fully equipped indoor theatres as well as substantial workshop space for the design and building of sets, costumes, and properties. Bristol allowed him flexibility in staging and, for the first time, the ability to produce a one-a-week stock season. Frequently referred to by critics as a "gentleman of the old school," Hartwig chose his repertoire from traditional favorites of the late nineteenth and early twentieth centuries, such as *Trelawny of the Wells* by Arthur Wing Pinero and James M. Barrie's *Dear Brutus*, intermixed with the occasional new play presented in the hopes of an eventual Broadway opening. Although he produced and directed one such piece, *Loose Moments*, by Courtney Savage and Bertram Hobbs, on Broadway following the 1934 summer season, the show failed miserably. A critic identified as W. G. K. at the *New York Sun* said, "Mr. Hartwig, who is a man of long experience in show business, tried out the piece at his summer theater and he should have known better."[31] This failure did not deter Hartwig from testing other new shows in summer stock, but until his death in 1941, he never made a second Broadway attempt.

The move to Bristol and, three years later, to Ogunquit, Maine, instigated a more pronounced split between the professional and student companies, but there is every indication that the quality of the school training did not diminish. In fact, the students were afforded their own fully equipped theatre where they produced a full season of their own to paying audiences. Though many other summer theatres willfully exploited their students, commonly known as apprentices and interns, for their tuition dollars while providing little education in return (see chapter 5 for a full discussion of the "apprentice racket"), the Manhattan Theatre Colony Workshop maintained high standards through its final summer school in 1965. Samuel Marx, in a 1939 *Variety* report, deemed the program "the best that I saw" on the summer circuit, one in which students "really performed their own plays in their own theatres" as promised in the school's brochure.[32] The brochure also provides testimonials from major stars who, while in residence at the professional house, made it a point to see the students perform. Actress Ruth Gordon, for instance, is quoted as saying that the Ogunquit school and the one at the Old Vic in London were the only two programs she honestly could recommend to students seeking quality training.[33]

The Ogunquit camp continues in the twenty-first century as the Ogunquit Playhouse. Although the small seaside village of Ogunquit was not known for its arty culture and the theatre ran a deficit for its first several Maine seasons, Hartwig believed in the power of tourism and summer residents to provide an audience. Neither Peterborough nor Bristol are tourist meccas, but Ogunquit, in southern Maine 17 miles from the New Hampshire border, seemed to have tourism potential in its wide sandy beaches and easy accessibility from Boston and other New England and New York cities. Unlike the colony's two earlier homes, however, Ogunquit offered no theatre building nor auxiliary structures for housing, set building, and the like. Hartwig operated his first four seasons in a converted garage and service station near the center of town, and although he managed to lure major stars like Ethel Barrymore and Maude Adams to the makeshift stage, the audiences were not as easily attracted. According to one local journalist, "the stars that Mr. Hartwig engaged to play for him drew a smart limousine audience, but they would come only once. They didn't feel happy in the quaint old garage even if Ethel Barrymore was trying to entertain them on the stage."[34]

A terminally leaky roof prompted Hartwig to buy a prime piece of real estate on U.S. Route 1, the main tourist thoroughfare, and build the company a new theatre, designed by Alexander Wycoff, which opened in July 1937. Boston critic Elliot Norton commended the well-equipped new theatre for its 600 deeply cushioned seats, all of which, thanks to a carefully raked floor, command a perfect view of the stage; the commodious stage itself, which was as large as that of Boston's Colonial Theatre and "so completely equipped that it could readily accommodate the D'Oyly Carte Opera Company, with their eleven sets of scenery and costumes for eleven different plays," the dressing rooms, which were equipped with hot running water, apparently a rarity in 1937; and separate property and green rooms as well as a full scene shop and lots of convenient parking.[35] The new environment solved the problem of reluctant theatregoers, according to the local correspondent, who reported that "the limousine customers came back and brought countless others with them."[36]

With the opening of the new playhouse, Hartwig's company rapidly became one of the premiere summer stock theatres in America. Although it had enjoyed a solid artistic reputation since its Mariarden days, the relocation to Ogunquit, coupled with the outstanding new building, propelled it to a prominence that would continue into the next century. After Hartwig's death in 1941, his wife, Maude Hartwig, ran both the Playhouse and Theatre Colony until 1949. Under her leadership, the New Colony Theatre, a well-equipped building designed expressly for the students, whom Hartwig preferred to call the junior company, opened in 1946. Although they had maintained a separate stock theatre for the student company since the Bristol days, this was the first time they had a purpose-built theatre. Per long-standing tradition, the junior company performed a stock repertory at least seven weekends during the summer season.

John Lane, an actor who had performed at Ogunquit and who had assisted Mrs. Hartwig with day-to-day operations since the late 1940s, purchased the property after the close of the 1949 season and ran the school in the Hartwig tradition until 1965 and the theatre for the next 49 years. In 2000, the Ogunquit Playhouse became, for the first time in its history, solely a musical theatre, under the leadership of producing director Roy Rogosin, and in 2001, in another first, it was awarded not-for-profit status.

The Berkshire Playhouse

The second of the pioneer theatres, the Berkshire Playhouse in Stockbridge, Massachusetts, also boasts a complex history, which dates back to 1886 with the formation of the Stockbridge Casino Company. During the Gilded Age of the late nineteenth century, wealthy industrialists built summer mansions, known ironically as "cottages," in and around Stockbridge in the heart of the Berkshire mountains of western Massachusetts. These elite summer residents commissioned the noted architect Stanford White, of the New York City firm of McKim, Mead, and White, to design a private club where they could gather for social events or repair to the reading or billiards rooms. The *Pittsfield (MA) Sun* reported that "the building of this Casino is the first Stockbridge symptom of dissipation and gaiety but it is such a little one and will be used so prudently and moderately that there is not much fear of de-moralization."[37]

The casino, in fact, was used very moderately, and no doubt prudently, in its early years, but after the turn of the century, it quickly blossomed into an active social center replete with dramatic and musical entertainments. Soon after, the decline in individual fortunes, particularly after the imposition of federal income tax in 1913, and the further institution of excise, inheritance, and excess-profits taxes after the U.S. entry into World War I promoted a parallel decline in the fortunes of the casino, which fell into disrepair and was put up for sale in 1926. A group of prominent artists and businessmen bought the building, moved it to its present location, and set about transforming it into a public theatre. In January 1928, the group formed the Three Arts Society, a nonprofit corporation promoting the arts of music, drama, painting and sculpture via performances, exhibitions, and other educational and benevolent means. The casino was thereafter called the Berkshire Playhouse, which opened on June 4 with a special performance of *The Cradle Song*, presented by Eva Le Gallienne's Civic Repertory Theatre.[38]

The first season of summer stock opened several weeks later on June 28, 1928, with a resident acting company, co-directed by Alexander Kirkland and F. Cowles Strickland, and a repertoire that included popular plays by A. A. Milne, Ferenc Molnar, and Bernard Shaw. The directors concurrently opened a dramatic school in accordance with the stated aims of the Three Arts Society, which, according to one newspaper correspondent, was "so arduous that it would discourage all but the most determined and best qualified" students.[39] In a structure similar to that set up by Walter Hartwig at the Manhattan Theatre Colony, classes in acting, voice, diction, fencing, and dancing were given in the morning while afternoons were reserved for rehearsing the students' own season of stock plays. After three years, Strickland, now operating the playhouse solo, changed the school to an apprentice program in the belief that a student would receive better theatre education by associating directly with the professional acting company. "He can obtain the theory of acting elsewhere," Strickland told a reporter, "but it is seldom that he can find an opportunity of working so closely with some of the best equipped players on the American stage." Students still had their own season of performances, however, and were occasionally engaged for bit parts in the mainstage productions.[40]

The Berkshire Playhouse had an unusual fiscal structure for a summer stock theatre because it was run as a subsidiary of a not-for-profit corporation. The managing director rented the playhouse from the Three Arts Society at a predetermined rate per week. If, at season's end, the theatre showed a profit, all additional money was turned over to the Fine Arts Building Fund of Stockbridge and used for artistic and philanthropic services. If, on the other hand, the theatre ran a deficit, as it did during the height of the Depression in the summer of 1932, the Friends of the Berkshire Playhouse, a support group formed in order to keep the theatre operational, pledged to underwrite any outstanding debts. The Friends either were no longer active or were unwilling to aid Strickland in 1934, when a decision to run a repertory rather than stock season caused a near financial collapse. The Three Arts Society, which was not endowed and therefore dependent on box office receipts for its survival, responded by hiring a new director, William "Billy" Miles, in 1935, who was known as an excellent business manager. Under Miles's leadership, financial stability was quickly restored, and the Berkshire Playhouse took its place as one of the principal summer stock theatres. Miles continued in that capacity until 1958 when changes in summer stock and in his personal life forced him to retire. He was followed by a succession of hapless managers, which prompted the Three Arts Society to sell the building and grounds in 1966 to the newly formed not-for-profit corporation, the Berkshire Theatre Festival, which continues to operate to the present day.[41]

The Cape Playhouse

The third of the durable pioneer theatres, the Cape Playhouse in Dennis, Massachusetts, was the first and ultimately the most successful of the many summer stocks that materialized on Cape Cod, one of the most popular of New England's vacationlands. Like the Berkshire Playhouse, the Cape gained prominence under its second director, Richard Aldrich, who, similar to Miles, was principally a businessman who did whatever was needed to keep the theatre financially sound. The Cape's founding, however, was a much more romantic tale, inspired by Provincetown's Wharf Players, who had flourished on the same peninsula just a decade earlier. Raymond Moore, who created the Cape Playhouse in 1927, began his theatrical life on Cape Cod as one of the second group of Provincetown Players, an amateur company that formed in homage to its New York City–based forebears (bearing in mind that the earlier company did not acquire that name until it was leaving Provincetown) and from a shared belief that, in the words of Mary Heaton Vorse, "there was a tradition to be carried on." Vorse, who was the owner of the Wharf Theatre, where the group she more properly called the Wharf Players had performed (see chapter 1), was one of a handful of people who had been members of both companies, and she is clear in delineating the two. The earlier troupe "had come together almost by chance," she declares, and had as their foundation "the plays that many different people had written," adding that "they also had gaiety and spontaneity and earnestness." In contrast, "the new group at once thought of building a theater and having a publicity director. The Provincetown Players had nothing but plays and the new group had everything but plays. It had an ambition, which was to be a prominent summer theater. It was a strange thing to hear publicity discussed when there was nothing as yet about which to make publicity."[42]

The second group of players presented its first abbreviated season in a disused movie theatre in 1923 and the following season in Frank Shay's barn, another of the earliest barn theatres (see chapter 3). After only one bill at the barn, the group, which had profound ideological differences, split in two. As Vorse describes it, one faction, which consisted largely of members of the old Wharf Players, including Shay himself, was dedicated to presenting the work of Eugene O'Neill, while the other, which included Raymond Moore, was interested in more diversified, less weighty bills. A member of the latter group, a Mrs. Aldis, took matters into her own hands by breaking into the barn early one morning and carrying off all the theatre's effects—the benches, the props, and "even the light bulbs"—in the back of her truck. She established the renegade company in her studio by the water, while Frank Shay's group carried on in the barn and presented O'Neill's Glencairn cycle for the first time in its entirety.[43]

Shay enlarged and built a fly tower on his barn theatre for the 1925 season. It was during this time that Moore, "who looked like a young robin peering over the edge of his nest," was making his plans, according to Vorse. Although she had little regard for him as a playwright, she acknowledged that "this young man had the most profound sense of how to make a theatre succeed."[44] He rented the barn in 1926 and with his partner, Harry Winston, who served as director, formed his first company, the Winston-Moore Players. Although they were moderately successful, Provincetown, at the far end of Cape Cod, is not the most propitious locale for a theatre that hopes to attract a large audience. Moore consulted a map and determined that Dennis, which "was forty miles from everywhere on the Cape," close to what was known as "the Gold Coast" of the Cape's wealthiest towns, and readily accessible from Boston, was the ideal location for a summer theatre. He purchased the eighteenth-century

Nobscusset Meeting House, transformed it into a working theatre, and opened for business on July 4, 1927.

In order to pay for renovations and support his first season, Moore launched a subscription campaign in the spring of 1927. He published a prospectus outlining his plans for the season of plays, to be selected from a published list that ranged from "high light comedies" to poetic plays to favorite revivals, and presented by a professional resident company. He also discussed his intentions for future development, including a writers workshop, junior company, and affiliated gallery featuring the work of local artists. In what could be characterized as a mission statement, Moore contended that although the Cape Playhouse "is not a Little Theatre movement" and assured "there will be no room for an 'arty' element," he did hope for it "to stand for the best in the field of art, and to establish something infinitely more important than a mere commercial theatre." He expected to "offer the public something of definite value, and to receive in return the public's interest, cooperation, and its financial support at the box-office."[45] These statements indicate Moore's desire to disassociate himself from the amateur Provincetown endeavors and to establish himself as a serious businessman capable of operating a fully professional theatre, an ambition that he admits can be realized only through the support of an enthusiastic, ticket-buying public.

Moore achieved success rapidly. Midway through his second successful summer season, he conceived the idea of incorporating the playhouse and its surrounding land and selling $50,000 of preferred stock in lots of between $100 and $2,500 to friends and subscribers.[46] He needed operating capital, not only to run the theatre, but to expand his holdings into a center for the arts, which ultimately included the junior theatre and art gallery, as promised, and a scene shop, administration buildings, actors' cottages, restaurant, and extensive gardens that served as the setting for music concerts, puppet shows, and other outdoor events. The complex also included the Cape Cinema, built in 1930, which became noted as the home of the world's largest single indoor canvas as well as for its films. The painting, a 6,400-square-foot modernistic mural of the heavens, designed and executed by Rockwell Kent in collaboration with scenic artist Jo Mielziner, turned the cinema into a tourist attraction. The cinema's film schedule was equally impressive. It included many world premieres, among them *The Wizard of Oz* in 1939, featuring former playhouse actress Margaret Hamilton.[47]

After Moore completed his empire in the early 1930s, he seemed to lose interest in its day-to-day operations. He hired Richard Aldrich, who had begun his career as the business manager for the Jitney Players but soon had graduated to producing plays on Broadway, to serve as business manager for the playhouse in 1935. Aldrich left after one year, only to return again in 1938 and, upon Moore's death in 1940, to succeed to the position of managing director. Aldrich remained at the helm through 1955. In the interim, he brought ever greater fame to the Cape via his marriage to Gertrude Lawrence in 1940, the year following his coup in bringing the international star to Dennis to play the lead in *Skylark*. As the wife of the producer, Lawrence starred in one play each season through the summer of 1950. She also teamed with Aldrich to open the Cape Cod Music Circus, devoted to the production of musical comedies and operettas, in Hyannis, on the south shore of the Cape, in 1950. The music circus (later renamed the Melody Tent), created in emulation of St. John Terrell's Lambertville, New Jersey, Music Circus, which opened in 1949, will be discussed in chapter 7.

The Cape Playhouse, like other major summer stock operations, underwent several changes in management after Aldrich's retirement, some successful, some less so. Unlike other theatres, however, it managed to weather the business downturns that began in the 1960s when, for a variety of reasons, summer stock lost its popularity. It continues to the present day, as do its sister theatres in Ogunquit and Stockbridge, as a viable summer venue that has successfully reinvented itself with the changing times. Hence, all three have earned distinction as America's oldest continuously operating summer theatres.

3

Broadway in a Barn

"In Broadway parlance all summer theatres are known as barns whether they have marble halls like ours or not," wrote Charlotte Harmon as the epigraph to her 1957 memoir as a summer stock entrepreneur.[1] Hence, the history of Harmon's tenure as producer of the Chapel Playhouse in Guilford, Connecticut, is titled *Broadway in a Barn*. The Chapel Playhouse was a renovated church, but, as Harmon contends, that was a minor point. Barn theatres are as associated with summer stock as bright lights, neon marquees, and fringed velvet curtains are with the Broadway stage.

Barns became the venue of choice for summer stock theatres for the simple reason that they were tall, commodious, solidly built wooden structures that were readily available for purchase or rental in rural areas. Their potential as performance spaces was obvious to anyone who had ever worked in a theatre. Most barns boasted large, wide-open floor space and a high ceiling, sturdy cross beams that could be used for hanging scenery and lights, haylofts that could be converted to balconies, and ample ventilation. If a barn did not already exist close to a newly developed vacationland, one could be found, purchased for a reasonable price, and moved there with relative ease. Since barns historically were redesigned and moved to suit the farmers' changing needs, the notion of renovating and relocating one to serve as a theatre was not unrealistic. Furthermore, since theatre groups invariably included carpenters and designers, there was in-house talent available to devise and carry out the conversion from barn to playhouse.

What began as a pragmatic choice for summer stock producers quickly turned to a cultural icon as barn theatres became emblematic of summer stock. Barns suited the summer resort ambience perfectly for city dwellers, who viewed them as classic symbols of agrarian society. Even back-to-nature vacationers could feel at ease attending theatre so long as it was housed within a humble, rough-hewn barn. "It was as if the drama were on holiday too," John Hutchens of *The New York Times* wrote in a 1938 article extolling summer theatres. "When you go to a rustic playhouse," he mused, "you are as removed from the Times Square hurly-burly as a pine tree from the Paramount clock. It may be an illusion, but it is an agreeable one."[2]

Barns provided different but equally powerful illusions for theatre producers who could not help but think of great theatres of the distant past as they entered these wood, straw, and earth environments. Shakespeare's Globe was popularly envisioned as a tall open space supported by wooden posts and beams upon an earthen floor, a space that bears marked similarities to a classic New England barn. One could go even further back in history to conjure up a vision of Thespis becoming the first actor as he stepped out of a circle of dancers onto a Greek threshing floor, considered by anthropologists to be an early performance space. The wide open space in the middle of early American barns that suited acting companies so well had a similar genesis—to provide a place for the flailing and winnowing of wheat to separate the grain—and barn historians still refer to it as a threshing floor. As farming became increasingly mechanized, these sizable floors became convenient places to unload hay but had little use except as glorified garages for farm equipment.[3] By the 1920s and 1930s, when theatrical impresarios were searching for just these kinds of spaces, farmers were building more efficient barns to meet the needs of modern agriculture, and older barns were readily available. Hence, a cursory knowledge of history and a glimmer of imagination were all that were needed to make the leap from Thespis through Shakespeare to the twentieth-century barn theatre.

Barn buildings have a natural capacity to inspire awe and wonderment. Barn aficionados frequently describe their love affairs with these noble structures in poetic terms. In his introduction to *An Age of Barns*, Eric Sloane's description of walking into an old barn at night is analogous to Judy Garland's similarly dramatic venture in the movie *Summer Stock*:

> I pushed open the half-collapsed door and stepped into the blackness. At once, I seemed to have an overwhelming sense of satisfaction and safeness: there was a welcome softness of hay underfoot, and although they could not be seen, the surrounding walls and the oversize beams made themselves felt, almost like something alive there in the darkness. The incense of seasoned wood and the perfume of dry hay mingled to create that distinctive fragrance which only an ancient barn possesses. I felt a strong affinity for the man who had built this barn. Perhaps some of his reverence passed on to me—perhaps that instant was the beginning of my regard and affection for old barns. It takes only an instant for a person to be directed to a path that he will follow for the rest of his life.[4]

Dean Hughes's poem "The Barn," in Arthur and Witney's historical homage to barns, is a grandiloquent testimonial reminiscent of Walt Whitman. Hughes beckons us to:

> Examine, if you will,
> These giant plates and beams,
> These stalwart loins and limbs and thighs.
> Each one was once upon a splendid time
> A giant pine
> Singing a hundred feet towards the skies.

He asks that we pause to envision the barn through his eyes:

> Stand with me
> a wondrous moment.
> In that crafted tree
> Is history enough of old great-grandsire times
> A century ago and more.

"There stands my barn!" he proclaims. "Monument to the past! Feast for the present! Song for the future!"[5]

The "giant plates and beams" which thrilled Hughes were, no doubt, equally thrilling for the theatre producer in search of the perfect space, which, as for the farmer, had the double allure of practicality and beauty. Arthur and Witney describe the sensation of entering a barn as "the kind of feeling the visitor gets standing in the nave of a cathedral like St. Paul's in London. He will be immediately conscious of space, the space provided by the lofty nave and flanking lower aisles, of shafts of light from seen and unseen sources, and, in the barn, of the warm glow on time-worn timbers."[6] The ideal theatre space would elicit a similar response from the audience, which producers hoped would react not only to its spacious beauty but also with a reverence appropriate to a majestic cathedral.

Barn Structures

The barns that most budding impresarios encountered were well suited to their ambitious task. New England barns featured timber-frame construction, which consisted of a heavy frame of hewn timbers. This type of construction, which is the most common for barns in eastern North America, is also known as post and beam, so named because all vertical structural members are referred to as posts and all horizontal members are types of beams.[7] The timbers in barns built prior to the mid-nineteenth century were generally hand hewn with a broadax or hatchet and then smoothed with an adze.[8] Sometimes one side of the timber would remain natural, with the bark intact. Theatre operators particularly prized barns with hand-hewn timbers because they, like the drama itself, celebrated the art of ancient and honorable craftsmen. The timber on these older barns also boasted a handsome patina that blended mellifluously into the surrounding environment.

Although it is doubtful that theatre producers were knowledgeable enough about barn architecture to be in search of particular styles, they obviously wanted rectangular structures with a lot of open space and as few obstructions as possible. Interestingly, although many purpose-built theatres do have structural support poles that impede audience sightlines, most barns selected for rebirth as theatres do not. This is because of the popularity in the Northeast of English-style barns (known variously as New England or Yankee barns) and, later, balloon-framed barns, both of which have large rectangular threshing floors and vaulted ceilings. The most desirable New England barns would have been those built with a swing beam, which was "large and strong enough to span the full width of the barn and support a hayloft without interim posts."[9] Not only did these beams provide a wide open space below, but they also ably supported hanging scenery and lighting. Many of these barns also featured a large gable-end entryway, often with a long transom above it to provide interior light (which would have to be shaded during performances), and that served admirably as a grand audience entrance.[10]

Those barns without sizable swing beams generally had roofs supported by a truss, which is an assemblage of posts and beams that span a much wider area than any one piece of wood by itself would allow. Trusses were common to purpose-built theatres as well, not only to ensure the wide open space through the house but also to provide a rigid framework for hanging lighting and other technical apparatus. Barns also frequently had a pitched truss that would conveniently follow the design of the pitched roof. This style would readily accommodate point loads, which are placed at evenly spaced locations along the length of the truss, as well as centerpoint loads, devised to support particularly heavy pieces of equipment. Hanging a batten on these trusses to suspend lighting instruments or scenery was simple because the pick-up points were obvious to any knowledgeable carpenter.[11]

Balloon-frame barns were developed in the Midwest during the second half of the nineteenth century and, not surprisingly, this popular style appeared in the Northeast shortly thereafter. Many of these were cheaper and easier to construct than post-and-beam frames because they could be made with hundreds of pieces of factory-produced lumber "cut to the same dimensions and joined by cheap nails" and could be assembled by people with rudimentary carpentry skills.[12] This style of barn proved ideal for theatres because the interior created an acoustically advantageous shell, such as those designed for symphony orchestras, and there were no support posts to obstruct sightlines. Lightweight trusses, made in the same fashion, were developed in the early twentieth century for barn roof frames, which also served theatre technicians admirably for hanging equipment.[13]

The cool, country barn theatres that were touted in advertising brochures actually were cool and, except on the hottest evenings, remained so because of their natural ventilation. Farm barns had to be well ventilated to ensure that the hay or other crops stored inside were properly preserved; animals sheltered there also required a healthy flow of clean air. Specific methods of ventilation frequently were part of the barn's design. Louvered panels, long narrow slits in the walls, roof cupolas, and martin, owl, or swallow holes that allowed both a draft and easy access for the small mice- and insect-eating birds for which these were named were among the most popular types.[14] Most timber-framed barns, however, were naturally ventilated by air flowing through the cracks between the timbers, which would get larger as the wood gradually shrank over time. "It must be confessed," say historians Arthur and Witney, "that in many old frame or clapboarded barns, which in a hundred and more years have never seen a coat of paint, light streams in between the boards and the wind whistles. Ventilation without cost or mechanical aids," they assert, "is thorough."[15]

Although barn theatres in America seem to be a twentieth-century phenomenon, barns historically were used for many purposes other than farming for the same reasons that they later served as theatres. Noble and Cleek cite their appropriation as "workplaces, dance halls, social centers for husking bees and similar activities, and even as religious sites, much as the Amish continue to use them even today."[16] Noted barn restorer Richard Babcock contends that almost every town in America used the local barn as a church until the parishioners could raise the money and labor to build a meeting house.[17] Since most churches are designed in what might be described as an end-stage configuration, with the congregation facing an altar area at the far end of a rectangular auditorium, it is a short leap from barn to church to theatre.

The Earliest Barn Theatres

It is impossible to declare with certitude what was the earliest playhouse to appropriate an old barn because aside from the most successful summer stock ventures, there is little documentation. The town of Madison, Connecticut, however, claims to have been the site of the first genuine barn theatre, known as the Madison Playbarn, which operated between 1920 and 1923. It was the creation of Constance Wilcox, the daughter of a wealthy summer resident who owned a sizable portion of the town's property, including the disused barn that Wilcox and her friend Alice Keating (who, as the wife of Bush Cheney, was a co-founder of the Jitney Players of Madison, discussed in chapter 2), decided to turn into a theatre. Wilcox had begun writing, directing, and producing her own plays in the woodland garden of her family's home in Madison some years earlier. Henry Holt & Company published five of those plays in 1920, which were favorably reviewed in the December 24 issue of *The Literary Review*: "In this pleasant volume Miss Wilcox has made a welcome contribution to the literature of the Little Theatre."[18] Perhaps the success of her plays persuaded her to find a roofed venue for her subsequent productions.

Wilcox related the playbarn's history in an unpublished typescript held at the Madison town archives, which began when she and Keating happened upon the barn on one of their walks. "It was deserted even then," she recalled, and "was still half full of hay in the old lofts—there were pitchforks and racks across the big old beams and a rusty high-wheeled buggy carriage and a farm cart in the center." Nevertheless, she and Keating envisioned that "it would make a perfect theatre by flooring over one side for the stage, and using the other just as it was [with its] old stalls and beams and loft, and center open space for the audience."

With the promise that all proceeds from her productions would be donated to the fledgling Madison Historical Society, Wilcox got permission from her father to proceed with the barn's transformation. A new half floor was built for the stage, although she fails to mention whether it was ground level or on a raised platform. A brightly painted proscenium arch with "a green and blue and silver dragon rearing up one side with his claws over the top and a high spindly-towered fairytale castle with pointed red roofs on the other" is the only other purpose-built component that she mentions. The audience was seated on about 100 "rickety" chairs that had been cast offs from the local movie house. The most expensive seats, which cost $1.50, were in the old barn stalls, which she rechristened as theatre boxes. Floor seats cost $1 and balcony seating, in the old hayloft, was only 50 cents although Wilcox contended that those were the best seats in the house; in the front row, the audience would dangle their feet on a long board "right opposite the stage and not too far above." Her mother's old rose-colored, long satin parlor curtains, strung up on pulleys and looking "quite grand," served as the act curtain. Lighting equipment was created out of old tin cans that "were rigged up by two electrically-minded students" from nearby Yale University. An old lean-to shed with a dirt floor and a door opening on to the back of the stage served as the tiny communal dressing room.[19]

The playbarn presented a total of seven plays—six one-acts and one full-length piece—over its four summers of existence. It was a great example of a classic "little theatre" run by enthusiastic amateurs, who contributed or built their own scenery, props, and costumes and performed without pay. All proceeds went to benefit charities and other worthy causes.

The second documented barn theatre was created by a like-minded but, perhaps, more famous group of amateurs. Theatre enthusiasts in Provincetown, Massachusetts, buoyed by the New York success of their old friends and neighbors who had premiered the plays of Eugene O'Neill at the old Wharf Theatre in Provincetown harbor decided to start a new little theatre in town, which they not surprisingly named the Provincetown Players. The second Provincetown Players (the original Players took that name only when moving to New York City—see chapter 1) presented their first two plays during the summer of 1923 in an empty movie house but in 1924 moved their theatre to Frank Shay's barn. Little is known of the theatre proper except that only one bill of plays was presented before the group split in two, with the renegades making off with all the benches, props, and light bulbs early one morning when Shay was temporarily away. Using Shay's furnishings, they set up a new little theatre in a studio on the water, while Shay regrouped as best as he could to finish presenting the first full production of his friend Eugene O'Neill's Glencairn cycle in his barn. By the following summer, Shay had enlarged the theater and "a tower was built" which probably accommodated a fly house.[20]

Although Mary Heaton Vorse provides little more detail about the space in her Provincetown memoir, she does assert that "there was always a vital feeling about this theater, something robustious [sic] and rollicking and alive."[21] In the summer of 1926, the barn was rented by Raymond Moore for his first summer stock season with a resident company before moving to Dennis, in the middle of Cape Cod, where, in 1927, he opened the Cape Playhouse. The fate of Shay's barn thereafter is unknown.

These early examples of how barns were quickly and, presumably, without much money or expertise turned into makeshift theatres testifies to how appropriate barns were to the task and why so many troupes chose to use them. For the pioneers who built fully functional theatres in old barns, it was a thrilling experience that produced sturdy, beautiful playhouses that have lasted into the twenty-first century. One of the earliest that is still an active theatre is the Dorset Playhouse, now known as the Dorset Theatre Festival, in the heart of Vermont's Green Mountains.

More Substantial Barn Theatres

The story of the Dorset Playhouse provides insight into both the practical and aesthetic qualities deemed essential to the barn theatre. Dorset was built in 1929 on a large tract of donated land at the edge of Cheney Wood, reputed locally as the most beautiful spot in town and a favorite haunt of artists. The playhouse erected there is an amalgam of three barns: two pre-Revolutionary barns donated by Ernest West that were dismantled and hauled by sleds four miles to Cheney Wood, and a third contributed by the Vermont Marble Company. The larger of West's buildings, which was 30 by 35 feet and constructed of hand-hewn timbers that measured 12 inches square by 12 feet long, was used as an auditorium that could seat 235 people. The second barn was 60 feet long, which made it possible for the stage to be 28 feet wide, still leaving room for 16-foot wings on each side. Carpenters constructed a proscenium arch where the two buildings came together. Washrooms, dressing rooms, property rooms, and storerooms were built in the wings.[22]

An unusual and charming distinction of Dorset are the interior walls. As the barns were reassembled, the boards, which were planed only on three sides, were placed outside-in, so the weathered surface would encase the audience and provide a constant reminder of their surroundings. As the audience stepped outdoors, they would leave the illusion of natural woods inside to enter the surrounding woodlands, which aptly served as the theatre lobby. In later years, a roofed porch was built to shelter patrons during inclement weather.

Dr. Edward H. Goodman, the founder of the Dorset Players, provided a lyrical report on the building of the theatre:

> It seemed a sacrilege to take the barn down, to break its stark grotesqueries, to transplant it from its solitudes to the promised activities of the Cheney Woods, to substitute for its emptiness of past years the cacophonies of to-day, but like those who ravage Mongolian caves for beauties hidden from view . . . we felt the acquisitive instinct born of love of beauty and possessed ourselves of the rare old structure. As tenderly as scientists handle precious treasures of by-gone days, so was this barn laid low, marking each peg, each rafter, each beam, each joist and carefully placing the structure to-gether again.[23]

Many of the barn theatres worked hard to retain their authenticity as barns, eschewing all but the most critical structural changes. The splendid New London Barn Playhouse in central New Hampshire, which is so proud of its heritage that it incorporates the barn into its name, is a converted barn originally built between 1815 and 1825. The founding producer, Mrs. Josephine Holmes, a Mount Holyoke professor who bought what was known as the Pressey barn in 1933 to convert it into a summer playhouse for her theatre students, compiled a history of the barn that was published in the 1955 season playbills. The barn was built by David Everett, the eldest son of Jonathan Everett Sr., who brought his family from Massachusetts to settle in New London about 1750. It is presumed that David built the barn shortly after he inherited the farm from his father, who died in 1816. According to local legend, David and his family cut the logs for the timber frame and hauled them to the barn's present location (unlike most barns, this one, apparently, was never moved). The logs for the braces, covering boards, and floor planks were sawed at an old water-power mill at Hominy Pot, known as Harvey's Mill. A carpenter from Newport, New Hampshire, was hired for $100 to hew the frame and rafters and set the braces; this task took him five months of "arduous labor not to mention his skillful planning with chalk line, square and pencil." Neighbors helped complete the construction for the price of "plenty of hard cider and a good dinner" in the best New England tradition.[24]

When Holmes engaged local workmen to convert the barn to a theatre in time for the opening of the 1934 summer season, great care was taken to maintain the integrity of the original structure. Once the space was renovated, it experienced few changes until long after Holmes's departure in 1948. During her final season, *New York Daily Mirror* drama critic Robert Coleman came to New London to review a show. He seemed equally impressed, however, by the theatre itself. "The New London Barn Players are one of the few summer theatres really playing in a barn—or former barn," he proclaimed. "The interior is illuminated with carriage lights. An oxen yoke hangs above the entrance. The cow stalls have given way to orchestra chairs. The hay loft is now a balcony. It's real straw hat."[25]

Holmes was succeeded as producing director by N. Warren Weldon, who, like his predecessor, made no further renovations. It wasn't until the third— and current—director, Norman Leger, that a few necessary changes were made. In 1957, a roofed front porch was built to serve as a fresh-air lobby for patrons. In 1961 a back porch was added, mercifully it seems, for the benefit of the actors who previously were forced to climb ladders to make stage-left entrances. The back porch also provided additional space for props storage and a convenient spot for fast changes, since the dressing rooms were in the basement. In the 1980s, the local fire department mandated that a separate outside stairway be constructed for the safe egress of balcony patrons, but a local contractor managed to design it so cleverly that theatregoers felt it was hardly noticeable.[26] An article in a 1987 playbill proudly proclaimed the integrity of the barn, which "other than the addition of a stage and a restructuring of the hayloft to provide a balcony" had remained essentially the same.[27]

Theatre-by-the-Sea and Other Quick Transformations

The reconstruction of Alice Jaynes Tyler's old barn into Rhode Island's Theatre-by-the-Sea was not as exacting an endeavor and is probably more typical of the way most summer theatre barns were transformed. When Tyler was widowed with three young children in 1928, she decided to supplement her income by opening a summer camp for girls at her Browning's Beach farm in Matunuck. After the economic effects of the Depression limited the appeal for summer camps, she decided to open a summer theatre, which she thought would be a much more profitable undertaking. To operate the theatre, she teamed with a Broadway producing triumvirate consisting of actor Leo Bulgakoff, late of the Moscow Art Theatre, British comedian Leslie Spiller, and lighting designer Abe Feder. Since Feder was the only one with design background, the job of converting the old barn fell to him. He arrived in Matunuck in April 1933 and hired a local contractor who, in turn, hired a crew of New Bedford, Massachusetts, ship builders. "Nobody looked at a plan. There was no plan," Feder recalled. "I said the box ought to be about forty-five-foot deep, from wall-to-wall about eighty, and the height at least fifty feet. He said, 'yup, that's all right,' and he goes ahead and he does it." Only the job took much longer than anyone had anticipated. "It got to be May and June and it was not going so fast and the money was limited. One day two people came in. I gave them both paint brushes and stain and they started staining the inside. One of the guys was John Houseman."[28]

Theatre-by-the-Sea's opening season ran only four weeks because the theatre wasn't completed until the end of July. As if in anticipation of the barn's tumultuous future, the opening production was a play called *Strictly Dynamite*. Although the building never suffered a weapons assault, it did weather two hurricanes, a fire, and years of neglect. Although the theatre was placed on the National Register of Historic Places in 1980, it had undergone several major transformations since its humble beginnings as the Browning barn. But few barn theatres have the distinction of having two such famous men—Feder, who is often credited with inventing the field of stage lighting design, and Houseman, who, the following year, became the producer for Orson Welles and the Mercury Theatre—be associated with their development.

Another quick barn transformation occurred at Forestburgh, New York, when John Grahame's winter company, which regularly played at New York City's Provincetown Playhouse, decided to open the Forestburgh Summer Theater in 1947. *PM* Magazine covered the event and did an amusing photo-essay-cum-primer on how to build a barn theatre in its June 23 edition. "First find the right barn," the article admonishes, as it proceeds to list four rules of thumb: "Make sure your barn is located in the middle of some good scenery; having chosen your barn, do not be daunted; especially, do not be daunted by a cow, it's your barn, not hers; and don't forget to have a stage."[29] Both the photos and captions clearly are written to be gay and amusing ("young stage folks never balk at trying to pass a miracle now and then") but it also is apparent that Grahame's theatre company itself was doing much of the hard labor. As in other barn theatres, the stage was built separately as an annex, necessitating the removal of the back wall and the structural reinforcement of the inside walls and roof. According to the estimates given, the troupe needed "16,000 feet of lumber, half a mile of electric cable, and half a mile of water pipes to get the barn theater ready to hold 250 people next month."[30] Apparently, company members finished on time to open their first summer season on July 8, 1947.

Pseudo Barn Theatres

Although summer stock tradition insists that the theatre be an authentic barn, it is important to remember Charlotte Harmon's declaration that all summer theatres are considered to be barns, regardless of their provenance. Hence, when entrepreneurs could not locate a real barn, they sought an old wooden building that fit in splendidly with the natural environment and, ideally, had the look, feel, and smell of agrarian society. Some barn theatres were created from scratch while others used different wooden structures, preferably bearing a charming patina of age, as the basis for their conversions.

"When you don't have a barn, build one," was presumably the thinking in Boothbay Harbor, Maine, in 1937, when the Boothbay Playhouse was designed and built in the style of an old New England barn. The advantage of designing and building a barn theatre was obvious, since one could determine its exact size and shape and ensure that no structural members would impede sightlines. Boothbay's designers chose an intimate yet commodious front-of-house measuring 30 by 60 feet that contained a lobby, box office, and restrooms as well as an auditorium and balcony which comfortably seated more than 300 patrons. The stage, which measured an ample 30 by 50 feet, was much larger than usual in a barn theatre. This spacious environment provided actors, directors, and designers with lots of playing and wing space, which was a veritable luxury in the summer stock business. The theatre also was equipped with louvered windows, which provided optimum ventilation, and an oversize double door for its main entrance, which, in the grand style of the Yankee barn, afforded the perfect finishing touch to the barn illusion.[31]

The Tamworth Barnstormers, who had been playing a circuit of barns and other ad hoc theatre spaces through the small border towns of eastern New Hampshire and western Maine since 1931, finally settled into their own theatre at their home base of Tamworth, New Hampshire, in 1935. Although not a barn, the 1824 wooden building, which had been used most recently as the town's general store, seemed a good candidate for conversion into a summer stock venue. According to the opening week playbill, the Barnstormers, like the theatre builders in New London, did their utmost to respect the integrity of the original structure. In this case, however, quite a bit more conversion had to occur because a general store is architecturally quite different from a barn—and even more different from a theatre. "The original uprights and beams are still in place," the company maintained, while assuring the audience that the old timbers had been "considerably strengthened and supported by new construction." The troupe retained the original windows and doors, used the paneling from the store counters below the stage and in the foyer, and floored the area below the orchestra seats with boards taken from the original second-floor hall. They built a balcony, "retiring rooms" for the audience as well as dressing rooms for the company, and a well-equipped scene shop. "The main floor is sloping, and the balcony is so terraced as to permit an excellent view of the stage from any one of the comfortable theatre seats," the Barnstormers happily informed their patrons.[32] True to their name, however, the troupe continued to barnstorm and, after the opening week in the new theatre, would appear in Tamworth only on Monday and Saturday evenings.

Converted gristmills built with logs also made good rustic theatres, as proprietors at the Mountain Playhouse in western Pennsylvania and at the Bucks County Playhouse at the eastern end of the commonwealth discovered. Once again, however, the barnlike quality of the building was key; one chronicler of Bucks County even confused the gristmill for a barn in the title of his book, *Local Barn Makes Good or a True Historie of the Coming of the Thespians.*[33] A western Pennsylvania journalist, however, delighted in what she characterized as a noteworthy distinction between New England and Pennsylvania summer stock theatres. "Not only is it typical of Pennsylvania, being built from an old log mill, but instead of being an old barn remodeled, as are those in the New England states, the old mill was taken down, moved nine miles, and entirely rebuilt to proper specifications for theatrical use."[34] The commonwealth seemed to agree since it erected an official historic landmark sign on the state highway adjacent to the theatre which reads: "LOG GRIST MILL. This reconstructed early log mill was built originally at Roxbury by a miller named Cronin in 1805. It was in operation until 1918. It is now used as the Mountain Playhouse. As restored, it is a fine example of an early mill."

The barn look melded with state-of-the-art technology was the goal of powerful producers at top-flight theatres such as the Theatre Guild's Lawrence Langner, who in 1931 founded the Westport Country Playhouse in Connecticut as a summer tryout house. Langner commissioned noted theatrical designer Cleon Throckmorton to build a barn theatre in emulation of Throckmorton's earlier summer venture, the Cape Playhouse, in Dennis, Massachusetts. Ironically, the Cape Playhouse, although a converted eighteenth-century building, had not been a barn but a religious meeting house. No matter—it had the requisite look and feel that Langner was attempting to capture, as he describes it in his 1951 autobiography, *The Magic Curtain*: "The Westport Country Playhouse is situated in a hundred-year-old orchard just off the Boston Post Road. A more attractive spot for a country theatre could hardly be imagined. This red barn nestling amid old, gnarled apple trees was a haven of peace and tranquility compared with Broadway, and some of the happiest days of my life have been spent driving to and from our farm to the Playhouse and rehearsing in the open air under the old trees."[35]

Langner wanted the playhouse's exterior and even the lobby and auditorium to retain a barn atmosphere, but he hired Throckmorton to create a fully modern stage and scene house that was the equal of the best New York theatres. Throckmorton went so far as to make the stage exactly the same size as the one at the Times Square Theatre so that Langner could easily move hit shows to Broadway without any scenic adjustment. Langner also wanted a taste of glamour in his country theatre so that patrons wouldn't forget that he was producing grand art, albeit in the country. As such he commissioned a "gay proscenium of bright red and gold" with a "bright red curtain and red-and-gold curtained side boxes" in emulation of the "tuppence-colored toy theatre of my youth."[36]

To complement Throckmorton's architectural prowess, Langner engaged scenic artist Rollo Peters to fashion brilliant sets and brought in New York carpenters and electricians to make sure the requisite technology was in place to realize them on stage. Langner felt that his Broadwayized barn gave Westport a distinction over most summer theatres in its ability to serve as an incubator for plays that easily could be transferred to city theatres.

Though Langner's model, the Cape Playhouse, also was interested in developing new work and providing a state-of-the-art environment in which to do so, it was equally intent on disassociating itself from the summer stock barn. When the Cape opened in the summer of 1927 in a converted eighteenth-century meeting house, it had no competition. As one of the first summer stock houses, it was largely responsible, albeit unwittingly, for establishing the rustic barn motif that would be copied by hundreds of imitators. And, even though the theatre proper was not a barn, proprietor Raymond Moore built a new scene and storage shop "deliberately barn-like in appearance" directly behind the theatre. Not only was its design "kept as simple as possible and in harmony with Cape Cod architecture" but it was built to be "high enough to lessen in appearance the height of the main theatre structure."[37]

When the Cape reopened with great fanfare in 1946 after a World War II hiatus, the playhouse advertised its distinction from other theatres of the straw hat circuit as *not* being a converted barn. "Patrons find themselves sitting in seats as comfortable as those in a Manhattan movie palace," a brochure proclaimed. "Further, the quality of performance and production that surrounds each play removes the Playhouse from the category of barnyard drama, with the care and skill that goes into the settings and costumes—as well as the direction and acting—comparing with the top in Broadway execution."[38] With lots of nearby competition, the Cape, not surprisingly, was searching for a distinction (it is important to remember, however, that the playhouse still looked like the charming rustic barn that incited the trend two decades earlier). Yet the notion of Broadway in a barn had become, by the 1940s, an established tradition, and the summer stock barn theatre look de rigueur for potential audiences.

The Architecture of Anticipation

The barn environment became, in fact, such a critical component of the theatre-going experience that it was equal to, if not more important than, the play being performed. The country barn became the perfect frame for the performance, creating what *New York Times* architecture critic Herbert Muschamp characterized as an "architecture of anticipation." Although he actually was discussing Broadway theatres in his article, his argument is equally valid for barn playhouses. "We go to Broadway for the frames," he posits, "or at least for the atmosphere they help conjure up" which he later describes as "red-and-gold disease." "The ornate whorls and swags of their sumptuous interiors," he proclaims, "capture an ethos, a state of mind as distinctive as those that pervade Greenwich Village, Harlem, SoHo or the Upper East Side." Equally important is the theatres' relationship to the street which, in most older houses is just beyond the tiny vestibules leading into the rear of the auditorium. "The streets of the theater district are themselves a lobby," he proclaims, "part of an urban procession that begins with Times Square." Although "the transition from exterior to interior is not seamless, it is fluid," he assures us, and acts as "an overture before the overture, a progression of visual and spatial links between the wild, wide-open spectacle of the city and the close focus of the proscenium stage."[39]

Just as the lavish accoutrements of the typical Broadway house provide theatregoers with an architecture of anticipation appropriate to the sophistication of New York City, the weathered barn, laden with old posts, cross beams, and the lingering scent of earth and hay provides an equally powerful architecture of anticipation to the rural vacationer. The sturdy, imposing barn, which, like most Broadway-style theatres, is tall and commodious, is as palpable a space to create the magic of theatre as any other. The barn theatres' lobbies—a roofed wooden porch leading to woods, lake, or seashore or, perhaps, just the natural environment with only stars and sky for a canopy—is, for the barn theatre, tantamount to the teeming streets of Times Square. And it suited the time, place, and mind-set of the average vacationer perfectly.

Susan Bennett, in her book-length investigation of theatre audiences, further explores the multiple levels of interaction vital to the theatre experience both on and off stage. She cites Wilfried Passow's focus on "the interaction of the audience with the 'make-believe world' of fictitious scenic interaction" as crucial, but notes that the audience's interpretation encompasses the performance on stage as well as its architectural environment.[40] Here she cites the work of Michael Hays, who argues that the choice of location is key to the conceptual and spatial structure of the theatre event. "Temporally, visually, and conceptually," Hays states, "the theatre itself provides us with an initial glimpse of the way in which the lived experience of the performance is organized as a structural whole."[41] In summarizing this research, Bennett asserts that "these physical and perceptual relationships are central to the audience's experience of a performance, and will always mediate readings of the fictional stage world."[42]

Summer theatre owners understood the importance of the audience's expectations and thus sought to create an environment that would meet, if not exceed, them. Consequently, many venues ended up being as much of a fiction as the play on stage. "The important thing in the country is the illusion," one canny producer proclaimed in a 1949 *New Yorker* profile on summer theatres titled, "Every Little Touch Helps." The little touches are the marks of antiquity or "respectable appearance of decay" that make a new building look old and a non-barn resemble a real one. "Whenever you *need* worms around here, you never get them," complained one theatre owner. "I thought nature would do the job for me free over the winter. Instead, I've got to go out and buy linseed oil and pay someone to rub it in." Another enterprising proprietor sold soft drinks at intermission from a wagon labeled "Iced Phosphates and Minerals" to provide a touch of nineteenth-century charm. A third owner, frustrated with unrelenting heat in what was, ostensibly, the fresh country air, attempted to make his hot theatre look cool by concocting an act curtain made out of artificial pine needles.[43]

The patrons in the barn may have craved a rustic illusion but not at the expense of personal comfort. This duality was a given of the summer resort industry which specialized in what *Architectural Forum* called "the mass-production of rustic comfort" in its 1948 review of the newly manufactured vacationlands. The magazine explained the delicate balance necessary for a successful enterprise:

> What these refugees from urban heat demand is two weeks' of active recreation in the heart of nature without any of nature's drawbacks. This calls for a delicate resort formula, in which waterfalls, birches, moonlight and woodsmoke are separated from their natural concomitants—boredom, mosquito bites, burned food and poison ivy. It calls for hot baths and cold martinis; scanty daytime dresses along with evening formality; a variety of sports when the weather's fair, plenty of indoor entertainment when it's foul.[44]

Concomitantly, summer stock audiences wished to gaze upon a homely country barn while sitting in plush, upholstered seats. They also wanted up-to-date lavatories that they could access without going outside, and cool country air, which on muggy nights had to be generated via mechanical air-conditioning. Pennsylvania's Bucks County Playhouse managed to combine the old and new brilliantly in its 200-year-old mill-turned-theatre, which retained a barnlike aura while maintaining a cool climate. This was accomplished by diverting the noisy millstream during performances through a sluiceway to the cellar, where it was used to operate an air-cooling mechanism. "We are old one minute and new the next," a proud staff member told the *New Yorker*.[45]

Siting the Barn

The perfectly conceived playhouse further required a perfectly situated locale to assure its success. That place, according to impresario Richard Aldrich, who owned and operated the three major summer venues on Cape Cod, was "the center of some vacationland."[46] His business manager, Harold Wise, explained the strategy further:

> Picking the right spot involves making careful surveys of population, that population's earnings and type of work. Ordinarily a summer influx is another consideration. If the location is Cape Cod, do the vacationists come from Boston or from the whole Eastern seaboard or from the entire country? Are they conservative Bostonians who see many shows and know professional work well? The Eastern seaboard generally may not be so familiar with top theatrical names, but may flock to see a big screen name. If the location is fashionable Long Island, nine-tenths of the summer populace come from New York City. They will have seen every play of any importance during the winter season. They want to swim and play tennis and eat hot dogs.[47]

A steady stream of theatre-hungry vacationers is vital to a thriving summer theatre, but even more essential, as Wise indicates, is the local population, known to producers as "the natives." In the inaugural edition of *Blueprint for Summer Theatre*, a how-to guide published under the auspices of ANTA between 1948 and 1954, authors Richard Beckhard and John Effrat advise prospective producers that once a suitable theatre building has been found, be sure there's a potential audience before signing the contract. The base of that audience, they assert, is the native population. "It is advisable to begin preparing the community at least three months in advance, preferably six," they admonish. "If you're not willing to devote that much time in preliminary spade work, the odds are you will lose your shirt."[48] Their game plan included getting accurate figures on the summer population of the chosen community, finding and assessing the competition within a hundred-mile radius, and determining what public transportation was available as well as the condition of local roads. If all those factors were positive, then the wise producer would ingratiate himself with community leaders, persuading them to take an active part in promoting the theatre. "The community wants to know and meet the head man," the authors advise. "They like the feeling of having a personal interest in the producer's welfare. Personal talks to organizations and clubs, and the producer's participation in community activities can sell a lot of tickets."[49] Before moving the barn in place, the wise impresario would know that it's the perfect location.

Farm Phraseology

The immediate association of summer stock with barns engendered a whole lexicon of specific terms, as noted in chapter 1, that refer more to farm culture than to the world of the theatre. As barn historians Noble and Cleek point out, the barn is "more than a vanishing, utilitarian building . . . it has become entrenched in our cultural symbolism." They note the many common expressions, such as "can't hit the broad side of a barn," "big as a barn door," and "barnyard humor" that are part of the everyday language of people who rarely, if ever, had actually seen a barn.[50] Similar to these more generic expressions of barn culture is one that has become as readily associated with summer stock as the barn theatre itself—the straw hat. It is difficult to pinpoint exactly when straw hat became a synonym for summer stock, but it no doubt involves more than just a witty journalist's search for another clever euphemism. The term began popping up in newspaper and magazine articles in the 1930s at precisely the same time that both the resort and summer theatre businesses were growing proportionately. The term probably referred to many types of straw hats—the more fashionable variety, frequently called boaters, traditionally worn by vacationers to protect themselves while cavorting in the sunshine as well as those larger, floppier kinds made of loosely woven straw and employed by farm workers, who also were subjected to the strong rays of the summer sun. Hence, straw hats carried a double allusion that neatly encompassed both the vacationers and the rural, agrarian milieu that enticed them. Some theatres, like Pennsylvania's Tamiment Playhouse, placed both kinds of hats on the heads of performers and capitalized on the term to advertise their shows. Although Tamiment was a summer camp theatre and not properly a member of the straw hat circuit of summer stock theatres, it happily borrowed the term when bringing the best of its summer season to Broadway in the fall of 1939. *The Straw Hat Revue*, which enjoyed a respectable three-month run in New York, certainly solidified the summer theatre/straw-hat affiliation.[51]

As summer stock evolved, the barnyard operations gradually were replaced by sophisticated production companies offering top-notch shows. Yet, the barn theatre as well as the rustic charm of the rural outing remained. John Hutchens described the allure perfectly: "You know how it is on Broadway.

You rush from dinner to a taxi and thence through a small lobby to find your place in an impersonal audience. It is otherwise in the country. You take your time. You dine at leisure, walk or drive to a playhouse which probably is smaller than even an intimate Broadway house, but seems larger because there are trees and space around it."[52] He goes on to describe a typical audience—one that even a stranger like himself could admire and enjoy being a part of: "People know one another. Many of them are summertime neighbors, they have come to the theatre in groups or parties, and they stand around talking amiably and at their ease, comfortably and informally dressed. Back on the Broadway whence many of them come their attitude can be summed up as 'show me,' but now they are in a mood to be amused. And when, the daylight still lingering outside, they drift into the theatre, they are the perfect audience—theatre-minded but receptive."[53]

These, then, are the patrons supporting Broadway in the barn—a felicitous mixture of a supportive local community with the summer residents and visitors they beckon to join them at their lovely rustic theatres. And even though the heyday is past, there are still numerous barn theatres operating in the twenty-first century, including a new theatre that opened in a converted barn as recently as 1998 (see chapter 9), attracting much the same kind of audience for all the same reasons.

4

The Men and Women in the Straw Top Hat

Independent theatres in the United States tend to be founded and built by single individuals. The messianic personalities who started summer stock theatres were a special breed of artist, entrepreneur, and guru who held equal attraction for the theatre workers they persuaded to come work for them, usually for multiple seasons, and for the often skeptical local residents who had never wanted a resident theatre but who ultimately would embrace both the playhouse and players. Most set up shop during the 1930s and the best of these dynamic and affable leaders founded theatres that largely have continued into the twenty-first century.

Zelda Fichandler's depiction of the individuals who built the regional theatre movement of the 1950s and '60s is equally applicable to those earlier theatrical pioneers who founded the summer stock houses, which were America's first regional theatres. Fichandler, a founder and driving force behind the Arena Stage in Washington, D.C., described their shared history: "In the old days, the theatre *was* its artistic director. It was the artistic director, propelled by a vision of burning intensity, who brought the theatre into being, assembled the meager economic and physical resources, and collected or already had available a group of artists ready to set out on a journey of undetermined length to a vaguely determined destination."[1] Since these people were self-appointed founders, directors, and visionaries, they rarely had a formal arrangement with the theatres they willed into being. As Fichandler put it, "the only contract the artistic director had was one with him/herself and that was unwritten and, therefore, binding, more-or-less until death do us part."[2] Not surprisingly, this figure was inextricably bound to the theatre, and vice versa, in the mind of the public; one could not exist without the other and, when discussed, both names appeared in the same paragraph, if not the same sentence. Hence, when the director died, retired, or simply decided to move on (a rare occurrence, but it happened on occasion), the theatre underwent a crisis. These individuals were literally irreplaceable, and although others would of necessity step into the jobs, they never managed to fully fit in their predecessors' shoes. In most instances, the successor would carry on in emulation of the departed guru for as long as possible until time, space, and fading memory allowed real change to occur.

A major distinction between the summer stock founders and their later counterparts in the regional movement was the latter's status as artists in their own right. Almost all regional theatres were developed by outstanding directors seeking a place to mount the work they wanted to produce; this was not true in summer stock. Although most stock pioneers participated in productions, usually as actors, directors, or designers, their more valuable contribution was in recognizing and nurturing those abilities in others. This capacity to discover and promote talent also extended to finding savvy businesspeople to handle the theatre's finances. Almost without exception, the founders were not good fiscal managers; they excelled at bringing the money in, but once the money was in hand, they didn't know how to budget it effectively.

Prototypical Jig Cook

The men and women in the straw top hats were primarily visionaries, instigators, and cheerleaders, all with a healthy dose of eccentricity, whose spiritual ancestor was, either directly or indirectly, George Cram "Jig" Cook. Cook, who is briefly profiled in chapter 1, was the motivating force behind the Provincetown Playhouse, a daunting task considering the caliber of the people he was mobilizing—John Reed, Susan Glaspell, Robert Edmond Jones, and Eugene O'Neill, to name the most prominent. Cook, however, was an exceptional human being—a true eccentric—who defied rational explanation. Provincetown Playhouse historian Robert Sarlós calls him "Dionysos in 1915" and cites playwright Mike Gold's testament to his "sublime, gallant, crazy theatrical faith" that seemed to be at the heart of his talent.[3] Cook's widow, Susan Glaspell, devotes an entire book, The Road to the Temple, to trying to substantiate her husband's unique gifts. "He was the center," she explained succinctly. "For the most part, he made the others want to do it, as well as persuaded them it could be done." He also trusted people fully and "valued them by the finest moment they showed him—sometimes largely a radiation from his own glow."[4]

Although Cook was quite unlike other founders in some ways—he was, for one, an aesthete obsessed with creating a utopian society—he shared their commitment to fulfilling the dual roles of guru and catalyst, spurring artistic excellence via joyous collective creation. He also functioned as a true collaborator among equals who would not hesitate to get his hands dirty, even if it meant scrubbing the toilets before the audience arrived. Sarlós describes Cook as "a spiritual inebriate who identifies himself with the creative act itself" and "attacked every task with gusto, with intoxicating enthusiasm, with self-annihilating commitment, without distinguishing between small and large issues."[5] He remained through it all, however, an intimidating force. Cook believed in collective will, but he also asserted his power as leader and could readily function "as a dictator as well as a prophet."[6] He had both the determination and authority to persuade others to see things his way, and he would pour all his energies "into keeping that fire of enthusiasm, or belief, from which all drew."[7]

Cook's ability to inspire and nurture talent, perhaps his greatest single asset for the players, is best exemplified by Mike Gold in his description of their first encounter:

> I had a play. It was a very naive one-act play—they produced it later. . . . I sat down. Minutes passed and he didn't say a word. Then he began talking like a character in a Dostoievsky novel. I had never heard such talk before. He talked as though he had known me for years. He glanced through the play, and I told him what I was trying to do. I was an assistant truck driver for the Adams Express Company, but he made me feel like a god! He told me what I was trying to do. It was what he did for everyone, great, small, dumb, or literate.[8]

This single quality is a hallmark of all great summer stock entrepreneurs.

Cook, however, was not the definitive role model for a successful theatre producer. He had, for instance, little interest in making money. When the Provincetown began, it was truly an art theatre, staffed by willing volunteers dedicated to producing poetic drama and plays with political and social ideologies. No one drew salaries, and what little money came in went to theatre upkeep. As soon as it became more of an official business operation, which seemed to threaten his idealistic vision of pure art via collective creation, he left. He wanted nothing to do with capitalism or anything that smacked of populist fare. Yet, his passion, energy, commitment, and dedication to the theatre collective was, in the 1910s, a new and noteworthy phenomenon in the American theatre. Certainly that ardor and dogged insistence on creating a truly independent, self-reliant organization that could set its own artistic agenda was an inspiration. He proved, indeed, that it could be done.

This chapter will focus on three exceptional summer stock entrepreneurs—"barnyard Belascos," as *Variety* smugly called them—who combined Cook's fervor and vision with enough practicality, courage, and "plain old horse sense" to ensure the continuing success of their institutions.[9] Although all three founded their theatres in rural outposts in the early 1930s, and each dealt with the vagaries imposed by the Depression, they all, like Cook, allowed their unique personalities to shape the feeling and form of their new enterprises. Also, like Cook, they did whatever was necessary to make their theatres work. Francis Grover Cleveland, the youngest son of U.S. President Grover Cleveland, headed the Barnstormers in Tamworth, New Hampshire, for a record 65 seasons; Edith Bond Stearns, the first of three generations of women to run the Peterborough Players in New Hampshire; and Robert Porterfield, the promotional genius behind the Barter Theatre in Abingdon, Virginia, the first officially designated state theatre in the United States, will be profiled in turn.

Francis Grover Cleveland

Driving into Tamworth, a village nestled between the White Mountains and lake district of eastern New Hampshire, you encounter this historic marker:

First Summer Playhouse

Nearby stands the Barnstormers' Summer Playhouse, the oldest in New Hampshire and one of the first in the nation. Opened in 1931, at one time the cast covered a weekly 80-mile circuit. Currently its performances are limited to this community. Founder of theatre was Francis Grover Cleveland, son of the 22nd President.

Although Cleveland characteristically would refer to this sign as "my premature obituary," the Barnstormers merited considerably more attention than the average summer stock theatre simply because one of its three founders was the son of President Grover Cleveland. In fact, he often humorously was declared the son of two U.S. presidents because his father was elected twice, his terms running 1885–89 and 1893–97. Ultimately, however, Francis Grover Cleveland became equally famous for his longevity at the helm of the Barnstormers, which he actively produced and directed until two months before his death in 1995. At that time, the company was the oldest professional theatre in the country under the same founding management, and the oldest to continue with one-a-week stock, mounting eight shows in eight weeks. Actors' Equity also told Cleveland that he maintained the lowest ticket prices nationally which, in 1993, had just been raised to a $15 top. "We don't make any money, in fact, we lose money," he declared, "but now that we're non-profit, it's OK. I want to keep it as cheap as possible so that people who don't have too much money can come."[10]

The spirit of making theatre accessible and affordable to as many people as possible infused the Barnstormers from its beginnings during the Depression. The company was the co-creation of Cleveland, his wife, Alice, and their friend Edward P. Goodnow, who had studied with Professor George Pierce Baker at Harvard as part of the famous 47 Workshop. "He was really the powerhouse behind this thing," Cleveland modestly averred, "and he directed every show up until the war."[11] Cleveland had been a character actor of some repute in Boston who, although only 28, specialized in older roles. After graduating in 1925 from Harvard, where he had done a little theatre, Cleveland taught English at the Browne and Nichols School in Cambridge. "I'd been teaching two and a half years without knowing much of anything, so I thought, why not act?"[12] He met Goodnow while working with the Cambridge Dramatic Club, and eventually they, along with Alice, decided to form a partnership. While the men handled artistic matters, Alice immediately took charge of finances, which she continued to oversee through the 1979 season.

Tamworth was chosen as the home for the new theatre because the Clevelands owned property there, thanks to Grover Cleveland's 1904 purchase of a large tract of land with several houses that became the family compound. Francis, who was born in 1903, spent every summer there from the age of one onward, so it was familiar territory. Although Tamworth proved to be "a bad theatre town if ever there was one" in those early years, the company chose to open and close there on Monday and Saturday of each week. In between, it trouped to a varying circuit of resort towns that included Wolfeboro, Conway, and Holderness in New Hampshire as well as the Maine hamlets of Poland Springs, Sugar Hill, and Harrison. Cleveland assessed each on the comfort and convenience of the performing venue, which seldom was an actual theatre, and for the number of swear words the townfolks would endure. "We had to watch the language," Cleveland said. "You could not say 'damn' at Holderness, so we had to take the show to Bald Peak Country Club because you could say 'damn' there. In Wolfeboro, you could say 'damn' and 'hell' but in Tamworth we had to cut those words out."[13]

Tamworth not only demanded cleaned-up scripts but offered little in the way of an adequate performance space. For its first four seasons, from 1931–34, the company set up an 18-foot stage and movable chairs in a converted barn known as Tamworth Gardens, so-called because the proprietor fancied himself a prizefight promoter and would train his prospective boxers there. Two olivette lights, simple box-shaped instruments that produced big, broad beams of light, were adequate to illuminate the tiny stage, which could accommodate only minimal scenery and an act curtain that made its initial appearance a half hour before the opening-night performance. The box office consisted of a table and umbrella out on the porch where Alice and her sister-in-law sold the tickets. Since Tamworth's "village virginity was not to be violated," the company had a hard time drawing an audience, and Cleveland recalled standing out on the porch at 8:30 (despite an announced 8 o'clock curtain) waiting for one more car to drive up to the door before starting the show.[14]

The paucity of Tamworth audiences forced the company out on the road Tuesdays through Fridays, hence the name "Barnstormers." The troupe packed up scenery, props, costumes, the two olivettes, and the light board in a big truck and, with two station wagons for actors and crew, headed off about 4 o'clock on Tuesday afternoons to the first stop. They would do the show, repack the truck, and return to Tamworth, arriving usually around midnight. Rehearsals began at 10 A.M. and would continue until late afternoon when the troupe would be off to its next performance, packing and repacking as usual. "We'd study lines whenever we could, frequently in the car going to and from shows," Cleveland recalled, "but we never knew them very well. There was a lot of prompting in those days."[15]

"You had to be young and eager and hardworking to do that kind of trouping," declared former props master and later Barnstormers' board president Betty Steele, who remembered the whole process as "exhausting."[16] Yet, during their first decade, the Barnstormers found their largest and most enthusiastic audiences on the road. Their favorite town was Wolfeboro, which they played every Friday to packed, friendly houses who would show up as early as 6:30 with picnic suppers in order to get a seat. "We looked forward all week to Friday night," Cleveland reminisced, "when we became the theatrical giants of our dreams."[17] The enthusiastic crowds made up for the perfunctory Masonic Hall Auditorium, which served as their stage and where they had to pay a weekly fee of $5 to hire a policeman to guard the building. Cleveland also recalled the men's dressing rooms in the basement, which were "foul smelling in the extreme and full of mosquitoes," but had grand acoustics that encouraged the gents to "raise their voices in fairly harmonious song" as they shed costumes and makeup.[18]

None of the theatres on the tour had lavatories, either for actors or for audiences, but some venues were even less well equipped. Cleveland recalled playing for just one summer in a movie theatre in Plymouth, New Hampshire, where "the only way to get on stage was by hoisting up a ladder from outside or by walking through the audience."[19] At Camp Rockywold in Holderness, the theatre itself was splendid but the dressing room was a little hut out back, which could be accessed only by crossing a treacherous series of tree roots in the dark and possibly the rain. The worst theatres, however, were in Conway, a popular tourist town and, thus, a standard stop on their tour. When the one bona fide theatre there, the Bijou, was sold and turned into a factory, the troupe was forced to purchase an old mill and turn it into a makeshift theatre. Audiences, fortunately, would still come despite the insistent problem caused by the stream underneath. Since the Barnstormers had purchased the water rights along with the mill, they would close the dam on playing nights so that the audience could actually hear the actors. Unfortunately, the stream also served the town as a sewer and, when shut off, its "drawbacks were odorous and visible." Eventually, the company took up residence at the Intervale Playground, which, like the movie theatre in Plymouth, had a stage accessible only by ladder, so the actors would have to get in place before the audience arrived. To make matters worse, the owner would lock Alice Cleveland inside the little box office until all the tickets were sold and proceeds counted, to ensure that he got his proper cut.[20]

Although the company continued to barnstorm to many theatres of this ilk until 1941, it did improve its home base. Mrs. Frances Cleveland Preston, Francis's mother and a dedicated patron who frequently trouped alongside her son, purchased an 1824 building in the middle of the village that had most recently been the site of a general store, replete with cracker barrel and pot-bellied stove. The building was converted to a working theatre that boasted rest rooms (although there was not yet running water), commodious dressing rooms, a workshop outfitted for scenic construction, and raked seating for the audience both on the main floor and in a newly constructed balcony. The Barnstormers opened its 1935 season in the new house and played there a full week before taking the show, once again, on the road.[21] The building housed all performances of the now permanently based troupe when the theatre reopened after World War II in 1946.

The Barnstormers' repertoire remained constant during Cleveland's 65-year stewardship, reflecting his predilection for plays of the 1920s, '30s, and '40s that tell a well-crafted story. "We have this theory that the great plays of that era need to be kept going," Cleveland explained, because they capture the "spirit of that time and give people an idea of what things were like then." Besides, he added with a smile, they are all "darn good plays."[22] Popular selections included *Springtime for Henry*, *June Moon*, *Our Town*,

Harvey, The Late George Apley, and, the Barnstormers' signature play, *Ghost Train,* a 1930 thriller that opened the theatre in 1931 and has been revived seven times since. Cleveland also liked the work of Chekhov and Shaw and frequently added *Uncle Vanya, The Seagull,* or *Arms and the Man* to a season's bill along with a few works by contemporary writers, such as Neil Simon, who specialize in well-made plays. Actor Will Cabell, who became a Barnstormer in 1970, characterized the repertory as "a living history of the American theater" and credited the company with "keeping these little plays alive."[23] He and other Barnstormers never seemed to mind that Cleveland chose each season single-handedly. "Suggestions are happily accepted," claimed one observer, "and more often than not promptly ignored."[24]

To say that the Barnstormers was Cleveland and that Cleveland was the Barnstormers is not an exaggeration. The company thrived because of the mutual respect and devotion that Cleveland shared with the members, who were there largely because he was there. Betty Steele, who was a Barnstormer for 60 years, affirmed that "Francis created an atmosphere of belonging, a feeling that this was your organization and that you were a very important part of it. The loyalty that everyone has to the company has been built up over the years, and it was almost entirely Francis's doing."[25] He was also a highly creative individual who would inspire creativity in others. "This place makes it possible to do your best work," said company veteran Susan Riskin, while Dan Rubinate, who joined the troupe in 1955, called the aura Francis created "an aphrodisiac." "For a creative actor, working under this kind of freedom is wonderful," he proclaimed.[26]

Although Cleveland officially directed most Barnstormer productions after 1946, his style could best be described as non-intrusive. He simply would allow the actors to rehearse as freely and openly as possible without directorial imposition. "I'd let them go ahead until something is blatantly wrong and then talk to them about it and see why it is," he said. He felt strongly that they were "comfortable and happy actors who really feel a sense of community here" and enjoyed a "togetherness thing" that afforded everyone a great sense of accomplishment.[27]

Until the 1960s, Cleveland's identification as heart and soul of the Barnstormers was not simply public perception—he was the legal owner of both its intellectual and physical property. This nearly drove him and his wife into bankruptcy, particularly in those seasons when the theatre either lost money or just managed to cover expenses. There was only one show in 1953 and none in 1960 because the couple could not afford to open. In August 1960, company members took action and reorganized the Barnstormers as a not-for-profit corporation. In 1969, Cleveland gave the theatre building to the company. These actions helped keep the troupe fiscally viable but hardly flush because box office receipts, even when houses were full, barely covered the weekly payroll. The Barnstormers had long counted on donations to pay the bills, and it was Cleveland's role to appeal to everyone who had ever purchased a theatre ticket for help. The thrust of the fundraising was via his annual letter, which patrons eagerly anticipated as one of the literary highlights of their year. Cleveland always penned a highly entertaining missive that talked about everything except money. In his 1979 edition, he glibly discussed the trials of being 75:

> I am sure that some of you must be seventy-five also, and that many of you have run the course with us. So you know how it is, once they start to tell you how young you look, you've had it. I have even tried to gild the lily, and for some years have been using Grecian Formula 16, which gives me a kind of peppery gray look, rather like an old wolf. I have not yet come to Geritol. Our dog, who is also seventy-five, takes Pet Tabs, which she likes, and I have often been tempted in times of stress, like now, to try them. But all of these things are a kind of shaky crutch. Father William is old, and let's not kid around.[28]

He closed by declaring that he had "fleeced" them "very effectively over the years" and if this were his last letter, he hoped that "1979's fleece would be golden." "You have been a wonderful audience," he commended them, and for his efforts he earned the company about $20,000.

Despite a history of economic hardship, Cleveland always paid salaries to all company members except apprentices. In the opening season of 1931, everyone got $15 per week and a share in the company's profits at the end of the summer. According to Alice Cleveland's account books, the troupe earned $6,514.30 and spent $6,392.77 that summer, leaving a surplus of $121.53, which was divided equally among the members. This practice continued until the Barnstormers was incorporated in 1960.

Although Cleveland was clearly irreplaceable, the Barnstormers were able to continue following his death because they had an obvious successor in Clapham "Cope" Murray. Murray had been barnstorming for 45 years and, in the last years of Cleveland's life when he was nearly blind, had served as his assistant. Hence, both the company and its loyal audiences felt that Cleveland's presence was still with them. Whether Murray, or anyone else, could ever have the combination of creativity, loyalty, perseverance, and humor that was Cleveland is debatable. Certainly it would be hard to find another producer-director willing to defend his audience against the likes of Katharine Hepburn and Henry Fonda. When the two stars were filming *On Golden Pond* near Tamworth in the early 1980s, their secretary called to get them tickets to an upcoming Barnstormers' show. The box office politely informed the secretary that the show was sold out. The undaunted secretary reminded the Barnstormers' agent that it was *the* Katharine Hepburn and *the* Henry Fonda requesting tickets. On appeal to Cleveland, he answered flatly, "we would never ask our subscribers to give up their seats."[29] The subscribers saw the show, and Hepburn and Fonda did not.

Edith Bond Stearns

Edith Bond Stearns, popularly known as EBS, created the Peterborough Players of Peterborough, New Hampshire, in 1933. Although she died in 1961, it reasonably can be argued that her philosophy and spirit continued to shape the theatre's operation until 1995, when the last of the three women who had maintained the family tradition for 62 years left. Although the third, Ellen M. Dinerstein, was not EBS's blood relation, she was the heir apparent to the directorship upon the 1983 death of Sally Stearns Brown, a Yale-trained lighting designer who had taken over for her mother in 1962. Dinerstein, who had been Brown's assistant and had variously functioned as stage manager, general manager, and managing director since coming to the theatre as an intern in 1971, was committed to keeping the Players in the family. Her board of trustees included EBS's son, John Stearns, and daughter Isabelle Stearns Gay, as well as Sally's daughter, Lulu Brown Weathers, who from 1984 through 1987 also served as the playhouse technical director. Who then was this grand matriarch who inspired such a long and productive family-run playhouse?

Edith Bond Stearns perfectly fit the profile of a summer stock pioneer, and had she settled in Peterborough a decade earlier, she certainly would have numbered among their ranks. She was the daughter of a prominent Boston businessman and patron of the arts, Charles Henry Bond, who owned a large amount of prime real estate along the city's main thoroughfare, Commonwealth Avenue. In an early display of the zest and daring that would distinguish her 28 years at the helm of the Playhouse, EBS became the first woman in Boston to qualify for a driver's license. Happily ensconced behind the wheel, she delighted in shocking staid society by cruising all over town. She further startled eminent Bostonians by becoming a divorcée with three young children in the early 1920s.

Stearns first visited Peterborough in 1925 at the behest of the MacDowell Colony, a prominent artists' retreat founded in 1907, for the dedication ceremony of Bond Hall honoring her father. Although charmed by the area, she did not return until the early 1930s after much of her inheritance had dissipated during the early years of the Depression. According to an old family story, EBS marched into the Peterborough Town Hall and asked what was the least expensive property in town.[30] She immediately purchased that property, the old Hadley Farm on Middle Hancock Road, just down the lane from the MacDowell Colony and not far from Mariarden, the performing arts complex founded by another Boston society matron, Marie Glass Buress Currier, in 1920. EBS moved her family there in 1932 and coerced her 17-year-old son, John, and a houseguest, the young director-designer Emile Beliveau, to transform her 150-year-old barn into a theatre, which she immediately christened "Our Playhouse." It was a minimalist affair with a painfully narrow stage (John Stearns later quipped that "it was so narrow, you had to go offstage to turn around"), a motley assortment of chairs and sofas dragged over from the main house for the audience, and lighting provided by kerosene lanterns and candelabras.[31] Yet, it would prove an adequate venue to begin experimenting with a new kind of American theatre that would aspire to artistic rather than commercial success.

"Our Playhouse" (the name always carried the quotation marks) opened with great fanfare, and considerable press notice, on June 18, 1933, with the premiere of *Manikin and Minikin*, a poetic drama by the well-known writer Alfred Kreymbourg, who was currently an artist-in-residence at the MacDowell Colony. The production was truly a family affair with a little help from their friend Beliveau, who served as director, set designer, and leading man. EBS produced, daughter Isabelle co-starred with Beliveau, John handled the props, and Sally did the lighting. An encore performance, augmented by a few songs and monologues, was presented on July 2 "especially for those who have worked here to help us make this old farm over into our home and 'Our Playhouse.' "[32] Kreymbourg, who was very pleased with the results, wrote to EBS: "Somehow, I feel that something really worth-while is on the way: something I've been watching for many years. Here's more than hoping!"[33]

An article in the *Peterboro Transcript* attributed the theatre's founding to a meeting of Edith Bond Stearns, Emile Beliveau, and Alfred Kreymbourg at which it became clear that "these three people, each in his own way, had been thinking along the lines of a poetic renaissance in American drama."[34] The plays were described as "a new kind of dramatic art, made up of elements of the old pantomime drama, of painting, of the dance, of poetry, of music" that could challenge and stimulate "minds that are still open" with "a promise of something new and beautiful in the theatre."[35] Stearns was credited with "devoting her life to the ideal" of producing modern poetic dramas either in verse or prose, as per the mission of "Our Playhouse," via her "cordial encouragement" of Kreymbourg and Beliveau's work.[36]

The second bill of the 1933 summer season featured two new works by Kreymbourg, *People Who Die*, "an echo play," and *Jack's House*, "a cubic play." A critic for the *Peterboro Transcript* assayed an explanation: "Each is related to a central love motive, to the problem of human relations, to the tragic comedy of man and woman, and each approaches the problem through a different dramatic medium and through a rhythmic form in the theatre originating out of the curious psyche of Alfred Kreymbourg."[37] The *Keene Sentinel*, a New Hampshire paper, in reviewing the August 2 performance, applauded Isabelle Stearns's and Beliveau's performances for rising to the challenge of "working out the thought sequences with facility of expression, artfully combining verbal utterance, bodily movement and stage lights, colors and music to form pictures of telling beauty."[38]

EBS was quickly distinguishing herself as an art theatre producer of some stature; her audiences included artists and writers at MacDowell as well as from Boston; Ogunquit, Maine; and Putney and Dorset, Vermont.[39] Dancer-choreographer Ruth St. Denis, who had affiliations both with Kreymbourg and the earlier art productions at Mariarden, saw the August 2 performance and agreed to become part of the theatre's advisory board. Playwright Mary Young read her new play at Peterborough and solicited suggestions for improvement from EBS and other members of the company. She wrote Sally Stearns a note extolling EBS as "a real woman, a real friend and a real mother" whose "wonderful work will spread to all the corners of God's world."[40]

For the 1934 season, EBS added a theatre school, with a tuition fee of $200. Although, like other producers, she may have viewed this as a way to underwrite playhouse operations, the school seems to have been well organized and staffed. The daily class schedule included body technique, diction, stagecraft, lectures, and several slots reserved for rehearsal with private classes available in French, painting, and dancing. Beliveau, Kreymbourg, and Kreymbourg's wife, Dorothy, all of whom were on the faculty at Briarcliffe Junior College in New York, taught there, as did other specialists in music and design.

"Our Playhouse" was rechristened the Peterborough Players in 1935, but the core company, as well as poetical mission of the theatre, remained the

same, although the repertoire expanded to include such classic plays as
Molière's *School for Wives*. Starting in 1936, however, everything changed.
EBS brought in a new staff, headed by the distinguished former Moscow Art
Theatre actress and Stanislavsky-trained teacher Maria Ouspenskaya, and
assisted by the up-and-coming actor-director Norman Lloyd; she switched
the programming to a much less experimental, more populist season; and the
theatre became an affiliate of the Actors' Equity Association. Stearns had
come to understand that the theatre couldn't survive with only MacDowell
colonists and their ilk in the audience; she needed a much wider base of support. "The townspeople really didn't want such arty presentations—they
wanted straight theatre," she declared, "and I wanted them to have what they
wanted."[41] She also must have felt the need to provide financial security for
the company, which was likely making little money from its highly experimental productions. Although there is little mention of finances in the extant
scrapbooks, there is a 1933 letter from Kreymbourg reassuring EBS that she
shouldn't worry about the Depression. "If we all work very simply and faithfully," he maintained, "the best results will follow."[42] This may have worked
for a few seasons, but by 1936 EBS recognized the need for change.

It isn't clear what happened personally or professionally during the transition period from a "coterie, closet theatre" with a narrow appeal to a professional summer stock house that responded to the tastes of the greater
Peterborough community.[43] Given EBS's reputation as a warm and loving
individual, however, the shift likely was smoothly executed. Although not an
artist herself, she had the gift of recognizing and nurturing potential in others.
She "made you believe you were important" and "saw more in you than you
saw in yourself," according to longtime Peterborough Player Rosanna Cox,
who first came to the theatre as an apprentice in 1939 and finally retired from
performing in 1994. Cox recalls being invited to sit at the foot of Stearns's
bed and share everything she had done, thought, and felt during the day.
Stearns would prop herself up in bed and listen for hours, all the while
exhibiting keen attention, compassion, and encouragement. Although Cox
could not attest that EBS invited all the Players to bedside chats, she did characterize her as "the center of a wheel that would radiate to everyone involved
in the production—the director, designers, actors, technicians, everyone." She
would inspire and stimulate the artists working for her, and was known to
make calls to directors at 2 A.M. to share an idea, but she never interfered
with the artistic process. "She would give over the reins to whomever had the
talent," Cox said, content to be the one who made sure that everyone had
what they needed to excel.[44]

In the same way that she showed sensitivity to the theatre artists, she was extremely receptive to her audiences. As J. Wesley Ziegler characterized it in a brief 1963 history, "the goal was to make the Players a place which the town would come to know and love, and which would maintain its hometown's traditions of high purpose and integrity."[45] Cox said that "the Barn," as the theatre was known, was "an extension of people's living rooms. EBS was close to the essential feelings and ideas of the people in her audience and it was important to her to always respond to them."[46] No doubt this was at the core of her 1936 decision to transform the theatre into a more populist place, offering a wider selection of comedies, dramas, and, later, musical entertainments. Yet EBS was committed to retaining the penchant for serious art that characterized the theatre's founding and gave it a distinction from other summer stock operations. Hence, she and her successors punctuated each season with classics such as *She Stoops to Conquer*, *Antigone*, *Peer Gynt*, *Uncle Vanya*, and many by Shakespeare and Shaw; serious modern dramas like *All My Sons*, *The Hostage*, and *The Glass Menagerie* and more experimental work including *The Caretaker*, *Rhinoceros*, and *Waiting for Godot*; and, especially during EBS's regime, premieres of new plays and musicals. The players also maintained its ties with the MacDowell Colony, producing another play penned by an artist-in-residence that was a thinly disguised portrait of Peterborough itself. Although Thornton Wilder's *Our Town* wasn't presented by the players until 1940, two years after both its 1938 Broadway debut and Pulitzer Prize, it was an obvious choice for the company, sweetened by Wilder's presence at rehearsals and performances.

As she developed "Our Playhouse," EBS also developed her children as theatre professionals. John and Isabelle eventually had successful acting careers in New York and Hollywood, while Sally became the first woman to earn an M.F.A. in lighting design at Yale, despite the fact that she never formally matriculated. Yale turned down her application repeatedly with no justification beyond its dogmatic refusal to admit women. Undaunted, EBS told Sally to pack her bags, because "we're going to New Haven." Dutiful, shy Sally, who always did exactly what her mother asked, complied and, at her mother's urging, began attending classes. In recognition of her talent and perseverance, Yale finally agreed to let her stay, and eventually awarded her a degree.[47]

Having lost two children to the lure of the entertainment industry, EBS was determined to make sure that Sally stayed with her theatre. Although during World War II Sally worked as an architectural lighting designer on U.S. Navy ships and then served with the Red Cross in Europe, EBS made sure that she got back as soon as possible to help reopen the theatre in 1946. In yet another example of EBS's legendary spunk, Sally received, without explanation, an emergency call to return home immediately after she served at the liberation of Dachau. As her ship was entering U.S. territorial waters, she heard her mother's voice boom out over the ship-to-shore radio's microphone: "I'm so glad you're here, I'm waiting for you. We're opening the Peterborough Players again!"[48]

EBS ran the theatre until her death in 1961 which, not surprisingly, precipitated a crisis. The 1962 season consisted of one show only, and after each performance the audience was invited to share their suggestions for the future of the theatre. Sally, who was "mother's stalwart assistant," reluctantly agreed to try to fill her mother's shoes. Although unlike her mother in some ways—she was as shy as her mother was flamboyant—Sally shared her mother's compassion and love for others, as well as the ability to convince people that they were wonderful, special individuals with the potential for greatness. She also, like her mother, eschewed any remuneration—neither woman ever drew a salary for her endeavors—and continued to use their dining room table as an office and meeting place for the theatre staff. Sally, in fact, hardly changed anything, including the arrangement of furniture in the house since, for so many people, it provided comfort and assurance that they were still a part of this wonderful extended family.

The barn, too, looked much as it did when, in 1933, EBS convinced her son and Beliveau to make it into a theatre. Other than the addition of a backstage scene shop in 1942 and the need to reinforce the roof and support beams, there were no major changes until 1983 when the back of the house expanded to accommodate an additional four rows of chairs, bringing the seating from a cramped space for 144 patrons to a slightly more commodious one that would accommodate 200 seats. The theatre building itself, plus 11 adjacent acres of land containing various outbuildings, including a costume shop and living quarters for company members, were deeded to the Peterborough Playhouse corporation by the Stearns-Brown family, which had retained private ownership until 1989.

History repeated itself when Sally's assistant and close friend, Ellen M. Dinerstein, assumed the duties of producing director after her death in 1983. Dinerstein stayed on at the Players until 1995, making much-needed alterations to what was clearly a failing physical plant and implementing managerial changes necessary with the transferal of ownership. Yet, she felt compelled to carry on the grand tradition of the Players as founded by EBS over a half century earlier. When asked about the succession of women who had always controlled the theatre, she maintained that there was no great plan or design to make it so. "I don't think of myself as Mother Courage," she laughed, while admitting that there "are a lot of people who think this is a mystical, magical, woman-centered place." Although she doesn't necessarily agree with that assessment, she does believe there is something special about the Players that has to do with its history as a woman-run operation. "It is a business, and it has always functioned as a business, but it is also a family-based and - run theatre. There might be something about women—in a lot of ways, the emotional, family-like nature of this theatre, what it has taken to keep it going, is the role that women more often play in the world than men. And perhaps that has made all the difference."[49]

Robert Huffard Porterfield

The most famous and, possibly, most dashing of the summer stock gurus was Robert Huffard Porterfield, the "Mr. P" of Virginia's Barter Theatre. Mr. P epitomized the classic founder/artistic director/guiding spirit of the summer stock universe with his magnetic charm, courtly manner, and "smile that was out of this world."[50] Like his fellow leaders, he was an ardent, nurturing parental figure who made people believe that they were invaluable members of the Barter family, whether on stage or in the audience. "When you were talking to him, he was absolutely riveted to you, and outside things didn't matter," recalled Rex Partington, who became Porterfield's successor. "And it didn't matter who you were; whether a peer, an underling, or royalty, you got the same attention."[51]

Porterfield, however, had a fervor and ambition that set him apart, and the Barter was truly a one-of-a-kind operation that reflected his singular person-ality. The theatre was created at the height of the Depression on the premise that farmers, with a surplus of food they could not sell, would be willing to swap produce for entertainment. Although one could purchase a ticket for 30 cents, most patrons bartered for their admission with offerings of vegetables, fruit, eggs, honey, hams, or other foodstuffs. It was an audacious scheme, but it worked, thanks to Porterfield's talent as a promoter extraordinaire. He married his ability as a fine public speaker with his innate political savvy, consummate charm, and an actorly flair to become "the greatest promotion expert" Rex Partington had ever met in his life. "But," he quickly added, "it wasn't hard sell. He could get you to do anything by being so sweet and warm, and it was impossible to say no."[52] Porterfield's gift of persuasion, combined with tireless ingenuity, not only gave birth to the Barter but allowed it to continue, albeit on a shoestring budget, for years. How else could a town of 4,000 in a remote corner of southwestern Virginia support one of the most active producing theatres in the nation? The Barter, which evolved from a summer stock operation to a fully fledged regional theatre by the early 1980s, producing 14 plays in two theatres each season, celebrated its seventieth anniversary in 2003. And it is still very much the house that Bob Porterfield built.

Part of Mr. P's promotional flair lay in his ability to "take a small notion and make it into a great story," according to the Barter's current artistic director, Richard Rose, a man whom many liken to the great Mr. P himself. "He was very good at spinning those stories into legendary proportions," Rose asserted, and "that's largely why this theatre is still here today."[53] It is also why the theatre's history is filled with amusing apocrypha that are now reported as fact. Most of these stories were widely circulated during the Depression by journalists eager for funny, uplifting news. Porterfield actively solicited the coverage (according to Rose, in later years Porterfield inspired the wire service to station a reporter right in Abingdon) since it helped to build the theatre's reputation and to sell—or barter—more tickets at the box office.

As one might suspect, even his personal history is littered with tall tales that were built around nuggets of truth. Robert Huffard Porterfield was born in 1905 and raised in southwest Virginia, which was an agrarian, conservative, churchgoing society. He got the theatrical bug early on but didn't decide to seek his fortune as an actor until after seeing his first professional production, a road company of *Rose Marie*, which was playing in Richmond, the state capitol, while he was in town for a debate tournament. Under strong protestations from his father, he left Hampden-Sydney College, where he was preparing for the ministry, and headed to New York City to study at the American Academy of Dramatic Arts. In an oft-quoted phrase, he allegedly told one of his theology professors, "I'd rather entertain souls than save them."

Porterfield spent the next seven years in New York, working at odd jobs and landing several small roles in Broadway and touring shows. In 1931, while on tour with Walter Hampden's popular production of *Cyrano de Bergerac*, he conceived the idea for the Barter. As the company was crossing midwestern wheat fields, Porterfield thought about all the farmers, both there and in his home state, producing literally tons of food that few people could afford to buy. A lot of theatre people were hungry and needed food; why not barter the best of what each could produce? Bartering goods was common practice in the farm communities where he grew up, and he knew that in times of economic hardship it was even more widespread. He discussed the idea with Hampden, who was not very enthusiastic, but Porterfield pursued it nonetheless. When the tour ended, he went back to Virginia to investigate the possibilities. He was pleased to discover that there were perfect buildings for a theatre available in downtown Abingdon—the long vacant Oprey House Theatre, originally built as the Sinking Spring Presbyterian Church in 1830 and transformed to a theatre sometime in the mid-nineteenth century by the Sons of Temperance, and dormitories and classrooms of the recently defunct Martha Washington College right across the street, which could be used for housing company members, rehearsals, and offices. The harder part would be to convince this Bible Belt community that having a theatre in its midst would be a wonderful thing. As Porterfield's widow, Mary Dudley, put it, "it is important to remember that to these people, theatre was the cesspool of iniquity, tantamount to the devil's playground."[54] His modus operandi was to give a promotional talk disguised as a lecture at the local college, Emory and Henry, where he succeeded in getting everyone excited about doing and seeing theatre. He even helped to mount a production of Noël Coward's *Hay Fever* to make sure that the students could experience the fun and excitement first-hand. With a solid foothold in at least one sector of the populace, Porterfield followed up his on-site investigations with letters to the Abingdon Town Council. To his surprise, they liked his proposal and offered him free use of the theatre and the defunct college so long as he maintained the properties, paid the utility bills, and agreed to never play on Sunday. He also was given the opportunity to rent additional space at the likewise defunct Stonewall Jackson Institute up the hill for a nominal fee.[55]

Sufficiently energized by local enthusiasm, he set out to convince the New York theatre community that founding a new theatre in an isolated outpost hours from the nearest metropolis was an idea whose time had come. Since he conceived of the Barter as a fully professional operation, yet one that would operate on little, if any, money, he needed to use his increasingly famous powers of persuasion to induce Actors' Equity, as well as the Dramatists Guild, to engage in some bartering. Equity agreed to allow its members to work with him, so long as he provided room and board and donated any monetary proceeds to the Actors' Relief Fund. The Dramatists Guild was equally congenial, allowing Porterfield to pay members' royalties in the form of Virginia smoked hams. This was, at once, a much-needed benefit for the theatre and a terrific opportunity for unusual publicity since such noted playwrights as Noël Coward, Maxwell Anderson, Thornton Wilder, and Robert E. Sherwood agreed to accept hams in lieu of dollars. Bernard Shaw, a vegetarian, returned his to the theatre, but when the company requested the rights to produce another Shavian play several years later, he supposedly suggested that spinach would be a welcome substitute. Although the tale may be apocryphal, Porterfield ostensibly sent Shaw the spinach, and along with the rights for *Pygmalion*, he got wonderful publicity in return.

With all the arrangements in place, Porterfield convinced 22 actors to leave New York and accompany him to Abingdon to launch the new theatre. One of their first tasks was to go, en masse, to the Presbyterian church on Sunday morning. Always the promoter, Porterfield knew that he still had to convince the wary locals that the players were friendly, decent folk, just like them. As the legend goes, it was the booming baritone of actor H. H. McCollum, singing the classic Christian hymn "Rock of Ages" so movingly and without having to read the lyric ("as only a real Christian could") that persuaded the congregation to give the troupe a chance. After the service, the actors were invited to different congregants' homes for Sunday dinner, and, having been duly charmed, the churchgoers showed up at the theatre on opening night. Although McCollum later told Mr. P that he hadn't been to church in 25 years and only knew the hymn because he had performed it in a play the previous year, it didn't matter. The Barter Theatre "was a hit before the first play was presented," according to Porterfield, and "no amount of public relations could ever match what that one trip to church accomplished."[56]

The theatre's first season of seven plays was successful enough to ensure a second season in 1934, with a company that had grown to 28, and an expanded repertoire of ten plays. The 1933 net profit included $4.30 in cash and two barrels of jams and jellies, all of which were promptly sent to the Actors' Relief Fund in New York. Porterfield also estimated that by the end of that first summer, the troupe had collectively gained 300 pounds via their daily consumption of box office receipts.

A great part of the theatre's allure for people in this farm community was their ability to buy tickets in barter, and they showed up with an amazing array of food and other goods at the box office. "With vegetables you cannot sell, you can buy a good laugh," they were assured on the troupe's advertisements, so they came with vegetables and fruits, both fresh and canned, as well as ham, bacon, eggs, and live chickens, hens, rabbits, sheep, and even larger cattle. Others offered honeycombs, baked goods, candy, flowers, wine, snakes, puppies, toothpaste, and motor oil. There also were the unique offerings that automatically became the stuff of playhouse lore. There was the pig, which had been admission for eight people, that got away, and the calf that didn't because a nimble company member caught it and brought it back before curtain. There was the coffin maker who, when told that the troupe had little use for coffins, decided that he could also make walking sticks. He must have enjoyed the shows a lot because by the end of the season, every cast member was the proud owner of a hand-carved cane. One of Porterfield's favorite stories was of the farmer and his wife who brought a cow to the theatre on the back of their truck. The man asked how much milk could be exchanged for a ticket and he quickly produced two quarts. When the ticket seller asked if his wife would also be seeing the show, the farmer replied, "she can milk her own ticket."

The Barter's box office looked more like a general store than a theatre lobby. On a table situated along one side was a scale and a list of the prices of various commodities at the local stores so that box office personnel could weigh the produce and determine a fair exchange. Surrounding the table were shelves and plenty of open space to store the day's receipts. Al Hirschfeld's 1939 cartoon of the lobby for the *New York Times* depicted a smiling, if slightly frazzled, Porterfield surveying the lively scene from down left, and extant photographs confirm that Hirschfeld's humorous interpretation wasn't far from the truth.

When media interest in this most unusual of theatres began to wane, Porterfield worked hard to keep the playhouse in the national news. In 1939, he devised the Barter Theatre Award, which initially recognized what he deemed had been the best performance of the New York theatre season but later extended to honor major directors and producers as well. At that time, there were few awards of this kind and even fewer opportunities to bring the professional theatre community together for a gala celebration. The award consisted of an acre of land on Porterfield's dairy farm, a Virginia ham, and "a platter to eat it off of" that was specially made by the Cumbow China Decorating Company of Abingdon and was emblazoned with the theatre's logo. The winner also would hold a special audition to select two actors—one male, one female—to spend the following summer in Abingdon as part of the Barter company. With his penchant for garnering top-drawer publicity, Porterfield launched his award by having the first lady of the United States, Eleanor Roosevelt, bestow the acre of land, the ham, and the platter at a gala luncheon for Laurette Taylor, known as the first lady of American theatre. Mrs. Roosevelt promptly memorialized the occasion in her syndicated newspaper column, *My Day*, and was invited back to give subsequent awards, including one to the third winner, Ethel Barrymore. The annual event soon became a popular addition to the New York social season that continued to keep the Barter in the news. Several of the actors who were selected to go to Abingdon went on to notable careers that garnered even more publicity for the theatre. Most famous among them were Gregory Peck, Rosemary Murphy, and Gerome Ragni, best known as the co-author of the rock musical *Hair*.

Porterfield's promotional skills benefited not only the Barter. He concurrently would champion southwestern Virginia, advocating its potential for scenic vacations and comfortable retirement homes, and the development of the American theatre as a national, rather than an exclusively New York City, phenomenon. The Barter Award is a perfect example of how he ingeniously could promote all three simultaneously, by having a small regional playhouse honor a Broadway actor with Virginia-made gifts bestowed in the folksy dialect of that region. The ham was always accompanied by a platter "to eat it off of," a phrase that was designed to provoke laughter in the New York audience along with a feeling of down-home sincerity and love that only folks from rural America could provide. Porterfield adeptly maintained the delicate balance between sophistication and innocence that portrayed the Barter as a serious art theatre that still embodied the stalwart, homespun values of American popular mythology. Hence, he would hold the ceremonies in New York but not without taking two actors back home with him to prove that quality theatre could be done in a non-urban environment.

This philosophy compelled him to join forces with Robert Breen, who became one of the founders of the American National Theatre and Academy (ANTA), to advocate for an American national theatre. They published an article, "Toward a National Theatre," in the October 1945 issue of *Theatre Arts* magazine, which argued that "the only way we can have a truly national theatre" was via decentralization. They called for "touring companies, resident companies, civic centre theatres, and regional theatres" to provide "high standard, professional theatre to the 90 percent of our people who have never had the opportunity of seeing it" and recommended that a U.S. Public Theatre Foundation be established to subsidize the plan.[57] Their call to action was followed by another in 1949, also published in *Theatre Arts* but this time spearheaded by two U.S. congressmen. Although neither effort succeeded immediately, both helped to validate the need for change. The subsequent launching of the regional theatre movement with substantial subsidies from the Ford and Rockefeller Foundations as well as the newly formed National Endowment for the Arts in 1965 helped to realize their dream of producing theatres all over the country, providing entertainment for all Americans.

At the same time he was writing, Porterfield was trying to establish the Barter as the official state theatre of Virginia, an action that he hoped would serve as an impetus for like-minded ventures throughout the country. He began his campaign for recognition before World War II, principally by ensuring that the full name of his playhouse, The Barter Theatre of Virginia, was always fully articulated in print and in radio promotions, a fact he would bring to the attention of as many politicians as possible. It was not until 1946, however, that the Virginia state legislature acceded to his wishes. Rex Partington described how Porterfield went to Richmond with several gunnysacks filled with feature stories and reviews, all of which highlighted the words Barter Theatre of Virginia, "and dumped them all over the desks of the legislators." He argued that they were doing such a wonderful public relations job for the state, that the theatre ought to have an annual appropriation.[58] The lawmakers were convinced and drew up an official agreement that afforded the company $10,000 per year in return for a nine-month season of 12 plays to be produced in Abingdon for the three summer months and on tour throughout Virginia for the following six. The agreement, which was administered by the Virginia Conservation Commission, solidified the Barter's position as an ambassador for the state:

> That for the consideration hereinafter stated, the Theater hereby undertakes, agrees and promises to further and assist the Commission in its work of advertising and promoting the educational, cultural, and economic interests of the Commonwealth of Virginia, and in attracting and encouraging people from other states and countries to visit in the Commonwealth where so many shrines and historic sites of national and international interest are located. The Theatre, having established a nationwide reputation for furnishing entertainment and educational and cultural services of rare quality on a barter basis, is in a unique position to render such service as is hereby undertaken.[59]

Virginia continues to support the Barter to the present day and several other states, including New Jersey and Pennsylvania, also have designated official state theaters. Porterfield's considerable contributions to the American theatre, however, were duly recognized in 1948 when he received a special Antoinette Perry "Tony" award and also was granted an honorary doctorate from Hampden-Sydney College.

The approbation and much-needed funds from the state were instrumental in revitalizing the Barter after World War II. During the theatre's wartime hiatus, a tornado destroyed much of the building and its property. When Porterfield returned from service with the U.S. Air Force in 1945, his initial inclination was to abandon the project. Pressure from both the local and theatrical communities convinced him to reopen the theatre, but only with an overhaul of its business operation. Actors' Equity was no longer willing to allow members to work for room and barter; actors would now have to sign contracts and be paid union scale. Dramatists Guild members, not surprisingly, also preferred dollars to ham. Although the name remained, the use of barter as payment was declared a thing of the past; the theatre needed cash to remain viable. Porterfield's announcement stunned the local community, which eagerly had awaited the opportunity to, once again, exchange "hams for Hamlet." One woman, upon hearing that the theatre was going to reopen in the summer of 1946, planted an extra row of beans in her garden to ensure her admission for the full season. Porterfield allowed some long-standing patrons to continue to use barter, but only in Abingdon and never on tour. There were still times, however, that unusual barter was accepted, particularly if the story had potential for good public relations. In the mid-'60s, a patron arrived at the box office wanting to exchange Civil War scrip for a ticket. Porterfield quickly agreed, and the story was out on the wire services within the hour.[60]

Mr. P died suddenly of a heart attack in October 1971, just shy of celebrating his fortieth anniversary at the theatre. Rex Partington, who had assisted him with production duties the previous summer, took over as artistic director, a position he held until 1992 when he retired and Richard Rose was hired as the third director in the theatre's history. Partington, who business manager Pearl Hayter contended was Mr. P's choice as successor, continued to operate the Barter in the style and spirit of his mentor. The Barter quickly became a living memorial to Mr. P, who, Hayter claimed, "has become something of a saint since his death, but I don't think that's the way he'd want to be remembered."[61]

For Barter audiences, Porterfield's image lived in his famous, often lengthy, curtain speeches that preceded each performance. Hayter surmised that many people came to the theatre "just to hear him talk" since his appearance was a de rigueur component of the show.[62] He would chat them up in his inimitable way, sharing choice tidbits of the Barter legend and lore, and would always hold a contest for the patron who had traveled the farthest to the theatre. In the early years, the prize was a pair of silk stockings, courtesy of the local hosiery mill that donated them. After the mill went bankrupt, the gift became a stoneware mug, likewise donated by a nearby factory. Part of the amusement of this warm-up act was to watch Mr. P poked and prodded through the curtain by eager cast members waiting to perform. He wouldn't leave the stage, however, until delivering his standard closing line, "If ya' like us, talk about us. If ya' don't, jes keep ya' mouth shut." "That's when he put them in his pocket," according to Fritz Weaver, and the evening's success was assured.[63]

A Code of Ethics

In 1957, Robert Porterfield published a "Code of Ethics for People in the Theatre," which he prepared with the help of several New York theatre friends. Although it was not widely disseminated, it captures the spirit, dedication, and integrity of the men and women in the straw top hat who devoted their lives to running artistically and financially sound theatres. The best of these managers, like Cleveland, Stearns, and Porterfield, created artistic homes for an ever-growing family of devotees, both behind and in front of the curtain. They inspired creativity, rigor, and love in equal measure and quietly demanded, through personal example, an ethical deportment as articulated by Porterfield below.

A Code of Ethics for People in the Theatre

Dramatic art is the most human of all the arts. We are servants of humanity—the producer, director, dramatist and actor—pledge unanimity in giving the audience the best theatre possible.

We pledge complete loyalty to the theatre, our great and noble profession.

We pledge ourselves not to let our position or our name be used in any way which will bring discredit to the theatre.

We will not speak derogatorily to the layman about our fellow actors, producers, dramatists. It is bad business to talk bad business in show business.

In theatre, where illusion is the first of all pleasures, we pledge our God-given talent for the reflection of life in all its respects, through comedy and tragedy, magic and glamour, and the world of make-believe.

We pledge ourselves to do everything possible to enhance our art and artistry and the theatre as an institution.

We recognize the producer as the autocratic head.

We pledge our talent to the dramatist in portraying his story of yesterday, today and tomorrow.

We pledge our acquiescence to the interpretation of the director.

We pledge ourselves to respect, cherish, and nourish the artistry of the actor.

It is our duty to appeal to the gregariousness of man, and to him we pledge the propagation of the eternal verities.

In humility we recognize the pleasure of our audience as the final criterion because without an audience we cannot have theatre.[64]

5

Judy and Mickey Join the Union: The Regulation of Summer Stock

The prevalent mythology—largely invented by Hollywood—of the genesis of summer stock conjures up images of Judy Garland, Mickey Rooney, and their fresh-faced band of "babes in arms" eagerly heading off to the neighborhood barn to put on a show. Although many tyro talents did get their start in stock, which the host theatres would use to lure audiences to barn theatres on the gamble that they would see the "stars of tomorrow," this formative period was short-lived. As soon as stock became monetarily successful and the largest annual employer of actors in the United States—a distinction held until the 1960s—Actors' Equity took a keen interest, and regulation soon followed. When summer stock became unionized, the era of big business began.

The Formative Years

The halcyon days of summer stock, what Morton Eustis described as "the hope of a national theatre that shall be vibrantly alive and exciting throughout each year of its existence," lasted from the early 1920s through 1935, the last season prior to the imposition of Actors' Equity regulations. Eustis, writing in *Theatre Arts Monthly* in June 1933, heralded the opportunities that summer stock gave to the young to learn their craft because "the summer season is primarily dedicated to the youth of the theatre." He credited young people with bringing what he characterized as "the summer stock movement" to life so that they could "become professional in deed rather than in fancy": "They can put into practice what they have learned in the dramatic schools; they can test their own professional quality under professional auspices in a varied repertory, and they can undergo in concentrated form almost every useful experience of Broadway. It is small wonder that they look upon the summer season as their season."[1]

This was all possible, of course, because the production costs were infinitesimal compared to those on Broadway. A summer show could be mounted for between $50 and $1,000 whereas the same show would require a budget of at least $10,000 in a Broadway house. Eustis also noted the low cost of theatre rentals, which ranged from gratis to $500 for the entire season. Finally, technicians and other support personnel could be hired for modest amounts, and might even work for little more than the price of room and board.[2]

Two of the best examples of Eustis's youthfully exuberant theatres were the Jitney Players and the University Players Guild (UPG), both profiled in chapter 2. The UPG, in fact, was most frequently heralded by critics as the stellar example of a short-lived but eminently successful summer stock venture that produced some of the great talents of mid-century theatre and cinema, notably Henry Fonda, Margaret Sullavan, Joshua Logan, and Bretaigne Windust. Both companies were run by well-educated young people from socially prominent families who had important connections to the worlds of industry, banking, and the mass media. Although everyone in these troupes worked hard and maintained a certain pride and integrity in meeting expenses and repaying loans, the fact remains that neither theatre would have gotten started without family support. Several years later, the Depression economy made it even more difficult for young people who did not have significant resources at their disposal to launch a summer theatre. The notable exception was Robert Porterfield and his Barter Theatre in Abingdon, Virginia (chapter 4), which operated through a unique series of union concessions, generous gifts of space and furnishings from the town of Abingdon, and the trading of performances for food, which kept the company fed throughout the summer months. The Barter, however, was a one-of-a-kind operation involving people who already had professional stage experience and were far from "babes in arms." If there were summer theatres that truly reflected the Judy and Mickey mythology, they have not become part of the historic record.

There were, of course, many summer stocks founded in these formative years by seasoned professionals who, for a variety of reasons, decided to take advantage of the new opportunities in the vacationlands. Certainly the economic hardships of the Depression significantly reduced the opportunities for productions in New York and on the road, while summer stock cost much less money. Professionals also wanted the same artistic freedom that lured young people to remote areas. In addition to those theatres begun in the 1920s at Ogunquit, Maine, and in Dennis and Stockbridge, Massachusetts (chapter 2), and in the early 1930s at Tamworth and Peterborough, New Hampshire (chapter 4), there were significant new operations in Connecticut at Guilford and Ivoryton; in Maine at Bar Harbor, Boothbay Harbor, and Surry; in Massachusetts at Cohasset and Fitchburg; in New York at Mount Kisco, Schenectady, Southampton, Suffern, and White Plains; in Rhode Island at Matunuck and Newport; in Pennsylvania at Deer Lake and Nuangola; and outside of the Northeast in such places as Wisconsin (the Peninsula Players in Fish Creek), Michigan (Ann Arbor Drama Festival), and Colorado (Central City Opera House). All of these ventures, which were increasingly touted in the local and national press, helped to draw the attention of not only the theatre-going public, but also the professional theatre world, which had hitherto not paid the new stock theatres much heed.

The most famous of the recognized professionals to launch a summer stock operation was Lawrence Langner, the eminent producer and co-founder of the Washington Square Players and the Theatre Guild. In 1931, he and his wife, Armina Marshall, an actress with whom Langner co-wrote several plays, opened the Westport Country Playhouse in Connecticut as a tryout house for new plays and for a permanent repertory company that they planned to move to New York for a fall season. Langner hired Cleon Throckmorton to design a rustic barn theatre that perfectly emulated the dimensions of New York's Times Square Theatre to ensure an easy transfer of productions (see chapter 3) and engaged a distinguished acting company that included Dorothy Gish, Armina Marshall, and Rollo Peters, who doubled as scenic designer. Langner explained his rationale for opening the playhouse in his memoir, *The Magic Curtain*: "There we were free to try out our creative ideas without interference, and without facing financial disaster if they failed. New plays and the classics could be essayed without reference to the tastes of Broadway. Actors could attempt new roles without facing the terrors of the New York opening nights, and new directors and scenic artists could be given a first chance to show their talents. And furthermore, the younger generation could have an opportunity to gain experience in the theatre."[3] If an established New York producer such as Lawrence Langner was seeking to escape from the constraints of show business, it is obvious why not-so-well connected people would want to do likewise.

Whether run by ambitious youngsters or more seasoned professionals, new summer stock theatres appeared each year. Since no official records were kept until Actors' Equity got involved (and even then the union did not publish full lists of its member theatres), it is difficult to determine exactly how many theatres were operating during this period. Articles in *Theatre Arts Monthly*, which championed the new venues from their earliest days, enthusiastically declared that there were more summer houses every season, but seldom provided actual statistics. In the August 1932 issue, the magazine printed production calendars for 32 theatres, but it is doubtful that this represented all of the operating houses. In what appears to be the first comprehensive listing, *Variety* enumerated 104 producing stages in 1935 and in 1936 proclaimed a new record of 126 summer stock houses.[4] This figure, which was supported by a list of all the theatres, topped seasonal estimates given by Actors' Equity, which presumed that in addition to the 50 houses now operating under its aegis, there were perhaps just as many theatres functioning independently.[5]

The business model for these ventures, which had been buoyed by the success of the art theatres and an influx of newly trained theatre students pouring out of the universities, was the new crop of independent stock theatres that appeared in cities during the first decades of the twentieth century. Although the golden era of first-class stock was over with the rise of the combination companies that glutted the American stage in the 1870s, stock had begun to make a comeback by the turn of the century. *The New York Dramatic Mirror* announced that more than 40 companies were founded between 1896 and 1899; by 1910, there were well over a hundred, with any sizable city boasting one, if not two, full-time companies.[6] Historians are quick to point out, however, that these new stock houses were vastly inferior to their nineteenth-century predecessors. They were no longer elite entertainments located in the fashionable districts of town but were situated among the lower-class amusements, which included burlesque shows, nickelodeons, and dime museums. The "new" stock, which was subject to the vicissitudes of the first-class commercial theatres that were domineered by the Syndicate and the Shuberts, was unable to attract better than second-rate actors and second-class plays to its stages except during the summer months when the combination companies would suspend production.[7] Accordingly, Alfred Bernheim in his landmark study, *The Business of Theatre*, published in 1932, labeled these "summer stock theatres," but they need to be distinguished from the later summer stocks, which are the focus of this book, for several reasons. First, most were located in cities and operated, or tried to operate, all year long. Second, these theatres were largely run by local managers who were either unable or unwilling to sign with the two controlling monopolies and were trying to stay solvent by booking better-quality plays and players during the time when "the road" went on holiday. Their business was bolstered with the advent of World War I, when higher transportation costs severely hampered the ability of the combination shows to tour. Third, and most important, the early-twentieth-century stock revival was truly that—a resuscitation of an old form of theatre presented in the traditional way. It didn't have the vibrancy of true summer stock, which was nurtured by the art theatre, the universities, and the back-to-nature movement and was by design a limited, summertime affair.

It was expressly because of the restricted playing seasons, along with the casual holiday environments, that the new summer theatres could make the business model provided by the old-line stock operations work. It was tough to sustain a continuously operating theatre with a sizable permanent company offering a weekly change of bill for nine to twelve months, but relatively easy to employ the same formula for a season of three to four months. It was even easier to do so in a summer resort environment where the theatre buildings were naturally small and rustic and where overhead costs were limited to little more than the price of electricity. In harmony with the pastoral ambience of summer stock, the scenography was simple; audiences didn't anticipate lavish sets and lighting in a converted barn. Salaries, which constitute the principal portion of any stock theatre's budget, were kept at a minimum since no one, except the occasional producer, relied on summer stock as annual income, and many theatre artists, particularly during the Depression, were simply happy to have work. They also, as Langner described it, relished the opportunity to work in an unfettered environment in which everyone had a voice in artistic decisions.[8] Actors, particularly those who generally were cast to type, could attempt new kinds of roles or even try their hand at directing, designing, or handling technical jobs; directors could act, designers could direct, and technicians could design. Still others enjoyed the relative luxury of being able to work and vacation simultaneously. Most of the summer stock theatres were situated at beautiful beaches, lakes, and mountains where the theatre staff could periodically enjoy the surrounding amenities. Dorothy Stickney affectionately described her seven summers at Lakewood: "It was a perfect place to spend the summer and the work was comparatively easy— only one matinee a week . . . . We had free use of the canoes and boats, and about all we ever thought of buying was an occasional soft drink or a candy bar or hot buttered popcorn from the little store just outside the theatre. The whole place had a distinctly holiday atmosphere. We lived in summer cabins and had our meals at a long table in the community cottage."[9]

No one was making a lot of money in summer stock and, in most cases, no one cared since money was not the primary reason for being there. Theatre managers relied on box office receipts to pay the bills and hoped that enough money would be left over to cover building improvements and start-up costs for the following season. The focus, in the early years, was on presenting good plays, done well, in as frugal a manner as possible. The pizzazz came from the performers, not the milieu. Since these charmingly rustic productions were equally novel to potential audiences, they were happy to patronize the new theatres, particularly since most stock companies kept ticket prices low. Furthermore, the possibility of seeing tomorrow's star today in his or her straw-hat debut was an inducement to buy a ticket. Katharine Hepburn played her first leading roles at Connecticut's Ivoryton Playhouse in 1931 by persuading producer Milton Stiefel to give a local girl a chance (he initially said no); Gregory Peck appeared at the Barter, where he was the recipient of its 1940 promising performer award and at the Cape Playhouse in 1942, while still an unknown, to play supporting roles; and the legend of the much-touted UPG all-stars lived on. Who might be next?

The summer theatres not only succeeded in making a stock system work but did so, at least in these formative years prior to unionization, as noncommercially driven enterprises. This was possible largely because of stock's paltry reputation among the show business elite; hence, no one paid the new summer stocks much attention, and managers were free to conduct business as they wished. As Alfred Bernheim explained in the early 1930s, "it matters not a jot how artistically perfect a stock company of today may be—it is still a stock company, and that means of the lower order in the minds of the public." Bernheim classified stock as "déclassé," offering as proof that "actors who can make Broadway do not play in stock. Dramatists present their scripts to Broadway producers. Directors, scenic artists, designers flock to Broadway. Broadway and long runs—that is the goal."[10] Although Bernheim was willing to admit that there were a few laudatory summer stock operations, others, like Alfred Harding of Actors' Equity, described the early years of summer stock in a decidedly derogatory tone:

> In the beginning, it was a wild scramble, undertaken in the main by men and women who did not know too much about the patrons' tastes, or from their behavior, much about the theatre either. Almost anything was considered good enough for actors and audiences at that time. It was a lark, an adventure, into which every one concerned was supposed to enter in the spirit of children playing games. It was the era in which no barn was considered safe from the forays of groups of wild-eyed enthusiasts. There were too many theatres and they, and their plays and productions, were not good enough.[11]

Hence, until the likes of Lawrence Langner and notable actors who were members in good standing of Actors' Equity became involved, most people were content in leaving this reputedly substandard entertainment alone.

Historically, however, theatres that begin as noncommercially driven ventures tend to become increasingly profit-driven as they realize success. Jack Poggi describes this phenomenon in *Theater in America: The Impact of Economic Forces*. In the early days the theatre can "get by in cheap quarters, paying actors little or nothing and skimping on scenery and costumes. If it fails, it fails, and nobody ever hears of it." However, success brings certain expectations of professional growth that, in turn, generate additional expenses and the need for greater income.[12] In the case of the new summer stocks, success brought union regulations that forced the theatres not only to pay higher salaries, but also to improve (or build) dressing rooms, lavatories, staircases, and other enhancements to be in compliance with Actors' Equity standards. Artists working under union contracts also had higher expectations for overall production quality, which engendered a vicious cycle of more expenses being met by increasingly higher ticket prices. "Finally," Poggi argues, "a point is reached at which a noncommercial theatre is no longer free to do whatever it wants. It has become so successful that it can no longer afford failure." Ultimately, it "either becomes commercial or dies. Or both."[13]

Actors' Equity and the Beginning of Big Business

Enter the Actors' Equity Association, the labor union representing actors, stage managers, and, at that time, directors and choreographers, in the legitimate theatre.[14] In 1934, when Equity began its investigation of summer stock theatre, the union was 21 years old. It had begun in 1913 as a group of 112 men who had gathered to contest a long list of abuses regularly suffered by actors since the American theatre's late-nineteenth-century transformation from a largely artistic enterprise run by theatre professionals to a predominantly commercial one run by businessmen. Their complaints included a lack of standard contracts, irregular wage payments and frequently no payment for work performed, unlimited rehearsal periods without pay, the stranding of road companies that closed suddenly with no provisions for sending actors home, the need for actors to provide their own transportation and wardrobe without compensation, the ability of managers to fire actors at will, and the lack of recourse for actors to challenge management short of prolonged and costly legal battles. Despite these egregious working conditions, it took six years for Equity to gain recognition as an official union because of complications within the labor community and a national atmosphere that favored business interests over those of individual workers. Finally, in 1919, the American Federation of Labor granted a charter to Equity's parent organization, the Associated Actors and Artistes of America (known as the Four A's), to over-see the group of unions representing performers in live entertainment, and the Four A's designated Equity as the official representative for actors in the legit-imate theatre. In August of that same year, Equity held its first and largest strike to date, which lasted 30 days. The strike shut down 37 shows in eight cities and prevented 16 other shows from opening. As a result, the Producing Managers' Association (PMA), which represented most major theatrical pro-ducers, signed a five-year contract with the union that agreed to all of Equity's demands and, more important, recognized its authority as a collective bargaining unit. Despite this significant victory, Equity still had major struggles with the producers throughout the 1920s, as well as with a rival actors' union, the Actors' Fidelity Association, which was supported by the PMA in an effort to undermine Equity's power. In 1924, the union estab-lished the Equity Shop policy, which, after prolonged negotiations with man-agers, guaranteed that 80 percent of all casts would be composed of Equity members in good standing while the remaining 20 percent could be non-union actors (but not former members who had been dropped or expelled from Equity). Major provisions passed thereafter included the 1929 rules protecting actors from unscrupulous agents, a 1933 minimum wage agreement, and the establishment of minimum rehearsal pay in 1935.[15]

Given the union's brief but tempestuous history, it is understandable that Equity would investigate every situation in which professional actors were employed to ensure that its hard-fought regulations were being upheld. This was especially true during the Great Depression when many members were out of work and may have been willing to accept paying positions outside of Equity's purview. Yet because the summer stock houses were viewed neither as commercial theatre nor as legitimate professional theatre, Equity had all but ignored them. The two notable exceptions were the Barter and the Westport Country Playhouse, both of which operated under special dispensa-tions from the union in order to maintain a status as respectable producing theatres despite their inability or unwillingness to pay Equity scale. Up until 1936, there were no summer stock theatres operating under union contracts.

Equity's initial inquiries into summer stock began when a few actors com-plained of bad working conditions in theatres during the summer of 1934. Specifically which or how many theatres remains ambiguous; *Equity*, the official organ for the union, never published the details. In an editorial,

"Summer Theatre: Boon or Bane?" in the September 1934, issue, Alfred Harding mused on conditions in summer stock, which, he contended, "have been as varied as their offerings," and ranged from "delightful" to "miserable": "But just what the field as a whole had to offer to the actors who have played in it remains something of a puzzle. Each actor, obviously knew those conditions he encountered. And, human nature being what it is, those who were ill used and disappointed have been much more vocal about their experiences than those who were happy and satisfied."[16] Consequently, he was directed by Equity Council to interview actors who had worked in stock the previous summer and report back the findings. A follow-up article in the October issue expressed his disappointment that so few members had responded, and he asked that they contact him as soon as possible. He assured them that "Equity is going into this investigation without any preconceived prejudices, without any conviction as to what it will find or ought to find in this important sector of the theatre" and reiterated that this was simply a request for information.[17] In the November issue, Harding declared that he had received few responses, and he chastised union members for withholding information: "Now this is a matter of very real interest to all members. The Council is probably going to legislate with regard to these companies when it is satisfied that it has the entire picture. It is for the Equity members who will be affected by that legislation to see that the Council has a correct picture. If they do not report their experiences and their convictions and the Council does not include some provision they believe to be essential to this type of work, whose fault will that be?"[18]

Given Harding's pejorative attitude toward summer stock, which becomes increasingly vitriolic over time, it is difficult to ascertain his motives in badgering the members for information. Was he looking for negative feedback that would substantiate the complaints Equity received prior to the beginning of the investigation or was he truly attempting to be equitable? On the one hand, he claimed that "there is already sufficient information on hand to indicate that some of these theatres were well run and that, all things considered, the actors who played there were not ill paid" while continuing to aver that "the amount of evidence on hand is not what it should be to give such places a sweeping bill of clean health."[19] It seems that he did want more information, but his tone, and the ostensible dearth of responses, indicate a wariness on the part of actors to cooperate. Did they perhaps fear for the continuance of their summer artist retreats?

Harding was silent until April 1935, when he published a stern editorial, "Regulation for the Summer Theatres," which demanded that Equity Council take immediate action "to begin policing" the summer operations in the same manner as it did the regular stock companies. Although his findings were still minimal, he nevertheless arrived at a classification system for the summer companies. While admitting that some theatres transcended his categories, he asserted that all theatres could be divided as follows:

Class 1. An established group, in a community able and willing to support a theatre; with reasonable equipment; fair, sometimes adequate pay; and a businesslike and courteous attitude towards its players; or
Class 2. A group in which some of these conditions do not exist or where they are deficient, but which probably could be made adequate through proper regulation and supervision; and, finally,
Class 3. A group where conditions are so unfavorable; where equipment is so inadequate, and where the management is so lacking in experience, or is so callous and indifferent to its players that no consideration is deserved or should be accorded. For groups in this classification the best that ought to be afforded is swift and merciless extinction.[20]

Harding's complaint was especially directed at summer stocks that tried out new plays but failed to adequately compensate and protect the interests of the actors who premiered them. At one or more of these theatres—again the number is indeterminate—actors received only room and board and no guarantee that they would retain their roles should the show move to Broadway, while managers enjoyed lucrative payoffs of $200 or more from Broadway producers who wanted to see the work performed. Harding pointed out that there used to be a separate contract specifically for tryouts; now, actors were not even getting paid.[21]

It would take a full year, but by the winter of 1936, Equity Council had acted on Harding's recommendations. A new contract created specifically for summer stock engagements was mandated for all Equity actors effective March 31, 1936. Theatre managers were to submit an application and questionnaire that Equity would use to classify the house as either an "A" or "B" company, thus determining operational guidelines. Any manager who employed Equity members but failed to comply with the union's regulations would have the actors forcibly withdrawn from the company and would have to pay their salaries and return transportation.

The new rules and regulations, which Harding reported in the April issue of *Equity*, were a result of his 1934 survey and on-site investigations of 38 companies conducted during the summer of 1935 by Lyster Chambers, an experienced actor and longtime Equity member. Chambers's inquiries uncovered abuses in what he termed the "board and lodging" and "dramatic school" rackets. In the first, actors would be required to pay for room and board provided by the management, which, in many instances, roughly equaled their weekly wages. At one theatre, actors ostensibly received $40 in salary, but $35 of it was immediately expensed in fees, netting them only $5 a week. Chambers found this situation particularly egregious since cheaper living arrangements had been available. He also took to task the "so-called dramatic schools" affiliated with summer stock theatres in which students were required to pay living expenses, instructional fees, and special privilege fees that allowed them to watch rehearsals and take part in productions. Chambers viewed this as little more than a managerial scheme to get rich quick. He also challenged the quality of instruction at these institutions since at least one teacher he encountered was a theatre neophyte himself.[22]

Unfortunately, Chambers's full report was not published; hence, it is difficult to determine if the problems enumerated represented the exception or the rule. Were these abuses widespread among the summer venues, all of which were independent operations, or were they isolated incidents? Since Harding wrote all the articles on summer stock for *Equity* magazine during this period, there is no counterbalance to his allegations. As the editor for the official union organ, was he the mouthpiece for Equity Council or were his editorials more representative of personal bias? How instrumental was he in promoting, if not actually crafting, Equity's new legislation? Surely had Equity Council disagreed with him, it would have insisted that he temper his language or would have removed him as editor. Perhaps the council did temporarily silence him: there is no mention of summer stock in *Equity* for a full year following Harding's incendiary 1935 editorial.

Regardless of their evolution, Equity's new rules governing summer stock changed the face of the summer theatre forever. No more could Equity actors legally work in unsanctioned venues without fear of reprisal, if not ejection, from the union. Producers wishing to employ Equity actors either would have to comply with the regulations, thus necessitating both budget and box office increases, or risk public censure and hefty fines. The problems that typically confronted producers who brought their theatres from small, experimental venues to recognized professional houses descended on the summer stocks quickly. Although, as Harding pointed out, "responsible summer theatre managers" would not find the new rules onerous because they had been observing them all along, they did have a major effect on producers who lacked the resources and political clout of more established managers.[23] Although one could still open a barn theatre with a young group of unknowns, the atmosphere had changed. Summer stock was now a recognized industry rather than a bold experiment. Despite the fact that Hollywood had not yet made the film, the era of Judy and Mickey's "hey, kids, let's put on a show!" was over.

The Regulation of Summer Stock

Equity's new "Managers' Summer Stock Company Application, Question-naire and Agreement" was a one-page, straightforward document that accomplished four things at once. It served to identify and officially register the summer stock theatre with the union; it informed the theatre management of the standard minimum conditions under which Equity members could be employed; it allowed Equity to determine the theatre's classification; and, once co-signed by the theatre manager and the union, it functioned as a legally binding agreement. The form consisted of six questions and eight general regulations that pertained to all types of companies. The theatre was required to divulge its terms of employment (salary, board, and lodging); whether it planned to produce new or old plays, or a combination of both; whether it had an affiliated school; a list of other companies in the vicinity, including their location and professional or nonprofessional status; and the drawing population of its audiences among permanent residents, summer residents, and vacationers. Equity designated those theatres at what it deemed to be an established location, operating within 40 miles of a regular stock company, and producing any new play during its season as Class "A" companies. Class "B" theatres were located in noncompetitive areas (in Equity's opinion) and produced revivals only. In both cases, regular stock conditions, as modified by the "Minimum Contract for Summer Stock Companies Only," would apply, whereas salaries would differ. Class "A" theatres were required to employ at least six Equity members as part of its resident company and to pay actors minimum union scale, which in 1936 was $40 weekly for senior members, $25 for junior members, and $25 for those holding jobbing contracts.[24] Class "B" theatres could pay as little as $5 per week to all actors but had to provide free room and board.

Regardless of classification, all theatre managers were subject to the eight stipulations listed below the questionnaire. The order of these requirements is alogical (the designated dates of the summer season, for instance, do not appear until number 13), but seems to reflect Equity's desire to rectify the most egregious abuses suffered by actors first, followed by more general guidelines. The top requirement, therefore, attempted to solve the board and lodging problem by assuring that members not be obligated to live and eat at any particular place. If it was impossible to obtain suitable accommodations other than from the theatre management, the cost could not exceed $3 per day. Rule 2 required theatres to notify the union every Tuesday of the full cast list, including jobbers, for the following week, thus permitting Equity to keep track of its members and actors who might become members. Rule 3 specifically protected jobbers who were engaged to perform at a location other than their place of employment. In such cases, the manager had to provide free room and board during the rehearsal week.[25]

Additional requirements involved the company's classification and Equity's right to change it at any time. The union also insisted that the theatres print their classification status prominently on the front of all contracts so that members would immediately know their terms of employment. The final stipulations ensured that managers would abide by the rules, would use official contracts in employing Equity members, and would agree that any and all disputes were to be arbitrated as outlined in the standard stock contract. Last, Equity, which had hitherto ignored summer stock as a special category of theatre, designated that the official summer season would run from May 1 through September 15. No doubt if September 15 fell on a Friday and a manager wished to close his season on Saturday night, she or he would have required special dispensation from the union.

In its April report on the new Equity rules, *Variety* predicted dire consequences for many summer stocks, which, it presumed, would be unable to operate with the additional expenses imposed by unionization. "It is generally understood that there is little profit margin in the sticks," *Variety* said, "and the salary requirement may force the reduction of summer spots." It also noted that overall, the importance of summer theatres had "become minimized," citing the fact that no new successes had arrived on Broadway that season.[26] Only three months later, *Variety* contradicted its earlier pronouncement by proclaiming a new record number of 126 summer stock theatres; 47 of those were registered with the union, and most of those operated as Class "A" enterprises.[27] The summer houses also were continuing to try out new shows, and although most failed to become Broadway blockbusters, several would enjoy modest success in New York. Lewis Nichols, writing in the *New York Times*, estimated that 150 new plays were tried out each summer, and statistics that he provided indicated a greater success rate the previous season than *Variety* had reported. Nichols counted 89 Broadway premieres during the 1935–36 season, 8 of which had come from summer stock theatres. Of those, 3 ran for more than 100 performances, which was the standard test of a Broadway success. Although, as he pointed out, that was not a high percentage, "it must be remembered that the O'Neills, Sherwoods and Kaufmans of this world are not tried out in the rustic playhouses."[28] The most celebrated summer stock transfer—*Life with Father* from Maine's Lakewood Playhouse—was still three years away, and in the interim, Lakewood, Westport, and other Class "A" theatres were continuing to experiment with new scripts.

At the same time that *Variety* published its record-breaking list of stock houses, Alfred Harding cautiously announced the success of the new summer theatre policy in the July issue of *Equity* magazine. He expressed the hope that at the peak of the season, there would be 75 approved theatres employing more than 500 union members. He also credited Equity with bringing a new measure of respect to what he still maintained was a lower form of entertainment. Displaying, once again, his penchant for hyperbole, Harding launched into another tirade on this "new form of summer theatre so distinct from that which had preceded it as to seem to present a new social phenomenon and which threatened, unless speedily curbed, to become a social problem." He asserted that "many of the managers of this new theatre were not professional theatre men; they came from the amateur theatre; from dramatic schools; from the colleges," adding, "heaven only knows from what cracks they crawled to become producers in the summer theatre." Harding accused them of wanting only to discover the next smash hit—from which they could reap substantial monetary benefits—by mounting "cheap tryouts of new plays" where actors would achieve little more "than a bare living and a high quota of humiliation."[29] As always, Harding made sweeping generalizations with little evidence to substantiate his claims. Given that Harding represented as distinguished a professional body as the Actors' Equity Association, it is no wonder that summer stock continued to suffer from a negative reputation.

Once Equity had officially recognized summer stock as a legitimate category of employment, it regularly would remind members of the rules and would request their cooperation in helping to maintain standards. "We recognize that no manager can evade the conditions of the Equity contract unless some actors help in that evasion," Harry Lane admonished in the May 1938 issue of *Equity*, while reminding members that ignorance was not a legitimate defense in eluding rules that had been in effect for two years.[30] To ensure compliance, the union conducted annual inspections of the summer stock houses and warned both managers and actors "that the Equity policeman may catch you if you don't watch out."[31] Despite these repeated warnings and assertions that members regularly complained each autumn about sins perpetrated the previous summer, there was little solid evidence of problems. This was confirmed by Robert Keith, a member of Equity Council and "an important actor who carries with him into this troubled field more personal and professional prestige than any representative Equity has ever had for this work," who agreed to conduct a widespread inspection of summer stock houses during the summer of 1939 that was to last until Labor Day.[32] Keith resigned his post on June 13, declaring that his position had been "a superfluous expense to our organization." Of the more than 20 theatres he had visited, only one had unacceptable conditions, and for those he blamed Equity members:

> The special policing of the Summer Theatres might result in some benefit, although it is doubtful that anyone could unearth the connivance between managers and members of our organization. Working daily with our office has demonstrated that we have machinery to handle any situation that can possibly arise in the Summer Theatre. All that is necessary to set that machinery in motion is the cooperation of our members, without which the office is helpless. It must be remembered that the guilt of connivance cannot be placed solely on the manager.[33]

Keith recommended that his position be abolished. Although Equity Council did not appoint a replacement for Keith that summer, it would continue to conduct periodic inspections of summer stock houses in the ensuing years.

In 1938, Equity published its first rule book devoted specifically to summer stock employment. It was largely a replication of the 1936 regulations with additional explanations and clarifications of those points that had been open to interpretation. There were some new guidelines on travel and meals, as well as a section devoted to "connivance." Although the rule book described in legal terms the various infringements that could occur between or among Equity members, agents, and stock managers, it also translated them into "simple language": "Working under other than the regular Equity form contract, securing engagement through non-accredited agents, accepting less than Equity conditions, [and] failure to demand and obtain minimum conditions established by Equity, may result in loss of membership, revocation of the agent's permit and declaring the manager unfair."[34]

It is easy to understand why Equity members, given the expensive new regulations demanded by the union, would be tempted to work in a cash poor but ideologically rich summer stock company that was necessarily functioning outside of the rules. No doubt, there were some unscrupulous managers who, as Harding was wont to describe them, were realizing hefty profits at the expense of underpaid, self-sacrificing actors. More likely, however, "connivances" that were illegal in the union's eyes were simply theatre companies wishing to remain financially solvent and independent of any and all controlling factions.

Summer Stock Managers Organize

Summer stock managers were no longer able to operate their theatres according to a simple business model. Their basic financial and managerial requirements grew in complexity as Equity introduced periodic rises in minimum salaries and tightened its rules governing working conditions during the late 1930s and 1940s. In seeking ways to minimize costs and maximize box office revenues, the managers joined forces with high-profile actors to reinvent the star system, which evolved into the combination company, both in emulation of nineteenth-century stock practice (to be discussed in chapter 6). The managers also formed a professional alliance in 1941 known as the Summer Stock Managers Association (SSMA), which claimed 42 charter members at its first convention at the Hotel Algonquin in April 1942. All of the major class "A" producing houses were represented, and the SSMA's board of governors was a veritable who's who of summer producers, including Milton Stiefel of the Ivoryton Playhouse as president, Richard Aldrich of the Cape Playhouse as vice-president, and William Miles of the Berkshire Playhouse as treasurer.

The Algonquin conference provided a forum to discuss shared concerns that affected the health of both summer stock and the American theatre in general. A critical issue was the potential effects of World War II, which the United States had entered the previous December after the Japanese attack on Pearl Harbor, on the coming summer season. Producers correctly anticipated that nationwide gas rationing and a severe shortage of tires would hinder patrons from getting to the theatres, most of which were in remote areas that were not accessible by public transportation. They also discussed the importance of holding benefit performances for war relief, both to support American efforts abroad and to help raise public opinion of professional theatre at home. The recent congressional hearings held by the Dies Committee on Un-American Activities, which effectively had ended the Federal Theatre Project in June 1939, had cast a negative light on all theatre artists, regardless of their politics. Hence, the producers felt that every opportunity to promote patriotic fervor and pro-American sentiments should be exploited. In a *New York Post* article covering the convention, Wilella Waldorf wrote:

> After the attacks on the theatre and artists in general in Congress and elsewhere, it is felt all along Broadway that some means must be taken to

control the avalanche of demands for patriotic service on the part of show folk, and to see that the theatre gets credit for the work its people are doing and will continue to do. Navy Relief, Army Relief, the USO, and the myriad of war drives will, as always, get the utmost in aid from entertainers, some of whom haven't had a paying job in months. But the Theatre Wing will run the business and see that the theatre as an institution gets credit for it.[35]

Waldorf added a spirited quip that no doubt represented the feelings of many legitimate theatre workers regarding the congressional allegations: "When the war is finally over, we should enjoy the spectacle of watching several loud-mouthed legislators publicly obliged to eat large sections of the Congressional Record devoted to statements on the uselessness of show people."[36]

The other major topic of discussion was the virtual disappearance of new scripts in the summer stock houses in the past few seasons. Thornton Wilder, who spoke at the closing dinner, chided the managers for putting on too much "shallow stuff" and for being timid in their selection of plays. "Since the early pioneering times, some of the courage has gone out of the summer theatre movement," he declared, observing that the more prosperous the theatres had become, the less tendency there was to experiment with new scripts. Waldorf defended the managers who, she declared, were "not in the business for their health" and were forced to cater to the tastes of their audiences or face annihilation. She did agree with Wilder, however, that some experimenting would be good for the summer theatre as an institution. "A more crusading spirit abroad in the erstwhile 'cowbarns' is something devoutly to be wished, with the Broadway district becoming increasingly conservative," she asserted.[37]

Although it would deal with timely issues as necessary, the SSMA's main function was to provide a place for producers to share frustrations and advice. As John Huntington, who served as president in the early 1950s, reminisced about the first convention:

After spending about five or ten minutes with these other and now brother managers, it came upon me with something of a shock that if I had had the opportunity to talk shop with these men before my partners and I opened up at Brattle Hall, one of two things would have happened: either we would not have opened at all, or, in opening, we would have been far better prepared for the manifold and painful rigors of our first summer stock season. The information, the hints, the friendly help that was offered, the exchange of opinion with men whose opinion I valued very, very highly, was, to me, one of the most gratifying and satisfactory experiences I have ever had.[38]

In the mid-1950s, the SSMA, which had become the Stock Managers' Association (SMA) in 1950 in order to extend membership to all stock theatres, disbanded and re-formed as two separate organizations: the Council of Stock Theatres (COST), representing both summer and winter "star" stock managements, and, for those theatres that maintained resident stock companies, the Council of Resident Stock Theatres (CORST). The SMA had evolved from a support group to a recognized collective bargaining association that negotiated contracts and conditions with Equity and other labor unions. While this status continued under the new organizational structure, COST also maintained a central booking office to tour shows from one theatre to the next.

Apprentice Programs

Almost every theatre had some kind of apprentice program in place, since the energetic young students provided an inexpensive, reliable labor force, which, in many cases, was necessary for companies to function. The apprentices would be employed in virtually every facet of making theatre, from building sets to cleaning lavatories, and proved particularly valuable during performances to service the patrons' needs, from parking cars to ushering to selling refreshments at intermission. Those with developed skills might operate follow spots, work as dressers, or change sets and properties. In recompense for their labors, apprentices generally received free room and board and a good theatre education in a wide variety of subjects, from acting and text analysis through set and lighting design. The better houses also afforded apprentices the opportunity to mount their own productions and take on smaller roles in main stage performances. Generally, however, a tuition fee was charged, which, depending on the theatre, could range from a few hundred dollars to as much as one thousand at places that advertised as dramatic schools.

The apprentice programs, like every other facet of summer stock, were only as good as the theatres that ran them. Charges of exploitation frequently were leveled at all apprentice programs, since the students worked very hard and rarely received a salary. Since most summer theatres had minimal professional staffs and everyone, including the managers, worked overtime, it is doubtful that most apprentices worked harder or longer than anyone else. Certainly, however, there were abuses. In the most egregious cases, the apprentices were treated as unpaid labor who were expected to function 24 hours a day, seven days a week; it was generally at those same theatres that they were charged the most money, ostensibly for the privilege of working with seasoned professionals. Less respectable managers also provided little or no formal training and performance experiences, and, all too often, what training was available was conducted by unqualified teachers. To Equity's mind, however, the most heinous part of the apprentice racket was the promise, by some managers, that the starry-eyed hopefuls would become full-fledged Equity members by the end of the season. As at least one critic pointed out, however, this cunning inducement was largely the fault of the union itself, which until 1949 had a rule that any apprentice who appeared in four plays during the summer would be required to join Equity.[39] To a novice actor who dreamed of becoming a professional quickly, this "requirement" was a palpable enticement to work as an apprentice, no matter how deplorable the conditions. In 1943, the summer stock committee of Equity Council made a formal recommendation to stop this practice by rewriting the rule so that "no apprentice student or non-Equity jobber can qualify for membership in his first season" no matter how often he or she appeared on stage. To become a member, the apprentice would have to play at least three weeks in a succeeding season or any engagement at all in a third. The committee felt that the new ruling would solve two ills at once by undermining unscrupulous managers using the promise of an Equity card as a lure to unsuspecting students and also by assuring that acting companies would maintain a high degree of professionalism. The more apprentices who appeared on stage, Equity reasoned, the fewer union members who would be employed.[40]

The committee's recommendation was tabled, possibly because so few summer stocks operated during the summer of 1943, until 1948 when these issues again were raised as a serious concern. Although a revision of the apprentice rules was included in the new guidelines sent to all actors, agents, and managers in February 1948, it, along with two of the other mandated changes, was reversed after complaints filed by managers propelled the council to reconsider. The only important change to take effect immediately was that managers were required to register the names and addresses of all apprentices and dramatic students connected with the theatre no later than one week after the opening of the season.[41] An ensuing investigation resulted in new rules being passed by Equity Council the following year that were virtually the same as the summer stock committee's 1943 recommendations. As of summer 1949, apprentices, students, and non-Equity jobbers would be ineligible for membership during their first season of stock, regardless of the number of plays in which they appeared. During the second season, actors had to be given an Equity contract once cast in their fourth show, at which time they became eligible to join the union. The third summer, any former apprentice who was being hired to act or stage-manage had to be signed under an Equity contract.[42]

Although some predicted that "apprentices, unable to join Equity forthwith, should prove a little less eager to shell out their dough," there is no indication that the number of apprentices diminished.[43] If anything, apprentices became more ubiquitous than ever during the 1950s since, by that time, apprenticing in summer stock was widely considered to be the best way to gain a professional theatre education. Paul Barry, an experienced summer stock manager, penned a defense of the apprentice system that compared it to a requirement of European repertory theatres that new members serve as apprentices for several seasons before accepting them as "journeyman" members of the company. The apprentices were paid little or nothing, were expected to perform menial duties, and would "advance from spear carrying to better roles as their talent warrants." The only other option to apprenticing in the United States was to attend acting schools, which, as Barry pointed out, may or may not provide the full production experience that he considered essential to professional training. "The processes by which they learn [in summer stock] are so fundamental," he contended, "that it's agonizing to think they are so often ignored or denied":

> The apprentice is immersed in theatre twenty-four hours a day for twelve or more weeks. Several plays are produced, built from the printed page to the finished product and sold to an audience. The plays are cast and rehearsed, costumed, propped, lit, played on sets, designed and directed by professionals, acted in the principal roles by professionals. All the other elements of the theatre are present as well, the promotion, the administration, the ballyhoo and the selling, the complete business of theatre. The Apprentice learns by osmosis. If the Producer is conscientious enough to conduct classes, then the training is more complete than anywhere else; the combination of study and practice are invaluable to the Apprentice's development.[44]

When producers did abuse the apprentice system, problems should be addressed and rectified. "Criticize these," he declared, but not the system. The professional theatres need apprentices for economic survival, Barry argued, just as the theatre novice needs to work as an apprentice to mature as an artist.

To help potential applicants, the American National Theatre and Academy (ANTA) published guidelines on apprenticing in summer stock, which included advice on who should apply, how to select a theatre, and what to expect once engaged. By the 1950s, most apprentices, except for those receiving scholarships, had to pay for the privilege of working with professional companies. Both tuition and room-and-board fees were to be expected, and could range anywhere from $100 to $400 for the summer. Meager salaries were paid in some cases to scholarship students, but usually only "to males who can double as truck drivers." ANTA provided a long list of possible duties and reminded students that everyone was expected to work long hours that "precluded a vigorous social life." As to whether to apply to Equity or non-Equity theatres, ANTA advised that the opportunity to work with a fully professional company was immeasurable, particularly since it could provide important contacts for future employment. On the other hand, since most of the non-Equity theatres were smaller, they might provide more acting opportunities for apprentices. In either case, only serious students were encouraged to apply. "The production of summer theatre is such that there is no longer any place for the dabbler," ANTA warned, adding that unless the apprentice "is prepared to accept complete responsibility for the jobs, big and small, assigned to him," he "will be both unhappy and a dead weight" to the company.[45]

A final and not inconsiderable advantage of having apprentices at a theatre was the subsequent publicity benefit should the young unknown become a star. Summer stock brochures delighted in reminding audiences that a particular actor apprenticed at that theatre before she or he was famous, thus enticing the reader to buy a ticket or season subscription to discover this year's budding stars. Patricia Neal lied about her age so that she could apprentice at the Barter Theatre when only 16; Joanne Woodward claims to have gotten the richest theatre education possible while an apprentice at the Monomoy Theatre on Cape Cod; and Bette Davis would have been an apprentice at the Cape Playhouse had she arrived sooner. Since all the apprentice slots were filled, she agreed to work with front-of-house staff during the summer of 1928, thus becoming the theatre's most famous usher.

The Summer Theatre Grows Up

As Alfred Harding finally admitted in 1941, "the summer theatre has grown up and is largely in the hands of people who have become professionals at the game."[46] If this was true before World War II, it certainly was true in the boom years following the war. Immediately after the World War II hiatus, summer stock returned in force with 99 Equity-sanctioned theatres operating in 1946. In 1947, the number jumped to 125.[47] The *Blueprint for Summer Theatre 1953 Supplement* reported more than 500 summer theatres of all types, playing in 39 states plus Washington, D.C., Bermuda, and Canada. Of these, about 140 had posted Equity bonds and were functioning as stock operations. The popularity of summer stock had spurred the creation of all sorts of theatrical entertainments that operated exclusively in the summer months. In addition to the Equity, Non-Equity, professional, and amateur stock companies all over the country, there were college and university groups, repertory companies, pageants, spectacles, and drama schools offering a wide variety of shows and services. Productions occurred both indoors and outdoors in conventional proscenium theatres as well as in arenas, tents, stadiums, and, in a few cases, on stages completely surrounded by water. Although summer theatre was continuing to spread throughout the country, largely via a new influx of arena stages, the bulk of the stock houses remained in the northeastern part of the country. In 1952, there were more than 225 theatres operating along the Atlantic seaboard from Maine to North Carolina.[48]

The fact that summer stock had become big business was corroborated by Richard Beckhard and John Effrat via their popular series of how-to books. The *Blueprint for Summer Theatre*, published in 1948 and described by *Equity* as an "indispensable source for any summer stock manager,"[49] was the first of seven annual editions detailing all facets of operating summer stock theatres. In addition to providing complete lists of both summer and winter houses as well as updated rules and regulations from Actors' Equity, the *Blueprints* included articles on handling publicity and community relations, preparing budgets, instituting proper accounting procedures, and solving technical problems. These volumes were not only crammed with sage advise by the most experienced and successful producers, but also provided a venue for public debate on topics of common concern, such as the vagaries of the star system and the new music theatre tents, both of which profoundly changed the industry during the 1940s and 1950s.

As new business models changed the way that summer stock operated, they simultaneously changed the way in which these theatres were perceived. Initially, the new polish evident in the theatres was deemed, by at least one major critic, as a positive improvement. Elliot Norton, the major Boston drama critic from 1934 until his retirement in 1982, also recognized a certain integrity in the summer houses that was not apparent in regular commercial theatres. In a 1940 column for the *Boston Post*, he discussed the changes in stock from its earliest days as a disparate band of small, struggling companies of varying talents, through the middle 1930s, when it flourished as a laboratory in which to try out new plays, to 1940, when "most of the companies worth visiting are now doing good things, or at least interesting things, with good and sometimes great players." He pointed out that very few of these theatres made any money and truly were operating as nonprofit institutions, using any bonus income to make improvements for the following season: "This is, admittedly, so contrary to the American commercial spirit that it may be hard to believe. Actually—and here is one fundamental reason why the summer theatre setup is so encouraging to most of us—the people involved are preparing themselves for higher places in the wider realms of theatre."[50] He continued by profiling the decency, if not nobility, of the practitioners: "They have come into the theatre, these summer folks, with clean hands. They are not pirates, to whom the drama is something to be exploited. They are enthusiasts, who find something deep and stirring in the pleasure of their work. They have high ambitions, high ideals, high notions of the standards of their business."[51] Norton asserted that they already had made their work felt in the wider theatrical world and that alumni were garnering distinguished positions on Broadway. He closed with the hope that these "spirited, gifted enthusiasts" would become theatre's new leaders, adding that "those involved in operating the better theatres are among the nicest people in the world."[52]

Writing ten years later for the *Blueprint for Summer Theatre 1949 Supplement*, Vernon Rice, a critic for the *New York Post*, was not as optimistic. He wondered what had become of those idyllic groups of yore who boasted talent plus high ideals and did not worry about making money. Citing the University Players Guild as the ideal company, he reminisced how "in those days when they all were ambitious and not at all famous, [they] did everything from painting the scenery to playing walk-ons, with each one getting his chance at a fat, juicy part." "Now," he moaned, "we've got fine protective rulings, a minimum wage and everybody has turned specialist." Although he admitted that summer stock's main function was not as a training ground but as a locus for first-class entertainment, he lamented the recent changes that propelled a rise in ticket prices as tyro talents were banished from summer stages in favor of established and expensive stars.[53]

Despite the four-year hiatus during World War II, the face of summer stock had changed radically in the decade between Norton's and Rice's assessments. Although Rice longed for a return to "the simple things in the good old summer time," it was not to be, for the "clean hands" that Norton praised in 1940 were becoming increasingly besmirched by commercial incentives. If Actors' Equity permanently changed the way in which summer stock theatres conducted business, the star invasion of stock would finish its transformation from a venue for young hopefuls to a lucrative haven for big-name stars. The barn theatres had discovered a new cash cow.

6

The Barn's New Cash Cow

In marketing nomenclature, a "cash cow" is a well-established, reliable product that will consistently produce high revenues. No doubt the term originated with dairy farmers who would stake their income on their prized cattle herds. Once the farmers sold out to the theatre folk and the real cows were evicted from the barns, it was up to the producers to find their own special breed of cash cow. Summer stock discovered it in the visiting star performers who invaded the barn theatres beginning in the mid-1930s. What initially was known as "star stock" rapidly evolved into a "star system" that included the "star circuit" or "package tour," a revival of the nineteenth-century combination companies that transformed summer stock for many of the largest and best-known venues. By the 1940s, the lure of seeing the potential stars of tomorrow had waned in favor of seeing the biggest stars of today appearing in person at the barn down the lane. What was now clearly a summer stock industry engaged in an ongoing debate over the merits of the new package shows versus "old-fashioned stock." Many managers ultimately regretted their decision to embrace the star system since, as one critic astutely commented, "every week you whoop up a star you minimize the importance of a week without one."[1]

It was common knowledge that the star system, which had displaced the venerable stock companies throughout the United States during the nineteenth century, promoted the rise of the combination company—a move that led, in turn, to the commercialization of the American theatre. Even if there were naïve summer stock managers who refused to heed the danger of history repeating itself, there were plenty of critics to enlighten them. The complications inherent in scheduling a star circuit in 1939 "were not very different from those of sixty years or more ago, when the visiting star system was not a mere midsummer madness but standard practice in the theatre," remarked Helen Ormsbee in the *New York Herald Tribune*.[2] Though Burns Mantle, writing in the *New York Daily News*, considered the revival of the star system "an experiment" in 1940, it was, to some, a clearly established threat by

1949.[3] In a piece for the *New York Times* that year, summer stock director Melville Burke wrote: "It is my belief that summer stock companies may be ruined in the next decade by their concentration on stars. This wholesale destruction may descend on the rustic circuit unless summer theatre companies realize that their theatrical firmament is greater than any stars therein. For proof, let me cite the record."[4]

The Demise of Nineteenth-Century Stock

The historic record had been established nearly 20 years earlier when the first economic history of the American theatre, written on commission by Alfred L. Bernheim for the Actors' Equity Association, was serialized in 20 consecutive issues of *Equity* magazine between 1930 and 1932. The collected articles were subsequently published by Benjamin Blom in one volume, titled *The Business of the Theatre: An Economic History of the American Theatre, 1750–1932*. In his chapter, "Twinkle, Twinkle, Little Star," Bernheim traced the evolution of the star-stock system back to the late seventeenth century when the practice began in England. By the end of the eighteenth century, a few British stars were coming to America on generous contracts, but the great influx did not begin until the 1820s, when such prominent actors as Edmund and Charles Kean, Junius Brutus Booth, William Charles Macready, and Charles and Fanny Kemble embarked on lucrative U.S. tours. They were soon joined by native-born artists such as Edwin Forrest, James H. Hackett, and, a few decades later, Charlotte Cushman, all of who, with Yankee pride, were pleased to provide homespun competition for the alien attractions in their playhouses. In all instances, they were independent, freelance agents who would guest-star for one or more performances with resident stock companies. There was no attempt at integration or the more modern notion of ensemble acting; the stars were billed and pampered as luminaries, separate and apart from the rest of the company, and were paid handsomely for their efforts.

So long as the visiting stars were an anomaly, they were welcome adjuncts to many stock companies, whose regular audiences would pack the house and thus fill the coffers whenever a famous guest artist appeared. Problems arose when the stars became ubiquitous and managers booked them every week; this left little opportunity to return to a normal stock season, where the companies' principal actors could resume the leading roles. Patrons, however, grew accustomed to star turns and would shun performances without them. Bernheim quoted an 1828 article in the *New York Mirror, and Ladies Literary Gazette*, which criticized this practice: "The effect has been, that, by the highly-seasoned intellectual banquets served up to them (the public), their appetites have been so pampered and spoiled, that, like practiced *gourmands*, they have lost all relish for simple, wholesome food, and now think no more of going to see a good comedy, well played by the regular company, than the *gourmand* would of making a hearty dinner on a plain roast beef."[5]

The deleterious effects of this star surfeit on the resident companies came fast and furious. Managers found themselves in fierce competition for the most popular attractions, who, fully cognizant of the prevailing marketplace, were steadily increasing their fees. In order to save money, managers would reduce the salaries of their full-time actors or replace the more seasoned, higher-priced ones with lesser, cheaper talents. Since the star was the thing, the supporting company had been reduced simply to that: supporters whose function was to showcase the celebrities' talents but otherwise stay out of their way. Hence, the quality of resident companies decreased markedly as strong, experienced actors either were fired or quit in protest, since their talents were being little used and frequently much abused.

The stars likewise had a negative effect on the development of American drama which, with the exception of new plays commissioned by Edwin Forrest, stagnated during this period. Most stars were not interested in experimenting with untested scripts, which ultimately might not display them to their best advantage. Instead, they relied on the stable repertoire on which they had established their reputations and that featured plays with star parts geared to their particular talents.

Ironically, the stars who, at first, brought fame and considerable profit to theatre managers eventually prompted their undoing. When riches grow commonplace, customers have a surfeit of them and grow tired of seeing the same stars week after week. Edwin Forrest, who became notorious for bullying managers into giving him lucrative engagements, cost the Louisville Theatre in Kentucky money when audiences failed to materialize. On one night during his 1848 engagement, box office receipts totaled a mere $150. Yet Forrest, who was under contract for $200, insisted that he be paid in full despite the fact that to do so cost the manager $50 plus operating expenses.[6] While playing at the American Theatre in New Orleans that same season, Forrest made a profit of $7,643 for a 30-day engagement that cost the management more than $800. The manager might have made a meager profit had Forrest sustained an injury that resulted in the cancellation of one performance and the return of $1,000 in ticket sales.[7]

Forrest was only one of many overpaid performers whose notorious fees virtually bankrupted theatres. By the mid-nineteenth century, a few managers had stopped hiring stars, and were returning to what was now deemed the old-fashioned resident stock company featuring talented, experienced actors. For the majority of theatres, however, there was no turning back. The fashion for stars had become so well established that the stars themselves were inventing new ways to improve production quality, minimize their own labors, and maximize profits. As such, they began hiring a few additional actors to tour with them, thus ensuring a high quality supporting cast in principal roles. Although this practice evolved in response to the diminished state of resident stock—there were very few quality actors left in the house companies—it proved especially advantageous to the star, who could now spend less time in rehearsal and still be assured of strong support in critical roles. This development weakened the stock company further; the next logical step was full annihilation, which happened with the advent of the combination company. Here, the star would travel with a full cast and all the appurtenances necessary to production—sets, costumes, properties, and even stagehands. This arrangement afforded stars complete control over their productions and avoided the vagaries of unknown managers, actors, and production personnel along the road. The new combination companies were not only artistically stronger than star stock; they also were far more lucrative. As Bernheim argued, actor-managers would not have been so eager to take on the additional financial risks and managerial concerns of touring a full company if the earning potential were not significantly higher.[8] Also, the combination companies took over rapidly, almost immediately replacing the star-stock system.

It was at this juncture that some outside businessmen, who knew nothing about theatre but a lot about money, became involved in professional theatre. The old stock system, which consisted of independently owned and operated theatres that largely self-produced their seasons, did not have major revenue potential for investors. Combination companies, on the other hand, which centralized production, booking, and management, were inherently structured to promote commercial interests, a fact that readily became apparent to savvy businessmen. As Bernheim maintained, however, it was not the venture capitalists who transformed the nineteenth-century stage—it was the theatre artists themselves. "The theatre was prepared for commercial exploitation by internal forces," Bernheim stated, contending that businessmen appeared only "to reap the fruits of the new organization." The evolution from resident stock to star-stock to the combination company was driven by managers, stars, and, later, actor-managers, who kept discovering new ways to enhance their own careers and personal earnings. "What followed was dictated by the logic of the economic background," Bernheim explained, and the eventual monopolies created in the theatre mimicked those in other major industries, such as oil, railroads, iron, and steel.[9] It is true that, once in place, businessmen viciously exploited the new system for commercial gains, with little regard for artistic integrity, and thus propelled the unionization of the professional theatre as well as the rising costs of production throughout the twentieth and twenty-first centuries. They did not, however, create the monster; they merely kept it fed.

Bernheim ended this discussion by speculating as to whether the stars and managers would have so thoroughly destroyed resident stock if they could have foreseen the consequences of their actions. In light of the star invasion of summer stock, which occurred with full knowledge of the events of just half a century earlier, one could confidently answer, Yes. History repeated itself so quickly because only a few individuals, generally theatre critics whose salaries weren't dependent on box office revenue, protested at first; it was not until later, when the managers and stars were no longer making fistful of dollars, that they regretted their actions. Human nature suggests that people, be they theatre artists or oil barons, will do whatever is possible to reap personal gain, regardless of the cost to the larger entity. Hence, the barn doors readily swung open to give the star system a new home.

The Star System in Summer Stock

In an industry without a unified history and in which aggressive self-promotion was common practice, it is difficult to determine the absolute truth. Although Lewis Nichols claimed that stars, such as Maude Adams, were touring the barn theatres as early as 1934,[10] the more popular tale of the beginnings of the new star stock names the instigator as Richard Aldrich, credited in a 1955 *New Yorker* profile as "undoubtedly the best-known summer-theatre producer in America."[11] Twenty years before that profile, when he unwittingly instituted the star system, he was doing what turned out to be a one-year stint as business manager at the Cape Playhouse. Raymond Moore, who had founded the Dennis, Massachusetts, theatre in 1927, was in serious debt, and he hired Aldrich, who by that time had gained a substantial reputation on Broadway as a financial wizard, to help turn things around. To Moore's horror, Aldrich's solution was to hire the popular star Jane Cowl at the unheard-of summer stock salary of $1,000 a week to revitalize the playhouse's reputation. The scheme worked, and the Cape ended the 1935 season with all debts paid and money in the bank.

Aldrich's prowess initially put him out of a job since Moore, apparently believing that it was Cowl's and not Aldrich's genius that had resuscitated his theatre, fired Aldrich and resumed management himself for the next two seasons. He re-hired Aldrich in 1938, who immediately took over as the Cape's producer-director and went on to become the managerial star of the summer circuit.

Aldrich's coup of 1935, however, was emulated rapidly by other summer stock producers who saw the possibilities for fame and profit. Likewise, the stars were eager to follow Cowl's example of taking a working holiday with a large paycheck attached. Soon Ethel Barrymore, Gladys Cooper, Helen Hayes, Gertrude Lawrence, Philip Merrivale, Walter Hampden, Florence Reed, Ruth Gordon, Clifton Webb, Libby Holman, Nance O'Neill, and Ruth Chatterton—just to name some of the more popular stage stars of the era—were touring the barns to great acclaim and earnings. They also were pleased to have the opportunity to try out roles they may not have had the occasion to perform in New York—many were particularly keen to do Shakespeare—and, in these earliest years, some were anxious to premiere new scripts that possibly could transfer to Broadway. Others were happy to revive favorite roles and present them to new audiences, thus solidifying reputations won on material for which they had become famous.

In the first few seasons of summer star stock, the guest artists would rehearse with the resident company for a full week, thus promoting strong ensemble performances. The arrangement was beneficial to the stars, who were enjoying their busman's holidays; to the audiences, which were seeing quality theatre with major performers in picturesque surroundings; to the managers, who usually could wreak only a small profit from an expensive star's engagement but who considered the attendant publicity more than adequate compensation; and to members of the resident stock company, who relished the opportunity to appear on stage with important stars and hoped to capitalize on their newfound acquaintances during the winter season in New York. The stars also brought nationwide prominence to the summer stock houses, which, with few exceptions, had been principally regional phenomena.

"Let's have stars," proclaimed director-producer John O'Shaugnessy. "They add excitement, glitter, glamour, and audiences like them. But let us make sure, as producers, managers, and directors we handle them well and get the most out of their very great values to our summer theatres."[12] By the time O'Shaugnessy penned this advice, star stock had ballooned into several types, all of which had evolved simultaneously in the late 1930s and had been attempted with greater or lesser degrees of success during the following decade. The first, what business manager Richard Highley termed the "personal appearance star system," was the perverse stepchild of the original star stock.[13] As the demand for stars became greater, Hollywood film actors, who were great favorites with the public, found they, too, could garner lucrative summer contracts by touring the barns. Most, however, were not interested in spending half the summer rehearsing with the resident companies, which would have reduced their incomes proportionately. Instead, they wanted to arrive at the last possible moment, have a quick dress rehearsal with the company, and then perform. This scheme proved detrimental on several levels. First, there was no time to build an ensemble performance until, with any luck, the end of the engagement, at which point the star and the company had had a week of "rehearsals" before a paying audience. Second, many opening nights were a shambles because there had been little or no rehearsal and the stars were busy being stars rather than actors engaging in a role. Third, many Hollywood and, in the 1950s, television actors lacked stage training and could not really act. Their inadequacies were all the more prominent when supported by experienced performers. Audiences eventually tired of seeing celebrities who were not theatre artists attempting to do legitimate drama, and they exhibited their discontent by staying away in droves, causing some theatres to fold.

The trend for arriving at engagements at the last minute was not limited to media stars, however. Legitimate stage actors indulged in this practice more and more as they discovered that managers were still eager to engage them, with or without full company rehearsals. The results were much the same as with the non-acting celebrities. A strong theatre performance requires some semblance of ensemble. Without it, you have little more than a star posturing and preening without benefit of a dramatic context.

Raymond Bramley, a member of the Fairhaven Summer Theatre, a resident star-stock company in Massachusetts, wrote to the Summer Theatre Committee of Actors' Equity in 1948 detailing the problems of late-arriving stars. Although his letter was remarkably fair to all parties—he cited the difficulties and emotional strains experienced both by the star and by members of the resident company—he was clearly asking Equity to discourage the practice since the ultimate loser was the public, who was paying to see bad performances. He described the process: "At the present time, a resident company rehearses without the Stars, their parts being read by inexperienced apprentices, or by a director reading one or more long parts, and trying at the same time to direct. Then, when the Stars do arrive, they invariably change business, and many times cues;

yes, and sometimes suggest changing characterizations."[14] As substantiation for his remarks, Bramley included a review by E. J. Dias of the New Bedford, Massachusetts, *Sunday Standard-Times*, that described one critic's reaction to this deplorable practice:

> The proceedings at Fairhaven last week made us more than a little fed up with "name" stars, such as Mischa Auer, who do not have enough professional responsibility to arrive in time for sufficient rehearsals with the resident company. The play "20th Century" is a farce filled with numerous exits and entrances and situations that call for careful timing—in short, it demands meticulous preparation.
>
> Mr. Auer did not arrive in Fairhaven until the afternoon of the opening performance. This belated appearance of the famed comedian was unfair to the Fairhaven resident company (who had been rehearsing all week), inasmuch as they had inadequate time to acquaint themselves with Mr. Auer's acting style. As a result, on last Monday night, he upset them constantly on lines and stage business, so that the result was a ragged, uninspired performance.[15]

Dias praised the "inherent excellence" of the resident company for keeping the show from being "a complete fiasco," and he admonished Auer for his unprofessionalism. "Not only was Mr. Auer's dilatory arrival unfair to the cast, but also to the audience who pay good money to see a professional production and not something resembling a dress rehearsal of the West Cupcake Dramatic Society." In contrast, Dias praised film star Barry Sullivan, who had arrived in Fairhaven for a half week's rehearsal of *The Second Man*, the theatre's subsequent attraction. "This careful preparation should insure a smoothly functioning opening night performance," Dias predicted.[16]

Some stars, however, chose not to travel alone and, either in deliberate or unwitting emulation of their nineteenth-century forebears, reinvented the partial package tour. Stars would choose an appropriate vehicle to showcase their particular talents, hire several actors to fulfill the major supporting roles, engage a director to rehearse the mini-cast in New York, and then embark on a summer-long tour of resident stock houses. Clarence Derwent, the president of Actors' Equity in the early 1950s, described the procedure as akin to the problems outlined by Bramley in solo star stock: "The star and perhaps a couple of supporting players arrive in town on Sunday (occasionally Monday) and after a scampered run through with the resident company, ring up each week on a nervous first night and spend the rest of their stay complaining of the inability of the harassed company to adapt itself in one rehearsal to their temperamental requirements."[17]

It was only a short leap to the reincarnation of the nineteenth-century combination company, rechristened as the package tour or star circuit for twentieth-century summer stock. Just as they had a century earlier, stars gradually expanded their supporting cast to include all but walk-ons. A notable change from the earlier practice, however, was that summer package tours usually did not travel with scenery or lighting; it was the responsibility of the host theatre to supply those elements based on detailed floor plans and designs provided by the packager (either the star himself or herself or someone hired to organize and manage the tour). The summer houses also maintained a full technical staff so that the packages could tour without stagehands and other backstage personnel. Those venues which changed over to booking package shows exclusively were now called "summer theatres" as opposed to "summer stock theatres" since a resident company was no longer needed and walk-on roles could be played by apprentices or other support staff. Hence, although the terms "summer theatre" and "summer stock" had been used interchangeably until the early 1950s, these were now very specific designations, with differing contractual relationships, between Actors' Equity and the theatre managements.

The first of the star package tours was such a novelty that at least one theatre did not understand exactly what it had booked. Edward Everett Horton organized his inaugural tour of Benn Levy's popular farce, *Springtime for Henry*, for the summer of 1938. *Variety* reported that a theatre at Clinton (possibly either the Clinton, Connecticut, or Bayshore Theatre in Clinton, New Jersey, but the author doesn't specify), had hired Mr. Horton without realizing that he was not traveling alone. Hence, it dutifully rehearsed its resident company, using a substitute for the missing star. "When the whole outfit showed up," *Variety* mused, "they were greeted with blank astonishment."[18] Nevertheless, the show proved so successful that Horton revived it the following summer and then continued the tour throughout the winter months, eventually performing it throughout the Midwest and South, as well as in Cuba.[19] *Henry* went on to become a staple of summer stock in the following decades, playing for a total of 2,700 performances.[20] It also became Horton's signature piece and assured him the distinction of being "the first great legend of the summer theatre," according to William Miles of the Berkshire Theatre who contended that "every summer theater that could scrape together his not inconsiderable fee" booked the show "at least once."[21]

Horton's 1938 success persuaded a passel of other stars to follow his lead during the 1939 summer season. The most prominent of these was Ethel

Barrymore, who also effected a summer stock first by bringing the full company of *Whiteoaks*, which had been on the road since the previous September, to the summer barns to wrap up a 40-week national tour. They appeared at the Westchester Playhouse in Mount Kisco, New York; the nearby Ridgeway Theatre in White Plains, New York; the Berkshire Playhouse in Stockbridge, Massachusetts; the Deertrees Theatre in Harrison, Maine; the Cape Playhouse in Dennis, Massachusetts; and possibly others.[22] The success of *Whiteoaks* in 1939 prompted Barrymore to try *The School for Scandal* in 1940, replete with a full company, costumes, and even scenery. In what became a much-emulated financial arrangement for the early package tours, Barrymore contracted with theatre managers to receive 20 percent of the week's box office net, with a guarantee of $500 as her personal fee, $800 for the rest of the company, and $200 to cover royalties, transportation costs, insurance, and related items. As one reporter put it, "a $1,500 guarantee is terrific for a summer theatre manager under the most auspicious circumstances," particularly since other stars were charging $1,000 and more for personal fees alone.[23]

Many theatres that subscribed to the star system did not restrict themselves to one form of star engagement. Most maintained a resident company, at least through the early 1950s when it still was required for Equity sanction, and employed a combination of two or more types of guest-star engagements throughout the summer, ranging from the star who arrived early to rehearse with the company to booking in full package tours. Other managers maintained one specific kind of star production throughout a single summer but would change operating strategies from season to season, usually depending on the degree of success both they and other star system venues enjoyed the previous year. By the middle to late 1950s, a number of theatres banned stars altogether and returned to what was then regarded as old-fashioned stock. Their story will be told in chapter 8.

Star System Economics

The economics of star system theatres depended on whether the package included one, several, or a full company of actors and also on the location, seating capacity, and drawing power of the host theatre. William Miles, the managing director of the Berkshire Playhouse when it operated as a star-stock house in the 1930s, wrote an article in which he devised a sample weekly budget for a medium-sized theatre with a capacity of 350 to 400, in a good locale. His estimate of $1,717, which included a relatively modest fee of $300

Entrance to the Elitch's Garden Theatre, 1890s. (Photo courtesy The Denver Public Library Western History Department, Denver, Colorado)

Entrance to the Elitch Gardens' Theatre (note the slight change of name) in the late 1940s. (Photo courtesy The Denver Public Library Western History Department, Denver, Colorado)

The Jitney Players' truck containing the portable stage, 1923. (Photo courtesy The Charlotte L. Evarts Memorial Archives, Madison, Connecticut)

The Jitney Players' truck being converted to a stage, 1923. (Photo courtesy The Charlotte L. Evarts Memorial Archives, Madison, Connecticut)

The fully assembled stage with an unidentified play in progress, The Jitney Players, 1923. (Photo courtesy The Charlotte L. Evarts Memorial Archives, Madison, Connecticut)

The Shakespeare Stage at Mariarden, Peterborough, New Hampshire, 1922. (Photo courtesy Peterborough Historical Society, Peterborough, New Hampshire)

The old Stockbridge Casino, designed by architect Stanford White of the New York City firm of McKim, Mead, and White, before it became the Berkshire Playhouse. (Photo courtesy Berkshire Theatre Festival Archive, Stockbridge, Massachusetts and Heather Rose, Studio Two, Lenox, Massachusetts)

The Berkshire Playhouse, now known as the Berkshire Theatre Festival, celebrating its 75th anniversary season in 2003. (Photo courtesy Berkshire Theatre Festival Archive, Stockbridge, Massachusetts and Heather Rose, Studio Two, Lenox, Massachusetts)

The opening production of the Berkshire Playhouse, The Cradle Song, presented by Eva LeGallienne's Civic Repertory Theatre, June 1928. (Photo courtesy Berkshire Theatre Festival Archive, Stockbridge, Massachusetts and Heather Rose, Studio Two, Lenox, Massachusetts)

Basil Rathbone greets some of the backstage workers, Vern Coleman, Whitey Lutz, Brant Ellis, and Albert Gazverde, in 1927, when he was appearing in The Guardsman, the opening production at the new Cape Playhouse. (Photo courtesy of The Cape Playhouse Archive, Dennis, Massachusetts)

Gregory Peck took time off from his role in Playboy of the Western World at the Cape Playhouse in 1946 to play horseshoes on the beach in Dennis. (Photo courtesy of The Cape Playhouse Archive, Dennis, Massachusetts)

The Cape Playhouse scene shop in 1957. Joe Hazzard, Helen Pond, Bob Brand, Herbert Senn, and John Jenkins. (Photo courtesy of The Cape Playhouse Archive, Dennis, Massachusetts)

The last production as viewed from the back of the house in the old Westport Country Playhouse, September 2003, prior to the renovation. (Photo courtesy Chance Farago, Westport Country Playhouse Archive)

The Westport Country Playhouse, circa its founding in 1931, with grazing sheep maintaining the true barn theatre atmosphere. (Photo courtesy Chance Farago, Westport Country Playhouse Archive)

Westport Country Playhouse, rendering of proposed renovation and expansion for summer 2005 reopening and 75th anniversary season. (Photo courtesy Ford Farewell Mills & Gatsch, Architects, LLC)

The New London Barn Playhouse, one of the oldest and most authentic of the summer stock barns, in 1934 shortly after it was converted to a theatre. (Photo courtesy Norman Leger, owner/producer)

The New London Barn Playhouse in 1940, now an established summer stock theatre featuring the New London Players, but with little change to the barn except for a ticket window, a bit of landscaping, and proud new sign. (Photo courtesy Norman Leger, owner/producer)

The New London Barn Playhouse in 1982 is still essentially the same rustic barn with the addition of a front porch to keep the patrons dry at intermission. (Photo courtesy Norman Leger, owner/producer)

A matinee audience exchanging "barter" for tickets at The Barter Theatre, Abingdon, Virginia in 1937. (Photo courtesy The Barter Theatre Archive, Abingdon, Virginia)

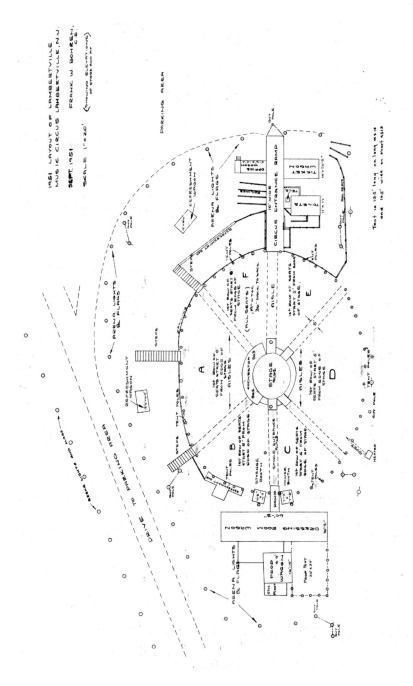

The layout of Lambertville Music Circus showing elevations of the stage and pit, 1951. (Photo credit: Wisconsin Historical Society, Madison, Wisconsin, image number WHi-23332, St. John Terrell Papers)

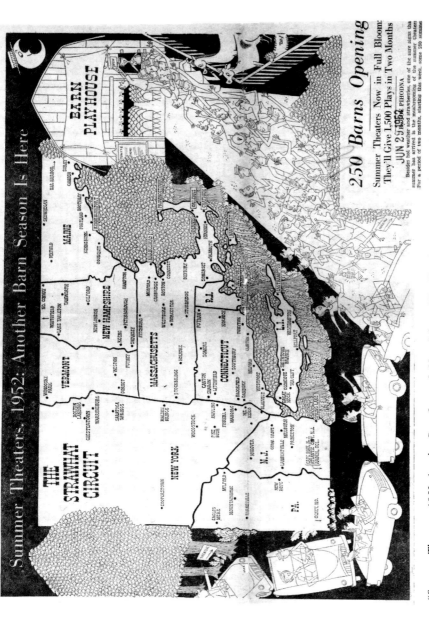

"Summer Theaters, 1952: Another Barn Season Is Here," Straw Hat Circuit map, New York Herald Tribune, 29 June 1952. Maps like this were published by all the major northeast newspapers from the 1930s through 1960s at the beginning of the annual summer theatre season. (Photo courtesy The Center for American History, The University of Texas at Austin, Austin, Texas, New York Herald Tribune Morgue, CN 11767)

Lon McAllister, Ruth Manning, and John Kenley appear in the Kenley Players' production of The Poor Nut in Deer Lake, Pennsylvania, 1939. (Photo courtesy Mr. John Kenley)

The cast studying their scripts on the lawn in front of the Boothbay Playhouse, Boothbay Harbor, Maine, early 1960s. (Photo courtesy Franklyn Lenthall and James Wilmot, Boothbay Harbor, Maine)

Producer Adrienne Grant in front of the 1888 barn she transformed into the Arundel Barn Playhouse, Arundel, Maine, in 1997. Staff photo by Gregory Rec, Portland Press Herald. (Photo courtesy Portland Press Herald, Portland, Maine)

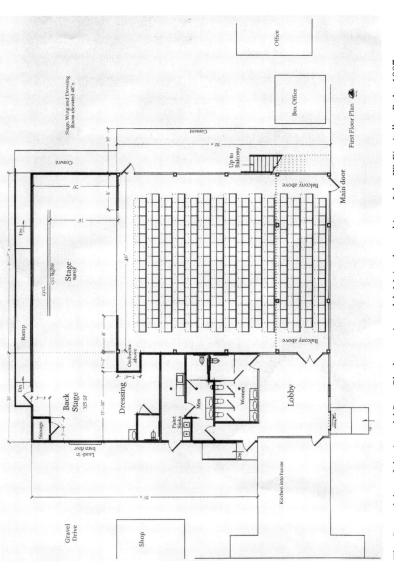

The Groundplan of the Arundel Barn Playhouse, Arundel, Maine by architect John W. Einsiedler, R.A., 1997. (Photo courtesy John W. Einsiedler, R.A., Kennebunk, Maine)

for the guest star, was itemized as follows:

Rental of Theatre	$100
Director's Salary	50
Designer's Salary	50
Business Manager's Salary	40
Press Agent's Salary	40
Box Office Treasurer's Salary	30
Doorman, janitor, and ushers' salaries	40
Salaries 3 crew men	75
Star's salary (average)	300
Cast Salary (8 actors, one of them the Stage Manager)	320
Royalty on Play	125
Newspaper advertising	50
Posters and postcards	50
Tickets	12
Transportation	20
Scenery, props and lights	150
Rental of costumes (prorated)	25
Public liability and workman's compensation insurance	15
House Expenses (phone, light, cleaning supplies, gas for company cars, etc.)	75
Proration of preliminary expenses of $1500 incurred before season opened	150
TOTAL	$1717

Miles estimated that if the theatre could guarantee approximately 1,500 customers per week, paying between 75 cents and $1.50 per ticket, it would break even. "Experience has taught us that sixty per cent capacity is a fair operating figure" that will cover expenses, Miles confirmed, while "the top forty per cent can represent profit." He warned potential managers to expect week-to-week fluctuations both in costs—for instance, some stars will charge more, royalties vary widely, and certain plays demand extensive props and scenery, while others require little—and in box office receipts, since variables like the weather can sabotage the best-laid plans.[24]

Budgets would change accordingly for a personal appearance or partial star package, both of which necessitated an advance director who would arrive at theatres one week ahead to rehearse the resident company and ensure that the scenic requirements were being prepared to specification. In these cases, the packager usually would negotiate a certain minimum plus a percentage of any profits over the net box office receipts. The early full package shows, such as those run by Barrymore and Horton, were financed similarly, but by the 1950s, when the packages became slick commercial operations like the old combination companies of the 1800s, the economics changed. According to accountant Edward Lutz, whose firm, Lutz & Carr, handled 80 percent of the summer stock theatres and worked to regularize all of the summer theatre contracts in the 1950s and 1960s, the producer would hire a show for a fixed price that would include everything but personnel for the nonspeaking roles. The agreed price was a percentage of the gross box office receipts and "the traveling show had a right to go into the box office and check the computation of the tickets sold," Lutz said.[25] Although producers still had house personnel on salary as well as basic maintenance and advertising expenses, they were now functioning as managers of roadhouses rather than as directors of self-producing theatres. These were the kinds of venues that Equity reclassified as "summer theatres," to distinguish them from the stock houses that still maintained resident companies.

The Star Package Summer Theatres

Despite the fact that this new classification of theatre did not produce its own shows, these venues were large, sophisticated enterprises that could afford to book the costly package shows and still turn a profit. They also had to market and comport themselves in the same manner as any summer operation that was dependent on the local community for survival. Stephen Langley, the author of *Theatre Management and Production in America*, gained his administrative expertise at the Falmouth Playhouse, where, for nearly 20 years, he served as managing director. The Falmouth, the second of impresario Richard Aldrich's successful Cape Cod summer theatres, was conceived and operated exclusively for package tours. Langley maintained a staff of 20 and a dozen unpaid apprentices to handle all technical and managerial duties in operating the theatre; to clean and perform maintenance on the cottages housing the star, the acting company, and the apprentices; to tend the lawns; to make shopping trips into town, which was half an hour's drive each way; to sell concessions and to help keep the gallery of 20 arts and crafts and food shops running; and to assist the visiting actors with whatever they needed done. There was also a large restaurant on the premises, which had a separate staff but was still Langley's responsibility.

Langley's schedule afforded him, at most, five or six hours of sleep a night. He would rise by 7 o'clock, get a doughnut at the pro shop (there was a golf course on the property), and accomplish whatever he needed to do in the relative quiet of the early morning before the box office opened at 10. "It was my only time to think," he recalled, "so, if I had to write press releases, or check contracts, or do bank deposits, I would do it then. The rest of the day was dealing with emergencies." He would change clothes four or five times a day as appropriate for different appearances and would try to grab an afternoon nap "to keep my sanity." Langley would have dinner at the theatre "which was always interrupted," greet the audience, and see that the curtain went up without mishap. "I almost never saw the entire show," he reminisced, "it was just impossible. I was surprised at one point when someone accused me of never giving the actors the courtesy to sit through a performance, which left me speechless. What could I do?"[26]

Langley outlined the typical workweek at the theatre, which would begin on Saturday night when a show closed. The staff and crew would stay up all night striking the old set and loading in the new one. The previous company would leave by noon on Sunday, while the new troupe would arrive sometime between noon and five, and would immediately rush in to check out the set and their dressing rooms. "There could be terrible explosions if they were not happy," Langley winced. "I always said it was terrific to get a company from a lousy theatre where they were all unhappy, because then it was easy to please them. If they came from a great theatre like Elitch's (in Denver, Colorado), where it was heaven on earth and they were wined and dined, God help us all."

Once acclimated in the theatre, the company members were taken to their accommodations. There was an actors' cottage, "with thin walls and shared bathrooms," that could house up to nine performers, and also a star's cottage right on the grounds. Alternatively, or if the cast was large, some members might be placed in local motels, but since they needed to be transported back and forth, Langley tried to keep them on site. After they were settled, Langley gathered his management staff with as many cars as needed and took everyone out to dinner. "Once they had a few good drinks and some good food, everybody would be a little happier," Langley said, and would then be ready for Sunday night rehearsal. Depending on the nature of the show, and how long they had been doing it, there might be a full dress or just a simple run-through. If it was a musical or intricate costume show, the crews would rehearse with all the changes before the dress or, if needed, would have a full technical rehearsal on Sunday followed by a dress rehearsal on Monday afternoon.

Monday night openings were formal affairs at Falmouth, as well as at many other summer houses, when the bulk of the subscribers and other prominent local citizens would come to see the premiere of the new show and to meet the actors at a gala party following the performance. The caché of rubbing noses with the great and near great was critical to sustaining loyal audiences, and the actors were expected "to do some of this personal appeal—it's the least they could have done," Langley commented.

On Tuesdays, the staff, apprentices, and crew had off until the evening performance. "I never made an exception to that of which I am very proud," Langley beamed. Langley himself did not have off, however, because Tuesdays he prepared press releases and other publicity materials for the following two weeks. He also would take the current star out for personal appearances to local hospitals, shops, or perhaps for a radio or television interview. After the show, the staff usually threw the cast a big party down by the lake.

There were two performances, matinee and evening, on Wednesdays, as well as a 9 A.M. staff meeting to welcome the advance director for the next show and discuss schedules, budgets, and any problems. After the meeting, the staff would distribute assignments to the apprentices, and work on next week's show would commence. Thursdays and Fridays were devoted to building the scenery and props, and on Fridays the cast usually gave a party for the staff. At one point, Langley offered Friday matinees, but he halted those in favor of two shows on Saturdays, a 6 P.M. twilight performance followed by a 9 P.M. closing show. He also maintained a late-night cabaret for several years (cabarets are a standard adjunct to many summer stock houses), which presented a revue by a company of five or six young performers who remained in residence for the entire season. Langley claimed that it was in one of those companies that the young Joan Rivers got her start as a comedienne.[27]

John Oblak, who served as technical director at the Lakewood Playhouse in Maine in the late 1960s, described the star package routine in terms of physical production. A detailed ground plan, property list, and color swatches would be sent to the theatre in advance, thus giving the resident designer time to create a floor plan and painters' elevations for the setting prior to the arrival of the advance director. The degree of creative license afforded to designers would vary from show to show, but in all cases they would try to keep the size and shape of the playing space as consistent as possible to assure the acting company a smooth transition from one theatre to the next. Since a discrepancy of even a few feet can radically affect timing and cues, Oblak was pleased that Lakewood's stage was large enough to accommodate even the most ample set dimensions, unlike some theatres on the star circuit where significant reductions in size would have to be made. Color selections, both for scenery and props, would be chosen to complement the palette established by the costume designer, since the costumes traveled with the actors. The advance director brought the detailed promptbook and a light plot for the house stage manager, who would work with the resident lighting and sound directors on the technical requirements for the new show. Like Falmouth, Lakewood was on a Monday-through-Saturday performance schedule, and the routine was similar: Saturday night and early Sunday morning would be devoted to striking the previous set and loading in the next, followed by rehearsals on Sunday or Monday.[28] Mondays, which in most locales heralded the arrival of a new onslaught of tourists, were the traditional opening nights along much of the summer circuit.

"It is only through the use of stock scenery that the summer theatre functioning under the package system can survive," Oblak avowed, since in one-a-week stock, there were only a few days available to build any special units needed for a given show. Most of the flats, which were used to construct the walls, and platforms would be pulled from the theatre's inventory and assembled to conform to the designer's plans. By Friday afternoon, the full set would receive its base coat of paint, and on Saturday the painting would be completed and any preliminary rigging prepared. Oblak described the difficulties of intricate scenic rigging at Lakewood, which was a "hemp house" with no counterweight system, meaning that raising and lowering the scenery was accomplished by the "brute force" of stagehands carefully pulling on and releasing ropes with the aid of an occasional sandbag. He described the exhaustion of the crew, who had to perform technical duties for the eight performances of the current week's show while building the special scenery and props for the next. The weekend turnovers were especially difficult because one production had to be completely dismantled and another put in place in the span of a single Saturday night. It is not surprising that Lakewood's crews generally consisted of university students who had the benefit of youth, energy, and strength to endure the long workweeks.[29]

The Great Star System Debate

Almost as soon as the star system began, people began to debate its merits and detriments. They also wondered why and how the summer stocks had changed over so rapidly from being training grounds for ambitious novices to well-paid semiholidays for established stars. Elinor Hughes, in a 1941 article in the *Boston Herald*, mused that audiences must have grown "tired of giggling amateurishness" and had begun "to look for the names of players they had heard of and plays that they knew about but had, perhaps, missed or overlooked during the winter season." She also cited a survey conducted by

the North Shore Playhouse, a summer stock theatre in Marblehead,
Massachusetts, in which 90 percent of the playgoers queried said that the star
was what attracted them to a play. Other theatres must have made the same
discovery for, as Hughes observed, "if you look around, you'll find stars
galore, some traveling with their own units, some in solitary grandeur moving from stop to stop on the strawhat circuit, but unquestionably, the name's
the thing."[30]

Charlotte Harmon, who was producer at Connecticut's Chapel and, later,
Clinton, Playhouses in the 1950s, had an interesting theory on why women
went to see female stars in summer stock, particularly older film stars like
Constance Bennett. She overheard women at one performance commenting,
" 'It's remarkable! Why I saw her when I was a little girl. She was a big star
then. She must be almost sixty.' " Harmon researched Bennett's age at the
time—she was only 51. She surmised that watching an older woman who still
appears glamorous and alluring to men made the women in the audience feel
good. "And women certainly sell our theatre tickets," Harmon declared.
"They decide what shows they want to see, they order the tickets, and then
they make their husbands take them to the performance."[31]

Richard Aldrich, heralded as the most successful summer theatre producer
ever and the man credited with inventing the star system, explained the transformation very simply—people want to see stars. He cited the many letters he
received from people, "city folk included," who had seen their first legitimate
stage play at the Cape or Falmouth Playhouses and had so enjoyed the experience that they planned to see more. "And these people were not youngsters
either," he said. "What had brought them," Aldrich wrote, "as well as a good
part of our audiences, was the star. Their curiosity, which bade them take a
first-hand look at a nationwide celebrity, later turns into avid interest in theatre." Aldrich used this rationale not only for preserving the star system but
for sustaining summer theatres since they "are one of the best stimulants of
year-round theatregoing that I know."[32] The question remains, however,
whether these same people ever cultivated a true theatre-going habit—one in
which the presence of a star is immaterial so long as the play and production
are strong.

Aldrich's argument was often cited as a principal reason for maintaining
the star system, despite there being no statistics to support the claim. People
pointed to the relative successes and failures of star-system versus no-star
houses as corroboration, although in summer stock, just as with any form of
public entertainment, there are a multitude of variables that suggest that no
one element makes or breaks a theatre's fortunes. Certainly star-system

theatres that were in a prime location, with a large seating capacity, and offering reasonable ticket prices could succeed, but there was no guarantee. "Too many managers expect the mere announcement that 'Miss Glamour' will appear next week to create a stampede of business and subsequent success," Herman Krawitz, a summer stock manager and producer, observed, adding that "it will not." A good manager, "whether he runs a star theatre or not" still "must run a theatre," he said.[33]

Krawitz learned his trade working for Richard Aldrich, who seemed to possess the golden touch in managing stars as well as theatres. Stars are "worth the money," Aldrich declared, even those who command about $1,500 per week plus a percentage of the gross. He cited Helen Hayes, Gertrude Lawrence (his wife), and Tallulah Bankhead as three examples who "attract S.R.O. [standing room only] business everywhere they appear and so prove beneficial to the entire season's gross income." He admitted that a star theatre needed a lot of seats—between 600 and 900—to keep ticket prices affordable, but he felt the allure to the public was palpable. "Where else, one may ask, can you see nine or ten top stars consecutively in an intimate theatre at such reasonable prices?"[34]

Bill Ross, an active director and producer and longtime member of the Equity Council, supported a star system in summer stock but not the one that was prevailing in the early 1950s. He felt that stars, if properly handled, could positively boost the popularity of summer stock theatres, all of which should aspire to:

(A) Make a profit for management
(B) Give employment to actors during a traditionally slow season
(C) Help in the de-centralization of the theatre and help people stay in the habit of going to the theatre.[35]

This could not happen, however, when the stars were being "exhibited as freaks rather than actors." If stars were willing to rehearse and become integrated into a strong resident ensemble, he felt, it would be beneficial to everyone. The theory that "the audience will return time and time again just to see a star and will go away satisfied without seeing an integrated and coordinated performance" was simply "outmoded," he declared.[36]

Traveling with star package shows could be advantageous to young actors seeking both experience and an opportunity to develop as performers. Diana Herbert, one such actor, enjoyed the benefits of performing for a wide array of managers at various playhouses who potentially could offer her a job in future seasons. "What better way is there to audition than this?" she asked.

Herbert also explained how a star could transform a "mild little comedy" into an "hilarious farce" via the strength of his performance, citing as an example her two occasions of performing the same role in Benn Levy's *Clutterbuck*. In the first and lesser production she had appeared with a small resident stock company; the second time, she was supporting Arthur Treacher in star stock. "I learned many a lesson from playing the same scenes with him," she said.[37]

Certainly the strongest support for the star system came from the stars themselves, many of whom made a lot of money working in summer stock. "When the wolf's at the door, run to the barns," advised Tallulah Bankhead in a much-quoted remark exhorting her fellow stars to pay off their debts by touring the summer circuit. Many took her advice, and, according to Sidney Whipple, who was no fan of the star system, they got away with it because so many producers were willing to hire them despite the deleterious effect they often had on the quality of production. "Stars elderly and passé, stars who haven't had an acting role on Broadway in years, and stars in need of what they call pin money, have come to believe that the summer theater business is a sort of polite racket," he complained. "Many of these actors have nothing to offer but a name, and sometimes it is a tarnished name at that."[38]

Greed was the number one complaint against the star system, and it was leveled against both the stars and the theatre managers who, if they were savvy administrators, also stood to make a sizable profit. Actor Donald Cook characterized it as "larceny—petty on the part of the manager and grand on the part of the star—because neither is in good faith. The manager cheats his patrons with a flea circus geared to the carriage trade while the star cheats both management and public with a mediocre performance at best for a wage far above what he could earn for his best efforts elsewhere."[39] Most criticisms, however, were directed solely at the stars, whose often exorbitant fees were seen as detrimental to everything but their personal bank accounts. Jeff Morrow, a popular leading man in stock and touring companies who was not considered a star, felt the system particularly hurt people like him whose salaries were reduced because the stars cost too much. "Experienced featured actors frequently just cannot afford to work at the lessened salaries offered due to the prominence of the star item in the budget," he complained, "despite our desire to stretch our acting muscles in good parts."[40] Donald Cook concurred, remembering "with considerable embarrassment" a package tour where he supported a star "who demanded and got $5,000 per week, regardless of theatre size or location" which, he contended, "meant financial sacrifice for everyone else concerned."[41]

Lewis Harmon, who co-produced at the Chapel Playhouse with his wife Charlotte, viewed the star system as "a bad force in summer theatre," because "it blatantly proclaims 'the play is NOT the thing.' " He described how after four seasons, the star system had gotten too expensive for their small theatre, which seated fewer than 400 patrons, and where even with full houses all week they were hard pressed to cover operating expenses. They decided to return to resident stock for the 1950 season and, in order to attract audiences, lowered their ticket prices to $1 top on weekdays and $1.50 on Saturday evenings. "We had a good Equity company but it took some selling to convince the public this was a good professional group—no stars, low prices—they had to be convinced these were not amateurs."[42] Charlotte, in her book about their travails, *Broadway in a Barn*, described phone conversations she had with potential patrons: " 'What's playing?' they'd demand when they phoned. We'd tell them. '*Who's* in it?' they'd want to know. We'd name the actors. 'Oh,' they'd say, when they didn't recognize any big Hollywood stars, and hang up."[43] Her husband, who had been a Broadway press agent, moaned, "The star system has so degraded the profession that in certain areas you have to publicize and advertise to the utmost to make the public realize there are good actors, darn fine actors, who will act as a group without benefit of so called 'names.' "[44] The Harmons disagreed in print as to how they fared that season—Lewis contended that they ended in the black, while Charlotte maintained that they lost money—but nevertheless they decided to return to the star system, but at a larger house. They sold the theatre at Guilford and took their operation seven miles away, to Clinton, Connecticut, where an additional 119 seats made a star-stock operation viable.

The price of stars "climbed ridiculously" in a relatively short time, according to producer Theron Bamberger. In 1940, when he began his association with Pennsylvania's Bucks County Playhouse, Bamberger paid more than $300 for a star performer only twice. After World War II, the standard rate was $1,000 per week. "Not even the swank and successful Cape Playhouse paid more, and they attracted the biggest stars," Bamberger claimed. By 1951, however, fees were completely out of hand. "Agents have been calling up to offer their star clients and without a quiver have quoted $2,000 or $2,500 or even more. Furthermore some of the theatres are paying it," he lamented. He related how one particular star had failed to attract audiences when charging $750 a week two years earlier. That same star, remarkably, was now asking $1,500.[45]

A second major drawback of the star system was the growing disinclination of the stars to rehearse with the resident company, which fed a related woe: the stars' propensity to rewrite the scripts, usually illegally, and not bother to inform the host theatres. Arthur Sircom, who directed at many major summer stock houses, wrote a letter to Actors' Equity complaining about this very situation. He had been contracted by the Olney Playhouse in Maryland to direct a partial package production of *Meet the Wife* with Mary Boland, a popular stage and screen comedienne. Sircom arrived to discover that Boland and her principal supporting cast were not arriving until the end of the rehearsal period. He was set to prepare the rest of the company when they discovered that the script they had been sent by the play broker "did not correspond in any way to the version she had concocted over the years." As a result, he bemoaned, "I had no working script, she did not seem to think it was her responsibility to see that we had one, the poor actors trying to learn the play in a week's time were on the spot, and I was helpless." The producer allowed Sircom to withdraw, but was left with a bad situation since "contracts had been signed with Miss Boland and she made it difficult for anyone to present a good production."[46]

Lillian Ross told a similar story in a *New Yorker* article about summer stock. Hollywood star Signe Hasso was touring the summer circuit in *Love with a Stranger* with her leading man in tow. They closed the play at the John Drew Theatre in East Hampton, Long Island, on a Saturday night, and drove all night and through the next morning to reach the Cape Playhouse in Dennis, Massachusetts, by noon on Sunday. Upon their arrival, they discovered that the script the resident company had been rehearsing was somewhere in between their version and the author's original. Ross reported that "at four o'clock Monday morning, Miss Hasso, the supporting cast, and the director were still at work taking East Hampton lines out of Miss Hasso's script and putting Dennis lines in."[47]

The increasing emphasis on stars prompted a significant decrease in the number of companies without them, which was one of the most discouraging consequences of the star system. "The summer theatre is the only existing training ground for young actors and young directors," said actor Paula Laurence, "and the star system does not afford them the proper opportunity."[48] It was equally detrimental to resident stock which, as Jeff Morrow noted above, hired fewer solid repertory actors in order to better afford the guest star performers. Ultimately, replacing resident stock actors with transient stars hurt the theatres themselves as their all-important community relations began to erode. Ben Irving, a staff associate at Actors' Equity who toured the summer stocks in 1949 observed that the healthiest town-theatre relations occurred where there were resident stock companies that were known to their audiences: "The 'natives,' once having identified a performer, are interested and eager to follow his or her growth through varied and contrasting roles each week. The actor, in turn, stimulated by this interest, is spurred on to the use of his most creative abilities. The knowledge of public support sufficed to give him security in his work, and this contributed to heightened and unified performances."[49] In such circumstances, Irving found, the community supported the theatre itself, even to the extent of underwriting its operations. In contrast, the star-package houses did not engender a continuing actor–audience relationship because performer turnover was high. Patrons coming to see a star often had little or no alliance to the theatre itself and tended to be single-ticket buyers rather than subscribers. When their interest waned in seeing a succession of stars in lackluster performances, the box offices suffered precipitously.[50]

Although the stars were some of the biggest advocates for sustaining a system that seemed designed to augment their annual salaries handsomely, they also lodged their own complaints against it. Many had problems with incompetent managers who seemed willfully determined to make their lives difficult. Henry Morgan discussed how at one theatre, the on-stage bar, which was always positioned stage left, had ended up stage right for no apparent reason other than to raise havoc with his blocking. "It would take me a week to figure out what these people were all about," he reminisced, "and then it was time to go on to the next place."[51] John Carradine, who appeared in 15 assorted plays under 28 different summer stock managers within the span of six years, attributed any failures to "managerial amateurism, incompetence, egotism, stubbornness, cupidity, fraud and immorality." He likewise blamed "stars" who had no business advertising themselves as such or those who accepted that billing without consideration of "the responsibilities attendant upon that privileged position." They shirked those responsibilities by giving slipshod or ill-prepared performances, by casting themselves in unsuitable roles or in dated, time-worn vehicles, by surrounding themselves with incompetent support, and by appearing before the public in an unfit condition. "I have yet to see a failure in an enterprise where the 'star' was competent, popular, and conscientious, and the management business-like, intelligent and theatre-wise," he asserted.[52]

Besides carping at managements, which may have been as unruly as described by a perhaps equally unruly star, stars also realized the problems inherent in the solo or partial package system when they are thrust together with a resident company in the eleventh hour before opening. Edward Everett Horton was touring one summer with a supporting company of four in

Noël Coward's *Present Laughter*. Six resident actors at the various theatres on the circuit would join them to complete the cast. "We're prepared for inconveniences, but some of the inconveniences are *too* inconvenient," Horton told Lillian Ross. "We want to play it quick. The newcomers are always slow on the upbeat."[53] Robert Perry, an actor, director, and manager in stock for 25 years, witnessed the same problem from a slightly different perspective. "Too often the star disregards the fact that the first class stock company is as important a phase of the artistic theatrical world as any other," and thus fails to see the difficulty of its position in trying to acclimate quickly and appropriately to the visiting star's needs.[54] Ultimately, the amount of rehearsal time could make or break the quality of a production. Paula Laurence, who played in various stock situations for years, repeated the prevalent wisdom: "We're all familiar with the star who arrives late Sunday night, rehearses once with a company which has been rehearsing without him all week, and opens Monday night. It's bad for the cast. It's bad for the star. And it's bad for business."[55]

Stars Will Be Stars

The complaints against stars, as well as the plethora of anecdotes about their often eccentric and even outrageous behavior, are the stuff of numerous theatrical memoirs. Harold J. Kennedy, a veteran director, playwright, and actor, penned *No Pickle, No Performance* to divulge backstage war stories, many of which occurred in summer stock. Charlotte Harmon's *Broadway in a Barn* is dedicated exclusively to anecdotes gleaned from operating a summer stock theatre for ten years. Virtually every article of some length or book chapter dealing with summer stock will include at least one pithy tale of a star's antics, on or off the stage. These stories are typical of theatre in general, and the stars whose behavior shocked out-of-the-way summer theatre communities tended to be just as mischievous when playing on Broadway. The two stars who accrued the most summer stock legends are Edward Everett Horton, no doubt because he was a fixture of the summer stock circuit for more than 30 years, and Tallulah Bankhead, no doubt because she was as famous for impetuous behavior as she was for her acting abilities.

Horton enjoyed a wonderful reputation on the summer circuit as a charming and affable man who was friendly when people approached him and always willing to help promote the show. Charlotte Harmon recalled that whenever she booked him, local chambers of commerce, Kiwanis, Rotary, and Lions clubs for miles around would ask to have him as a guest speaker, and he would always oblige. She also credited him as one of the few stars who, despite his considerable fees, cared whether the management made any money. When budgets became particularly tight in the 1950s, Horton was one of the first stars to change his contract from one-third of the gross box office receipts to a flat salary plus a percentage. He, like all stars, did have his eccentricities, however, and Harmon told one tale about his refusal to perform in slightly wrinkled pants on a very hot summer evening. At 7:15 P.M. on a Saturday night, she frantically sought someone capable of ironing them to his satisfaction, and at 8:35 P.M., returned the rejuvenated slacks just in time for his 8:40 P.M. entrance.[56] In another tale, Lillian Ross described how Horton would dash out of the theatre with his makeup on and drive 100 or more miles back to his New York apartment just to avoid sleeping in a strange bed at a summer stock house. "I don't mind," he said, "if I can wash my face with good city water."[57]

Although her disposition on the summer circuit may have been no better or worse than it was elsewhere, Tallulah Bankhead stories abound and, as Harold Kennedy proclaimed, "everything that has been said about her is true, I suppose, and she would be the last to deny it."[58] He related one summer stock experience when he was directing her in *The Second Mrs. Tanqueray*. When she arrived at the theatre and saw the set, she "screamed the place down." There was a gorgeous Victorian staircase leading up to a magnificent center door, but she would have no part of it. "I cannot act on steps," she declared and insisted they be removed at once. Since this was not to be easily accomplished, particularly within the abbreviated time frame afforded by summer stock, Kennedy persuaded her "after a few soothing martinis" to try the stairs. During dress rehearsal she understood the power the ascent up the staircase could add to her performance and "the steps were never mentioned again," he said. "But as I passed her dressing room the next night I heard her giving instructions to her advance director who was preceding the company to the next stop at Ogunquit, Maine. 'And darling, tell them I must have steps. I cannot act without steps.'"[59]

Lawrence Langner described how Tallulah arrived at Westport for the first rehearsal of *Her Cardboard Lover* with a lion cub, which was her constant companion. Although he didn't actually appear in the play, the lion did join her for curtain calls:

> On the opening night, Tallulah took her first curtain call alone. The next curtain call she appeared with the baby lion in her arms, her tawny hair picking up the color from his, or *vice versa*, but in any event making a pleasing picture of actress and lion meet audience. Naturally, the curtain calls multiplied, for with each call Tallulah displayed her lion in a more imaginative manner. Tallulah

carried the lion on stage with her as she toured from one summer theatre to another, until by the end of the season the lion had grown almost as large as a St. Bernard and weighed over thirty pounds, and under these conditions he was led, not carried, to the footlights.[60]

Richard Aldrich, who had hired Bankhead at the astounding sum of $5,000 a week to open the Falmouth Playhouse with Noël Coward's *Private Lives* in 1949, received in return a sold-out run, an auspicious beginning for his new theatre, and a classic Tallulah story. She had refused to rehearse since "I know this play so well I can do it underwater," despite the pleas of the technical crew, who were understandably nervous about their "*first* first night." When the curtain puller tried to persuade her to at least run the curtain calls, she retorted, "You just hold that curtain for a long time between the second and third acts. The third act takes only twenty-seven minutes, and I don't want the audience to think they've been cheated." After a successful opening performance, Bankhead produced a very large bottle of vintage champagne during the final curtain call. She wished the theatre a successful season and christened it by breaking the bottle over a phonograph cabinet on the set—and breaking the cabinet, too.[61]

The New Look for Summer Stock

In the years following World War II, Actors' Equity changed its summer stock rules and classifications several times to reflect the complex and varied modes of production that were becoming increasingly more common. It also was looking out for its constituency, which, in the flush of summer stock popularity, was finding more employment in the summer than at any other time during the year. Equity councilor Alan Hewitt compiled statistics for the 1949 season, which established that almost three in ten Equity members worked in the ten weeks between June 28 and Labor Day. Although this figure attests to the vitality of summer stock, it did not presage the health of theatre in general. Of the 2,924 members who played at least one week of summer stock, 2,147 played only in summer stock that year. "It is a sad commentary on the state of employment in the theatre," Hewitt remarked, "that this represents the highest level of the year."[62]

In March 1948, Equity announced its "New Look for Summer Stock" which eliminated Class "B" operations (see chapter 5); mandated rehearsal pay, for the first time, of $20 per week; raised the minimum salaries from $40 to $50 per week; and required that all companies operating within a 25-mile radius of New York, Chicago, Los Angeles, and San Francisco must be 100 percent

Equity shops. The Equity Council also defined a package show as "a 100% Equity attraction playing for more than one theatre or management, which includes all the members of the cast, not including extras, required for that attraction."[63] As the package and partial package tours became more prevalent, Equity revised its rules in 1953 to encourage the redevelopment of resident stock and to persuade managements to seek Equity jurisdiction. Accordingly, although all theatres still needed to have six resident members, the union reduced the percentage requirement of Equity to non-Equity actors from 70-30 to 50-50 in theatres seating fewer than 300 patrons. It also eliminated the need for houses that exclusively booked star packages to retain a resident company; this is when the new designation of "summer theatre" entered the lexicon.[64]

In the summer of 1952, Equity's Paul G. Jones created a profile of the 128 theatres operating under Equity contracts. He reported that there were 65 small budget stock companies that used resident companies exclusively or jobbed in one or two people a week; 38 large budget stock companies that used resident companies but employed either full or partial package companies, or a number of jobbers, during the majority of the season; six summer theatres that jobbed in full package shows only; two rotary stock circuits that sent out five and nine companies respectively;[65] seven large civic or open air light opera companies, most operating in the Midwest and including such venerable houses as the St. Louis Municipal Outdoor Theatre (MUNY) and the Kansas City Starlight Theatre; and ten "musical tents."[66] These tents, which first appeared on the summer scene in 1949, were rapidly becoming formidable competition to all summer entertainments. "Look what the music tents are doing to us," bewailed Lewis Harmon as he decided to leave summer stock producing for good in 1955.[67] As the star system battle raged on, this new form of entertainment, housed in a special tent with a patented design that could seat 2,000 patrons, would soon create a new cash cow.

7
Musicals, Tents, and Terrell

While the star system was being hotly debated in the old barns, St. John (pronounced and spelled "Sinjun" or "Sinjin") Terrell was busy inventing a whole new form of summer stock. Inspired by the advent of the new Broadway musical via Rodgers and Hammerstein's smash hit *Oklahoma!* (1943) and its many formulaic successors as well as the enduring popularity of operetta, Terrell foresaw the tremendous potential of offering musicals to summer audiences. The old barn theatres, however, were too small to accommodate the large casts and sizable orchestras required by these entertainments. Simultaneously, audience sizes and box office revenues would need to increase so that the expanding operating costs could be met. Rather than creating large new theatre buildings, Terrell advocated circus tents as perfect short-term, mobile theatres for warm-weather performances. He dubbed his invention, which came with a patented design for the ideal tent, a "music circus," in acknowledgment not only of the traditional big-top housing but also because his programs included live carnival and animal acts within an atmosphere reminiscent of Barnum and Bailey. He also had the musical plays reconceived so that they could be presented, just like the circus, with arena staging. The inaugural tent theatre, the Lambertville (New Jersey) Music Circus, opened in 1949. By 1955, with the founding of the Musical Arena Theatres Association, for which Terrell served as the first president, there were 15 highly successful tent theatres in operation across the country.

If summer stock theatre was a uniquely American invention, then Terrell's music circus was its most quintessentially American element. The pioneer summer stock theatres were the brainchildren of enterprising, independent-minded gurus who dared to challenge the theatrical status quo by inventing a new form of theatre from shards of the usable past. They borrowed ideas from nineteenth-century theatre practice and appropriated old venues, disused barns and other rustic, inexpensive structures, and reconceived and repackaged these in a new locale at a propitious moment in economic and artistic history. Terrell, who was a spiritual descendant of these messianic personalities who are profiled in chapter 4, possessed the vision of Jig Cook, the practical know-how of Francis Cleveland, the audacious energy of Edith Bond Stearns, and the promotional genius of Robert Porterfield. Unlike them, however, his tastes and talents were less influenced by the legitimate stage and more directly attributable to the spectacle and ballyhoo of P. T. Barnum, who, for many, epitomized American show business. Terrell formulated his new divertisement also by borrowing from the past, but he chose circus, carnival, tent, and popular musical entertainments as his inspirations and from these concocted a package worthy of Barnum's "greatest show on earth." In fact, *New York Daily Mirror* critic Robert Coleman employed Barnumesque language to herald Terrell's music circus as "one of the wonders of the East."[1]

Like the founders of traditional summer stock before him, Terrell created the perfect entertainment to fit the temperament of the times, which in the years immediately following World War II was a desire to revel in the real and imagined glories of bygone America. By combining the new musical comedies, which frequently were set in the romanticized past, with the iconography and style of some of America's most cherished nineteenth-century amusements, Terrell fashioned a diversion that, like most American commodities, owed its success as much to its packaging as to its substance. One could see musical comedies on Broadway and on tour in traditional proscenium theatres but where else could audiences find *Annie Get Your Gun* or *Carousel* performed in an environment that encapsulated the American spirit celebrated in the play? The circus big top imbued the grandeur and freshness of wide-open space and the great outdoors, which, indeed, was just beyond the canvas flaps that served as doorways; the arena-style staging promoted intimacy between audience and performers and, without benefit of curtains and other masking devices, laid bare the process of artistic creation, which proved fascinating to audiences accustomed to proscenium-house theatres where the raw mechanics of mounting shows were hidden from view; and the decoration, seating, flooring, support structures, and side show exhibits and diversions all bespoke the festive, casual atmosphere of carnival rather than the staid, often opulent rigidity of big-city theatres. The fact that Terrell himself was a fire-eater who frequently performed between the acts and, on occasion, even during the shows, helped solidify the music circus as a circus. Audiences were invited to wear casual clothes—men were even welcome in their shirt sleeves—eat peanuts and popcorn, which were hawked up and down the aisles, and, at times, shake hands with the performers as they whisked by. It was still recognizably theatre but with a decidedly American flavor that engendered frivolity, gaiety, and a rollicking good time. By the close of the first summer season, Terrell had a bona fide hit, and everyone predicted that "music circus was going to sweep the country."[2]

St. John Terrell, Impresario

St. John Terrell was the stage name of George Clinton Eccles Jr., who was born in Chicago, Illinois, in 1916. His parents, who were perfume manufacturers, frequently took him to Europe during his childhood, where he would delight in the sensationalistic theatre of horror at the Grand-Guignol in Paris. Back in Chicago, he began acting professionally and claimed to have been the first to play the title role in the daily radio serial *Jack Armstrong, the All-American Boy*, which was syndicated nationally. He also spent a summer traveling with "Joe Wright's Carnival," where he learned his flame-swallowing trick and the delights of carnival entertainments. Terrell played summer stock and also a few Broadway engagements, where he had minor roles in such shows as *Judgement Day* (1934–35) and *Winterset* (1935–36). Despite his theatrical inclinations, he spent three years majoring in chemistry at Columbia University in anticipation of taking over the family perfume business. He eventually received his degree at Northwestern, where he finished his baccalaureate after serving in the Army Air Force during World War II.

Before entering the service, however, Terrell, at the age of 21, embarked on his career as a theatre impresario. While attending a party in New Hope, Pennsylvania, during the summer of 1938, Terrell, along with actor Richard Bennett (with whom he had appeared in *Winterset*), playwright Kenyon Nicholson, and music arranger and orchestrator Donald Walker, conceived the idea of starting a summer stock playhouse at the old gristmill in the center of town. As Walker described the evening later, he and Nicholson had met "a promotional genius who could take an inch and blow it up into a mile. If anyone could start a theatre in New Hope," he said, "it was Terrell." He was already "imbued with an unquenchable yearning to run a theatrical operation—anywhere, anytime, anyhow" and had enlisted Bennett, who was a famous actor and popular local resident, to support him in his quest.[3]

Walker, who was the first to characterize Terrell as a "disciple of P. T. Barnum," stood in awe of his promotional genius. He describes how Sinjun managed to have his glowing press releases of the as-yet-unrealized theatre printed "as if they were gospel" by theatrical editors who normally were skeptical of such blatant puffery. "The cold facts—that the 'theatre' was still a dusty, old broken-down grist mill and the financing all soap bubbles—did not bother Terrell," Walker said. Sinjun similarly managed a successful fundraising appeal to the conservative members of the local Rotary Club who, after listening to his sales pitch for five minutes, were eagerly signing on to the project. Walker found this feat particularly remarkable since Sinjun was "a rather young man" who "possessed a Barrymore profile, a lot of wavy chestnut hair, a weakness for loud sport jackets and a talent for fire-eating," which did not fit the profile of the standard Rotary member.[4] Sinjun's charm and handsome good looks were, no doubt, a major part of his appeal, as was his ability to be "eloquent, warm, and witty."[5] Lester Trauch, a local newspaper editor, recalls Sinjun's allure for theatregoers:

> During Terrell's one-year reign, he always appeared on the porch of the Playhouse before performances, giving theatergoers their money's worth even when he wasn't on stage. A fashion plate, he invariably wore his hat rakishly, at just the right angle. One evening when my best friend, writer Grace Chandler, and I approached the theater, she suddenly stopped in her tracks. "Lester," she said, shocked. "St. John has no shirt on!" I looked over at Terrell greeting people on the porch, and he did indeed appear to be shirtless. When we got close enough, we saw that he was actually wearing a shirt of the faintest, palest pink. That was Terrell for you, always ready to be different. Every other man in the crowd was wearing a conventional white shirt.[6]

In order to assure the playhouse investors of Terrell's sincerity and before giving him a lease to the property, Walker had him draft a letter of intent. In it, Terrell describes himself as "the first impulse that started this project" and declares his will to succeed: "I am going to have a theatre, and a successful one, in your locality before I go on to other things in my life. If it cannot be your theatre, it will be another one. On this I am determined. My determination, with a modicum of intelligence, both native and theatrical, has been the essence of what success I have had in the theatre."[7] Terrell subsequently was hired to produce the summer season for the next two years with "an escape clause" in his contract should the board determine they wanted a change.[8] Although there is widespread disagreement as to exactly what happened, a change apparently was desired because Terrell left after the first season. Although he ended the summer with money in the bank, and the new Bucks County Playhouse was widely considered a grand success, he probably was forced out. The official statement declared that Sinjun "wanted to move on to other challenges," but he flatly denied it. "I didn't want to leave the theatre at all," he told historian Gilda Morigi, blaming one powerful stockholder who wanted more artistic control for forcing him out. "I was a rather tempestuous young man at the time," Terrell admitted, and "perhaps I should have been more concerned with people's egos and sensitivities. But as far as I was concerned, these people had nothing to do with the artistic aspect of my creation, of which I was naturally jealous."[9]

His next opportunity for theatrical artistry was while stationed in the South Pacific during World War II. After suffering a back injury, he was assigned to a USO troupe that was performing musical comedies and revues in war-ravaged Manila in the Philippines in 1944. There were no usable theatres, so the company played on a flat piece of land with G.I.s jostling for a viewing space in front of them. It was then that Terrell conceived the idea of an arena theatre in a tent as a quick, easy way to create an instant theatre with available materials. "I figured all they had to do was make a few passes at the ground with a bulldozer, and they could dig out a bowl and seat 4,000 soldiers around it and have a music circus," Terrell said.[10] The army rejected his idea as "silly," but he held onto it for future use back at home. After the war, he finished his degree, moved the perfume business, which he now co-owned with his mother Reta Terrell (Terrell was her birth name), to New York, bought a summer home near Lambertville, New Jersey, just across the Delaware River from the thriving Bucks County Playhouse in New Hope, Pennsylvania, and, in 1949, finally returned to his music circus idea. He persuaded a group of investors to advance him $35,000 in start-up money, rented 12 acres of land on a hilltop overlooking the river, and hired a bull-dozer to dig out a crater that would become the stage. He blasted solid rock to create the orchestra pit, created tiered seating for 700 (he would add 500 seats by the end of the summer), and covered it all with the tent he had purchased. Although his backers "backed out" at the last minute, Terrell culled funds from a variety of sources—he borrowed money from the perfume business, cashed in his war bonds, and dug into his stash of winnings from crap games—and opened for business.

Although no success is ever certain, Sinjun felt his investment would pay off and for good reason. Musical entertainments had always been popular draws for widely diverse audiences throughout the country but the post–World War II years were an especially fruitful period. In 1943, the new composer/lyricist-librettist team of Richard Rodgers and Oscar Hammerstein II premiered the first of a series of hit musicals that would revolutionize musical comedy. Although both were seasoned professionals who had successfully teamed with other noted writers and composers such as Lorenz Hart and Jerome Kern, their collaboration sparked a new brand of stirring yet sentimental, patriotic celebrations of Americana that proved the perfect antidote for a nation that had just suffered the dual devastations of the Great Depression and a world war. Their work also featured a tighter integration of music and plot than generally had been achieved in musicals and introduced dance as a means of storytelling and character revelation. This newly enhanced formula for structuring the musical play combined with sober plots devoid of the cynicism, flashiness, and topicality typical of prewar theatricals to produce entertainments that reaffirmed basic American values. Rodgers and Hammerstein's own string of successes, *Oklahoma!* (1943), *Carousel* (1945), *South Pacific* (1949), *The King and I* (1951), *Flower Drum Song* (1958), and *The Sound of Music* (1959), promoted a series of equally successful copycats by other writing teams. *Annie Get Your Gun* (1946) by Irving Berlin and Herbert and Dorothy Fields, *Brigadoon* (1947) by Alan J. Lerner and Frederick Loewe, *Guys and Dolls* (1950) by Frank Loesser, Jo Swerling, and Abe Burrows, *Wonderful Town* (1953) by Leonard Bernstein, Betty Comden, and Adolph Green, and *Pajama Game* (1954) by Richard Adler and Jerry Ross, all proved successful at the music circuses. Equally popular fare were revivals of operettas dating from the earlier part of the century, which, like their more recent counterparts, were romantic, fanciful excursions into a kinder, gentler era. Franz Lehar's *The Merry Widow* (1907), Victor Herbert's *Naughty Marietta* (1910), Rudolf Friml's *The Vagabond King* (1925), and Sigmund Romberg's *The Desert Song* (1926) and *The New Moon* (1928) were enduring favorites.

Prior to Terrell's innovation, musicals had seldom been attempted in summer stock because they required so much space and money. Most musicals needed too large a cast, too big an orchestra, and inflated ticket prices to meet the considerable expense of doing a musical in theatres where there were few seats. When enterprising producers did mount them, however, they invariably were successful, even with minimal staging, higher ticket prices, and an orchestra consisting of two pianos. One producer, in fact, suggested that musicals were so popular in 1951 that the public would come to see them whether or not the cast featured star performers. She told of a group of producers who, in 1950, had shared preproduction expenses to mount and tour several musicals to each of their theatres. A few had used high-priced stars while others had engaged average performers with good singing voices. All the shows were equally well received, and the stars seemed merely "incidental" to the success of the productions.[11] Although the allure of stars was important in later years to keep audiences coming to the tents, it is remarkable that in the midst of the star system invasion of summer stock in the 1950s, the tents flourished without star talent. As producer Steve Slane described it, "the shows themselves are so strong in name value that the producer is able to feature the title as the star attraction." He added that at the time, "musical comedy names with strong box-office pull are unbelievably few in number. The budget does not permit the use of an Ethel Merman or Alfred Drake, and surprisingly enough, below this top bracket there seems to be little value in names for the off-Broadway public." The situation changed as productions of musicals proliferated and more and more singing and dancing stars emerged, but at least until the middle 1950s, music tent producers did not share the "star" problem experienced by their counterparts in regular summer stock.[12]

The idea of using a tent was equally rooted in American theatre and entertainment history and perfectly fit the ambience of gay, summertime fun that Terrell wished to capture. Although tents are commonly associated with circus, there was a long tradition of legitimate theatre in a tent during the late nineteenth and early twentieth centuries. Tent shows, in fact, were a popular style of theatrical presentation whereby plays or variety shows would troupe from town to town with their portable canvas theatres. Although companies initially employed circus tents with central poles, most eventually switched to tents that emulated proscenium-style theatres with a stage at one end and free of any obstructions to audience sightlines.

The most highbrow of the tent entertainments were those appearing on the Chautauqua circuit at the turn of the twentieth century. Chautauqua was founded on the shores of Lake Chautauqua in upper New York State in 1904 as a tent meeting that offered religious instruction. It rapidly expanded into a culturally refined variety show which offered respectable vaudeville sketches, dramatic skits, monodramas, lectures, and other high-tone entertainments. By 1912, there were more than 1,000 Chautauqua tents, which were characteristically brown to distinguish them from the white big tops of the circus, touring the country throughout the summer months. There were also hundreds of tent repertory companies, spelled in this context "repertoire" and generally simplified to "tent rep," which provided more homespun, less refined entertainments than the Chautauquas, designed for rural audiences. Many shows featured the comic character Toby, who, along with his tomboyish sidekick Susie were the familiar hero and heroine of these rustic amusements. While tent rep survived into the 1930s, most of the Chautauquas closed during the 1920s as a result of competition from movie houses and radio and, later, the effects of the Depression.

Terrell's adoption of tents for his new music presentations drew from both the traveling tent show and circus traditions. He was presenting fully scripted shows, like the tent reps, but opted to use circus-style arena staging rather than end-stage configurations. Although the central poles presented some problems during his first season, he soon discarded them in favor of an umbrella-style tent with the poles going upward and no sightline impediments, an original design that he patented and had built for the following summer. Terrell was a great believer in theatre-in-the-round, which he described as an "ancient idea that promoted truer performances" than could be realized in an "artificial picture-frame stage." The latter he considered "merely a passing phase, about 250 years old," while "the arena is the original." He elaborated: "About 25,000 years ago while the neighbors were squatting around the fire in the cave, some showoff, probably an ancestor of mine, had to cut up. Made funny faces, stood on his paws. That was theater. In the round. It stayed round for ages. Now it's going round again, as it should. All we need is to get people into it."[13] Sinjun argued that arenas provided everyone with good seats, no farther than 20 rows from the stage, and excellent sightlines, which promoted an intimacy that was equally attractive to audiences and performers. Audiences felt as if they were in the most expensive orchestra seats and that no other section was getting a better view than theirs. Most proscenium-trained performers, once they became accustomed to it, relished the close actor–audience relationship of the arena, where they felt they were playing directly to a group of devoted friends. They also enjoyed the resounding accolades, which, as one comedian commented, allowed you "to hear applause coming from four sides."[14] Producers liked arenas because scenery was necessarily kept to a minimum so that audiences would have unobstructed views. Since other operating costs were significantly higher than in dramatic stock, purveyors of music circus appreciated having one budget area where they readily could save money. Finally, directors enjoyed the challenge of staging and choreographing shows that originally had been created for picture-frame theatres in an open environment, unimpeded by walls, doors, and other bulky scenic items. This allowed for a wider choice of entrances and exits, a new fluidity of movement and actor positions, and a possibility for invention generally unavailable in proscenium houses where the permanent architecture narrows the scope of feasible choices.

Although Terrell does not claim to have rediscovered arena staging for legitimate theatre, he also does not mention—nor does anyone writing about the music circus phenomenon—that theatre-in-the-round was undergoing a renaissance in America. In June 1947, Margo Jones, one of the pioneers of the new regional theatre movement, had founded a permanent arena theatre in Dallas, Texas, that was christened Theatre '47 but would change names annually on New Year's Eve "in order to remain contemporary at all times."[15] Theatres '47 through '50 produced 18 premieres and 11 classic plays in arena fashion. Jones used her experiences to write the seminal work *Theatre-in-the-Round*, published by Greenwood Press in 1951, which influenced scores of imitators. In the interim, however, at least two other important arena theatres had begun—Nina Vance's Alley Theatre in Houston, Texas, in November of 1947 and the Arena Stage in Washington, D.C., founded by six people affiliated with George Washington University in 1950 but soon spearheaded by Zelda Fichandler, who remained producing director until 1991. These three women, frequently characterized as the founding mothers of American regional theatre, staunchly believed that only by creating cost-effective theatres-in-the-round out of any available space could theatre truly be decentralized and achieve a national presence throughout the United States. All three were also directors who proved by example that any play could be produced successfully via arena staging. They did not use tents—their arenas were in hard-walled buildings—but otherwise their concepts were those employed by Terrell when he opened his music circus in 1949. Whether these ideas were simply practical solutions to potentially expensive building plans that were conceived simultaneously by many (although Vance and Fichandler both admit their indebtedness to Jones) in the lean years immediately following World War II or were just "in the air" is difficult to determine. It is interesting, however, that enthusiasm for this rarely employed style of staging in America should blossom in so many places at once.

While excitement for arena staging ran high in some circles, many traditionally trained theatre practitioners were skeptical that actors could readily adapt to the challenge of playing 360 degrees or that audiences would embrace actors' backsides happily. Actors' Equity warned their members that working in arenas would prove difficult for those who lacked training "in this round kind of acting." It further advised that there would be no more "turning upstage to cough" since, technically speaking, "upstage" does not exist in an arena. With a snide nod to producers who, the union felt, were now saving lots of money thanks to the absence of scenery, Equity predicted that "a new breed of coughless actors may have to be developed."[16] Lots of critics also grumbled about the unattractiveness of watching an actor's back, but complaints subsided once directors and choreographers became more comfortable with arena staging. Noted dance critic Walter Terry professed admiration for Rex Cooper's choreographic feats both in *Gentlemen Prefer Blondes* and *Die Fledermaus* during Lambertville's 1953 season. "It is hardly a secret that a dance image, a specific movement, a group design customarily looks better from one angle than from another and one of the attributes of a great choreographer is that he is a master of directional design," Terry said, acknowledging that this is a special challenge in theatre-in-the-round, where "only designs which are as pleasant from back, side or diagonal as they are to the front may be employed." He cited Cooper's clever approach to the ballet in *Die Fledermaus*, saying he "managed to fill the comparatively small stage with broad, uncluttered action" that complemented and even extended "the equally careful movement patterns of the singing actors." Cooper also "selected such turns and lifts as would best fill out a circle of interest for all onlookers."[17] Terrell, of course, felt that the arena stage promoted the most natural of performances and eliminated the awkwardness typical of proscenium staging. To make his point, he physically demonstrated an action for one interviewer:

> "Look." He faced his interviewer. "In the conventional theater, two actors who are supposed to be talking to each other stand side by side, facing the audience. Like this." He side-stepped two paces. "See? One here"—his hand indicated where—"and one here." He pointed to himself. "They don't talk to each other. They talk to the audience, like a vaudeville team." On an oval stage—he sketched one in the air—"movements and dialogue can be more realistic. The groupings are natural. And the audience's view, your view, is never blocked."[18]

He also felt that acting arena-style was difficult only "for hokum players." "The scene-stealers," he explained, "can't upstage anybody. If they're upstage in one direction, they're downstage in another."[19]

The major challenge of tent theatre, and the one thing over which producers had no control, was the weather. Rain, wind, cold, and major storms are all problematic and, depending on their severity, can range from a slight interruption during a performance to major disaster. Only one tent was completely demolished by a storm, the Milwaukee music tent in 1956 (luckily, without loss of life), while others had to temporarily suspend operations because of weather damage.[20] The resourceful nature of music circus operators, however, combined with the informal, festive atmosphere of the tents helped to ameliorate difficult situations. Heavy rain, for instance, could be a literal show stopper because water causes the canvas roof to tighten like a drumhead and "a million pelting drumsticks can offer serious opposition to the human voice even when amplified," said one longtime summer stock producer.[21] Terrell described an unscheduled hiatus during a performance of *The Merry Widow* during his first season, but fortunately the rain abated after only ten minutes. Edward Lutz, who as a founder of the Musical Arena Theatre Association and longtime summer stock theatre accountant sat through many a music circus performance, recalled one occasion where pouring rain stopped the show in Cohasset, Massachusetts, for almost half an hour. "I will never forget this Italian singer in that show," he reminisced, "who, when the storm broke out, was in a scene with food on the table where he would peel grapes." During the deluge, the singer circulated through the audience, handing out grapes to everyone. "He did this by himself so the audience wouldn't leave, and they didn't. They loved it! And he couldn't even announce anything because no one could hear him over the rain."[22] In a famous tale from the Cape Cod Melody Tent, when the rain began to wet the feet of an elderly patron, one gallant actor leaped from the stage, picked her up and carried her to a dry seat. Back in Lambertville in a later season, audience and actors joined together in a community sing while the rain poured down.[23] How they were heard over the din is not recounted, but no doubt a thousand people united in song could rise above it. Most casts, however, were not nearly as large and needed to rely on ingenuity to keep audiences attentive.

The standard life of a tent, which suffered considerable wear and tear even when the weather was mild, was about three years, and operators needed to replace it regularly. Over the years, however, Terrell continued to refine the tent design and construction to accommodate weather-related exigencies. His tents were fully fireproofed and he helped write the national fire safety code to ensure that all manufacturers would take the same precautions. He kept experimenting with different kinds of canvas to improve acoustics and claims to have tried at least 15. In a 1953 interview, he announced that he was using specially treated cloth that "makes [the tent] so hard that the sound bounces right off and gives us excellent acoustics."[24] Terrell also dealt with severe drops in temperature, which could make sitting for three hours in a tent a most uncomfortable experience, by installing a heating system that would blow warm air up through openings in the aisles. This innovation also allowed the music circus to extend its season to include late spring and early autumn performances.[25]

The Lambertville Music Circus

When Terrell launched his first music circus at Lambertville in July 1949, it was a new idea that took some getting used to for audiences accustomed to seeing musical comedies in fashionable proscenium theatres. There was sufficient curiosity to fill houses for the first few performances of *The Merry Widow*, which was the opening attraction, but attendance petered out over the next several weeks. Sinjun's gift for outrageous promotion helped resuscitate the theatre so that by the end of the season, he had turned a healthy profit. He had discovered that the more he distinguished the music circus as its own peculiar breed of entertainment, far removed from the stodgy theatres that normally housed major musicals, the more successful he became. Hence, he added more and more circus, carnival, and fun fair attractions to the gay and gaudy package. The refreshment stands, ticket office, and other administrative buildings were painted bright red and yellow and built to resemble circus wagons; over time, he acquired real wagons, which he added to the mix. Pennants waved from the roof of the tent, which each season acquired a fresh coat of bright paint in a varying array of greens, yellows, tangerines, and whites.[26] He purchased hand-carved animals and fanciful seats from an amusement park carousel and placed them around the grounds for people to sit and enjoy refreshments during intermission and before the show.[27] Six-by-eight-foot banners, patterned on the "old circus banner line" and displaying the theme of the season's shows, were specially commissioned and displayed outside the tent.[28] The music circus grounds were filled with lights, and he eventually added a ferris wheel, all of which could be seen for miles at night. He featured sideshow entertainments, such as juggling, clowning, and, occasionally, a personal demonstration of fire-eating. For the 1955 season, he built a special outdoor stage for these attractions and inaugurated an "olio revival of between-the-acts shows," which had been customary in legitimate theatre and other entertainments for hundreds of years. One of the acts was billed as Jim Daring with Ko-Ko and Bongo, the human chimpanzees. "These chimpanzees do everything but talk," the promoter promised, "and have been seen at all the leading amusement parks throughout the country and were featured with the Ringling Brothers and Cole Brothers circuses."[29]

Sinjun also devised special promotional gimmicks to bring crowds to the theatre, such as a "show train" to transport audiences from Philadelphia to Lambertville and back on which they would be entertained by Otto Griebling, a popular veteran clown, a live band, and a cognac-tasting, courtesy of Hennessy liquors.[30] In conjunction with a 1955 production of *Li'l Abner*, he held a Daisy Mae look-alike contest, a "Sadie Hawkins Day race" renamed for Daisy Mae, and special area appearances by Jan Chaney, the actress playing Daisy Mae, all of which were co-sponsored by the *Trenton Times*, a major New Jersey daily, which promised lots of newspaper coverage.[31] When he was not plugging a particular show, Sinjun would hire Army balloons and helicopters to cruise overhead to spark curiosity and attention from casual onlookers. "He goes for promotion stunts in a big way," quipped one local reporter who had seen it all.[32]

The music circus repertory expanded considerably after Terrell's first Lambertville season, when he was relegated to reviving older musicals and operettas that were in the public domain. Contemporary writers were leery of having their plays produced in the round, which they feared would distort their carefully wrought works and mar the performances, and so they refused to grant him production rights. Thanks to the efforts of composer Sigmund Romberg, many of whose operettas were produced at Lambertville later that season, feelings began to change. Romberg, who shared an attorney with Oscar Hammerstein II, came to Sinjun's opening night of *The Merry Widow* and loved the results. He promptly told his lawyer that arena staging worked beautifully, thus encouraging Hammerstein and others to reconsider their position. It also did not hurt that Lambertville's premiere season, which was being carefully monitored by the theatre cognoscenti, proved a resounding success, with audiences demonstrably enchanted by the novel approach to old favorites. Hammerstein was so impressed that he rewrote his 1928 hit *Showboat* to accommodate the new style. The revised *Showboat* opened to great acclaim in September 1950 at the end of Terrell's second season and was revived four times during the decade, prompting Sinjun to proclaim it the "all-time great" for the music circus.[33]

From 1950 onward, neither Terrell nor other music circus producers ever had a problem attaining rights to a show. The commodious tents, which by the mid-1950s regularly seated at least 1,500 patrons, assured large new audiences for musical comedy and, consequently, composers and writers were justly rewarded via a steady stream of handsome royalty checks. The tents also offered writers an opportunity to revive and even revise shows in a welcoming environment that did not carry the pressures nor expectations of a comparable revival on Broadway. Members of the original creative team of *Cabin in the Sky*, which premiered in 1940, were pleased to have the opportunity to restage it at Lambertville in 1959. Vernon Duke, George Balanchine, and Boris Aronson all worked with Terrell and his artistic team in reshaping the show for arena staging.[34]

A Music Circus Industry

News of the success of the original music circus spread rapidly, and Terrell recognized the potential profit in marketing his concept and expertise to likely impresarios. He applied for and received in 1953 an official U.S. trademark for the term "music circus," which he defined as "limited to the production of musicals, musical comedies, light operettas or similar productions under a tent or in an arena theatre."[35] He also incorporated as the Music Circus of America and devised a do-it-yourself music circus kit, which came with the promise of "on-the-spot advice and assistance." In the contractual memo of agreement, Terrell pledged to provide "information, data, and know-how in connection with the establishment of a Music Circus" in return for a flat fee of $500. Should the interested party decide to open a tent theatre, the $500 would be applied against royalties (a minimum of $250 plus 3 percent of the gross receipts above $13,000) paid to Terrell during each week of operation. Terrell was obligated to provide a blueprint and seating diagram of the arena theatre; scenic and lighting plots; permission to purchase a tent, such as the one designed and patented by Terrell and Ernest Chandler, without additional royalty payment; sample budget and operating statements from his Lambertville theatre; consultation regarding the selection of plays, players, and artistic staff; photographs of plays already produced and copies of Terrell's own cut versions of scripts; and the right to use the phrase "music circus" in the name of the enterprise. He also guaranteed at least one visit to the music circus location to make on-site recommendations.[36]

The accompanying packet sent to the prospective producer consisted of a series of chatty pieces of advice, presumably dictated by Terrell and recorded as spoken without benefit of change in grammar, syntax, or other stylistic considerations, and duplicated on Lambertville stationery. It begins with "A Short Word Picture and Set-Up of the Lambertville Music Circus" which is a one-page advertisement for the genius of Terrell's concept. "In the face of constantly rising production costs," he begins, "I have developed a *new* method of presenting first rate Summer Musicals with top-drawer talent thru-out [sic] at one-fourth their current costs." He lists five components—central staging, arena theatre, music, location, and financial setup—that are critical to his argument. "By employing central staging," he contends, "the fabulous building costs are cut almost completely; with it also goes the designer, scenery painters, stage hands, grips, etc.," which, he asserts, is "the greatest money saving device ever proposed for Theatre's current financial dilemma." While saving money, one can actually earn greater profits in an arena since "two-fifths more people can be seated at the same cost" as in a conventional theatre. Further cost-cutting can occur with the help of Terrell's music director, Robert Zeller, who developed a nine-man, ten-piece orchestra that emulates the sound of a 22-piece orchestra. Saying that "the Musician's Union has agreed to our plans," Terrell provides accompanying sheets describing the specific instrumentation and recommendations on how to cut corners and make substitutions in both instruments and personnel. They suggest, for instance, using an electric organ to emulate reeds and horns and to employ a harp "only when a very good harpist" is available. Other personnel could be reduced if the conductor, organist, and choral director all can play the piano and double as rehearsal pianists and vocal coaches during the day.

Location, which is Terrell's fourth element, was key to Lambertville's continuing success; there was a population of 3.5 million people within a 35-mile radius of the tent, thus assuring a sizable audience pool. He notes that "the location is recognized as a theatre and entertainment area" with "seven top restaurants" that afford the theatre "enthusiastic cooperation."[37] The future success or failure of other music circuses relied heavily on their location because most had more than 1,000 seats to fill, which, with seven or eight performances a week, was possible only in a densely populated area. When Lambertville began, however, it was relatively modest in size. Terrell's attendant financial data is based on 700 seats which, he points out, could be raised to 838 seats by opening a tent flap and extending seating outside. Since this was impractical on rainy nights, Terrell and Chandler's new tent design, patented in 1951, accommodated twice as many patrons.

Terrell's budget of fixed weekly production costs, which totaled $5,855, was based upon data compiled from his 1949 opening season:[38]

Production costs—weekly fixed costs

Royalty (average)	$450.00
Printing (average)	25.00
Subscription campaign	25.00
Tickets	40.00
Legal	15.00
Audit	30.00
Transportation	20.00
Sound	12.00
Phone	25.00
Light	25.00
Electrical equipment	25.00
Advertising	200.00
Supplies	10.00
Canvas	5.00
Trucking	20.00
Insurance	8.00
Postage	5.00
Costumes 20 costumes @$6.00	120.00

(*Continued*)

(*Continued*)

Staff	
Janitor, watchman	30.00
Secretary	35.00
Box Office (two men)	125.00
Director	165.00
Music—8 men, 2 pianos, 1 electric organ—rented,1 conductor	1,200.00
Stage Manager	100.00
One electrician	60.00
Two stars	800.00
Nine ballet dancers, costumes	400.00
Twelve chorus (average)	500.00
Ten principals	1,000.00
One business manager	65.00
One prop	50.00
Three technicians	65.00
Press Agent	75.00
Designer	75.00
Props	50.00
TOTAL EXPENSES	$5,855.00

He computed weekly grosses, based on an average cost of $2 per ticket, on a sellout of a 700-seat house, with potential earnings of $9,800 per week, and an 800-seat house, which could bring in up to $11,900. Terrell lists a figure of $9,845, which he fails to itemize, in opening costs for the season and also considers potential income from the sale of concessions ($200 per week) and program advertising which, after subtracting advertising costs, nets roughly $1,000. Hence, with full houses over a 12-week season, a music circus could boast a handsome profit of between $49,000 and $75,000.[39] Once the audience capacity doubled in size, these figures theoretically could be twice as high.

It is instructive to compare Terrell's sample budget for a music circus operating in 1949 with a similar budget compiled by William Miles for operating a dramatic stock company a decade earlier (see chapter 6). Miles estimates average weekly expenses of $1,717 for a medium-sized theatre with a capacity of 350 to 400 in a good locale. With 1,500 patrons a week paying between 75 cents and $1.50 per ticket, Miles calculates that a producer could break even.[40] Using Miles's figures, the highest revenue, given a continual sellout over a 12-week season, would total only about $18,000. Although inflation and other financial factors must be taken into consideration in comparing these figures—the post-Depression economy of 1939 was very different from the post–World War II economy of 1949—the differences exhibit why a capital-driven producer would prefer to operate a music tent over a standard summer stock theatre. Both operations eschew high-priced star talent—the salary for the lead performers rose only $100 in the intervening decade, from $300 to $400—and both propose modest expenditures for scenography. The earning potential for a summer stock house, however, was constrained by space limitations. Short of knocking down a wall to afford more patrons a view, only so large an audience could fit inside a permanent building. When the stock houses tried to increase revenue by hiring well-known stars, they found their expenses rising exponentially and their box office sales not as lucrative as they had hoped. The music tents, on the other hand, so long as they could resist the high-priced stars that were bankrupting the dramatic houses, managed to limit expenses while maximizing profits. Add to the equation that musicals were the guaranteed hot commodity of the theatre world in the late 1940s and 1950s, and the choice was obvious. St. John Terrell's idea really did look like a pot of gold, and others were eager to partake of the prize.

The first producer to join Terrell in the music circus business was, not surprisingly, Richard Aldrich. The widely heralded "dean of American summer stock theatres," opened his new star-stock theatre, the Falmouth Playhouse, the same summer that Terrell was establishing his Lambertville tent, and both proved box office successes. Yet, Aldrich's weekly operating costs far exceeded Terrell's, particularly when he engaged a star like Tallulah Bankhead, whose salary alone cost $5,000 a week. Furthermore, since the seating capacity was significantly lower, Falmouth could never realize the income imaginable at a music circus.

Aldrich, ever the shrewd businessman, seized the opportunity to repeat his recent success at Falmouth with a new music circus venture in yet another part of Cape Cod. He had an excellent managing director at Falmouth, Herman E. Krawitz, who had proven his administrative talent a few years earlier under Aldrich's watchful eye. After serving in World War II, Krawitz had returned to college where, as a sophomore, he founded and ran his own summer company, the University Playhouse at Mashpee on Cape Cod, designed in emulation of the legendary University Players Group (UPG) of the 1920s. Aldrich had admired Krawitz's work and during the University Playhouse's second season, wrote a flattering article about the up-and-coming troupe, which he published in the playbills of his long-established Cape Playhouse in Dennis, Massachusetts, exhorting his audiences to support the fledgling group. The following season, however, the University Players disbanded because Aldrich had announced plans to open at Falmouth, just five miles away, and the players felt they could not compete with such a formidable neighbor. Aldrich immediately offered Krawitz, who had just received his degree from City College of New York, the management of the new theatre and Krawitz agreed on the condition that he could hire 11 members of his former company who were now out of work.[41] Thus Aldrich cannily acquired an experienced staff and proven location for his new venture. He now owned two one-a-week star-stock theatres on the Cape that could both function successfully because they were 30 miles apart and served different population centers. Neither of them, however, produced musicals. The idea of starting a music circus with a no-star policy that offered Cape audiences a very different theatre experience must have seemed irresistible. Aldrich asked Krawitz to "get into the music theatre business for us," arranged with Terrell to provide working plans and "know-how," and enlisted the help of his wife, Gertrude Lawrence, who imbued the project with her class, glamour, and fame, to launch the new theatre. Krawitz and company found a propitious location in the bustling town of Hyannis, at least 20 miles from both Dennis and Falmouth, and the Cape Cod Music Circus opened the following summer in July 1950. Like its predecessor in Lambertville, it was an instant success.

Despite the public's willingness to embrace the new tent theatre, there was trouble brewing backstage. There were two groups claiming credit for its success, the Krawitz and Terrell factions, and neither had positive reactions to the other. Richard Aldrich, as was his wont, had initiated the project and then largely absented himself from the minutiae involved in bringing it to fruition. He provided the concept, financing (with partners), name prestige, and the initial contact with Terrell, but left the day-to-day business details to his staff; hence, Krawitz, as general manager, was in charge of building and operating the theatre. Krawitz recalls meetings with Terrell during the spring when he was given full descriptions and plans of how the theatre was to be built. "Sinjun is a lovely man but he gave us stupid advice," Krawitz said. For example, "we couldn't believe the plans for the pit—it was like we were digging to China, and we'd never see the orchestra again." On the other hand, his basic ideas for the music circus and his eye for talent proved invaluable. Terrell, for instance, sent Lambertville's director, Robert Jarvis, to restage his work of the 1949 season in Hyannis the following summer. "He was sensational," Krawitz said, "and his ideas worked beautifully. The plays were well prepared and by simply remounting and repackaging them, we opened with an enormous bang."

Krawitz is quick to credit Terrell for his ingenuity and showmanship and is convinced that without him, the Hyannis tent never would have happened. He maintains, however, that "we were more skilled as managers and smart enough to know when Terrell was telling us wrong things, so we didn't do them. Terrell would shout, 'no, my plans are right—do it!' and I would say, 'we do that, and we're going to be in trouble.' "[42] From the perspective of Terrell and his associates, however, the problems lay with the inexperience and ineptitude of the Hyannis staff. Terrell's general manager, Cornelius P. Cotter, described the difficulties they experienced in trying to set up the new theatre to their attorney, Justin Golenbock:

> Bobby [Robert Jarvis] and I went up at the start of the season to find amateurs making the scenery, working on the lights, and trying to blame us for their lack of knowledge. But we pitched in and opened with a fine production of *New Moon* which started Hyannis off to success. Then too soon, we ran into inter- ference, hijacking of authority that had been definitely agreed to be sure; engag- ing of actors over our heads, firing of the ballet without notification; all around seemingly intentional sabotage. In spite of this we went ahead—fought with— intrigued against—shunted off from Dick Aldrich . . . details bore. And when we finally mentioned contract—the Music Circus of America's contract with Hyannis—Holtzmann [David Holtzmann, Aldrich's attorney] said "What con- tract?" Only then did I find out that the agreement settled on between all of us in your office had never been finished, never been signed.[43]

What had begun as a disagreement over working methodologies and exper- tise had escalated into threats of litigation by 1951. Holtzmann regularly sent royalty checks, per the contractual agreement, to Terrell during Hyannis's first summer of operation. Sometime in the spring of 1951, however, Holtzmann discovered that the contract was not legally binding—apparently Aldrich had never signed it—and he threatened Terrell with legal action if he attempted to claim that Aldrich had breached contract. What was particu- larly upsetting to Terrell was that his crew had worked industriously with the Hyannis group, despite all the "maddening fumbling opposition" they encountered, on the presumption that they were honoring a five-year contract and that "the four years to follow would make up for the first year in which we gave our all in know-how and actual direction."[44] Also, by 1951 Aldrich was running two music circus operations—one in Hyannis and one in Cohasset, across the Cape Cod canal on the south shore of Massachusetts below Boston. Ultimately, no lawsuits were filed by either party, but Aldrich changed the name of the Hyannis operation to the Cape Cod Melody Tent to avoid further conflicts with Terrell. The Cohasset tent, which continued to be called the South Shore Music Circus, was owned by the South Shore Playhouse Associates, Inc., a community-based group that had contracted with Aldrich to provide the shows, most of which had been hits in Hyannis the previous season. Terrell allowed South Shore to advertise as a music circus without remuneration, probably because it was a not-for-profit organization. It was the only theatre using the epithet "music circus" that remained unaffiliated with Terrell when the Musical Arena Theatres Association was founded in 1955.

The only producer to officially sign a contract with the Music Circus of America and to pay regular royalties was the Sacramento Music Circus in California, which opened in 1951. A winter tent, established in Miami Beach, Florida, in 1950 by Terrell's associate Laurence Schwab, was billed as "Laurence Schwab presents St. John Terrell's Music Circus, Robert C. Jarvis, General Stage Director," and featured the productions staged by Jarvis in Lambertville the previous summer. In the next few years, Terrell opened two more tents which, together with his flagship theatre in Lambertville, formed a three-theatre circuit tour. He also attempted a "motor music circus," which was a custom-designed arena theatre that could set up and break down quickly, thus allowing his shows to travel. The motor music circus provided an orchestra pit plus the regular big top, which Terrell borrowed from his Lambertville theatre, a "dressing top," which was a smaller tent for the actors, a 26-by-21-foot oval stage, seating platforms and chairs to accommodate 1,780 patrons, a ticket office, a power plant, and a "light ring" truss for the equipment mounted above the stage, all of which compacted into eight trailer trucks. The stage crew traveled in the trucks, while the 40 cast members accompanied the entourage in their own bus.[45] Terrell's circus on wheels premiered in Dallas at the Texas State Fair in October 1952 with a one-hour version of *Show Boat* which performed five times a day for a 16-day engagement. Despite or perhaps because of the number of performances, the show lost money.[46] The company was scheduled to travel to Florida for the winter months where it planned full-length productions of both *Show Boat* and *Carnival*. Although Terrell had hoped to slowly make his way back up the coast to play in Philadelphia sometime during the spring of 1953, there is no indication that the show ever arrived. He returned the tent borrowed from Lambertville and reopened the following summer as usual, without further mention of his mobile circus.

Though the motorized version did not prove successful, the permanently constructed music circuses flourished. There were 15 successful arena tent theatres spread across the country from Massachusetts to California when the producers came together to form the Musical Arena Theatres Association in November of 1955. The alliance served to represent their mutual interests to Actors' Equity, with which they created a new standard contract expressly for music circus engagements, and to encourage the continued growth and development of the form. By 1958, there were 10 more arena tents and by the early 1960s, when this type of entertainment reached its zenith, there were more than 30.[47]

What had begun as St. John Terrell's innovation was rapidly adopted by other producers eager to make their own success and not have to pay Terrell royalties. After his ill-fated attempts to coerce Aldrich into submission, Terrell seemed resigned to the fact that others would copy his idea without compensating him. Thanks to the trademarking of the term "music circus," however, the later tents employed different titles such as musical tent, musical and music theatre, music fair, music carnival, lyric circus, melody circus, and melody circle, to distinguish them from Terrell's original. All followed Sinjun's basic prescription for success, however, and capitalized on what one reporter called "the al fresco touch," which separated the tents from the regular proscenium theatres on "the strawhat circuit."[48] The expense of starting a tent theatre, however, rose significantly over a relatively short period of time. What had cost Terrell $35,000 in 1949 was capitalized at between $175,000 and $250,000, depending on location, by the opening of the 1958 season. Because the tents were much larger, however, producers potentially could earn a much higher profit. Whereas Terrell began with only 700 seats, the average tent by the mid-1950s seated 1,600 patrons, with some as large as 2,100 seats. Also, the tents usually played for an extended season of at least 15 weeks, three more than in Terrell's inaugural season.[49]

The higher cost of running a music circus necessitated a more sophisticated approach to attract new producers. Steven Slane, in the *1954 Supplement* to the annual *Blueprint for Summer Theatre*, provided a rationale for opening a tent theatre that combined astute business advice with an appeal to the civic-minded individual. Slane, who had begun as Herman Krawitz's treasurer in Hyannis, went on to manage the South Shore Music Circus from 1951 to 1953, and then left to start his own arena, the North Shore Music Theater in Beverly, Massachusetts, which, when it opened in 1955, was the first music circus to build a permanent roof over traditional canvas walls. In his article, "Why a Music Tent?" Slane fashions an argument that considers why the investor, the producer, and the audience all find this form of entertainment attractive. He divides investors into two categories: those who are outside the local community and those who live within driving distance of the proposed theatre. The first group, he contends, is interested solely in making a profit and thus must be convinced that investing in a music circus is a more attractive prospect than investing in, for instance, a Broadway production. While the latter is "a one-shot deal" that terminates when the show closes, a tent will operate for many seasons, thus affording an investor the opportunity to enjoy a continuing income. Local "angels," as financiers of new ventures are commonly called, typically have a more personal interest in their investments because they directly benefit their community. The investors reap double rewards from their investment, gaining both money and, in the case of a new theatre venture, the personal satisfaction of providing good entertainment in their own backyard for their family, friends, and neighbors. "In all probability," Slane asserts, they will prove excellent boosters for the theatre since "they will attend every production . . . some more than once" and encourage others to do likewise.

Slane's inducement to producers was a latter-day version of Terrell's original solicitation, which, given the expanded number of seats and proven allure of musical theatre over the intervening five years, promised even greater monetary rewards. He recommends a change of bill every other week rather than every week because most musicals can sustain a two-week run at the box office. By cutting the number of attractions by half, it will reduce production expenses proportionately plus afford a longer rehearsal period for the next attraction. Slane also suggests that a civic-minded producer can, without much monetary outlay, spread goodwill and reap some "psychic income" as well by inviting audiences, who ordinarily would not be able to attend live performances, to come either at significantly reduced prices or as "guests" of the management. Teenagers, nursery school children, and handicapped children are good target populations for this charitable gesture, which could continue to pay off for the producer: by introducing young people to theatre, he is building future audiences. As long as the remainder of the house is filled with paying customers, Slane believes a producer could extend these invitations without suffering a significant loss of income.

The spirit of reinforcing community harmony is likewise extended to all audiences where the egalitarian architecture of the arena in which "every seat is an orchestra seat" brings people together in a warm, intimate atmosphere that is difficult to attain in a regular proscenium house. Slane also affirms that music circus is truly a family affair where multiple generations can attend as a group and share their enjoyment. "Here is an opportunity, not easily found elsewhere, for this generation to see a performance of *Merry Widow*, *Chocolate Soldier*, or any of the almost-classical operettas" while members of "an earlier generation, whose Marilyn Monroe may have been Marilyn Miller, all want to see *Sunny* once again." He also suggests that "a grandparent, with a youngster of six in tow, can attend a music tent production of *New Moon*, and both will find enjoyment."[50]

The music circus concept continued to evolve with slight adaptations to the established formula by different groups of producers. A quartet of Boston-area investors—two businessmen, a public relations specialist, and an experienced producer/director—united to open the Carousel Theatre in Framingham, Massachusetts. They calculated that a music circus could "flourish on the outskirts of a large metropolitan area if it was easily accessible to the right people" and set out to find the ideal location. By employing sophisticated market analysis, they found a propitious site just off Exit 13 of the new Massachusetts Turnpike that was accessible to other major highways and within a 25-minute drive for more than three million people. Their theatre was the largest built to date and seated 3,000 people. It also distinguished itself by offering for its opening season two straight plays to complement a season of seven musicals, all of which employed star performers. The premiere summer season in 1958 was so successful that the American Marketing Association invited them to its fall meeting to talk about their success strategies. The association commented, "the idea is as old as the Acropolis, and it would have been as dead if it were not marketed properly!"[51]

Decline

In 1961, Sinjun Terrell granted an interview to the *New York World-Telegram* in which he predicted that in a very short time there would be "arenas all over." "In about three years every respectable shopping center will have an arena theater with real actors and honest shows," Terrell told reporter Frank Aston, who characterized him as "the grandpa of summer tents" and "the fire-eater frequently seen in Jack Paar commercials" so his readers would recognize him.[52] Terrell was speaking at the height of the music circus craze; within the next few years, the tents would begin to experience the difficulties that would drive most out of business during the 1970s. The warning signs, however, had appeared a few years earlier. In an August 1956 letter to the editor of the *Wall Street Journal*, Robert H. Bishop III, who was president of Musicarnival Inc. of Cleveland, Ohio, contested a recent article that "enhanced the popular impression that tent theatres are easy ways to fame and fortune." Bishop claimed that since the founding of Lambertville in 1949, approximately 30 tent theatres had been launched. Of these, ten had failed, others were experiencing difficulties, and only six had "a consistent record of profits." The profitable ventures were "founded early in the game when costs were low (\$40,000 to \$60,000 proved adequate capitalization) and the novelty value of arena staging under canvas was considerably greater than it now is." Most tents, he asserted, needed "to raise substantial amounts of fresh capital in order to complete their first season or to provide working capital to start their second." He attributed weather problems as well as competition from mediated entertainments—radio, movies, and television—as factors in keeping audiences away.[53] William Miles, in a 1957 article on "Summer Theatres as a Business," articulated other problems faced by the music circuses. In addition to weather—always the number one factor—he mentioned the lack of both air-conditioning and repertory as principal obstacles. By the mid-1950s, most traditional theatres, including many summer stock theatres, had installed air-cooling systems for the comfort of their patrons, who had become accustomed to air-conditioning in restaurants, movie houses, shops, hotels, and even in their own homes. Summer evenings, even in rural areas, are not necessarily cool, and if there is no breeze, a tent can be a stifling environment. An even greater concern was the limited repertory of musical comedies. As Miles points out, "for every ten straight plays suitable for stock that come out on Broadway each season, there is usually only one good musical," hence "the problem of a repertory becomes apparent." He adds that "nothing ages faster or more irretrievably than the book of a musical comedy" and that theatres can sustain only so many revivals of the top shows since "it is rare that the second showing finds the audience that the first one did."[54]

If these were problems in the mid-1950s, it is easy to imagine that they had grown much worse by the 1960s. Of particular concern, as Miles had predicted, was the lack of new shows. Although there were important musicals that premiered in the 1960s that would find success at the summer tents— notably *Camelot*, *A Funny Thing Happened on the Way to the Forum*, *Hello, Dolly!*, and particularly *Fiddler on the Roof*—the 1964–65 season is considered the last of the "great era of musical plays."[55] Thereafter, the political and cultural fabric of American society changed irrevocably, as did its musical theatre. The new musicals, aptly reflecting the times, were serious-minded explorations of issues, both personal and societal, facing a troubled people. These were inappropriate choices for the gay, circus like atmosphere provided by the music tents where the promise of giddy happiness, not thoughtful contemplation, sold tickets. The solution for many producers was to offer concert performances by popular musicians such as Louis Armstrong and

Paul Whiteman, and to recycle musical comedy favorites by offering star attractions. A few years earlier, merely the mention of the show's title would have been enough to ensure full houses every night.

The Guber-Gross Circuit

Although St. John Terrell is the undisputed founder of the music circus, the greatest success story belongs to Music Fair Enterprises Inc., or what is more familiarly known as the Guber-Gross circuit. Originally, it was Guber-Ford-Gross, named for the three Philadelphia school chums—Lee Guber, Shelly Gross, and Frank Ford—who pooled their resources to open the Valley Forge Music Fair in Devon, Pennsylvania, just outside of Philadelphia, in 1955. At their height, they had a chain of six successful music circuses operating in Pennsylvania, Massachusetts, New York, New Jersey, and Maryland, two of which—Valley Forge and the Westbury Music Fair on Long Island, New York—are still running. Ford left the partnership in 1967, but Guber and Gross continued producing theatre in the tents as well as on Broadway, off Broadway, and on road tours throughout the country, until Lee Guber's death in 1988. In a 1973 interview, Guber credited their success with their ability to change with the changing tastes of their audiences. "People do want to go out and be entertained," he averred, "but we've got to stop trying to fit the people to the system and start fitting the system to the people—making it easier and more attractive to go to the theater." He labeled their enterprises as "entertainment centers," and contended that he and Gross were in "show business, not in theater." They had attempted serious theatre by bringing, for instance, the New York–based Negro Ensemble Company to their tent theatre in Shady Grove, Maryland, but had "failed badly." "With 2,800 seats, we can't do the serious things," Guber said. He explained their philosophy further:

> I like to think there's something festive, escapist about what we do. Let's say it's what happens on television between 8 and 10 at night, as opposed to what happens on Sunday afternoon. We're also doing more and more concert and variety events for a couple of reasons. One, we're playing a longer season, and two, the output of musical comedies has dwindled in the past few years. There isn't as much to choose from as there was.[56]

Guber-Gross also were committed from the start to booking all-star attractions on the belief that "the bigger the star, the righter you are."[57] They always adhered to this policy but noted the precipitous rise in fees over the years. Shelly Gross explained how uneasy they were in the 1950s paying

Constance Bennett "all of $1,000 a week" to do *Wonderful Town.* "Now we pay $500,000 and $600,000 to Frank Sinatra and Diana Ross," Gross said, commenting that "only the biggest attractions can make that profitable."[58]

All of the Guber-Gross music theatres began as tents, and all converted to hard-top arenas, appropriate for year-round use, with far greater seating capacities. The Westbury theatre, for instance, opened in June 1956 in a striped tent holding 1,700 seats. In 1965, at a cost of more than $1 million, it was converted to a permanent structure seating 2,862.[59] Most other producers followed suit and converted tents such as the Cape Cod Melody Tent and South Shore Music Circus into permanent structures. Although still operating, these venues now book only concert performances, and most have not offered a legitimate musical in years. The only music arena to persevere as a tent, and to continue to offer musical theatre, is the Sacramento Music Circus in California. It was founded, under Terrell's tutelage, in 1951 as a 1,800-seat theatre. In 1969, it expanded to seat 2,500 while still retaining the tent ambience. The theatre's most recent renovation, completed in 2002, incorporated "a double layer tent-like fabric" in a fully enclosed, clear-span arena designed for year-round use. Despite the high-tech components, the Sacramento Music Circus claims to be "the last remaining tent theater in the United States," and assures its patrons that "these renovations will not make any changes to what Sacramento audiences have come to know as a wonderfully unique theater experience."[60]

Terrell himself never eschewed the tent ambience. In addition to his Lambertville progenitor, he opened three additional music circuses—the Neptune in Neptune, New Jersey, in 1952; the Brandywine in Concordville, Pennsylvania, in 1958; and the Sterling Forest Gardens, near Tuxedo, New York, in 1960. Because Terrell adhered strongly to his original concept, all four closed by 1970, victims of the changing times. "We just didn't sell enough tickets," he reminisced to a reporter the year before his death in 1998.[61] Although he pursued other professions after leaving the music circus business, he continued to nurture flamboyantly theatrical schemes that kept him frequently in the news. He was, for instance, a champion of the historic King Richard III who, he believed, was ill served by Shakespeare's tempestuous play that portrays him as a murderous thug. In 1983, on the 500th anniversary of Richard's accession to the throne, he arranged a memorial mass in St. Patrick's Cathedral in New York, followed by a medieval banquet in his honor at the Players' Club. Two years later, Terrell commemorated Richard's death at the battle of Bosworth Field by holding an even more elaborate medieval feast at Sardi's, which featured wooden spoons, pewter dishes, and a menu that included quail, suckling pig, ale, and mead.[62] An even more famous bit of theatricality—and one which he managed to repeat for 25 years—was his annual impersonation of George Washington crossing the Delaware River. The headline in his *New York Times'* obituary heralds him as "a Re-Enactor of History" and features a photograph of Terrell, garbed in a tricorn and cape and accompanied by six "soldiers" in a small boat, portraying General Washington in his legendary Christmas Day crossing with 2,400 members of the Continental Army to attack a Hessian stronghold at Trenton, New Jersey. What began as a publicity stunt for the music circus in 1953 became a much-anticipated annual event that is still carried on by the Washington Crossing Historic Park Foundation in Pennsylvania.

8

A New Definition of the Small Summer Barn

You know, I don't understand the theatre. These hams come down here, work their cans off for a dollar-eighty a week, live in places that a cockroach would turn up his nose at—and for what? Just to act. So help me God, actors will act anywhere, in anything, and for anything—all they want to do is to act.

The epigraph above, a monologue taken from Moss Hart and George S. Kaufman's 1940 comedy *George Washington Slept Here*, is delivered by the character Rena Leslie—the wife of the leading man—who is relegated to playing bit parts in summer stock.[1] Although she's really not interested in theatre and is only there to keep a watchful eye on her straying husband, who appears as a minor character in Hart and Kaufman's play, Leslie's astute observation of actors is critical to understanding how and why summer stock stayed alive. Actors needed a place to act, and summer stock provided the best available opportunity. At least through the 1960s, summer stock theatres in the aggregate remained the number one employer of professional actors in America. *Equity* editor Dick Moore estimated in 1961 that there were twice as many actors employed during the summer as during the winter, despite the growing hardships experienced by many summer theatres.[2] Leslie's comment relates equally well to anyone involved in operating a summer playhouse: producers needed a place to produce, directors sought plays to direct, and designers and technicians longed to create theatrical environments to design and build. In short, artists needed an artistic home, and they would do virtually anything in order to maintain it. Most summer stock theatres remained viable so long as there was an audience willing to support them, enough cash to keep producing shows, and enough energy and dedication, generally on the part of the producers, to keep returning for another season. In the play, Leslie eventually quits. "I don't mind an occasional rustic touch," she contends, "but when you walk into your dressing room and find that a couple of birds have built a nest in your brassiere—it's time to go back to the city."[3] Most summer theatre folk in real life were not so easily deterred, as witnessed by their creative strategies to keep their theatres alive.

New Definitions of Small—and Not So Small—Summer Barns

In its final press release of the 1958 season, the Bucks County Playhouse proclaimed "New Definition of Small Summer Barn Seen." When producer Michael Ellis took over this widely respected theatre in southeastern Pennsylvania in 1954, he announced his intention to mostly do new plays, and over his 11-year tenure at the playhouse, he premiered nearly 50. The previous producer, Theron Bamberger, had been forced to give up the theatre because of diminishing receipts, despite employing fine companies of actors, well-known star performers, and solid revivals of recent Broadway hits. Although Ellis retained Bamberger's penchant for hiring stars, he felt he could reverse his malaise by offering new plays interspersed with revivals of major works, such as T. S. Eliot's *The Cocktail Party*, with exceptional casts. Ellis engaged Ilka Chase, Uta Hagen, Edna Best, Murray Matheson, Philip Bourneuf, Jerome Cowan, and Richard Waring, all major stars, to perform in Eliot's play, which enjoyed a sold-out two-week run, probably a first for a straight play in summer stock.[4] After several seasons of this experiment, Ellis was ready to declare that this formula was the best possible avenue for summer stock success, thus arriving at his "new definition" of the "small summer barn":

> Now that the 1500 seat summer tents and theatres have invaded the once rustic and primitive summer circuit, and can pay higher royalties to playwrights and stars, theatres such as the Bucks County Playhouse find themselves drawn more and more to the new play, the novelty approach, and, always, the finest possible casting, direction, and staging. If such should be the case, the summer theatre in the 400-seat bracket can be counted on to make a vital contribution in the direction of productions of new scripts.[5]

This was not the first time new plays had opened in summer stock; in the 1930s, premieres were considered a vital component of the summertime experience. After World War II, however, when the summer theatres returned with a flourish, few new scripts were in evidence, much to the disappointment of many longtime critics who had welcomed the opportunity to see new plays in a relaxed summertime environment. Hence Ellis was actually reviving one of the elements that had made summer stock a lively force in its first decade and, at least at Bucks County, it proved a successful means of bringing audiences back to the theatre.

What worked for Ellis in Bucks County was not the same formula that would work for John Kenley in rural Pennsylvania and, later, in industrial cities in Ohio and Michigan. Like Ellis, Kenley took over a small theatre in Pennsylvania, but his was in a very different section of the state where theatregoing was an anomaly and there were no summer tourists to fill the auditorium. To attract audiences to his new enterprise at Deer Lake, which was near Pottsville in northeastern Pennsylvania's "coal region," he had to invent his own definition of summer stock. Although Kenley had worked in New York as a casting director for the Shubert brothers during the 1920s and 30s—he liked to call himself Lee Shubert's "left-hand man"—he had no previous producing experience.[6] He did know a lot of actors, however, and he persuaded 12 young hopefuls to pay him $250 each to work as apprentices at his theatre, which gave him the requisite capital to open for business. He equally relied on his friendships with famous actors, whom he lured to Pennsylvania as star attractions in his shows with the promise of handsome salaries. Kenley established a successful operating model, which he used for the next 50 years: hire top-name star attractions, selected for their box office appeal, who were willing to mingle with audiences and sign autographs after the show; maintain a strong resident company of well-trained repertory actors who "could act rings around the stars" but who would do whatever was necessary to showcase the leading attraction; refurbish scripts with careful editing and often major rewrites to give maximum exposure to the star; and keep ticket prices low and on a par with the admission charged at the local movie house. This method continued to work, despite rising costs and extraordinary salaries of $30,000 a week to his biggest stars, because he rented larger theatres over the years, which would seat 3,000 paying customers. Hence, Kenley's new definition of the small summer barn was to abandon it for a large civic auditorium. He was also the first summer stock producer to regularly hire television stars, many of whom, as frequent guests on the popular evening talk shows hosted by Jack Paar and later, Johnny Carson, would give Kenley free advertising as well as nationwide exposure by mentioning their forthcoming appearances at his theatres.[7]

The key to success for Ellis, Kenley, and other producers in the latter years of summer stock seemed to be the simple admonition to know your audience. Historically, the most successful summer stock theatres consistently addressed the tastes and entertainment needs of their local communities, which provided the critical base of support that sustained these theatres from year to year. Bucks County audiences were a case in point. Long known as "the genius belt," Bucks County boasted a rarefied mix of artists, writers, and intellectuals, many of whom also had homes in New York City. They attended Broadway productions regularly and thus had seen the important new plays in their premiere productions with the original casts. It is not surprising that they were not interested in attending revivals of the same plays they had seen the previous winter with an all-new cast, no matter how prestigious the actors. New plays, however, were attractive commodities, particularly to artists who confronted the challenge of creating new work in their daily lives. Hence, Ellis was reinventing his theatre based on an acute knowledge of audience predilections. John Kenley, addressing a very different group of theatregoers in rural and industrial areas, knew his audiences equally well. These people, who lived far from New York City and other arts-oriented metropolises that presented live theatre, were more attuned to the populist entertainment offered by the new medium of television. The opportunity to see stars from their favorite TV shows in person, shake their hands, and obtain their autographs was the primary attraction; the play, in this instance, was definitely not the thing. Hence, Kenley did everything he could to showcase the star attractions to their best advantage since they were keeping his huge auditoriums filled to capacity.

These men, and others like them, were classic small-business owners, functioning in a time-honored tradition in which success depends "primarily on the skill of the manager and secondarily on the location of the business."[8] In summer stock, one could argue that a slight variation of this rule is more accurate: an excellent location is paramount but it will succeed only if the manager understands exactly what kind of paying customers that location engenders. Furthermore, if the local demographics change, the manager must be willing to change with the changing population, defining and redefining his "small summer barn" as often as necessary. Very few summer stock theatres had become indispensable institutions that garnered unflinching community support in the face of economic fluctuations. Although local citizens did, on occasion, band together to seek various ways to keep their theatres functioning, they did not always succeed (the closing of the Boothbay Playhouse is a good example, to be discussed later in this chapter). Since theatre is a precarious product that suffers, more than most commodities, from the vicissitudes of public taste, producers must diligently monitor that taste and, ideally, help to mold and shape it via consistently excellent productions. They also must understand their limitations—most small summer barns ultimately succeeded because they remained small—and handle their finances with a deft hand.

Small Theatre Economics

Thomas Gale Moore, who published an economic study of the American theatre in 1968, declared summer stock to be "the strongest branch of the theater outside of New York."[9] His research dates from the early 1960s, a period that can now be considered the final gasp of summer stock's golden era before the steady decline in numbers of theatres and profits eliminated all but the most tenacious operations. Gale's statistics are, nonetheless, impressive, and they demonstrate just how powerful a force summer stock was in twentieth-century American theatre. Although he used a relatively small sample of theatres and admittedly had difficulty obtaining accurate information, he estimated that the attendance at summer stock theatres during the summer of 1962—a period of three to four months—exceeded that of either Broadway or road tours for their entire 9- to 10-month seasons by one to almost three million people. Gross receipts in these latter two classifications reflected their much higher ticket prices—he lists $43.5 million for Broadway and $31.5 million for the road respectively—while summer stock earned between $22.6 million and $30.6 million, which are substantial sums for an abbreviated season. The attendance figures, however, are staggering—7.6 million on Broadway, 7.8 million on the road, and between 8.8 million and 10.2 million in summer stock—which leads one to question why something ostensibly so popular could decline so rapidly. Broadway and, by extension, the road, which was dependent on Broadway for its product, was experiencing a slump because of the cultural, political, and philosophical transformation of American society in the 1960s, which had rendered the old plays and musicals obsolete but had not yet discovered a worthy substitute.[10] This "lack of product," an oft-used expression by theatrical producers, eventually affected summer stock as well, but since most of these houses were in rural areas, the trickle-down effect took longer. Also, because the summer stocks were smaller and necessarily attuned to a specific community, they featured more diverse offerings than Broadway, which specialized in a very particular kind of play or musical that would have mass appeal to a broad-based audience.

Moore's study of summer stock, which consisted of questionnaires and visits to only 12 theatres, led him to three interesting conclusions. First, he could discern no economy of scale in size of operation for nonmusical houses. In other words, large theatres proved to be no more profitable than small ones, and he foresaw no trend toward expansion. (Kenley, who was just developing his large-scale theatre circuit when Moore was doing his research, is not mentioned in this study; furthermore, Kenley's operation was virtually one of a kind and he had few imitators.) Moore's second observation was that profitability seemed to be unrelated to the type of plays produced, since he found that comedies, dramas, and musicals were equally successful at the box office. Finally, summer stock theatre seemed to be a "break-even proposition," with as many shows making money as not. Hence, over the course of a season, most producers, in his limited study, managed to remain solvent.[11] Unfortunately, Moore, who was an economist and not a theatre professional, failed to list the theatres surveyed, but the offhand mention of two—the Bucks County Playhouse and the Olney Theatre in Maryland—leads one to suspect that he chose only well-established operations that would have an economic history worth studying. As such, his suppositions may indicate that these managements were especially tuned to the likes and dislikes of their audiences, handled their finances carefully, and were fully cognizant of what their theatre was and was not. Since numerous operations bearing these attributes ultimately failed, it is important to conduct a more incisive and inclusive investigation than Moore's.

When asked what contributed most forcefully to the declining fortunes of summer stock, producers cited the following culprits: rising costs, particularly those imposed by Actors' Equity; the hegemony of the star system; competition from television and, to a lesser extent, film; competition from the music tents; and a growing lack of product in the paucity of suitable new scripts. Although most of these issues have been examined in previous chapters as problems encountered in the early development of stock, the fact remains that, with the exception of the music tents, which mostly had closed by the 1980s, all continued to be serious challenges throughout summer stock's history. One must also consider that the U.S. economy was extremely volatile during this period, suffering, in addition to spiraling inflation, from a panoply of socioeconomic problems, which included environmental decay, energy shortages, discriminatory hiring practices (especially for nonwhites and women), poverty, urban decline, population pressure, and rising crime.[12] All of these had an influence on how people chose to spend their leisure time, which included taking vacations, day travel to resort and amusement areas, and, of course, going to the theatre.

It was certain that the price of lumber, hardware, paint, fabric, lighting equipment, and all the other required nuts and bolts of running a theatre, continued to escalate. What most concerned summer stock producers, however, was the nearly annual rise in cost of doing business with Actors' Equity. For many, the prestige of running an Equity theatre, as well as the promise of a professional, talented company, who had earned their union cards by dint of merit, outweighed the financial burden. Certainly, all star theatres had to be Equity houses, and others that still maintained resident companies preferred the union affiliation. It was possible, however, to hire a company of professionals who were "known in the business," a phrase used to designate respected experienced actors whose names were not familiar to the general public, at the designated Equity minimum wage and save considerable money. Other producers chose not to affiliate with Equity at all, either by running exclusively amateur operations or by hiring experienced or promising actors who were not union members. Occasionally, these theatres would supplement their acting company to fulfill a demanding star role with a visiting Equity guest artist, known as a "jobber," who had to be hired under an official contract and paid union scale. The theatre, however, was not required to embark on any other arrangement with the union, although invariably Equity representatives would work hard to bring the producer into the fold.

A producer's dilemma as to whether to become an Equity house extended far beyond the actor's, stage manager's, and until 1959, director's and choreographer's minimum wages. Over time, the union imposed additional costs that could potentially break a modestly capitalized theatre's budget. The most prominent of these was a practice known as "bonding," whereby before a theatre could open, the producer would have to send Equity a check covering a full two weeks' salary for all Equity members in the company's employ, one week's salary for each jobber hired for the first three productions, and an additional hundred dollars to cover possible bookkeeping charges, assessments, transportation costs, and the like.[13] Most or all of the money was returned at the end of the season so long as everything had gone well, and all members had been able to fulfill their contracts, per the stipulated terms. Should the theatre close unexpectedly, however, or actors not receive what was agreed upon, money would be paid out of the bond. For many small theatres, the several thousand dollars needed to post bond at the beginning of the season was beyond their meager budgets.

Another unexpected hardship came with the 1963 Equity ruling regarding pension plans, which were now being included in stock contracts. Depending on the theatre's classification, which, at that time, included the Association of Civic Music Theatres (large outdoor musical theatres), the Musical Arena Theatres Association (indoor musical theatres, including the tents), the Council of Stock Theatres, known as COST, which covered the larger dramatic stock companies, and the Council of Resident Stock Theatres or CORST, which oversaw intermediate and small dramatic companies, there was a different scale of pension contributions. All theatres began with

1 percent of payroll in 1963, with various maximum cutoff points, but all were scheduled to grow by several percentage points in subsequent seasons. Also, beginning in 1965, contracts would be subject to cost-of-living increases, but this would apply only if the annual rise in minimum wage was less than the figures published annually by the U.S. Bureau of Labor Statistics revised Consumers' Price Index. All producers also had required payments for transportation and wardrobe cleaning costs, while others, depending on the size of their theatre, had illness and hospitalization insurance, worker's compensation, and matching Social Security contributions.[14]

Given these conditions, it is easy to understand why some producers chose not to seek Equity affiliation or, in some cases, drop it in order to stay in business. In a 1954 article titled, "Summer Theatre at the Crossroads," Thomas Ratcliffe, the producer of the Sea Cliff, New York, summer theatre and president of the Stock Managers' Association, predicted that his peers would "do everything to cut down costs," resulting in a decrease in jobs for the majority of the union's membership, more theatres opting to "go non-Equity," and more managers making an effort to do small cast plays, cut parts, and use local amateurs and apprentices whenever possible. He cited the Pawling, New York, summer theatre as one that had just become non-Equity and both the Westhampton, New York, and Boothbay Harbor, Maine, theatres as ones that eschewed resident companies altogether and became community theatres hosting a series of visiting amateur groups.[15] Rowena Stevens, the producing director of the Pocono Playhouse in Mountainhome, Pennsylvania, maintained her Equity affiliation but made the decision to eliminate stars and offer solid repertory players beginning in 1953. She reported that her experimental first production under the new scheme, *The Moon is Blue*, proved a big hit with audiences and earned higher box office rewards than if she had featured "a name."[16]

Some theatres wished to cooperate with Equity, as in the case of the Wingspread Theatre of Colon, Michigan, but found the union intransigent and unwilling to embark on what the theatre viewed as creative problem solving. The Wingspread was a 225-seat theatre that offered religious drama in a small town in the southwest sector of the state. It had contracted with a New York–based company specializing in religious drama, the Broadway Chapel Players, all of whose members held Equity cards, to come to Michigan for the summer. The company, which was eager to have an opportunity to play together for an entire summer season, had agreed to a salary of $55 per week plus transportation costs for each actor, which had been the Equity minimum the previous year. Wingspread's producer, Eleanor E. Walton, wrote to Equity to request a waiver, so that her non-Equity house could legitimately employ these actors without their suffering any chastisement from the union. Mrs. Walton received what appeared to be a boilerplate reply from the Equity office, which informed her of the new Equity minimum wage, the bonding requirement, and other rules and regulations pertinent to operating an Equity stock company. Nowhere did it mention or even allude to her question regarding the possibility of obtaining a waiver.

Walton's reply was respectful yet forthright and, no doubt, representative of the frustrations felt by many other small producing theatres across the country. "I'm sure it was not unintentional that the main purpose of my letter seemed to be disregarded," she stated, declaring that if the paltry raise of $2.50 in the minimum wage were "the only requirement to our meeting Equity demands, we would not hesitate a moment." She made clear, however, that her theatre was not and would not request consideration as an Equity theatre, despite their desire to have the Broadway Chapel group join them for the summer. She explained her position further:

> We have written Mr. Penn [the head of the Chapel group] that your answer has closed the door. We do feel it is regrettable, since it is hardly possible such a group of players can anywhere else find a spot for themselves this summer where they can work together as a group. Also, knowing the percentage of non-employment (even in the summertime) of Equity actors, most of whom depend on summer employment particularly for income, we feel this is regrettable. When the actors' union forces small theatres to look outside of Equity bounds for their summer companies (and there are many such of us who are forced to do so), Equity is hardly making the lot of the minimum-wage actor easier.

Walton then summarized the theatre's financial situation and proudly proclaimed its respected status in the local community, where "we have never failed to pay a bill at the end of the summer, salary or otherwise." The theatre's integrity and goodwill "is such that the security we offer our actors is even greater than the two week's wage assurance the Equity bonding affords; our actors come with a full-summer guarantee of employment at the salary stated," she averred. She closed with the following recommendation, which one can only wish had been published in *Equity* magazine for the contemplation of all: "If Actors' Equity Association has never made a study of why more and more of the small inland summer theatres have left the Equity fold or why they do not care to join with the union which was chartered for the same mutual interests which theatre administration desires, I feel they should make such a study. This small case history might add just one bit of interesting evidence."[17]

The Equity dilemma faced by producers ultimately affected actors in need of employment, who often found themselves in the unattractive position of debating whether to seek union affiliation or not. By joining the union, they could guarantee a certain minimum wage and benefits while employed, but an Equity card alone did not ensure a contract. Also, since many theatres changed their management style and repertories, sometimes more than once, it was difficult to predict hiring patterns and expectations from year to year. Actors who specialized in straight dramatic or comedy roles, for instance, were finding more opportunities for work as producers opted to forgo star engagements. The opposite occurred for musical comedy performers, however, since in the beginning, musicals drew substantial audiences on name recognition alone. People went to *Oklahoma!*, *Guys and Dolls*, and *Wonderful Town* simply because they wished to see these popular new musicals and producers would attract sizable houses for these shows regardless of who was appearing in them. Hence, known-in-the-business performers would have the opportunity to play major leading roles to appreciative audiences. Gradually, however, musical producers fell prey to the star syndrome as well. These respected unknowns, who used to play opposite each other, were now being hired to support famous performers like José Ferrer, Howard Keel, and Jayne Mansfield. Pretty soon audiences were demanding two star attractions, and these former leading actors were now out of work or relegated to taking character roles at lower salaries. Many went into the popular new entertainment medium that began in the 1960s, dinner theatre, which, as its own novelty waned, underwent the same devolution as summer stock.[18]

Producer Lee Falk outlined "What's Wrong With Summer Stock" for *Equity* in 1959 by decrying rising costs, by warning of diminishing creativity in light of financial realities—a charge taken up by those producers finding new definitions for their old barns—and by considering the question of subsidy. Given the considerable expense of staying in business and the formidable competition for audiences from television, movies, and radio, he perceived that the "living theatre" had "been dragged into the position of being an expensive side-show next to the main tent, facing the fate of opera, symphony and ballet," all of which, even by the 1950s, were heavily subsidized arts.[19] The idea of subsidy for theatre was not new—most people were aware of the considerable support, usually governmental, given to theatres in foreign countries—and the United States itself had even experimented with public subsidy via the Federal Theatre Project in the 1930s. Yet, there were few not-for-profit theatres, which according to their corporate structure were permitted to offer tax deductions to donors from the private, corporate, and foundation sectors, prior to the 1960s when the glamour and influence of the Kennedy administration made theatre and its allied arts a national priority. Private foundations, notably the Ford Foundation, under the inspired leadership of W. MacNeil Lowry, and later the Rockefeller Foundation, initiated major subsidies for the new regional theatres that were emerging in major cities across the country, and the U.S. government cautiously embarked on a plan for arts funding via the creation of the National Endowment for the Arts in 1965. Summer stock theatres, with few exceptions, did not enjoy the benefits of this largesse because these houses were seasonal enterprises and had operated, like all American theatres, as commercial businesses. The few summer operations that did opt for nonprofit status did so either because they literally had run out of money and had no other choice if they wished to go on (see the discussion of Francis Grover Cleveland and the Barnstormers in chapter 4) or because they wished to present plays of a serious and experimental nature, which would not guarantee survival via box office revenue alone (profiles of 2 such theatres, the Boothbay Playhouse and Williamstown Playhouse, will occur later in this chapter). In none of these instances, however, did the theatres become the kind of stultified institutions that Falk had feared. "In other entertainment fields," he posited, subsidy "appears to freeze creativity and limit activity to a comparative point just above absolute zero." He was not sure that this would happen in stock theatre, but he did not seem eager to test the waters even though, by his own admission, all five of the stock theatres he personally had managed were defunct. He contended, however, that subsidized theatre was already happening on Broadway "where we can see a play run eleven months, go on tour, and still not pay back a cent to backers. And in stock," he bemoaned, "we find three-quarters of our theatres losing money, being subsidized by people who can't afford it."[20] His point— that subsidy can and does come from the artists and producers themselves— is critical to an understanding of how many of the summer stock theatres, especially the smaller venues, survived. Actors and other stage personnel would willingly work for low, sometimes barely subsistence-level salaries, just to have the opportunity to practice their art. Similarly, some producers often were not earning enough money to cover operating costs, yet would make up deficits via their personal bank accounts, which, as Falk argued, they could ill afford. Falk believed that summer stock could be an exciting, viable business if only managers employed creative solutions. The story of four such managements—two of which chose not-for-profit status and two of which remained commercial—follows.

Boothbay Playhouse—"Kiss the Joy as It Flies"

Franklyn Lenthall and James Wilmot, the second and final owner/producers of Maine's Boothbay Playhouse in the seaside resort of Boothbay Harbor, lived by this motto, paraphrased from William Blake's poem "Eternity," for the 18 "exciting and frustrating years" between 1956 and 1974 when they operated the theatre. To better glean their philosophical perspectives on running a summer stock playhouse, the full quotation follows:

> He who binds to himself a joy
> Does the winged life destroy;
> But he who kisses the joy as it flies
> Lives in eternity's sun rise.[21]

"It's the philosophy we'd taken on because it was a wonderful period, not only for us, but for the Boothbay region and for summer theatre in Maine," Wilmot reminisced, willingly overlooking the frequent difficulties "and a lot of hard luck" they endured over the years in keeping the theatre open. "My thing about 'kiss the joy,' " Lenthall chimed in, "is relevant if you have a love affair or a summer stock theatre—don't hang on, don't mutilate it, just enjoy it while you can. The minute you tighten in on something, you lose it. And I really believe that." When maintaining the theatre ultimately became too expensive and more frustrating than rewarding, Lenthall and Wilmot put it up for sale. "We were working our fanny off," Lenthall winced, "and we just could not do it anymore."[22]

The history of the Boothbay Playhouse is especially interesting because it encompassed three distinctly different styles of operation under only two managements: a commercial, semiprofessional resident stock company offering a repertory of recent Broadway comedies, mysteries, and the occasional drama; several strictly amateur seasons, also run commercially, which were essentially little theatre festivals, as had been popular in the 1920s; and a not-for-profit resident Equity company of fine repertory actors, which presented an unusual selection of British, European, and experimental plays that made it unique among the summer houses. It also had a history of operating difficulties, despite auspicious beginnings, which predated Lenthall and Wilmot's tenure at the playhouse. Its sole former owner, Sherwood Keith Lacount, who used the stage name Sherwood Keith, was a Boston-based actor-singer and the scion of an insurance magnate who wished to help his son's career. A 100-acre piece of property, which had been a working farm, was purchased on a scenic highway linking the Maine resorts of Boothbay Harbor and Wiscasset.

The old barn was razed to make way for a new barnlike structure that would become the theatre and the farmhouse was appropriated as a dormitory for the actors. Boothbay was probably the first summer stock house to be designed and built from the ground up to emulate an old New England barn; as such, it afforded both charm and state-of-the-art theatrical equipment in a commodious, well-planned environment that even included an air ventilation system, which served players and audience equally well. Under Keith's management—he served both as executive director and as a leading man in the acting company—the playhouse seemed to be a fairly standard summer stock operation, featuring a 10-week season produced by a resident company with all scenic needs designed and built on the premises.

The company began to lose audiences and revenue about 1948, in the post–World War II period that were boom years for most summer stock enterprises. In a fall 1951 letter to his supporters, Keith sent a request for early subscribers to enable him to open the following season. He determined he needed $5,000 in start-up money which, at $22 per subscription, amounted to only 227 patrons. "Out of a region such as this, which boasts over some 40,000 people in the summer," he maintained, "it wouldn't appear that the above requirement was in excess." Statistics provided in the following paragraph, however, suggest that very few of those people had been supporting his playhouse. Although the theatre could seat 314, he was attracting only about 112 ticket buyers per performance, thus leaving 202 empty seats at each of the 289 shows presented during the previous four seasons.[23]

Although Keith ran a regular stock season in 1952, it would be his last. The following year, he and his wife, actress Louise Winter, concocted a scheme to present a series of community theatre groups—seven from Massachusetts and two from Maine—for 1-week engagements. Expenses for a dozen members of each company were covered by the playhouse, while any additional members would have to pay for themselves. Keith's production manager, Hunter Perry, declared "we have no idea where all this will lead, but we are certain of one thing, it will give a wonderful week's vacation to these wonderful people who carry the spear for the theatre during the winter."[24] The idea proved so successful the first season that Keith purchased a second house, the Deertrees Theatre in Harrison, Maine, so that he could offer engagements to twice as many worthy amateurs, who, not surprisingly, eagerly vied for an opportunity to have work that doubled as a seaside holiday. Keith claimed, in fact, that the community groups were "casting at least one play strictly on merit in the hope of being chosen," and that little theatres were "scouting" each other throughout the winter to compare talent, sets, costuming, and direction."[25] The experiment was heralded by critics such as Robert Coleman of the *New York Daily Mirror* who was pleased to see summer stock "getting back to basic principles," thus restoring "sanity and balance to the straw-hats."[26]

As they embarked on their second amateur season, Louise Winter claimed that the first year's success resulted in "doubled attendance and bigger grosses" at the box office and that the shows had been "far superior to the hurriedly rehearsed run of stock shows" that the theatre had been producing in previous years.[27] The couple continued the practice, however, for only three seasons, ending the third by co-starring in a production of *The Fourposter*, a two-person comedy well suited for a husband-wife team. What initially proved a popular novelty with the public lost favor all too rapidly, despite the support of noted New York critics. The theatre was dark in 1956 and was sold over the winter to Lenthall and Wilmot, who initially had a third partner, Jill McAnney, whom they bought out in 1963. They essentially were always a two-man operation, however, with Lenthall directing the shows and Wilmot serving as business manager in charge of all finances, box office, and maintenance.

To prepare for their new venture as summer stock producers, the pair made a tour of 22 summer theatres to determine how to newly define their (pseudo) barn playhouse by assessing the strengths and weaknesses of the competition. The most lasting impression—even 40 years later—was all the dirt; summer stock, it seemed, was rife with "bad housekeeping," which ranged from "absolutely not good to filthy, rotten dirty." Since they knew many of the performers, proprietors, and other stage personnel, they were given access everywhere, from backstage to the bathrooms to props' closets, and they generally were not pleased with what they saw. "You'd see comely girls on stage in lovely frocks," Lenthall reminisced, "and then they'd put their feet up and they were black on the bottom. Even worse was when the curtain would open and billows of dust would sweep out over the house." The exteriors of the playhouses proved equally uninviting. "There wasn't really anything attractive about the theatres to make someone want to go in," Wilmot remarked. "If you were driving by, there wasn't anything that would make you look." They also commented on the uncomfortable seats and quickly decided that they would have cushy seats in their theatre with lots of leg room. "We figured if the derriere is tired, you've lost your first critic," they agreed. Production quality was all over the place, but they discovered that more often than not the worst shows featured star performers. "We saw lots of famous stars not playing well or not handling problems that would happen," they said, adding that "of course, audiences love it when things go wrong, and they applaud." Finally, they determined that, given the type of repertoire they wanted to produce, they had to be nonprofit or risk losing everything.[28]

The tour proved essential in shaping the development of the refurbished Boothbay Playhouse which, under the new regime, was transformed into a pristine and beautifully appointed venue. The grounds were lush with thousands of brightly colored annuals, manicured lawns, and a hundred acres of woodland. Wilmot also designed and built a Japanese garden in later years, which added to the appeal. In 1963, they built an extension to the main theatre, which was the same size as the stage, to provide a rehearsal hall by day and commodious indoor lobby by night. New restrooms were also added exclusively for audience use, and a little pub for preshow and entr'acte refreshments (which never sold liquor, to Lenthall's regret; "if we had, we might have made it," he remarked). They eliminated 42 seats from the auditorium to create a cross aisle, thus reducing their house size from 314 to 272, truly a novelty on the summer circuit, where producers were constantly trying to figure out how and where to fit in more seats, but installed substantial padding on the remaining chairs to ensure their patrons' comfort. Interior decor was handled by Wilmot, who was a regional painter of some repute, and he frequently would mount lobby art shows of his own work and the work of other artists. The playhouse was also a showcase for Lenthall's impressive collection of theatrical memorabilia, dating from the eighteenth through twentieth centuries, which included stage jewelry, costumes, portraits, photographs, sculpture, playbills, figurines, set models, and toy theatres. After the playhouse closed in 1974, Lenthal and Wilmot purchased a nearby historic house that was a suitable environment for showcasing the collection and operated the Boothbay Theatre Museum as their summertime endeavor between 1975 and 1990.

The most noteworthy distinction between Boothbay and other summer stock theatres was its choice of repertory. Lenthall, who directed all 172 productions during their 18-year management, had a particular affinity for contemporary British plays which, with few exceptions, were not regularly produced in America. Twenty-six of these, by such writers as Enid Bagnold, Agatha Christie, Noël Coward, J. B. Priestly, Terence Rattigan, and Emlyn Williams, had their American premieres in Maine. He also enjoyed producing new European plays that were edgy and experimental, such as Harold Pinter's *The Birthday Party* and a double bill of Eugene Ionesco one-acts, *The Bald Soprano* and *The Lesson*. The latter shows sent at least 35 perplexed theatregoers per performance out of the house before curtain, one even accosting Lenthall in the lobby by grabbing his lapels and shouting "you're going to lose all your customers doing stuff like this!"[29] The great majority, according to one reviewer, "supported the talented cast with appropriate and abundant laughter and accorded them hearty applause at the curtain calls." The critic himself did not like the plays, but he admired the fine acting, directing, and setting, and declared that the quality of production "was as fine as any we've seen this summer."[30] Boothbay also regularly produced the classics, including Molière's *The School For Wives*, which they claimed was one of their most successful productions, and contemporary American dramas by playwrights who were rarely performed in summer stock, such as Edward Albee and Tennessee Williams.

The playhouse became nationally recognized as a straw hat noted for "more substantial offerings" than "the usual formula for warm-weather theater," which was deemed "as fluffy as cotton candy." Consequently, Boothbay headed *Time* magazine's list of theatres worth attending in its summer straw-hat listings.[31] Boston critic Eliot Norton, in reviewing the 1968 summer stock schedules, credited Boothbay with having "the most varied program of any summer theater in the country, with five American premieres in a season that will include American, English, French, Polish, and Russian plays," and he devoted a full column to discussing the unusual repertory.[32] A local critic, in reviewing the Maine summer season, proclaimed "the most exciting, stimulating, and provocative moments of theater came, as usual, at the Boothbay Playhouse," with this explanation: "I say 'as usual' because Franklyn Lenthall and Jim Wilmot are the only producers on the circuit who regularly delve into drama and, from my standpoint, a departure from a strict diet of comedies and musicals is most refreshing. I imply no criticism of any producers, understand. If I were running a summer theater I doubt that I'd have the courage to stage 'The Physicists,' 'The Poker Session' and 'The Holly and the Ivy' in one season, but I'm awfully glad someone does have that courage."[33]

Lenthall and Wilmot maintained a full payroll of 23 employees, consisting of a 12-member dramatic stock company, eight apprentices, two cooks, and a waitress. For the first two seasons, they brought their New York City–based company to Maine, but Lenthall was dissatisfied with the overall quality of the work. At that point, he decided to become an Equity house, and he contends that "it was the best decision I ever made," despite the constantly rising costs, because it assured him of a consistent standard of performance from individuals who could readily meld into a tight ensemble. It ultimately was the exorbitant cost of staying in business, however, that propelled them to sell the playhouse in 1974. Immediately after the season closed, a "self-appointed, voluntary and temporary committee" consisting of local residents and theatre devotees formed to investigate whether there was "sufficient enthusiasm and financial support in the community to warrant an attempt to raise funds sufficient to guarantee the Theatre's continuation." Lenthall and Wilmot provided a financial statement that indicated their distress. There was a net cash deficit of nearly $20,000 for the 1974 season with start-up expenses for opening in 1975 estimated at $40,000.[34] Although the theatre had incorporated as a not-for-profit foundation in 1957 and, throughout the years, had enjoyed generous donations from well-heeled summer residents, as well as a $10,000 grant from the National Endowment for the Arts the final season, it was not enough to defray costs. Box office receipts, at a $5.50 top ticket price in the final season and a maximum of only 272 seats, were never sufficient. "Our last season, we sold out every night but three and still lost $20,000," Lenthall lamented. But neither he nor Wilmot regret their wonderful years at the playhouse. "When you go to the theatre, you must be entertained, and I do think you should be educated, but painlessly," Lenthall said. "Our theatre was exciting, interesting, and never boring. People may not have liked everything, but our audience stayed with us. And that was a terrific thing."[35]

The Kenley Players—"Strictly Showbiz"

"It was all showbiz, strictly showbiz," John Kenley contended, "and they had to be *big* shows to fill those theatres."[36] The lone point of comparison between Lenthall/Wilmot's and Kenley's operations is that both believed in maintaining a strong resident company of Equity actors as the backbone of their productions. The only other thing they had in common is that both went out of business for the same reason—money. The exorbitant cost of producing summer stock in the late twentieth century affected small and large theatres, not-for-profit and commercial operations alike, the only difference being in degree. What Boothbay lost for its entire 1974 season was the same amount that Kenley would pay his star attraction in a single week. Otherwise, these theatres stood as far apart on the summer stock spectrum as possible, thus exemplifying the extreme diversity of the genre in its waning years.

From opening his first theatre, which seated 500, in Deer Lake, Pennsylvania, in 1940 to running a three-city circuit of theatres, playing to nearly 10,000 customers a night in the 1970s and '80s, Kenley was always in a class by himself. He succeeded by inventing his own methodology, which employed the philosophy of "showbiz," gleaned from his many years with the Shuberts, and a strict reliance on the star system within a summer stock milieu. As one of the Shuberts' casting directors, he developed a sharp eye for talented performers capable of wowing an audience, for which the Shuberts were justifiably famous, and which aptly served him in his own star-entrenched summer theatres. Although Kenley had worked for Lee Shubert, who was considered to be the more artistically inclined of the brothers, his own proclivities as a producer seemed closer to the style and temperament of J. J., who preferred big, splashy musical entertainments. He also seemed wedded to J. J.'s dictum of cramming as many patrons as possible in to see a show, regardless of their personal comfort. In what may be an apocryphal yet oft-repeated quote, J. J., when asked to describe what he did for a living, replied, "I put asses in seats." Kenley was a master at "putting asses in seats" and, even when the house ostensibly was full, he would find more chairs and set them up in any available space.[37] One might conjecture that Kenley's unusual choice of locale for summer stock, from rural communities in Pennsylvania to the industrial cities of Ohio, none of which had anything to do with tourism, allowed him to become a Shubert-like mogul himself in what was essentially virgin theatrical turf.

In another legacy of his Shubert years, he chose to incorporate as the Kenley Players, a name that originated while still casting for the Shuberts. "Every actor that came to New York had to come through me," he claimed, "so we used to all lunch together at Gilhooley's—Sardi's was too expensive. We'd walk together down Shubert Alley and call ourselves the Kenley Players, and I've used that name ever since." It served him well since he never owned a theatre, but the name, which he patented, would travel with him from venue to venue. Rather than purchasing playhouses, he would negotiate long-term lease agreements that freed him from the exigencies of building upkeep, particularly since he was in residence only three or four months. In Ohio and Michigan, where he rented large civic auditoriums and music halls, the building managements were happy to have Kenley for several lucrative months each summer, and equally happy to be able to rent to other producers during the rest of the year. This scheme also allowed Kenley to maintain his identity, no matter where his company was playing. "If my name were attached to a theatre building, I'd have lost it over and over," Kenley commented, "whereas everyone knew and respected the Kenley Players, wherever they appeared."[38]

Kenley was anything but an ordinary businessman, even among theatrical producers who were known for their eccentricities. He delights in tales of wild irregularities, which, particularly in the early years in Pennsylvania, helped to build his reputation into legendary proportions. As his empire grew, he necessarily became more conventional in his mode of operation, but the devil-may-care philosophy that distinguished his beginnings always lingered; in short, Kenley loved to be outrageous. "I did not have a bank account in my first years," Kenley reminisced, "so I operated on a cash basis, including paying my stars." The admission price to his first theatre was 99 cents a seat, so a star earning $500 a week would "end up with nearly 500 pieces of paper" to take home. He'd hide his earnings under the mattress of one of his female stars, selected because she was "one of the few who didn't sleep around." "I wouldn't tell her," he'd chuckle. "I'd just slip into her room in the morning and reach under her mattress and get the money to open up the box office. She slept soundly." He also loves to tell the story of Edward Everett Horton, whose $1,000 salary was paid in ones, fives, and a few tens. Horton stuffed the money in his socks and dashed back to New York City to join his friends at the Stork Club before it closed. "When the check was presented to Mr. Horton he created a panic of laughter (he loved laughter) getting the money out of his socks in that most elegant nightclub, to pay his check."[39]

Virtually everyone who worked for Kenley was a relative, and those who were not were trusted employees who became part of his extended family. As such, all the official personnel were fiercely loyal and of a like mind in protecting their mutual interests. Kenley's propensity to hire only bona fide and "adopted" family also allowed him to remain exclusively in charge of all aspects of his operations. Anyone who disagreed with him or tried to exert his or her own managerial or artistic will did not stay in Kenley's employ for long. He particularly had problems with directors and choreographers who insisted on stamping his productions with their own artistic imprint. Eventually, he made his longtime stage manager, Leslie Cutler, into his resident director as well, since his idea of directing was that "everyone put their hands in it."[40] No one's hand was more firmly entrenched than Kenley's, however, since he would never hesitate to offer his "suggestions" to whomever he felt required them, and Cutler, apparently, would willingly take them "in stride." Kenley would cast the plays and watch rehearsals from his box office window. "If all went well," he said, "I went back to selling tickets. Otherwise, I would come in and ADJUST" (capitals original).[41]

The most extraordinary of Kenley's business practices, which some, including the governing board of the Council of Stock Theatres (COST), would term egregious, was his hiring and handling of stars. Not only did he pay them exorbitant salaries of up to $30,000 per week (which, at one point, provoked COST to expel him from the organization), but he pampered them, both personally and professionally, to excess.[42] It is a tribute to the thousands of people who worked for Kenley in his 40-odd years as a producer that they endured such behavior, yet Kenley treated all of his employees well, particularly the resident actors who, for their considerable troubles in service of the stars, were paid reasonably above Equity minimums. Everyone must have ascribed to Kenley's philosophy that without the stars they all would have been out of work.

"I've never met a star, bad or indifferent, mean or sweet, that didn't deserve to be a star," Kenley contended. "They all had something very special that attracted audiences, as well as stamina and a certain ruthlessness." His definition of a star was someone whose name was "a household word," which largely meant television and, secondarily, movie personalities, and whose appearance would prompt long lines at the box office. Their talent and technical abilities as performers were immaterial since his resident company was prepared to do anything to ensure a smooth production. As Kenley told one reporter, "to make a star look good you have to have supporting actors who can pitch lines at them so well they can't miss."[43] Kenley's favorite example of his stock company salvaging a performance was when Zasu Pitts was engaged to star in a mystery thriller, *The Bat*. Pitts was a popular comedienne whose trademark was fluttering hands and a dejected expression, and Kenley thought she was perfect to play the part of the screaming, frightened maid trapped in a spooky house. For reasons known only to her, she did not arrive at the theatre until two hours before opening; she also had not read the script until earlier that afternoon. As Kenley described it:

> We had a very fast run-through. The curtain went up at eight thirty and she was pushed around the stage by Tom Poston [a member of the resident company]. All she did was scream during the entire show. Lines she was to speak were uttered by my fine stock actors in the third person. She emerged a hit. The audience thought she was great. Talk about surprises. At one point she mixed up the plot whereby the Bat actually did not have any place to exit. Tom Poston, who was playing the Bat, leaped into the audience and exited through my box office.[44]

Since Kenley's audiences came to his theatres to see their favorite stars in person, he gave them as much exposure to the star as possible by rewriting scripts, adding musical numbers, and giving them leading roles that were not necessarily suited to them. Needless to say, Kenley's shows were not known for their artistic integrity nor, necessarily, their quality. A unified production was not Kenley's priority because audiences intent on seeing the star were not all that interested in the rest of the show. They also were displeased if the star spent too much time offstage; hence, "adjustments," as only Kenley would concoct them, would be made. Kenley understood that all stars were not equal, however, and he had a remarkable ability to assess the drawing power of a particular star and would fix her or his salary based upon his estimated audience response. He could justify the $30,000 he paid Paul Lynde, Burt Reynolds, and Henry Winkler because they would draw capacity crowds, but most stars would earn far less, usually between $5,000 and $15,000 per week, because their audience appeal was somewhat less.[45] By any assessment, however, his stars were well paid and were expected to do little more than sell tickets. He also treated them regally off the stage, happily catering to their every whim. Many of these whims have afforded him a multitude of scandalous tales, with which, in the retelling, he gleefully attempts to shock his listeners. For Kenley, this was just part of the "showbiz" he made his life's work.[46]

The New London Barn Playhouse—"Hey, Kids, Let's Put on a Show!"

On yet another extreme of the theatrical spectrum is Norman Leger's charming barn theatre in the lake region of central New Hampshire. Because Leger, like Kenley, believes in operating his theatre as an independent, commercial venture, he would never have entertained the idea of subsidy. "Back in 1955 when we bought the theatre," Leger reminisced, "it never occurred to us to set up as a nonprofit." His perspectives on functioning within the not-for-profit universe are shared by many producers who relish their autonomy: "If you are nonprofit and you have a board, you need to deal with them. If it's a puppet board that's fine, but how long will they remain a puppet board? Because things can change, and you have people on the board saying, 'Norman, now you've done these musical comedies and this commercial stuff long enough. We've got to start doing Shakespeare.' I'm convinced that if the wrong management took over this theatre, it could be a dead issue in two or three years."[47] Since Leger, like Kenley, was dependent on box office revenue, they shared a basic philosophy of providing entertainment for the public and, not surprisingly, produced the same sorts of musicals and light comedies. The comparison stopped there, however. Leger eschewed both stars and Actors' Equity, except for the occasional guest artist (never a star) when he lacked a suitable lead in his young but enormously gifted resident company. Instead, he created the iconographic Mickey Rooney/Judy Garland summer stock experience of "hey, kids, let's put on a show!" that heretofore had existed only in the movies. The formula worked, attracting both the local and summertime populations in and around New London, and continues to thrive into the twenty-first century.

Leger's theatre is a nineteenth-century barn, which still exudes a beautiful rusticity that bespeaks an earlier century and thrives on the youth, energy, and exuberance of the young people who, metaphorically speaking, are "hoofin' in the hay." "These kids are good singers and dancers," Leger contends, "but even in the years when they weren't such good performers it was still their enthusiasm and energy that made the shows work. Audiences would say, 'They're having such a good time,' and they truly were. And that's what we capitalize on."[48] Almost all are either recent college graduates or are still in their junior or senior years with majors in theatre, music, or dance. They are selected principally from New York and regional auditions that cater to young performers seeking their first professional experience. All are considered interns, but they do receive a nominal weekly stipend plus room and board. They are housed in an old Greek revival style house adjacent to the theatre in men's and women's dormitories, with beds arrayed in double-layered berths that emulate the sleeping compartments in old railroad cars. There is a company cook and hired kitchen help, but otherwise the actors do everything for themselves, including putting in hours building and painting scenery, sewing costumes, doing publicity, and learning all facets of theatre production. It's a close-knit group that does everything together, including their laundry, which turns into a weekly party because the local laundromat opens specially for them between 11 P.M. and 1 A.M. on Friday nights. The company brings food, drinks, and music and "has a grand time entertaining each other as the washing and drying machines whirl."[49]

In addition to performing musicals and comedies in the evenings, the troupe presents daytime children's theatre throughout the summer. For most summer stock operations from the 1950s onward, children's programming became a standard component of the theatre's redefinition, for several reasons. "When we started it we thought we were doing it as a service to the public," Leger recalled, and indeed it strengthens the theatre's ties with the community and helps to build an audience, not only for the young people's shows but for the adult theatre as well. The parents become interested in attending the regular season and, once their children are old enough, they bring them along at night. Leger also has the acting company meet with the children after the performances; the actors hand out candy, sign autographs, answer questions, and help the kids distinguish between the actors themselves and the characters they portray. These are worthy rationales for doing children's theatre, but as Leger noted, they are not the only ones: "You can't ignore the money. We sell out two shows a day, and that brings in an additional $1,500, which is a nice amount of money that is particularly valuable when you're not doing as well with the evening shows as you would like."[50]

Whether a playhouse is commercial or not-for-profit, the subscribers are always the core of its audience and bank account. "They're the base of your support," Leger attests, "because they pay in advance and you know you've got that audience coming to the shows. They're a godsend to the theatre." Leger and his staff worked hard to boost the subscribers from fewer than a hundred to more than a thousand in the late 1980s by more accurately gauging the tastes and temperaments of New Londoners and planning the seasons' offerings accordingly. In a playbill article that describes the play selection process, Leger answers the question "How does a title get on the Players' schedule?":

> The answer is—whatever is adjudged by the producers as a title which the audiences want to see. Not "should see," mind you. Or "must see." The path to ruination, as anyone can guess, is scattered with titles which the audience "should see" or "must see," and those plays were probably fraught with "messages" in the content of the play. This particular producer has gotten *this* message after thirty-odd summers of producing: the man in the audience wants to see that which he finds the most entertaining. [emphasis original][51]

Leger admits that making that determination is no easy task and that he's made plenty of mistakes over the years. Knowing that his audiences had enjoyed Neil Simon's comedies in the past, Leger scheduled *California Suite* one summer. "The subsequent letters and phone calls made a startlingly clear and strong statement that the language used and the sometimes raunchy, often-times off-beat, humor of this three-taled comedy were offensive to our audience," he wrote.[52] He had similar problems with *A Chorus Line*, which he produced twice. The first time he did the script as written, a decision that generated an even greater volume of hate mail than elicited by *California Suite*. For the second production, all offensive language was expurgated from the show. "Audiences don't like the character if she or he uses strong language, especially 'the f word,' and particularly when it is said by a woman. Even worse, they tend to associate the character with the actor and when she comes off stage, she is looked at negatively."[53] Since the actors are in residence for the entire summer, the dislike can extend from one show to the next, which creates an uncomfortable situation for performers. Leger believes that his young actors deserve a positive experience, so he avoids subjecting them to potentially volatile situations.

Besides choosing his season cautiously, Leger further attracts his audience by offering a friendly, homespun ambience that "breaks down the formality of going to the theatre." Maintaining the rustic patina of the 150-year-old barn helps enormously. "This is a very informal theatre and just walking into the barn itself will give that to you," he says. He also sets up his support personnel along the path the audience takes to enter the theatre to help remove any remaining formality. Patrons first encounter "the hospital ladies selling pillow cushions for 5 cents," with all proceeds going to the local hospital charity. This tradition, begun when the theatre opened in 1933, is maintained to this day "and the pillows still cost only a nickel," Leger laughingly contends. The second breakdown occurs at the box office where the staff are primed to be friendly and chatty. Then, a cowbell, chosen from Leger's considerable collection, is rung to let the patrons know that the show is about to begin. The patrons enter the auditorium to encounter their friend, neighbor, or neighbor's child ushering them to their seats. "By the time they get to the seat, they've gone through this whole series of situations that break down the formality of the theatre. It's one of our great charms, and we've been very careful never to change that," he said.[54]

The informality and rusticity of the barn extends to the stage presentations as well. The locus of the show is the acting company, and it truly is their exuberance that makes the production successful. In keeping with the "hey, kids, let's put on a show" philosophy, sets, costumes, lighting, and other appurtenances of production are serviceable but remain in the background because the show is about the energy and talent of the young performers, who more than adequately fill the stage with their enthusiasm. Furthermore, there is no amplification; the actors employ old-fashioned projection techniques to be heard and, in old-style trouper fashion, remain undaunted by little things that may go amiss. During a 1993 performance of *Seven Brides for Seven Brothers*, the zipper popped on the dress of one of the leading ladies. Although she literally was falling out of her costume (since the show was set at the turn of the twentieth century, her flesh was completely covered), she kept singing and dancing through lively production numbers without missing a beat. Judy and Mickey, no doubt, would have been very proud, and certainly producer Norman Leger could not have been happier.

The Williamstown Theatre Festival—The French Restaurant Amid the Pizza Parlors

"We are not summer stock—we are a festival," declared Nikos Psacharopoulos, the man whose vision and energy commanded the Williamstown Theatre

Festival (WTF) for 33 years. "If you put twenty pizza parlors in a block and right in the middle open a French restaurant, you'll get people to come to it," he offered by way of analogy, adding that "last year 44,000 people came. We've created a habit, like a museum. Audiences know they can count on the caliber and depth of the company and the quality of the plays."[55]

Psacharopoulos's assessment is correct—WTF is not a summer stock theatre, nor, other than during its first season in 1955, could it ever have been classified as such, but it is probably America's most widely known and respected theatre to operate exclusively in summer. When he assumed the executive directorship at the beginning of its second year, WTF became a professional enclave for graduates of the Yale School of Drama, most of whom already were or were about to become major forces in the American theatre, including, of course, Psacharopoulos (known to one and all as "Nikos") himself. Soon WTF garnered a reputation as an actor's theatre that draws the finest talents from across the country to work for minimum wage in a small college town in northwestern Massachusetts. They are attracted by the repertory, which specializes in what Nikos termed "the modern classics"— Chekhov, Shaw, Brecht, Williams, and other playwrights of that caliber—and premieres of new works by recognized dramatists. The resident company, which includes directors, designers, and technicians as well as actors, numbers about 250 a season. The majority are well-known theatre artists, but none are billed or paid as stars. To enumerate just a few—Kate Burton, Dick Cavett, John Conklin, Blythe Danner, Colleen Dewhurst, Olympia Dukakis, Mildred Dunnock, Richard Easton, Geraldine Fitzgerald, Holly Hunter, Bill Irwin, Frank Langella, Santo Loquasto, Mary Tyler Moore, Carrie Nye, Maureen O'Sullivan, Austin Pendleton, Gwenyth Paltrow, Christopher Reeve, Rex Robbins, Ron Rifkin, Marian Seldes, Maria Tucci, Christopher Walken, Sam Waterston, Sigourney Weaver, and Joanne Woodward— demonstrates the extraordinary range of talent that is typical of any WTF season. Furthermore, many of these artists return year after year, presumably because it provides a one-of-a-kind retreat from commercial entertainment or, as actor Richard Thomas termed it, "a working sanitarium" where "you just put yourself in high gear and get ready for highly concentrated work."[56] "We do things here they can't do anywhere else," Nikos told one reporter in 1972. "Take Rex Robbins. He earns $50,000 a year doing television commercials—he grimaced—for Cool-Whip, for Safeguard that you put under your arms, for Timex watches, but artistically he is going dry. He is happy to spend six weeks here for practically no money to be an actor again."[57] Summer stock, even extraordinary summer stock, Williamstown is not.

Although WTF produces plays only in summer, its mode of operation is more akin to what is now classified as a resident nonprofit professional or regional theatre. When WTF was founded in 1955, the regional theatre movement was in its infancy and there were only a handful of such enterprising independent playhouses scattered across the country, all of which had full 9- or 10-month seasons between September and June. Generally, they took the summer off, whereas Williamstown simply reverses the timetable to three months on and nine off, thus affording artists the time to make money elsewhere so they can afford to return to WTF the following summer. The Antoinette Perry (Tony) award committee apparently agrees with this classification since WTF was afforded the prestigious Regional Theatre Tony Award in 2002, presented annually to a theatre company based outside of New York City that has displayed a continuous level of artistic achievement contributing to the growth of theatre nationally. Even though few regional theatres can boast as exemplary a list of alumni, WTF's season of main stage and second stage productions, supplemented with cabaret shows, new play readings, experimental pieces, children's theatre, lectures, postperformance discussions and special events, is typical of regional houses, as is the theatre's status as a not-for-profit institution. The big difference, of course, is that Williamstown compresses it all into three short months of intense activity.

WTF was conceived not by theatre people but by members of Williamstown's Board of Trade who were attempting to lure tourists to their sleepy but charming hamlet in the Berkshire mountains during the summer months when its only claim to fame—the prestigious campus in the center of town, Williams College—was on holiday. Not far to the south, there was a mecca of artistic enclaves that attracted visitors by the thousands, notably the Tanglewood Music Festival, which was the summer home of the Boston Symphony Orchestra; Jacob's Pillow, the nation's most prestigious summer venue for visiting national and international dance companies; and the Berkshire Playhouse in Stockbridge, a venerable summer stock theatre. A casual remark during a board meeting prompted Ralph Renzi, then news director for Williams College, to write a series of articles in the *Berkshire Eagle* championing the idea of a summer theatre. The Board of Trade responded by raising $9,653 as seed money and on 19 November 1954, the new playhouse was incorporated as the Williamstown Theatre Foundation, Inc. The foundation joined forces with Williams College, which provided the venue—the 479-seat Adams Memorial Theatre—dormitory and office space, and, initially, the personnel, and the theatre opened the following summer.[58]

The premiere summer season was run by David Bryant, the head of the Williams College theatre department. Although the quality of work was uneven, the choice of repertory proved that Williamstown could attract audiences to support serious theatre in the summer months. Although Bryant left the college shortly thereafter, his lasting legacy to WTF was to hire Nikos Psacharopoulos, a graduate student at the Yale School of Drama, who served as Bryant's associate during the first season. Upon his resignation, Nikos immediately was offered the position of executive director with the full commendation of the board, and his contract would be renewed annually for the next 33 years. His first request—to "bring a few friends from Yale" to work with him—was heartily granted, and the theatre began to be reshaped in Nikos's image.[59] From then on, the names Williamstown Theatre Festival and Nikos Psacharopoulos were inextricably entwined, and even after his death in 1989, his indelible imprint remained. A reporter, writing in commemoration of the theatre's twenty-fifth anniversary, described his influence on the theatre, a narrative as interesting for its perspective on what the writer characterizes as "traditional summer stock" as on Nikos himself:

> Two qualities mark Nikos's years with the theater. He will not compromise his basic philosophy of presenting the best plays. There is no interest in the commercial approach of traditional summer stock with the traveling big names appearing in second rate productions of light, unmeaningful offerings. The reputation of the theater, and the executive director's, was built on the standard of excellence and sophistication. Second, Nikos has that highly desirable ability of being able to watch over every facet of what goes on inside the Adams Memorial Theatre. He is watchdog of the dollar, he is fund raiser, he knows the value of good publicity. In short, he is the ideal combination of artist and businessman. Add to that the fact that he is a task-master, demanding every ounce from his colleagues and giving an ounce and a half in return.[60]

After his death, Nikos's longtime dramaturge, Steve Lawson, published a tribute in the *New York Times*, which not only concurs with the above but indicates that things never changed. Nikos "wasn't an easy man," Lawson declared, describing him as "a blend of Max Reinhardt, Ivan the Terrible, and P. T. Barnum." Yet, he inspired great loyalty, and many artists kept returning for the privilege of working within the special environment he had created. Lawson quotes Peter Hunt, Nikos's associate of 33 years, as saying: "We mostly yelled at each other. But it was so damned stimulating! He was like Toscanini; you never played as well with anyone else." Santo Loquasto, who had been designing for WTF since 1965, told Lawson: "It's *impossible* what Nikos asked you to do. He got you so excited about a project, you couldn't disappoint him—or yourself."[61] Actors also were fiercely loyal and, despite lack of billing and very little pay, would frequently drop everything and come whenever he called. "Nikos was notorious for calling on a Sunday," actor Dwight Schultz told a reporter, "and saying, 'Be here on Monday.' And you simply didn't question it—you went. Because not only were the productions of an exceptionally high caliber, but Nikos was so very actor-oriented. He hired actors first and then produced a season."[62]

Nikos's propensity for making WTF an actor-driven theatre also made the season's schedule a bit erratic since shows and personnel would change, perhaps more than once, in the eleventh hour. Although as Lawson commented, this habit "drove press and box office people to drink," Nikos considered it one of the great allures of Williamstown. "When I do announce [the season], everyone is eager to hear, anxious to buy our tickets. Nor is anyone surprised when I switch a show, as I did last season with *Sherlock Holmes*. On a Wednesday night, I knew we could extend it for a week. Thirty thousand flyers went out, ads appeared in all the papers, we set up phone banks to reshuffle all the tickets, and by the next Wednesday we were sold out." Tom Fontana, a playwright who served as Nikos's assistant in the late 1970s, declared that "all of the juggling, the changes, are part of what makes this place so different. Here you have elasticity. You know if something better comes along—he'll do it."[63]

Nikos died just before the theatre's thirty-fifth anniversary season and, as is typical at all theatres where the spirit of one individual predominates, difficulties ensued. Actor and director Austin Pendleton, who started at Williamstown in 1955 and who has returned perennially, described the effect of his death on the theatre as "like throwing a piece of meat to the dogs," and it took several seasons for the theatre to reestablish equilibrium. Michael Ritchie, who had served WTF as a stage manager for many seasons, was named producer in 1996, and he continues to hold the post. Although WTF continues to evolve, as any successful theatre will, it is still very much the house that Nikos built. Although it lacks the all-consuming dominance of a single personality, it thrives on the panoply of guest artists who share Nikos's values and may well be, as Frank Langella asserted, "the closest thing we have to an American repertory theater in this country."[64]

Still Here: Summer Stock in the Twenty-First Century

"I'm Still Here" from Stephen Sondheim's musical *Follies* has become the anthem of survival in the American theatre, where, for almost all artists, careers have swung capriciously from stellar success to unemployment through just getting by. That syncopation has been the rhythm for summer stock, which, despite the vicissitudes of entertainment tastes and economics, has managed to persevere into the twenty-first century. There are not as many venues as there were in the golden age from the 1930s through 1960s, but the form survives. There even have been a few new ventures, such as the Arundel Barn Theatre in Maine, which was launched in 1998 with a full awareness of the precarious nature of the business. The need to entertain and to be entertained is fundamental to human experience, and where the need appears to be unfilled, artists always will attempt to satisfy it.

The 2003 edition of *Summer Theatre Directory*, an annual publication of Theatre Directories of Dorset, Vermont, lists employment opportunities at more than 350 venues that offer theatrical entertainment in the United States during the summer months. From an assessment of their operating style, advertised season, and full-time personnel, 93 of these could be loosely characterized as summer stock, although very few maintain resident companies. Another 103 offer a wide variety of legitimate theatre experiences in large musical arenas and opera houses, outdoor theatres, showboats, and as summer extensions of university training programs, but are not stock operations per se. There are 25 historic and/or religious dramas and pageants; 47 three-quarter- or full-year operations that offer special programs in the summer; 34 Shakespeare festivals; 19 theatres that provide scripted entertainments in amusement parks; and four Renaissance fairs. The remaining venues are on cruise ships, which largely operate throughout the year and hence are not strictly summer theatres.

If one considers these statistics solely in terms of summertime employment opportunities for theatre artists, the numbers have not changed much since the 1950s. The fact that nearly 100 still function as a form of traditional stock is significant and indicative of the fact that the form, despite the hardships, will not easily go away. Why is that so? In order to answer that question, it's useful to investigate three stock theatres that are functioning successfully in 2003. One is a pioneer summer stock theatre, which has both financially and artistically reinvented itself to return to its original principles. The second, founded in 1950 in the midst of summer stock's prime, has maintained a steady development via superior management, consistent artistic excellence, and a transformation from commercial to not-for-profit status. The last is the newest summer stock theatre in the country, founded just six years ago and situated, in the grand tradition of the form, in a nineteenth-century barn, which, given the challenges of renovating old agricultural structures for public assembly in the late twentieth century, was a considerable feat.

The Westport Country Playhouse, Westport, Connecticut

In the fall of 2002, the name "Westport Country Playhouse" was emblazoned on the marquee of Broadway's Booth Theatre on West Forty-Fifth Street as the sole producer of a revival of Thornton Wilder's *Our Town* starring Paul Newman. The show, which was the opening production of the theatre's 2002 summer season, featured a distinguished roster of actors in addition to Mr. Newman—Frank Converse, Jane Curtin, Jeffrey DeMunn, Mia Dillon, and Stephen Spinella—and played to 97 percent capacity during its nine-week run in New York. It was subsequently videotaped for the cable network Showtime and the *Masterpiece Theatre American Collection* series for television viewings in 2003. "One of the strong reasons that we felt this transfer was important was that we wanted to be thought of as a theatre on the edge," said Anne Keefe, Westport's associate artistic director. "We wanted to propel a change in the caliber of scripts and artists that would come to us if we got this kind of national and, indeed, international exposure. We want to get offered the good scripts immediately, not after the Manhattan Theatre Club, Playwrights' Horizons, Williamstown, and every other New York producer has gotten them first." Playhouse Executive Director Alison Harris concurred: "It's a great time to be picking plays and looking for directors, designers, and actors, when they see the excellence of our work on Broadway. *Our Town* at the Booth is exactly the same production we did here. So we can tell them that if you come to work at Westport, this is the caliber of work you can expect."[1]

Harris characterizes Westport as "the oldest living emerging theatre," which is a good way of describing a distinguished American theatre that is attempting to return to its roots. As discussed in chapter 5, the Westport Country Playhouse was founded by one of the most prestigious theatre producers of the twentieth century, Lawrence Langner, and his wife, actress and playwright Armina Marshall, as a summer tryout house for the Theatre Guild, New York's famed enterprise dedicated to premiering significant European plays in America and, later, the works of emerging American dramatists. The current artistic director, actress and director Joanne Woodward, envisions the new Westport as "picking up where Lawrence and Armina started in 1931." "There's a link here," she noted, "because they gave Paul (Newman, her husband) and me our first job. We were in *Picnic* in 1953, which was a Theatre Guild production. And then of course we knew them and we used to see them when we moved up here in the '60s." Woodward recalled the pair fondly: "I loved their whole feeling about theatre—they had such enthusiasm for it. When you read Lawrence's memoirs about the beginnings of this place, it just sounded like such fun. A group of all these actors saying, 'let's buy a barn and we'll have a theatre, and we'll do all the plays we want to do, and we'll write plays and have a great time.' I think that's a good thought. And that kind of thought can enthuse the audience about the theatre instead of just saying, 'here we have another comedy.' "[2] Despite her admiration for Langner and Marshall and their theatre, Woodward never had any ambition to take over the theatre herself. "Never in my wildest imagination did I think I'd ever do something like this," Woodward laughed, contending that "nothing motivated me to take this on—I simply was dragged into it." As a longtime resident of Westport, she knew the theatre well, although she had never worked there. When the previous executive director, James B. McKenzie, announced his retirement in 2000, the town grew concerned that the playhouse might forcibly be retired with him. Rumors abounded about developers eyeing the property in central Westport, just off the Boston Post Road, as a prime piece of real estate that could be far more lucrative as a shopping mall than as a summer stock theatre. Woodward was asked by a community leader to lend her expertise as an advisor to the playhouse, and she in turn asked her old friend Anne Keefe, a seasoned stage manager, to join her. Both assumed that their roles were limited to "helping out." Soon they were asked to join the board of directors of the Connecticut Theatre Foundation, which actually owns the property and, shortly thereafter, they were at the artistic helm. "There was a really strong board, a committed board, that wanted to take that next step," Keefe said, "and it was very appealing. We weren't just playing at it. I don't think any other summer theatre has as strong a board as we do, except, perhaps, for Williamstown."[3]

McKenzie had been running the theatre since 1959 when he and two other men, Henry Weinstein and Lawrence Feldman, leased the property from Lawrence Langner's son Philip, who had become managing director in 1951. Within a few years McKenzie had become the sole producer, and he kept the theatre going for the next 41 years. He focused on attracting the affluent local populace, aged "between fifty and death," to the theatre via a soupcon of "entertainment and light message theatre." "This is not an experimental audience," McKenzie said in a 1992 interview. "They are success-oriented people and they want to be re-affirmed in that success." Hence, he kept the repertoire fairly light, avoiding plays that dealt with race or explicit sex or that employed foul language. He also made certain that the audience didn't sit longer than one hour at a stretch and could get home early with very little inconvenience. He employed lots of star performers, particularly those known to audiences from television and films, and ran what he called "an old-fashioned summer theatre." Many of the shows produced at Westport also traveled the COST (Council of Stock Theatres) circuit throughout New England, which in the 1960s numbered 52 theatres; he would round out his season by booking in shows produced at member houses. By 1992, there were only three remaining theatres on the circuit—Westport, Ogunquit, and Dennis—and McKenzie was forced to produce a lot more plays than he desired. "We didn't start out as institutions," he contended, "we were just fly-by-night summer theatres. This is now an institution but only by accident. Nobody set out to create an institution here."[4]

Harris has great admiration for McKenzie's stewardship of the playhouse, although his producing philosophy was far different than hers. "It had been run very much as a seat-of-your-pants operation," she said, where "cash comes in and you spend it, and then cash goes out. When you run out of money, you stop doing things and then you wait for more cash." Like other summer stock producers, McKenzie "didn't want to be burdened by the pressures that are brought to bear by donors" or by a board telling him how to run his business. "He wanted to be the sole producer, pick the material, and do what he thought was good," Harris maintains, "and the box office would show he was right and by and large, it was right, because he kept the place running." Keefe agreed, adding that although Westport audiences recently had begun to demand a bit more challenging material, there always remained "the truth" about summer theatre. "It's the summer, it should be entertainment, it should be enjoyable," Keefe said, "and there's always an element here that demands that. It's almost as though they are saying, 'We'll do our thinking at the regional theatres during the winter—please don't make us work too hard in summer.' "[5]

Despite this predilection, the new female triumvirate—actually a tetrarchy since board president Elisabeth Morten, has been a potent force in reshaping the theatre's future—is trying to move Westport's loyal audience into slightly deeper waters with a repertoire of plays that will challenge audiences without making them feel uncomfortable. "I do want to stir their heads up a bit and give them a surprise or two," Woodward said. Although audiences were mixed on what they liked and didn't in recent seasons, they were largely supportive and willing to give the new repertoire a chance. "If you come out of the theatre and you don't talk about what you saw," Woodward said, "it's hard to say that *that's* theatre. I like it when there are arguments and people are vigorously disagreeing—that's how it should be."[6] Westport also is reviving some mainstays of the traditional summer stock repertoire—well-made plays of the 1920s through '40s—that are a personal favorite of Woodward's. In addition to *Our Town*, recent seasons have included Sutton Vane's *Outward Bound*, John Van Druten's *The Voice of the Turtle*, and Arthur Miller's *All My Sons*.

The biggest change at Westport, however, will be the playhouse itself. The theatre is closing for extensive renovations and will reopen in summer 2005 to celebrate the seventy-fifth anniversary season. The stated objective of the plan is "to create a performance facility to fully support the revitalized artistic and educational mission of the Westport Country Playhouse while retaining the character and spirit of the historic Playhouse."[7] This will be realized by a major overhaul of the backstage, lobby, and orchestra areas of the playhouse, while keeping the look of an old red New England farm barn with a charming wrap-around white porch. It will be larger and there will be more and improved outbuildings housing a scene shop, rehearsal hall, and administrative offices, but the ambience will remain intact. "It's very important to Joanne that we preserve that," according to Harris and Keefe.[8] "I don't want any of it to be a modern, shiny, shiny thing," Woodward insists, "because that has nothing to do with the kind of theatre I think of when I think of summer theatre." Everyone agrees that the theatre needs serious work, since it virtually hasn't changed at all since it was built in 1931. Langner never improved it, and McKenzie claimed "all I did was take over and try to keep it the same, which was my own peculiarity. So, now we're sitting here with this antiquity."[9] Since the "antiquity" isn't up to code in some places and is literally falling down in others, the renovation is more a necessity than a choice. Also, although plans call for it to remain a summer theatre, the building is to be winterized and to have the potential for year-round programming. As Harris says:

> We're not preserving the building, because it's just too decrepit, it's too far gone. But what we are preserving is the heritage of the playhouse and the spirit of the playhouse and the ghosts of the playhouse. And the spirit of Lawrence Langner who cast this as a bold experiment. He started doing really exciting theatre in the boondocks and would try out things, and that's what we want to do. So this is going back to the roots of Langner and Marshall, and we want to express that and not be a modern fancy glass-and-steel theatre.[10]

"Joanne wants to revitalize the Westport Country Playhouse and bring it back to what it was in its heyday," Harris avers. "We want to put on our own artistic stamp, but we want it to be just as good."[11]

Totem Pole Playhouse, Fayetteville, Pennsylvania

"Why would anyone want to start a theatre here? What were they thinking?" chimed Carl Schurr and Wil Love, artistic and associate artistic directors, respectively, of the Totem Pole Playhouse in south central Pennsylvania. Despite its proximity to major urban areas—the theatre is one and a half hours from Baltimore, two hours from Washington, D.C., an hour south of Harrisburg, and three hours from Philadelphia—it is situated in a conservative rural area that theatre staffers characterize as the northern tip of the Bible Belt. "We have to be very cautious about what we do here," Schurr said. "We can say 'God' and we can say 'damn,' but we can't say the two words together. We can't say 'Jesus.' We can say 'horseshit,' because that's natural around here. But we can't say the f-word because people will walk out or else just shut down and not listen anymore." Even though planning the season is challenging, since so many contemporary plays are, thanks to their vocabulary, automatically rejected, both directors adore working there and would not want to spend their summers anywhere else. "Audiences respond very well here," Love affirms. "If a comedy is really clicking with them, they just scream and howl. And I think, 'My God, I don't get this response in city theatres.'" Moreover, the playhouse is located in Caledonia State Park, an idyllic woodland that the two men refer to as "the enchanted forest." "We gather together all these talented people, in whom we really believe, to come play in the woods—to play on stage and play a bit offstage. What could be better?"[12]

The answer to the question "Why here?" lies in the early history of summer stock when transportation companies created public parks to lure urban dwellers to the great outdoors. As described in chapter 1, the development of American trolleys, amusement parks, and the first summer theatres happened concurrently in many locales when the parks sought to offer additional entertainments to attract customers. Before it was purchased by the Commonwealth of Pennsylvania, Caledonia was owned by the Cumberland Valley Railroad, which ran an electric streetcar line between the park and the towns of Chambersburg and Shippensburg, Pennsylvania. For 25 cents, round-trip, pleasure seekers could go to the park to enjoy a day's outing, as well as an evening visit to the dance hall. The idea of creating a theatre, however, came relatively late to the area when, in 1950, a group of 13 local businessmen decided to open a theatre in a converted garage at Gardener, Pennsylvania, the following summer. In 1952, they incorporated as the Totem Pole Playhouse (TPP) and moved to the old dance hall in the park, which they duly converted into a playhouse. Their first director was Karl Genus, of the Harrisburg Community Theatre, who mounted productions for the first three seasons. When Genus decided to move on to other ventures, they advertised for a replacement and found the ideal candidate in a recent theatre graduate of Carnegie Institute of Technology, William H. Putch.[13] Putch rented the theatre from the TPP for 10 cents a ticket and quickly transformed the playhouse into an active one-a-week stock venue that became known as "the Cadillac of summer theatres."[14]

Putch was another of the classic summer stock producers who did it all—producing, directing, acting, designing, box office, technical work, marketing, public relations, and being on hand to greet the audience at every performance for his nightly curtain speech. "What Bill did as one person, now takes three or four," Wil Love commented after his death.[15] Within a few years of his arriving at Totem Pole, Putch committed himself to becoming a part of the community, and the theatre became his life. He brought his wife, actress Jean Stapleton, and their two children there every summer for 30 years and he spent much of the rest of the year at their home in Fayetteville planning the subsequent season. "I married a summer theatre," Stapleton told a reporter for *People* magazine,[16] and in her son John's documentary film of Putch's life, she described the dedication he demanded: "I used to do the payroll the first years I was there, and it was a very simple procedure in those days. It was early on a Friday morning that I said, 'We have to go but I haven't finished the payroll yet' and Bill said, 'wait a minute.' So, I had to finish the payroll before I went to the hospital to have our first child."[17]

Putch described his penchant for excellence and what he characterized as his summer stock philosophy in an article he wrote reflecting upon his thirtieth anniversary season. He recalled directing a new play some years earlier when one of the actresses—formerly a close friend—continued to break up during a scene, thus "ruining the true comedy" in the play and "knocking the audience out of their belief in what we were doing." After the third such incident, he stormed backstage to express his displeasure. "For God's sake, Bill, relax!" the actress told him. "It's only summer stock." Putch screamed, "Don't ever say that to me! I don't accept that! If it were only that, then there is no reason for me to come back here and do this each year." He then ordered her to "get off my stage," and they never spoke again. For Putch, "stock" was "not an obscene word nor the old cliché" that many thought it to be.[18] He was proud of his work and happy to imbue each production with what became known as the "Putch Touch," a bit of direction, acting, or stage business that character- ized the show as his own. Although it frequently involved a cheap laugh, "it almost always worked really well," recalled stage manager and designer Paul Mills Holmes, and it became one of the long-standing traditions that endeared local audiences to the playhouse.[19]

Totem Pole was a respected regional theatre that was propelled into national prominence in 1971 when Jean Stapleton became, for a time, the most well-known actress in America. The phenomenal success of the hit tele- vision series *All in the Family*, in which Stapleton played the lovable "ding- bat" wife, Edith Bunker, made her a popular interview subject for journalists, who described her long career as a working actress on Broadway, on tour, and at Totem Pole. "Although she had done at least 75 shows here before *All in the Family*, Jean really packed audiences in thereafter," Wil Love remem- bered. "In 1971, we did ten shows in 15 weeks, and she was in three of them, which were sold at 115 percent capacity," he said. "And that floated us for the rest of the season." For a time, Stapleton's fame "created the illusion that this was a star theatre, but it really wasn't; it was just a coincidence," Schurr said, adding, "it was great financially for Bill."[20] By the early 1980s, however, Putch, like other summer stock producers, began to experience monetary dif- ficulties because the daily costs of running the theatre were rising much faster than box office revenue, and he could only increase prices so much without losing his audience. He tried to convince the TPP to apply for not-for-profit status, but the stockholders would not hear of it. At the same time, Putch's health began to deteriorate, and in 1983, shortly after completing his thirtieth season, he died.

Schurr and Love, who had been with the theatre since 1971, were quickly designated the heirs to the Totem Pole directorship, and in the first season fol- lowing Putch's death, they joined forces with Putch's daughter, Pamela, in running the theatre. She left after the summer of 1984, secure in the knowledge that her trusted colleagues would ably continue her father's legacy. "The changeover went very smoothly," remarked Sue McMurtray, the theatre's managing director, "because Carl and Wil were well known to our audiences and were personal friends of the Putch family."[21] They also were committed to honoring Putch's 30-year tradition, and so introduced changes gradually. A major change that evolved out of Putch's own failed initiative was the transformation of the theatre from a commercial to a not-for-profit enterprise. "It became clear to us that there was no way, with the changing times, that this organization could continue as a profit-making venture because we weren't making a profit—in fact, we were going more into debt year after year," Schurr and Love said. In order to keep the theatre running, they floated loans against the mortgage on their Baltimore house until the banks finally told them they were seriously into debt and were no longer a good credit risk. "That's when we convinced them to form a not-for-profit corporation," Schurr said. "This was all new to these people, and they still don't understand why the theatre can't pay for itself. They just want to keep raising ticket prices. Well, that's a short-term fix, and we can't afford it around here. Every time we raise ticket—and subscription—prices, we lose subscribers."[22] Hence, Schurr and Love went to local business leaders to form the Caledonia Theatre Company, the nonprofit corporation that actually runs the theatre. In a rather complicated business arrangement, Caledonia leases the theatre from the TPP, which still owns the buildings and pays land rent to the state of Pennsylvania, and then contracts with Schurr's production company, Thunderbird Ltd., which he purchased from the Putches, to mount the theatre season. Thus, there are three governing bodies that have a controlling interest in the theatre, but ultimately the scheme works. "We're still here doing shows," Schurr proclaims, "but we wouldn't be had we not formed Caledonia. We would have been dead eight years ago. We just couldn't have gone on financially."[23]

In order to keep the theatre entrenched in the heart of the community, the playhouse mounts a wide range of activities and fundraisers each year beyond the main theatre season. There are a series of theatre camps for youth run all summer long; special Wednesday buffets under a tent erected next to the theatre which service post-matinee and pre-evening theatregoers; a "Friends of Totem Pole Playhouse" group, which provides ushers and hosts opening-night parties and other special events; an "Adopt a Barrel" initiative to pay for colorful plantings outside the theatre; an annual Fun Fest to attract families to the theatre for a picnic, games, and backstage tours just prior to the start of the summer season; special discount tickets for students on the day of the performance; weekly postshow discussions; and opportunities to make tax-deductible donations during the annual fund drive and, for as little as $10 a season, have your name printed in all the playbills. Although these types of activities are not unique to Totem Pole—most theatres, whether commercial or not-for-profit, need additional sources of revenue and support beyond ticket sales and proceeds from program advertisements—Totem Pole has an especially long and inventive list of ways to keep the community feel that this is, indeed, its very own theatre.

The spirit of community properly starts from within, and although most summer theatres profess to be close-knit family ventures, Totem Pole's camaraderie and ease of operation is truly exceptional. "This is Camp Carefree," proclaims production stage manager Paul Mills Holmes, who after 26 summers at Totem Pole described his yearly trek to Fayetteville as "coming home." "When you only have 14 weeks to mount an entire season, you have to approach it like this is going to be the best time ever. And we do."[24] Guest scenic designer Jason Rubin was impressed by the rare combination of professionalism and genial calm that pervades the working atmosphere, which is all the more unusual in a summer stock theatre where shows are mounted every other week. "They can afford this laidback schedule," Rubin claimed, "since they're on top of everything, they're ahead of schedule, and it's all working like clockwork."[25] McMurtray likens the experience of working there to being in Camelot. "I think it comes all the way from the top," she averred. "Carl is not an excitable person—he is calm. And he hires terrific people, and it all works beautifully."[26] For their part, Schurr and Love simply enjoy the opportunity to bring together an "incredibly talented" group of artists each season to "create something that wouldn't be here if we weren't doing it—high-quality professional theatre. And there are people who understand that they wouldn't have anything if we weren't here, and they are very grateful. So that makes us feel good." Both dream, however, of doing better business. "We want this to be a theatre where we're turning people away and can run plays for three weeks at S.R.O [standing room only]," they proclaim. "We sold 70 percent of our houses last summer, which certainly is respectable, but not as good as we'd like. But we're here, and the dream of more will always remain."[27]

The Arundel Barn Playhouse, Arundel, Maine

"We do fluff," announced producer Adrienne Wilson Grant. "I know we do fluff, and I love fluff."[28] Grant's primary goal in creating and operating the

Arundel Barn Playhouse was to entice people, many of whom may never have seen a live performance, to the theatre, show them a wonderful time and, consequently, instill in them a playgoing habit. "A staggering number of people in this country do not go to any live performance, ever," she laments. By offering a show that will delight rather than challenge or offend patrons and by providing a warm, welcoming environment, she believes she can attract new audiences. She particularly concentrates on groups she deems to be the hardest sells, such as men over 40 who never go to the theatre and who have no idea what to expect. Grant suspects that they don't know how to dress for the occasion and are worried that they may not like the show but will be trapped in the theatre against their will. "So, they come here and almost always enjoy both the show and the experience," she explains. "Later, they might be reading the paper and notice that Portland Stage or the University of Southern Maine is doing a play. And they might think, 'Should I go see that?' " She hopes that they not only will go but also will have deeper, more introspective theatre experiences as a consequence. "Our role is to give them the courage to take that first step, and I'm very happy with it. That's why we're here."[29]

Grant's mission may seem impossibly idealistic, but both Grant and the story of her playhouse are more the stuff of dreams than of the reality of making theatre in twenty-first century America. As a project for her retirement—she was a theatre educator and choreographer—she decided in 1997, at the age of 65, to start a summer stock theatre in a barn. Although she considered purchasing an existing theatre, she ended up creating one anew by transforming an 1888 barn into a working playhouse. As earlier chapters of this study attest, barn transformations were common occurrences in the 1920s and '30s when building materials were relatively cheap and building codes, restrictions, and inspections, at least of summer theatres, were rare. In the late twentieth century, not only were costs significantly higher, particularly to renovate old structures, but the laws governing commercial zoning, land use, and public safety had become highly restrictive. Despite all odds, Grant managed to open a fully functional, government-approved, environmentally friendly playhouse in slightly more than one year after purchasing a rundown barn and farmhouse, known locally as the Smith homestead. Furthermore, she planned and supervised the entire operation personally and paid for it with her own money. Staunchly true to summer stock tradition, the Arundel Barn Playhouse is owned and operated by a single messianic personality who runs it as a commercial, small family business. Outside of bank loans, she has had no outside funding, grants, or other monetary contributions.

"I guess I really was affected by the Judy Garland and Mickey Rooney movies," Grant reflects. "Even when I was a kid, I pretended I had their barn in my parents' garage. It had old-fashioned wooden doors that opened out, and I used to put on shows and plays there."[30] After purchasing a real, albeit dilapidated, barn and beginning to research the multifarious components of realizing her dream, she began to question her sanity. "Why did I think I could do this?" she laughed, "and why didn't I see failure as a part of this equation?" No doubt her sense of humor, tenacity, willingness to seek and respond to expert advice, and insistence on paying all bills promptly helped her to succeed remarkably quickly, since she bought the barn in April of 1997 and was open for business in June of the following year. Other than the Vermont firm, Engineering Ventures, engaged to do the renovation design, Grant hired all local craftspeople, which, it turned out, was a politic way of ingratiating herself with the community. She paid them faithfully every Friday, supported and encouraged their work throughout, and threw them a pre-opening night party at the playhouse. She also perennially reserves the two rows of balcony seats for the men who built the theatre. "Whenever they want to come, that's their private place," she avers; "we rarely ever put those seats up for sale."

A more persistent challenge was dealing with the various local, state, and federal agencies to ensure compliance with the law. "Every day it was something else," Grant said, "and most of it I did without any argument or grievance. But if something seemed wrong with what I was being required to do, I sought expert advice." A case in point was her dealings with the Maine State Water Authority, which initially insisted on an excessive number of gallons of water, determined by the number of theatre seats, to operate the flush toilets. Since there was no city sewage available, Grant had to install three cesspools and build a 70-foot leach field behind the playhouse to absorb the toilet water. She hired a soil scientist to determine the best locale for the field, and he advised her that the state was mandating more water than necessary. To make her case, Grant contacted dozens of theatres as well as their local water authorities to verify usage and did the arithmetic. She compiled a report and sent it to the state, which checked her statistics and, finding them accurate, readjusted its requirement. This was a blessing, since piping water to the theatre was a costly and difficult venture. Although the town water mains were only one-eighth of a mile away, it cost $60,000 to make the connection. This figure might have been much higher without the help of the town planner, who suggested that the theatre, which is open only in the warmest months, might be able to install a "summer water" system consisting of light pipes laid just below ground surface. This scheme saved Grant thousands of dollars by allowing her to substitute the shallowly placed "summer pipes" for the regular all-weather variety, which are not only considerably more expensive but also require installation below the frost line to combat Maine's frigid winters, which is another costly procedure.[31]

What money Grant saved on water she spent building a parking lot. This unanticipated expense—she assumed that people would simply park on the grass—was mandated per the guidelines of the Department of Environmental Protection and the Army Corps of Engineers, both of which showed up to take measurements, make recommendations, and bestow final approvals. This resulted in an intricate design to avoid disturbing the wetlands and what one journalist described as "an NFL stadium size lot" with a three-foot-deep layer of gravel.[32] During construction, she had the added cost of putting in bales of hay and plastic fences to minimize the dust blowing on to adjacent roads and private property. Finally, the town insisted that as a safety measure she install 30-foot-tall parking-lot lights, which she felt were ugly and unappealing. "I'm sure, liability-wise, it's to my benefit," she sighed.[33]

Despite unanticipated regulations and expenses, it is clear that Grant loved every minute of the building process. "I was the superintendent of the work," she proudly proclaims, "and was here at 7 A.M. before anyone else arrived. I also was the last person to leave at night." She laughs when remembering her early reputation as "the woman from New York driving the pink Cadillac" who was clearly an outsider mucking about with a beloved farm that had been in the same Yankee family for more than a hundred years. Grant rapidly proved that she was no slouch by being on site constantly, carrying lumber, and doing whatever task was at hand. She also earned the admiration and thanks of town officials who were pleased to see her create a much-needed new business in the community that was in keeping with Arundel's rustic character and dedication to the arts. "What she's doing there is contrary to so much of what we see happening along highways in southern Maine," Town Planner Roger Cole told a reporter for the *Portland Press Herald*. "She wants to preserve a barn and a farmstead and the land. A 7-Eleven could have gone in there, removed the house and the barn, and put up a 24-hour convenience store."[34] When Grant began the project, Arundel already boasted two schools focused on arts and crafts education, so the addition of a summer theatre was most welcome in enhancing its reputation as an arts center as well as its attraction to tourists.

Although the playhouse does attract vacationers, 75 percent of its audiences are Maine residents, both permanent and seasonal, from towns stretching from Kennebunk to Portland. Grant's sole year-round employee, Susan Jones, who works full-time at the theatre only during the summer months, admires what she describes as "Adrienne's knack for her audience." "There are a lot of people here who appreciate the effort she puts into this theatre," Jones attests," and they frequently stop her at the grocery store to thank her for bringing this playhouse to their community."[35] Yet, the theatre still has problems filling its 225 seats to capacity, despite positive newspaper reviews and a lot of goodwill from neighbors. After five summer seasons, Grant was still running a deficit. Advisors felt that the summer of 2002 was still experiencing the fallout from the scare of September 11, 2001, which hurt theatres all over the country. Grant spoke with one Broadway company manager who described the same ticket-buying syndrome in New York that she was experiencing in Maine. "In years past," Grant explained, "people made their plans ahead of time and made reservations over the phone. It was unusual to sell more than two tickets at the door for any performance. In 2002, we were selling lots of tickets at the door every night, and it was very stressful. We never knew whether we'd have an audience or not."[36] In preparation for the 2003 season, Grant "made economies everywhere" so that she wouldn't have to reduce the number of plays or bring in outside groups, which would be cheaper than self-producing and would cause less wear and tear to the property. She cut out all travel money, made fewer repairs to the buildings, and decided to forge ahead, scheduling such perennial favorites as *Grease* and *Godspell* in the hopes of attracting larger crowds. What she will not do is quit. "I think a lot of people who build theatres do it because they want to direct or act," Grant mused, "but that's not my bag. I could fill in for just about anyone, except the pianist, if she or he got sick, but I'm not interested in doing it otherwise. The people who work here have attached themselves to this dream and they feel that it is theirs, too. And I'll be forever grateful to them."[37]

An American Phenomenon that Is still Here

If America had learned to play by the 1930s, as Foster Dulles asserted,[38] it is still playing into the twenty-first century, and summer stock theatre continues to be one of its active playgrounds. Despite the extraordinary social, cultural, economic, and political changes of the past century, summer theatre—stock and otherwise—is still here. It also continues to be a uniquely American phenomenon: no other nation has developed an analogous entertainment. Why, in a culture that avidly seeks fresh and unusual entertainments and just as rapidly discards them as yesterday's news, has summer stock survived? Is there something so inherently American in its very nature that it has become an indestructible part of the fabric of this society, even a building block of our evolving cultural heritage? Herewith are a few ideas worth pondering.

A True American Enterprise

Although summer stock descended from the same European, and especially British, roots that were the basis for all American theatre until the mid-twentieth century, it distinguished itself as a uniquely American enterprise from its inception. It emulated the traditional structure and organization of theatrical stock and its repertoire of plays was, with few exceptions, unremarkable, consisting largely of light comedies, whodunits, and other populist fare that if not actually European in origin were American-penned imitations. What was exceptional, however, was the manner in which summer stock theatres established themselves economically and conducted business. Most were maverick operations, founded by theatre artists who either were excluded from or chose not to affiliate with the monopolistic businesses that controlled professional theatre in America. To use standard American phraseology, these men and women were independent spirits who were "bucking the system" and "doing their own thing" on the new frontier of the rural vacationlands. Although predominantly city dwellers, they learned how to cope in these rustic environments and, like true pioneers, boldly set up stakes in the artistic wilderness, using whatever structures and materials were at hand to most cheaply and expeditiously create their theatres. When the onslaught of star performers, profit-driven producers, and theatrical labor unions, all of whom were eager to capitalize on this economically successful new venture, began to impinge on their operations, they still remained independent. Although survival was a constant struggle and many theatres banded together in professional organizations like COST and CORST to help each other combat the increasing economic hardships, all ultimately remained autonomous. The model of artistic independence they established was adopted, either overtly or unconsciously, by the second wave of theatres created outside of New York's grasp, what became known as the resident or regional theatre movement. These houses, however, never attempted to survive commercially and were largely founded as not-for-profit operations. Only in the last years of the twentieth century did some summer stock producers, faced by potential bankruptcy, follow suit.

Certainly Europe had its own tradition of independent theatres that sprang up in major artistic centers in the late nineteenth and early twentieth centuries, and their proprietors were also declaring their freedom from the

prevalent theatre autocracies. These theatres, however, grew out of a desire
for artistic reform based on the massive societal changes brought on by indus-
trialization. Europe's Independent Theatre movement was also urban, experimental, and artistically confrontational, all qualities that American summer
stock was and is not. Its influence on the little theatre movement in the United
States, which in turn affected the development of summer stock, is undeniable. Here, however, the primary lesson for the summertime pioneers was
that theatres could be established and even flourish outside of the oligarchy
of show business.

A Populist Repertory

Although there were notable exceptions, the majority of summer stock theatres offered and continue to offer populist entertainments suitable to their
physical and philosophical milieu as resort venues catering to hot-weather
clientele. As Jim McKenzie, longtime producer at the Westport Country
Playhouse, described it, summer stock "is not the holy grail category of developing American art. What we do here is essentially entertain people. We give
them a reason to go out and have fun for an evening. I don't have to defend
that position. Why should I? It is a kind of theatre which is quite valid."[39]
Most of McKenzie's fellow producers shared his sentiments and focused their
concerns on high production standards rather than on an artistically adventuresome repertory. Even today, under Westport's ambitious new regime,
there is an acknowledgment that many audience members believe that "it's
the summer, it should be entertainment, it should be enjoyable."[40]

While savvy producers know what propels their audiences to the box
office, they also acknowledge the artistic yearnings of their resident companies. Bill Putch at Totem Pole regularly produced one play a season "for the
company and myself" that he knew would lose money. "You had to keep
your sanity," he would say while judiciously planning a season principally
devoted to his south-central Pennsylvania audience.[41] The continuing challenge for producers has been to remain populist while offering something of
especial artistic or social merit that justifies the time, money, and energies
expended. All of these decisions, however, hinge upon that slipperiest of
human value judgments—taste, which even among theatre people is vigorously debated. Lawrence Langner, in his early years at the helm at Westport,
humorously described the situation:

> During the first years at Westport, I always managed to lose a considerable sum
> each season, but I charged this off to personal enjoyment, and assumed that I
> would have lost considerably more had I been really interested in farming. I

produced many of the plays largely to please myself, and usually booked in plays to please that part of the audience whose taste differed from mine. I made several attempts to overcome the difficulty of operating without loss. One season George Abbott and Philip Dunning, distinguished producers of Broadway hits, shared the responsibility of the theatre with Armina and myself. They put on a play one week while I put on a play the next week. During the rehearsal of one of my plays, I saw George Abbott sitting in the auditorium with a pained expression on his face. "Don't you feel well?" I asked. "I was just wondering how on earth you can select such plays," he answered. "I know just how you feel," I replied. "Every other week I wonder the same thing about you."[42]

Theatrical Apprenticeship, American Style

One of the most enduring reasons for keeping summer stock not only alive but a vital part of professional American theatre is its continuing role as a training ground for young theatre artists. "There's no better way to learn than in summer stock," declared Megan Bell after spending a summer as part of the acting conservatory at the Dorset Theatre Festival in Vermont. "The production schedule is right in your face, and you don't have a choice. You can't say, 'Oh, I don't feel like doing my homework tonight.' You just do it."[43] Elizabeth Capinera, who interned at the Lost Nation Theatre in Montpelier, Vermont, in 2002, and was invited back as an actor and assistant company manager in 2003, concurred, underscoring both the need for discipline and integrity: "Something the summer reiterated for me was how disciplined you had to be because you had this incredibly busy schedule. I would be in rehearsal all day and either be in the show at night or working backstage. The whole company was professional actors, and I had an obligation to be up to their standards."[44]

Michele Fields, who worked as a carpentry intern at the Surflight Theatre in Beach Haven, New Jersey, in 2002, and at the Westport Country Playhouse in 2003, was pleased to be able to use the skills she learned in college in summer stock. She described the long work hours with a gleeful smile: "I worked in the scene shop from 10 A.M. to around 5:30 P.M. and we'd break for dinner and then we'd have to be back at the theatre to tech the children's shows at 6:30 and the regular shows at 8 P.M. On changeover weekends, the show would end at 10:30 and we'd immediately begin strike. We'd get back to the houses when the actors would be having their breakfast."[45] "As much as you were tired, some of the most memorable and fun moments were those all-night work crews," said Kristy Farrell, who was Westport's company management intern in 2002. Farrell, a musical comedy actor who spent the following summer performing at the Galveston Island Outdoor Musical

Theatre in Texas, enjoyed her summer at Westport where she learned "a lot of the different facets behind the scenes" and discovered that she "enjoyed working on the other side of the production." "The professionals knew we were there to learn, and they'd take the time to teach us new skills," she said, adding, "I now know how to make curtains and hang wallpaper thanks to my summer there. It was a really positive experience."[46]

All of these young artists majored in theatre at college, where they received a comprehensive education in dramatic history, theory, and practice. Although well-prepared at school—all four were praised by their summer stock employers for their exceptional knowledge, skills, and professional demeanor—it was ultimately these apprenticeships that gave them their entrée into the profession. Not only did they make valuable contacts but they came to understand the lifelong commitment of theatre artists who, despite low pay, minimal benefits, and erratic employment, will do anything to work in the profession they love. As Capinera noted: "It's such a wonderful opportunity to be part of an ensemble with people a lot older than you but all working for the same thing. And they are so passionate about it. You learn that it's really important to just keep going and work through it, no matter how difficult the task or how tired you are. You remember why you're there and why everyone else is there, too."[47]

One of those "older" people, Paul Mills Holmes, who returns to Totem Pole every summer "to rejuvenate," credits stock for his entire theatre education. "This is where I learned everything because I didn't study theatre at all in college; I was an art student," he said, underscoring his contention that summer stock "is the best training ground in the world." "In the wintertime at Louisville (Actors' Theatre of Louisville, where he serves as a production stage manager) I tell all the apprentices that they *must* get a season or two of stock under their belts because that's where they will really learn. Stock teaches you how to make choices fast and to be able to change on the spot. You learn so much here because you have to."[48] Another "older" person who returned to summer stock was Joanne Woodward. One of her missions as artistic director at Westport was to revitalize its apprentice program, which, as Fields's and Farrell's reflections above attest, she has succeeded in doing. Woodward fondly recalls her own summer at the Monomoy Theatre in Chatham, Massachusetts, where she was one of five apprentices:

> We did 10 plays in 11 weeks—unbelievable. We did things like *All My Sons*, *Liliom*, Pirandello's *Henry IV*, and a Noël Coward. I acted in five of them and stage managed some others—I'd never been a stage manager in my life. One time I ran the sound, and I made costumes for *Henry IV* including the full king's

costume with his crown. We built the sets, painted the flats, and did absolutely everything. It was one of the most exciting, terrifying, and exhausting things I have ever done in my life and I learned so much.[49]

"That's what I'd like to see for the apprentices here," she remarked. "Not to work them like dogs but to make sure that they come away with an *experience*. It's such a wonderful kind of theatre with a resident company, and that's what I think of when I think of summer theatre."[50]

Another undeniable element of the summer stock experience is that it is fun, which also makes it especially appealing to young people. "I hope your book doesn't ignore the extraordinary dose of good times that summer stock provided its inmates, those of us who worked ten or a dozen or fifteen straight weeks without a break," wrote Robert H. Nutt of his experiences at Pennsylvania's Bucks County Playhouse in the late 1940s. "It was maybe the hardest work I ever did, but probably the most rewarding." Nutt shared tales of postperformance antics, when the younger people would head off to the "prototypical ol' swimmin' hole, particularly on hot nights after the show and several beers." Grace Kelly, who "was probably about eighteen at the time" and making her professional acting debut during the same summer that her uncle George Kelly's popular play, *The Torchbearers*, was being performed, would join them on occasion. "I don't personally recall actual skinny-dipping," Nutt wrote. "I think we retained a small amount of modesty with shorts and bra-and-panties." He recalls the entire experience as "one wonderful summer that lasted three years."[51]

A typical summer stock apprenticeship introduces novices to a typically American work schedule. Summer stocks mount a large number of plays in a compressed period of time, with a limited group of people working terribly hard for long hours, and then it's all over. This schedule is foreign to most theatre companies, even American ones, where at least twice as much time and far more personnel are engaged. In Europe and other parts of the world, the rapidity of the creation is unheard of since the making of a single production could literally take years. Despite the fact that most theatres do not operate on such an accelerated schedule, people agree that the training that summer stock affords is invaluable. Holmes contends that "working fast on your feet is the purest form of theatre" and it's also what he particularly likes about working in stock. "Everything is over in two weeks, and then you repeat that cycle five or six times over the course of the summer. You only have two weeks to do it all, so you have your marks every week. Every day you have to get something accomplished until you get to the final dress." This engenders a great camaraderie of working together to get the first play open and then immediately start to rehearse for the next one. "It's all about theatre," he said, "and the outside world does begin to retreat."[52]

A Theatre for the Young

Morton Eustis, writing in *Theatre Arts Monthly* in 1933, proclaimed that "the summer season is primarily dedicated to the youth of the theatre," and he characterized summer stock as the place where young people could "become professional in deed rather than in fancy." What he predicted in 1933 is still being practiced 70 years later: "They can put into practice what they have learned in the dramatic schools; they can test their own professional quality under professional auspices in a varied repertory, and they can undergo in concentrated form almost every useful experience of Broadway. It is a small wonder that they look upon the summer season as their season."[53]

The energy and vitality of summer stock reflects the youth culture for which the United States is known worldwide. Perhaps this single element makes summer stock quintessentially American. Although older people still work in stock, many to their dying days, they always surround themselves with the young, who are usually responsible for ensuring that the show really does go on. Perhaps the Judy and Mickey mythology of "Hey, kids, let's put on a show!" is not so far from reality. As long as there are young people yearning to make theatre, summer stock is destined to stay.

Appendix
Partial List of Summer Stock Theatres

The following list of summer stock theatres gives names, locations, and dates for which there is confirmed activity. Specific dates are given only for those instances in which definite information is available. Many of these theatres were, no doubt, active for longer periods than listed here, and some may have experienced one or more changes of name and ownership. In addition, some were not exclusively stock theatres and may be better known for variety entertainments. Others were active at other times of the year but featured a distinct summer season of plays. There are omissions because many theatres operated for only a few seasons, and records, if extant, are locally held. Summer Shakespeare and opera festivals, Renaissance fairs, historic and religious dramas, amusement park, and cruise ship entertainments are not included. The author invites readers to correspond with more information. Should there be a second edition of this book, this appendix will be updated accordingly.

Theatre	Location	Active years
Actor's Theatre	Plainfield, New Jersey	1950s
Actors' Theatre	Nantasket, Massachusetts	1940s
Actors' Workshop Guild	San Francisco, California	1960s
Adelphi College Summer Theatre	Garden City, Long Island, NY	1940s
Adirondack Theatre Festival	Glens Falls, New York	1994–
Albany Stock Company	Albany, New York	1940s
Alden Theatre	Jamaica, Long Island, New York	1930s
Allegheny Highlands Regional Theatre	Ebensburg, Pennsylvania	1974–
Allenberry Playhouse	Boiling Springs, Pennsylvania	1948–

Theatre	Location	Active years
Ambassador Music Hall	Fallsburg, New York	1930s
American Players Theatre	Spring Green, Wisconsin	1979–
Andy's Summer Playhouse	Wilton, New Hampshire	1970–
Ann Arbor Drama Festival	Ann Arbor, Michigan	1930s
Antioch Area Theatre	Yellow Springs & Toledo, Ohio	1950s
Arena Summer Theatre	Williamsport, Pennsylvania	1964–
Arena Theatre	Orleans, Massachusetts	1950s
Arrow Rock Lyceum Theatre	Arrow Rock, Missouri	1961–
Artists' Theatre	Arden, Delaware	1950s
Artpark	Lewiston, New York	1974–
Arundel Barn Playhouse	Arundel, Maine	1998–
Arundel Opera Theatre	Kennebunk, Maine	1950s
Astor Theatre	East Hartford, Connecticut	1950s
Atlantic Repertory	Atlantic City, New Jersey	1930s
Attic Theatre	Appleton, Wisconsin	1950s
Avondale Playhouse	Laurel, Maine	1950s
Avondale Summer Theatre	Indianapolis, Indiana	1950s, '60s
Bakersfield Playhouse	Bakersfield, California	1950s
Band Box Theatre	Suffield, Connecticut	1930s
Bar Harbor Players	Bar Harbor, Maine	1930s–'50s
Bard Theatre	Annandale-on-Hudson, New York	1930s
Barn Playhouse	Bolton Landing, New York	1950s
Barn Theatre	Augusta, Michigan	1946–
Barnstages	Nantucket, Massachusetts	1950s
Barnstormers, The	Tamworth, New Hampshire	1931–
Barrington Stage Company	Great Barrington, Massachusetts	1995–
Barter Theatre	Abingdon, Virginia	1933–
Bass Rocks Theatre	Gloucester, Massachusetts	1930s, '40s
Batavia Summer Theatre	Batavia, New York	1950s
Bay Shore Community Players	Bay Shore, Long Island, New York	1930s
Bayshore Summer Theatre	Bay Shore, Long Island, New York	1950s
Beach Theatre	West Falmouth, Massachusetts	1930s
Beach Theatre	Ocean City, New Jersey	1940s
Beacon Summer Theatre	Beacon, New York	1950s
Bedford Springs Playhouse	Bedford Springs, Pennsylvania	1960s
Beechwood Theatre	Scarborough, New York	1930s
Belfry Players	Williams Bay, Wisconsin	1950s
Belgrade Lakes Playhouse	Belgrade Lakes, Maine	1950s
Beloit College Summer Theatre	Beloit, Wisconsin	1950s

Theatre	Location	Active years
Bennington Drama Festival	Bennington, Vermont	1940s
Berks Players	Reading, Pennsylvania	1950s
Berkshire Playhouse	Stockbridge, Massachusetts	1928–
Bigfork Summer Playhouse	Bigfork, Montana	1960–
Binghampton Theatre	Binghampton, New York	1930s
Birchwood Repertory Company	East Stroudsburg, Pennsylvania	1960s
Birmingham Summerfest, Inc.	Birmingham, Alabama	1979–
Bishop Lee School, Nell Gwyn Theatre	Malden Bridge, New York	1930s
Black Hills Playhouse	Rapid City, South Dakota	1946–
Bloomsburg Summer Theatre	Bloomsburg, New Jersey	1950s
Blowing Rock Stage Company	Blowing Rock, North Carolina	1986–
Bolton Landing Summer Playhouse	Bolton Landing, New York	1940s
Boothbay Playhouse	Boothbay Harbor, Maine	1937–74
Boston College Summer Theatre	Boston, Massachusetts	1950s
Boston Summer Theatre	Boston, Massachusetts	1940s–'60s
Boulevard Theatre	Jackson Heights, New York	1930s
Brae Manor Theatre	Knowlton, Quebec, Canada	1950s
Brandeis University Summer Theatre	Waltham, Massachusetts	1960s
Brandywine Music Circus	Concordville, Pennsylvania	1958–70
Brattleboro Theatre	Brattleboro, Vermont	1930s, '40s
Brewster Summer Theatre	Brewster, Masssachusetts	1950s
Brickman Summer Theater	Pleasant Valley, New York	1930s
Bridge Bay Summer Theatre	Redding, California	1960s
Brighton Theatre	Brighton Beach, New York	1930s
Bristol Valley Theater	Naples, New York	1986–
Broadway Playhouse	Biloxi, Mississippi	1950s
Broadway Rose Theatre Company	Tigard, Oregon	1992–
Broadway Theatre	North Haven, Connecticut	1950s
Brooke Hills Plahouse	Wellsburg, West Virginia	1971–
Brookside Playhouse	Petersburg, Pennsylvania	1950s
Brown County Playhouse	Nashville, Indiana	1949–
Brown Summer Theatre	Providence, Rhode Island	1969–
Brown Theatre	Louisville, Kentucky	1960s
Bryn Mawr College Summer Theatre	Bryn Mawr, Pennsylvania	1940s
Buck Hill Falls Summer Theatre	Buck Hill Falls, Pennsylvania	1950s
Buck Hill Players	Stroudsburg, Pennsylvania	1930s
Bucks County Playhouse	New Hope, Pennsylvania	1939–
Buddy Piper Players	Idaho Springs, Colorado	1950s
Burlington Theatre	Burlington, Vermont	1930s
Cain Park Theatre	Cleveland Heights, Ohio	1938–

Theatre	Location	Active years
Cambridge Summer Theatre	Brattle Hall, Cambridge, MA	1940s, '50s
Camden County Music Fair	Haddonfield, New Jersey	1960s
Camden Hall Theatre	Camden, Maine	1940s
Cameo Playhouse	Miami Beach, Florida	1950s
Canal-Fulton Summer Theatre	Canal Fulton, Ohio	1950s–'60s
Canonsburg Summer Theatre	Canonsburg, Pennsylvania	1950s
Canterbury Summer Theatre	Michigan City, Indiana	1969–
Cape Cod Melody Tent	Hyannis, Massachusetts	1950–
Cape May Playhouse	Cape May, New Jersey	1960s
Cape May Stage	Cape May, New Jersey	1988–
Cape May Theatre	Cape May, New Jersey	1940s, '50s
Cape Playhouse	Dennis, Massachusetts	1927–
Capitol Theatre Summerstage	Rome, New York	1990–
Capri Theatre	Atlantic Beach, New York	1950s
Carolina Arena Playhouse	Greensboro, North Carolina	1950s
Carolina Circle Theatre	Myrtle Beach, South Carolina	1950s
Carousel Music Theatre	Boothbay Harbor, Maine	1978–
Carousel Theatre	Framingham, Massachusetts	1958–'70s
Carter Barron Amphitheatre	Washington, D.C.	1950s
Casa Mañana Theatre	Fort Worth, Texas	1958–
Casino-in-the-Park Playhouse	Mt. Holyoke, Massachusetts	1960s
Castle Heights Summer Theatre	Castle Heights, New Hampshire	1950s
Catholic University Summer Theatre	Washington, D.C.	1950s
Cazenovia Summer Theatre	Cazenovia, New York	1950s
Cecilwood Theatre	Fishkill, New York	1970s
Cecilwood Theatre	Fitchburg, Massachusetts	1960s
Centennial Theater Festival	Simsbury, Connecticut	1990–
Centennial Theatre	Yosemite National Park, CA	1950s
Central City Opera House	Central City, Colorado	1932–
Central Piedmont Summer Theatre	Charlotte, North Carolina	1973–
Central Theatre	Passaic, New Jersey	1950s
Chagrin Falls Summer Theatre	Chagrin Falls, Ohio	1950s
Chain O'Lakes Playhouse	Inlet, New York	1950s
Chamberlain Brown Players	Bronxville, New York	1930s
Chapel Playhouse	Guilford, Connecticut	1930s–'60s
Charlotte Theatre Festival	Charlotte, Noth Carolina	1960s
Chase Barn Playhouse	Whitefield, New Hampshire	1940s–'50s
Chautauqua Repertory	Chautauqua, New York	1930s
Chelsea Playhouse	Atlantic City, New Jersey	1940s
Chemung County Theatre	Elmira, New York	1950s
Cherry County Playhouse	Traverse City, Michigan	1960s
Chevy Chase Summer Theatre	Wheeling, Illinois	1950s

Theatre	Location	Active years
Chicago Tenthouse Theatre	Chicago, Illinois	1950s, '60s
Chicopee Playhouse	Galilee, Pennsylvania	1940s
China Dragon Playhouse	Hooksett, New Hampshire	1960s
Christy Players	Rochester, Minnesota	1950s
Cincinnati Summer Playhouse	Cincinnati, Ohio	1950s
Civic Light Opera Company	Little Rock, Arkansas	1950s
Cliff Haven Summer Theatre	Cliff Haven, New York	1950s
Clinton Playhouse	Clinton, Connecticut	1950s
Coconut Grove Playhouse	Coconut Grove, Miami, Florida	1960s
Coeur D'Alene Summer Theatre/Carousel Players	Coeur d'Alene, Idaho	1968–
College Light Opera Company	Falmouth, Massachusetts	1969–
College Showboat Summer Theatre	Kent, Ohio	1950s
College Summer Theatre	Ventura, California	1950s
Collingwood Theatre	Washington, D.C.	1950s
Colonial Manor Playhouse	Irwin, Pennsylvania	1950s
Colonie Summer Theatre	Latham, New York	1960s
Columbia Gorge Repertory Theatre	White Salmon, Washington	1996–
Comedy Theatre	Duluth, Minnesota	1950s
Community House	Bedford Hills, New York	1950s
Concord Plaza Players	Kiamesha, New York	1930s
Concord Theatre Company	Lowell, Massachusetts	1940s
Connecticut Players	Milford, Connecticut	1930s
Connecticut Repertory Theatre	Storrs, Connecticut	1957–
Cornell University Playhouse	Ithaca, New York	1950s
Corning Summer Theatre	Corning, New York	1950s–'70s
Cortland Repertory Theatre	Cortland, New York	1972–
Country Club Theatre	Prospect Heights, Illinois	1960s
Country Theatre, The	Goshen, Connecticut	1940s
County Center Summer Theatre	White Plains, New York	1950s
County Players	Suffern, New York	1930s–'50s
Cragsmoor Players	Cragsmoor, New York	1930s, '40s
Creede Repertory Theatre	Creede, Colorado	1966–
Crossroads Theatre	Bailey's Crossroads, Virginia	1940s
Crystal Lake Lodge	Chestertown, New York	1950s
Dallas Summer Musicals	Dallas, Texas	1960s
Daytona Beach Stock Company	Daytona Beach, Florida	1940s
Deal Conservatoire	Deal, New Jersey	1930s
Deer Lake Theatre	Pottsville, Pennsylvania	1930s–'70s
Deerpath Theatre	Lake Forest, Illinois	1950s
Deertrees Theatre	Harrison, Maine	1950s
Delacorte Theater	New York, New York	1955–
Denison Summer Theatre	Granville, Ohio	1950s

Theatre	Location	Active years
Depot Theatre	Westport, New York	1979–
Diamond Circle Melodrama	Durango, Colorado	1961–
Dixfield Summer Theatre	Dixfield, Maine	1950s
Dog Team Playhouse	Middlebury, Vermont	1950s
Dorchester Club	Dolton, Illinois	1960s
Dorset Theatre Festival	Dorset, Vermont	1927–
Drury Lane Theatre	Evergreen Park, Illinois	1960s
Duke's Oak Theatre	Cooperstown, New York	1940s–'60s
Dunkirk Summer Playhouse	Dunkirk, New York	1950s
Duxbury Playhouse	Duxbury, Massachusetts	1940s
East Chop Playhouse	Martha's Vineyard, Massachusetts	1950s
Eastern Slope Playhouse	North Conway, New Hampshire	1950s, '60s
Easton Summer Theatre	Easton, Pennsylvania	1950s
Easton Summer Theatre	Easton, Connecticut	1950s
Ebensburg Summer Theatre	Ebensburg, Pennsylvania	1940s
ECU/Loessin Summer Theatre	Greenville, North Carolina	1964–
Edgewood Players	Livingston Manor, New York	1930s
El Teatro de Santa Fe	Santa Fe, New Mexico	1950s
Elitch's Gardens Theatre	Denver, Colorado	1893–1996
Ellensville Playhouse	Ellensville, New York	1930s
Elverhoj Theatre	Milton-on-Hudson, New York	1930s
Emerson College Summer Theatre	Boston, Massachusetts	1950s
Encore Theatre	Downey, California	1950s
Essex Players	Essex-on-Lake-Champlain, NY	1930s
Ethan Allen Players	Brandon, Vermont	1950s
Fair Players	Dunkirk, New York	1930s
Fairfax County Summer Theatre	Fairfax County, Virginia	1950s
Fairhaven Summer Theatre	Fairhaven, Massachusetts	1940s
Fairman Players	Buckingham and New Hope, PA	1930s
Falmouth Playhouse	Coonamessett, Massachusetts	1949–'90s
Famous Artist Playhouses	Fayetteville & East Rochester, NY	1950s
Famous Artists Playhouse	Syracuse, New York	1960s
Farragut Players	Rye Beach, New York	1930s
Fayetteville Country Playhouse	Fayetteville, New York	1960s
Festival Theatre	Oak Park, Illinois	1975–
Fifth Ave. Players, Lake Nipmuc Playhouse	Mendon, Massachusetts	1930s
Fine Arts Center	Colorado Springs, Colorado	1930s
Finger Lakes Drama Festival	Ithaca, New York	1940s

Theatre	Location	Active years
Finger Lakes Lyric Circus	Skaneateles, New York	1950s–'60s
Flagler Players	Fallsburg, New York	1930s
Flat Rock Playhouse	Flat Rock, North Carolina	1937–
Flint Musical Tent	Clio, Michigan	1950s–'60s
Foothill Playhouse	Bound Brook, New Jersey	1950s
Forestburgh Playhouse	Forestburgh, New York	1947–
Fort Salem Theatre	Salem, New York	1972–
Forty-Niners, Chase Barn	Whitefield, New Hampshire	1930s
Foundation Theatre	Pemberton, New Jersey	1975–
Framingham Country Playhouse	Framingham, Massachusetts	1950s
Franklin and Marshall College Summer Theatre	Lancaster, Pennsylvania	1950s
Franklin Trask Theatre	Wareham, Massachusetts	1950s
Fredericksburg Theater Company	Fredericksburg, Virginia	1976–
Free Little Theatre Players	New York, New York	1930s
Frontier Town Theatre	Helena, Montana	1950s
Fullerton Park Theatre	Chicago, Illinois	1950s
Galveston Island Outdoor Musicals	Galveston, Texas	1977–
Garden Center Theatre	Vineland, Ontario	1960s
Garden Court Dinner Theatre	San Francisco, California	1960s
Garrick Players	Kennebunkport, Maine	1930s
Gateway Playhouse	Bellport, Long Island, New York	1950s–
Gateway Summer Theatre	Gatlinburg, Tennessee	1950s
Gateway Theatre	Somers Point, New Jersey	1960s
Gateway Theatre	Bellport, New York	1950s–
Georgia Shore Players	St. Simon's Island, Georgia	1940s
Gilbert & Sullivan Festival Theatre	Monmouth, Maine	1950s
Gladiators Arena Theatre	Totowa, New Jersey	1960s
Glen Wild Players	Glen Wild, New York	1930s
Globe Theatre	Chatham, Ontario	1950s
Gloucester School of the Theatre	Gloucester, Massachusetts	1950s
Gotham Players	Highland Grange, New York	1940s
Grand Island Playhouse	Buffalo, New York	1950s
Grand Theatre	Sullivan, Illinois	1960s
Gravenshurst Summer Theatre	Gravenshurst, Ontario, Canada	1950s
Great Lakes Drama Festival	Saginaw, Michigan	1950s
Great Neck Playhouse	Great Neck, Long Island, NY	1950s
Greater Seattle Inc.	Seattle, Washington	1960s
Green Hills Theatre	Reading, Pennsylvania	1960s
Green Mansions	Warrensburg, New York	1930s–'50s
Green Mountain Playhouse	Middlebury, Vermont	1940s, '50s
Greenbush Theatre	Greenbush, New York	1940s

Theatre	Location	Active years
Greenfield Summer Theatre	Greenfield, Massachusetts	1950s
Greenville Summer Theatre	Greenville, Pennsylvania	1950s
Greenwich Guild	Greenwich, Connecticut	1930s
Greenwood Gardens Playhouse	Peaks Island, Maine	1940s
Greenwoods Theatre at Norfolk	Norfolk, Connecticut	1999–
Gregory St. Playhouse	Rochester, New York	1930s
Gretna Players	Mt. Gretna, Pennsylvania	1930s
Gretna Theatre	Mt. Gretna, Pennsylvania	1977–
Grist Mill Playhouse	Andover, New Jersey	1950s, '60s
Griswold Players	New London, Connecticut	1930s
Gross Ile Summer Theatre	Gross Ile, Michigan	1950s
Grossinger Playhouse	Ferndale, New York	1930s
Groton Playhouse	Groton, Connecticut	1950s
Group 20 Players, Theatre-on-the-Green	Wellesley, Massachusetts	1950s
Group, Pine Brook Club	Nichols, Connecticut	1930s
Grove Theatre	Nuangola, Pennsylvania	1930s
Guild Hall	Easthampton, Long Island, NY	1930s
Guthsville Playhouse	Guthsville, Pennsylvania	1950s-'80s
Hackmatack Playhouse	Berwick, Maine	1971–
Halloway Bay Playhouse	Sherkston, Ontario	1950s
Hamden Summer Theatre	Hamden, Connecticut	1950s
Hampton House	Bridgehampton, Long Island, NY	1940s
Hampton Playhouse	Hampton, New Hampshire	1950s-'90s
Hangar Theatre	Ithaca, New York	1967–
Harbor Playhouse	Marion, Massachusetts	1940s
Harbor Theatre	Governor's Island, New York	1930s
Harmony Playhouse	Johnson City, New York	1960s
Harry Bannister Theatre	Stewartville, New Jersey	1940s
Hartman Theatre	Columbus, Ohio	1940s
Harvey's Lake Theatre	Alderson, Pennsylvania	1930s, '40s
Harwick Junior Theatre	Harwick, Massachusetts	1950s
Hayloft Summer Theatre	Lincoln, Nebraska	1950s
Hayloft Summer Theatre	Allentown, Pennsylvania	1950s, '60s
Hedgerow Theatre (year-round theatre that performed summers)	Moylan-Rose, Pennsylvania	1923–
Heritage Repertory Theatre	Charlottesville, Virginia	1974–
Highfield Playhouse	Falmouth, Massachusetts	1950s
Highland Park Music Theatre	Highland Park, Illinois	1950s
Highland Summer Theatre	Mankato, Minnesota	1967–
Hilda Spong Players	Cape May, New Jersey	1930s

Theatre	Location	Active years
Hilltop Theatre	Lutherville, Maryland	1940s–'50s
Hinsdale Summer Theatre	Hinsdale, Illinois	1950s
Holiday Arena Theatre	Swartswood, New Jersey	1950s
Hollywood Players	West End, New Jersey	1930s
Hope Summer Repertory Theatre	Holland, Michigan	1972–
Hopkinton Playhouse	Hopkinton, New Hampshire	1950s
Horse Cave Theatre	Horse Cave, Kentucky	1977–
Horsefeathers & Applesauce Summer Dinner Theatre	Winfield, Kansas	1973–
Hot Summer Nights	Cincinnati, Ohio	1980–
Hotel Bostonian Theatre	Boston, Massachusetts	1960s
Houghton Lake Playhouse	Houghton Lake, Michigan	1960s
House Club Theatre	Crawford Notch, New Hampshire	1950s
Hummocks Circle Theatre	Providence, Rhode Island	1960s
Hunterdon Hills Playhouse	Clinton, New Jersey	1950s–'90s
Huron Playhouse	Bowling Green, Ohio	1949–
Hutchinson Summer Theatre	Raymond, New Hampshire	1950s
Hyde Park Playhouse	Hyde Park, New York	1950s
IASTA Theatre, University of Denver	Denver, Colorado	1960s
Idaho Repertory Theatre Company	Moscow, Idaho	1950–
Indiana State University Summer Stage	Terre Haute, Indiana	1965–
Institute of Arts in the Theatre	Lake George, New York	1930s
Intermont Outdoor Theatre	Bristol, Virginia	1950s
Iowa Summer Repertory (University of Iowa)	Iowa City, Iowa	1920–
Iroquois Park Amphitheatre	Louisville, Kentucky	1950s
Island Theatre	Nantucket, Massachusetts	1930s
Ithaca College Theatre	Ithaca, New York	1930s
Ivoryton Playhouse	Ivoryton, Connecticut	1931–
Ivy (or Ivory?) Tower Playhouse	Spring Lake, New Jersey	1950s
Ivy Players	Springfield, Massachusetts	1960s
Jack and Jill Players	Chicago, Illinois	1950s
Jatoma Players	Alpena, Michigan	1950s
Jekyll Island Musical Theatre Festival	Valdosta, Georgia	1970s–
Jenny Wiley Theatre	Prestonburg, Kentucky	1964–
Jitney Players	Madison, Connecticut	1923–39
John Drew Theatre of Guild Hall	East Hampton, Long Island, New York	1931–

Theatre	Location	Active years
Johns Hopkins Playhouse	Baltimore, Maryland	1950s
Kalamazoo Village Players	Kalamazoo, Michigan	1950s
Kansas City University Summer Theatre	Kansas City, Missouri	1950s
Keeweenaw Playhouse Guild	Calumet, Michigan	1960s
Kenley Players	Columbus, Ohio	1958–'80s
Kenley Players	Dayton, Ohio	1958–'80s
Kenley Players	Warren, Ohio	1958–'80s
Kenley Players	Barnesville, Pennsylvania	1940s–'50s
Kenne Summer Theatre	Keene, New Hampshire	1950s
Kennebunkport Playhouse	Kennebunkport, Maine	1950s
Keuka College Summer Theatre	Keuka Park, New York	1950s
Keystone Repertory Theatre (formerly Summer Theater-by-the-Grove)	Indiana, Pennsylvania	1952–
Kingston Repertory Theatre	Kingston, Ontario, Canada	1950s
Kitty Davis Playhouse	Miami Beach, Florida	1950s
Knickerbocker Theatre	South Williamsport, Pennsylvania	1940s
La Jolla Playhouse	La Jolla, California	1947–
Laguna Summer Theatre	Laguna Beach, California	1950s
Lake Front Players	Chicago, Illinois	1950s
Lake George Dinner Theatre	Lake George, New York	1968–
Lake Luzerne Playhouse	Lake Luzerne, New York	1960s
Lake Placid Players	Lake Placid, New York	1930s
Lake Shore Players	Westford, Massachusetts	1930s
Lake Shore Playhouse	Derby, New York	1940s, '50s
Lake Shore Playhouse	Shapleigh, Maine	1950s
Lake Summit Playhouse	Tuxedo, North Carolina	1940s, '50s
Lake Sunapee Playhouse	Geoges Mills, New Hampshire	1960s
Lake Whalom Playhouse	Fitchburg, Massachusetts	1897–1973
Lake Winnepesaukee Summer Theatre	Lake Winnepausaukee, New Hampshire	1950s
Lake Zurich Playhouse	Lake Zurich, Illinois	1950s
Lakes Region Playhouse	Gilford, New Hampshire	1950s–'60s
Lakes Region Summer Theatre	Meredith, New Hampshire	1991–
Lakeside Summer Theatre	Putnam, Connecticut	1950s
Lakeside Theatre	Hopatcong, New Jersey	1940s
Lakeside Theatre	Landing, New Jersey	1950s
Lakeville Players	Lakeville, Connecticut	1950s
Lakewood Theatre	Skowhegan, Maine	1901–
Laurel House Players	Haines Falls, New York	1930s
Leatherstocking Theatre Company	Cooperstown, New York	1991–

Theatre	Location	Active years
Lees-McRae College Summer Theatre	Banner Elk, North Carolina	1984–
Legion Star Playhouse	Ephrata, Pennsylvania	1960s
Lenawee Players	Adrian, Michigan	1950s
Lewis & Clark Theatre Company	Yankton, South Dakota	1961–
Lincoln Park Summer Theatre	Lincoln Park, New Jersey	1950s
Lincoln University Summer Theatre	Lincoln University, Pennsylvania	1950s
Litchfield Summer Theatre	Litchfield, Connecticut	1950s
Little Theatre of Duluth	Duluth, Minnesota	1930s
Little Theatre of the Rockies	Greeley, Colorado	1934–
Little Theatre on the Square	Sullivan, Illinois	1957–
Lobero Theatre	Santa Barbara, California	1960s
Long Beach Playhouse	Long Beach, New York	1950s
Los Angeles Summer Playhouse	Panorama City, California	1960s
Lost Nation Theatre	Montpelier, Vermont	1977–
Louisville Stock Company	Louisville, Kentucky	1940s
Lydia Mendelssohn Theatre	Ann Arbor, Michigan	1960s
Lyndhurst Footlight Theatre	Lyndhurst, New Jersey	1950s
Lynn Summer Theatre	Lynn, Massachusetts	1940s
MacArthur Theatre	Montpelier, Vermont	1950s
Mac-Haydn Theatre	Chatham, New York	1969–
Mad Anthony Players, Trail Playhouse	Toledo, Ohio	1950s
Mahopac Theatre	Lake Mahopac, New York	1930s
Maine State Music Theatre	Brunswick, Maine	1959–
Malden Bridge Playhouse	Malden Bridge, New York	1940s, '50s
Mammoth Lakes Summer Repertory Theatre	Mammoth Lakes, California	1998–
Manhasset Summer Theatre	Manhasset, Long Island, New York	1950
Manhattan Players	Fitchburg, Massachusetts	1930s
Manistee Summer Theatre	Manistee, Michigan	1950s
Manor Vail Playhouse	Lyndonville, Vermont	1950s
Maplewood Summer Theatre	Maplewood, New Jersey	1940s, '50s
Marblehead Playhouse	Marblehead, Massachusetts	1950s
Mariarden Theatre	Peterborough, New Hampshire	1923–26
Marion Harbor Playhouse	Marion, Massachusetts	1950s
Maritime Players	St. John, New Brunswick, Canada	1930s
Marshall House Theatre	York Harbor, Maine	1950s
Martha's Vineyard Summer Theatre	Oak Bluffs, Massachusetts	1950s
Matoaka Lake Amphitheatre	Williamsburg, Virginia	1950s
Maverick Players	Woodstock, New York	1930s

Theatre	Location	Active years
Maxinkuckee Playhouse	Culver, Indiana	1950s
McLean Summer Theatre	Falls Church, Virginia	1950s
McVey Summer Theatre	Richmond, Virginia	1950s
Meadowbrook Playhouse	Cedar Grove, New Jersey	1950s
Melody Circle	Allentown, Pennsylvania	1950s–'60s
Melody Circus	Detroit, Michigan	1950s
Melody Fair	North Tonawanda, New York	1960s
Melody Fair	Toronto, Ontario, Canada	1950s
Melody Theatre	Danbury, Connecticut	1950s
Melody Top	Hillside, Illinois	1960s
Melody Top	Milwaukee, Wisconsin	1960s
Melodyland	Berkeley, California	1960s
Melodyland Theatre	Anaheim, California	1960s
Memphis Open Air Theatre	Memphis, Tennessee	1940s
Meridian Drama Festival	Washington, D.C.	1950s
Merrimack Playhouse	Concord, New Hampshire	1950s
Merrimack Summer Theatre	Merrimack, Massachusetts	1950s
Merry-Go-Round Playhouse	Auburn, New York	1958–
Merry-Go-Round Theatre	Sturbridge, Massachusetts	1950s
Miami University Summer Theatre	Oxford, Ohio	1966–
Michiana Shores Summer Theatre	Michiana, Indiana	1950s
Michigan Open Air Theatre	Detroit, Michigan	1940s
Middlebury College Players Summer Theatre	Cape Cod, Massachusetts	1940s
Milford Playhouse	Milford, Connecticut	1950s
Mill Playhouse	Pleasant Mills, New Jersey	1950s
Millbrook Playhouse	Mill Hall, Pennsylvania	1963–
Millbrook Summer Theatre	Millbrook, New York	1930s
Miller Playhouse	Miller, Indiana	1950s
Millstream Playhouse	Sea Girt, New Jersey	1940s
Millville Playhouse	Millville, Pennsylvania	1950s
Miniature Theatre of Chester	Chester, Massachusetts	1990–
Mohawk Drama Festival, Union College	Schenectady, New York	1930s, '40s
Monmouth Community Players	Spring Lake, New Jersey	1930s
Monomoy Theatre	Chatham, Massachusetts	1950s–
Monson Summer Theatre	Monson, Massachusetts	1950s
Montclair Summer Theatre	Montclair, New Jersey	1950s
Monticello Playhouse	Lake Kiamesha, New York	1940s
Montowese Playhouse	Branford, Connecticut	1940s
Mount Washington Valley Theatre Company	North Conway, New Hampshire	1971–
Mountain Playhouse	Jennerstown, Pennsylvania	1939–

Theatre	Location	Active years
Mountain Playhouse	Montreal, Quebec, Canada	1950s
Mountain Theatre	Braddock Heights, Maryland	1950s
Mountainside Outdoor Theatre	Cherokee, North Carolina	1950s
Mt. Tom Playhouse	Holyoke, Massachusetts	1940s
Mt. Vernon Summer Theatre	Mt. Vernon, New York	1950s
Mt. Washington Hotel Summer Theatre	Bretton Woods, New Hampshire	1950s
Muhlenberg College Summer Music Theatre Festival	Allentown, Pennsylvania	1981–
Municipal Opera	Louisville, Kentucky	1940s
Municipal Theatre, Inc.	Atlanta, Georgia	1950s
Murat Theatre	Indianapolis, Indiana	1950s
Music Circus	Lambertville, New Jersey	1949–70
Music Theatre Louisville	Louisville, Kentucky	1981–
Music Theatre of Wichita	Wichita, Kansas	1972–
Musical Big Top	Oakridge, New Jersey	1950s
Musicarnival	Cleveland, Ohio	1954–75
Myrtle Beach Playhouse	Myrtle Beach, South Carolina	1950s
Nebraska Repertory Theatre	Lincoln, Nebraska	1968–
Neighborhood Players	Philadelphia, Pennsylvania	1930s
Neptune Music Circus	Neptune, New Jersey	1952–70
Neptune Theatre Foundation	Halifax, Nova Scotia, Canada	1960s
New Barn Players	Saugerties, New York	1930s
New Bedford Festival Theatre	New Bedford, Massachusetts	1990–
New Century Theatre	Northampton, Massachusetts	1991–
New Cockpit in Court Summer Theatre	Baltimore, Maryland	1972–
New Harmony Theatre	Evansville, Indiana	1987–
New Haven Drama Guild	Stoney Creek, Connecticut	1930s
New London Barn Players	New London, New Hampshire	1933–
New Paltz Summer Repertory Theatre	New Paltz, New York	1973–
New Playhouse	Syracuse, New York	1960s
New Rochelle Playhouse	New Rochelle, New York	1930s
Newport Casino Theatre	Newport, Rhode Island	1940s, '50s
Niagara Falls Summer Theatre	Niagara Falls, Ontario, Canada	1950s
Nisswa Summer Theatre	Nisswa, Minnesota	1950s
North Shore Music Theatre	Beverly, Massachusetts	1955–
Northeastern State University Sizzlin' Summer Showcase	Tahlequah, Oklahoma	1983–
Northern Lights Playhouse	Hazelhurst, Wisconsin	1976–
Northland Playhouse	Southfield, Michigan	1960s

Theatre	Location	Active years
Northwestern University Summer Drama Festival	Evanston, Illinois	1954–
Norwich Summer Theatre	Norwich, Connecticut	1940s, '50s
Nutmeg Playhouse	Brookfield Center, Connecticut	1950s
Oak Park Summer Theatre	Oak Park, Illinois	1950s
Oakdale Musical Theatre	Wallingford, Connecticut	1950s–
Ocean County Playhouse	Toms River, New Jersey	1950s
Oceanside Theatre	Magnolia, Massachusetts	1950s
Ogunquit Playhouse (orig. Manhattan Theatre Colony)	Ogunquit, Maine	1933–
Ohio Northern University	Ada, Ohio	1991–
Ohio Valley Summer Theatre	Athens, Ohio	1950s
Old Fort Players	Charleston, New Hampshire	1950s
Old Log Theatre	Excelsior, Minnesota	1950s, '60s
Old Lyric Repertory Company	Logan, Utah	1967–
Old Orchard Beach Playhouse	Old Orchard Beach, Maine	1950s
Old Stone Barn Playhouse	Virginia City, Montana	1950s
Old Town Theatre	Smithtown, Long Island, New York	1950s
Oldcastle Theatre Company	Bennington, Vermont	1972–
Olney Theatre	Olney, Maryland	1938–2000s
Omaha Theatre	Omaha, Nebraska	1930s
Open Sky Theatre	Castine, Maine	1950s
Orange County Playhouse	Westown, New York	1940s
Orchard Hill Summer Theatre	Baraboo, Wisconsin	1950s
Otterbein College Summer Theatre	Westerville, Ohio	1966–
Oval-in-the-Grove	Farmington, Connecticut	1950s
P.C.P.A. Theatrefest	Santa Maria, California	1964–
Pacific Repertory Theatre	Carmel, California	1983–
Painters Mill Music Fair	Owings Mills, Maryland	1960s
Palo Alto Community Players	Palo Alto, California	1930s
Pan American Summer Stock Theatre	Edinburg, Texas	1972–
Papermill Playhouse	Millburn, New Jersey	1950s–
Papermill Theatre/North Country Center for the Arts	Lincoln, New Hampshire	1986–
Park Playhouse	Albany, New York	1989–
Pasadena Community Playhouse	Pasadena, California	1930s
Patchwork Players	Roanoke, Virginia	1940s
Paul Bunyan Playhouse	Bemidji, Minnesota	1951–
Pavilion Summer Theatre	Alstead, New Hampshire	1950s
Pelican Players	Panama City Beach, Florida	1950s
Pendragon Theatre	Saranac Lake, New York	1980–

Theatre	Location	Active years
Penguin Theatre	Centerport, Long Island, NY	1950s
Peninsula Players	Fish Creek, Wisconsin	1935–
Penn Playhouse	Meadville, Pennsylvania	1950s
Pennsylvania Centre Stage	University Park, Pennsylvania	1957–
Periwinkle Players	Pelham, New York	1930s
Peterborough Players	Peterborough, New Hampshire	1933–
Peterborough Summer Theatre	Peterborough, Ontario, Canada	1950s
Petoskey Playhouse	Petoskey, Michigan	1950s
Phillipsburg Theatre	Phillipsburg, New Jersey	1930s
Pine Beach Playhouse	Brainerd, Minnesota	1950s
Pine Bush Theatre	Pine Bush, New York	1950s
Pioneer Playhouse	Danville, Kentucky	1950–
Pioneer Playhouse	Cumberland Falls, Kentucky	1950s
Pioneer Playhouse	Ft. Knox, Kentucky	1950s
Pioneer Playhouse	Gilbertsville, Kentucky	1950s
Pitchfork Playhouse	Sharon, Connecticut	1940s
Pittsburgh Civic Light Opera	Pittsburgh, Pennsylvania	1940s–
Players	Marshfield Hill, Massachusetts	1930s
Playhouse, The	Eagles Mere, Pennsylvania	1940s
Playhouse-in-the-Park	Cincinnati, Ohio	1960s
Playhouse-in-the-Park	Philadelphia, Pennsylvania	1960s
Playhouse-on-the-Green	Worthington, Ohio	1960s
Plays-in-the-Park	New Brunswick, New Jersey	1963–
Poche Theatre	New Orleans, Louisiana	1950s
Pocono Playhouse	Mountain Home, Pennsylvania	1955–
Point Pleasant Play Shop	Point Pleasant, New Jersey	1930s
Police Gazette Players	Tudor City, New York City	1930s
Pompton Lakes Summer Theatre	Pompton Lakes, New Jersey	1940s
Port Players	Oconomowoc, Wisconsin	1950s
Porthouse Theatre	Kent, Ohio	1968–
Post Playhouse	Crawford, Nebraska	1966–
Post Road Players	Madison, Connecticut	1930s
Potash Bowl Theatre	Swanzey Center, New Hampshire	1950s
Powerhouse Theater at Vassar	Poughkeepsie, New York	1985–
Princess Theatre	Niagara Falls, Ontario, Canada	1950s
Princeton Summer Theatre	Princeton, New Jersey	1950s
Priscilla Beach Theatre	Plymouth, Massachusetts	1940s
Prospect Theatre Company	Rome, Georgia	1998–
Provincetown Playhouse	Provincetown, Massachusetts	1950s, 1980s
Publick Theatre	Brighton, Massachusetts	1971–

Theatre	Location	Active years
Pullman Summer Palace	Pullman, Washington	1977–
Putnam County Playhouse	Mahopac, New York	1950s
Putney Summer Theatre	Putney, Vermont	1950s
Quarterdeck Theatre	Atlantic City, New Jersey	1950s
Queens College Summer Theatre	Flushing, New York	1970–
Rabbit Run Theatre	Madison, Ohio	1950s
Rainbow Stage Theatre	Winnipeg, Manitoba, Canada	1960s
Ramona Park Theatre	Grand Rapids, Michigan	1940s
Randall's Island Summer Theatre	New York, New York	1930s
Red Bank Playhouse	Red Bank, New Jersey	1940s
Red Barn Players	Locust Valley, Long Island, NY	1930s
Red Barn Playhouse	Saugatuck, Michigan	1948–
Red Barn Summer Theatre	Frankfort, Indiana	1968–
Red Barn Theatre	Jackson's Point, Ontario, Canada	1960s
Red Barn Theatre	Northport, Long Island, New York	1960s
Red Barn Theatre	Westboro, Massachusetts	1950s
Reginald Goode Players	Clinton Hollow, New York	1930s–'50s
Repertory Playhouse	Keene, New Hampshire	1930s
Rice Playhouse	Oak Bluffs, Massachusetts	1930s–'50s
Richmond Summer Theatre	Richmond, Illinois	1950s
Ricks College Summer Play Mill	Rexburg, Idaho	1950s
Ridgefield Summer Theatre	Ridgefield, Connecticut	1940s
Ridgeway Playhouse	White Plains, New York	1930s, '40s
Riverhead Summer Theatre	Riverhead, New York	1950s
Riverside Theatre	Bridgton, Maine	1950s
Roadside Playhouse	Washington, D.C.	1930s
Robin Hood Playhouse	Arden, Delaware	1930s
Rockland County Playhouse	Blauvelt, New York	1950s
Rockport Players	Rockport, Massachusetts	1960s
Rockridge Theatre	Carmel, New York	1930s
Roosevelt Players	Miami Beach, Florida	1950s
Round Barn Theatre at Amish Acres	Nappanee, Indiana	1986–
Sacandaga Summer Theatre	Sacandaga Park, New York	1950s
Sacramento Music Circus	Sacramento, California	1951–
Saddleback Civic Light Opera	Mission Viejo, California	1978–
Sail Loft Theatre	Germantown, New York	1950s
Saint Vincent Theatre	Latrobe, Pennsylvania	1969–
Salt Creek Summer Theatre	Henadale, Illinois	1950s
San Diego Circle Arts Theatre	San Diego, California	1960s
Sandwich Summer Theatre	Sandwich, Massachusetts	1940s

Theatre	Location	Active years
Saranac Lake Summer Theatre	Saranac Lake, New York	1950s
Savoy Theatre	Asbury Park, New Jersey	1950s
Saxtons River Playhouse	Saxtons River, Vermont	1988–
Sayville Playhouse	Sayville, Long Island, New York	1940s
Schroon Manor Players	Schroon Lake, New York	1930s
Sea Cliff Playhouse	Sea Cliff, Long Island, New York	1950s
Seaside Music Theater	Daytona Beach, Florida	1976–
Shadow Lawn Stage	West Long Branch, New Jersey	1979–
Shadowland	Ellenville, New York	1985–
Shady Grove Music Fair	Gaithersburg, Maryland	1962–77
Shady Lane Playhouse	Marengo, Illinois	1960s
Shariwood Lodge	Ware, Massachusetts	1940s
Sharon Playhouse	Sharon, Connecticut	1950s–
Shawnee Playhouse	Shawnee-on-Delaware, Pennsylvania	1978–
Shawnee Theatre of Greene County	Bloomfield, Indiana	1960–
Shirtsleeve Theatre	Lindenhurst, Long Island, New York	1950s
Show Shop	Canton, Connecticut	1940s
Showcase Theatre	Evanston, Illinois	1950s
Silvermine Guild Summer Theatre	Norwalk, Connecticut	1950s
Skaneateles Theatre	Skaneateles, New York	1940s
Skytop Summer Theatre	Flower Hill, Long Island, New York	1950s
Sombrero Playhouse	Phoenix, Arizona	1950s, '60s
Somers Playhouse	Somers, Connecticut	1950s
Somerset Players	Niantic, Connecticut	1930s
Somerset Playhouse	Somerset, Massachusetts	1950s
South Park Theatre	Bethel Park, Pennsylvania	1995–
South Shore Music Circus	Cohasset, Massachusetts	1951–
South Shore Players	Cohasset, Massachuetts	1930s, '40s
Southampton Players	Southampton, Long Island, New York	1930s
Southbury Playhouse	Southbury, Connecticut	1950s, '60s
Spa Theatre	Saratoga Springs, New York	1950s
Spofford Playhouse	Spofford, New Hampshire	1950s
Spring House Theatre	Poland Spring, Maine	1950s
Spring Valley Playhouse	Spring Valley, New York	1950s
St. Louis Municipal Theatre, MUNY	St. Louis, Missouri	1919–
St. Michael's Playhouse	Colchester, Vermont	1947–
Stage Door Summer Stock	San Gabriel, California	1950s

Theatre	Location	Active years
Stage, The—Atlanta Women's Club Auditorium	Atlanta, Georgia	1940s
Stagelight Theatre	Buffalo Grove, Illinois	1960s
Stages St. Louis	St. Louis, Missouri	1987–
Stamford Summer Theatre	Stamford, Connecticut	1950s
Standing Stone Playhouse	Petersburg, Pennsylvania	1950s
Stanley Woolf Players	Liberty, New York	1950s
Starlight Musical Theatre	San Diego, California	1946–
Starlight Musicals, Hilton Univ. Brown Theatre	Indianapolis, Indiana	1960s
Starlight Theatre	Pawling, New York	1930s–'60s
Starlight Theatre	Kansas City, Missouri	1950–
Starmakers—Music Hall Theatre	Clinton, New Jersey	1950s
State College Community Theatre	State College, Pennsylvania	1955–
Steamboat Springs Summer Theatre	Steamboat Springs, Colorado	1950s
Steel Pier Theatre	Long Branch, New Jersey	1930s
Sterling Forest Gardens	Tuxedo, New York	1960–1970
Stone & Hoff Theatre	Lake Echo, New York	1930s
Stony Creek Theatre	Stony Creek, Connecticut	1940s
Storrowton Music Fair	West Springfield, Massachusetts	1960s
Straight Wharf Theatre	Nantucket, Massachusetts	1950s, '60s
Strand Theatre	Wilmington, Delaware	1950s
Stratton Theatre	Middleton, New York	1940s
Straw Hat Players	Moorhead, Minnesota	1963–
Straw Hat Players	Fort Carling, Ontario, Canada	1960s
Struthers Library Theatre	Warren, Pennsylvania	1985–
Studio Theatre Players	Green's Lake, New York	1930s
Summer Music Theatre	Macomb, Illinois	1972–
Summer Players, Inc.	Charleston, West Virginia	1950s
Summer Repertory Theatre	Santa Rosa, California	1972–
Summer Theatre at Mount Holyoke College	South Hadley, Massachusetts	1970–
Summeraround Theatre— U.W.-Whitewater Theatre/Dance Dept.	Whitewater, Wisconsin	1990s–
Summerfest at the University of Illinois	Urbana, Illinois	1991–
Summerhouse Theatre	Albuquerque, New Mexico	1950s
Summerhouse Theatre	Santa Fe, New Mexico	1950s
Surf Playhouse	Atlantic City, New Jersey	1950s
Surflight Summer Theatre	Beach Haven, New Jersey	1950–

Theatre	Location	Active years
Surry Playhouse	Surry, Maine	1930s–'50s
Taconic Playhouse	Copake, New York	1950s
Tahoe Playhouse	Bijou, California	1950s
Tanglewood Theatre	Falmouth, Massachusetts	1940s
Tappen Zee Playhouse	Nyack, New York	1960s
Temple-Gates Theatre	Flushing, Long Island, New York	1930s
Tent Theatre	Montreal, Quebec, Canada	1950s
Theater at Lime Kiln	Lexington, Virginia	1983–
Theater Barn	New Lebanon, New York	1984–
Theatre Go Round	Virginia Beach, Virginia	1950s
Theatre Guild, Plaza Theatre	Reading, Pennsylvania	1940s
Theatre in the Dale	New Milford, Connecticut	1940s
Theatre in the Park	Petersburg, Illinois	1996–
Theatre in the Sky	Waynesville, North Carolina	1940s
Theatre in the Woods, Woodland Players	Boothbay Harbor, Maine	1920s
Theatre L'Homme Dieu	Alexandria, Minnesota	1960–
Theatre of Four Seasons	Roslyn, Long Island, New York	1930s
Theatre on the Hill	Westminster, Maryland	1982–
Theatre Showcase	Orange, New Jersey	1950s
Theatre West Virginia	Beckley, West Virginia	1955–
Theatre-by-the-Sea	Matunuck, Rhode Island	1933–
Theatre-by-the-Sea	Woods Hole, Massachusetts	1950s
Theatrefest	Upper Montclair, New Jersey	1986–
Theatre-in-the-Round	Worcester, Massachusetts	1950s
Theatre-in-the-Round	Salisbury, New Hampshire	1950s
Theatre-in-the-Woods	Norwalk, Connecticut	1930s
Theatre-under-the-Stars	Atlanta, Georgia	1960s
Theatre-under-the-Stars	Vancouver, British Colombia, Canada	1960s
Thousand Islands Playhouse	Alexandria Bay, New York	1950s
Tibbits Summer Theatre	Coldwater, Michigan	1963–
Tilton Stock Company	Sandwich, Illinois	1950s
Timber Lake Playhouse	Mt. Carroll, Illinois	1961–
Timbers Dinner Theatre	Mt. Gretna, Pennsylvania	1975–
Tinkers Pond Theatre	Woodbury, Long Island, New York	1960s
Tivoli Summer Theatre	Oak Bluffs, Massachusetts	1950s
Totem Pole Playhouse	Fayetteville, Pennsylvania	1951–
Tower Ranch Tenthouse Theatre	Rhinelander, Wisconsin	1950s
Towers Summer Theatre	Cedar Grove, New Jersey	1950s
Town and Country Musicals	East Rochester, New York	1960s

Theatre	Location	Active years
Town Hall Playhouse	Westboro, Massachusetts	1940s
Town 'n Country Playhouse	Bismarck, North Dakota	1950s
TriArts at the Sharon Playhouse	Sharon, Connecticut	1989–
Triple Cities Playhouse	Binghamton, New York	1950s
Tuacahn Amphitheater & Center for the Arts	Ivins, Utah	1995–
Tufts University Summer Theatre	Medford, Massachusetts	1940s–
Unionville Summer Theatre	Unionville, Connecticut	1950s
University of Findlay Summer Stock	Findlay, Ohio	1977–
University of Michigan Theatre	Ann Arbor, Michigan	1940s
University of Minnesota Theatre	Minneapolis, Minnesota	1950s
University of Missouri Summer Repertory Theatre	Columbia, Missouri	1969–
University of New Mexico Summer Theatre	Albuquerque, New Mexico	1950s
University of Texas Summer Theatre	Austin, Texas	1950s
University of Virginia Summer Theatre	Charlottesville, Virginia	1950s
University of Washington Summer Theatres	Seattle, Washington	1950s
University of Wyoming Summer Theatre	Laramie, Wyoming	1952–
University Players Guild (UPG)	Old Silver Beach, Falmouth, Massachusetts	1928–32
University Playhouse	Mashpee, Cape Cod, Massachusetts	1940s
University Theater: Summer Show Biz	Edwardsville, Illinois	1975–
University Theatre	Lenox, Massachusetts	1940s
University Theatre—UW-Madison	Madison, Wisconsin	1977–
Upper Darby Summer Stage	Drexel Hill, Pennsylvania	1976–
Urban Playhouse	Yonkers, New York	1930s
Utah Musical Theatre	Ogden, Utah	1980–
Vagabond Players	Tuxedo, New York	1950s
Valley Forge Music Fair	Devon, Pennsylvania	1954–
Valley Players	Holyoke, Massachusetts	1940s, '50s
Van Wyck Players	Fishkill, New York	1940s
Vanguard Players, Masonic Temple	Atlantic City, New Jersey	1930s
Vanguard Playhouse	Detroit, Michigan	1960s
Vineyard Playhouse	Vineyard Haven, Massachusetts	1982–
W.W.U. Summer Stock (Western Washington University)	Bellingham, Washington	1971–

Theatre	Location	Active years
Wagon Wheel Playhouse	Sewickley, Pennsylvania	1950s
Wagon Wheel Theatre	Warsaw, Indiana	1956–
Wagon Wheel Theatre	Rockton, Illinois	1950s
Wareham Music Circus	Wareham, Massachusetts	1950s
Warren Players	Spring Lake, New Jersey	1930s
Warwick Musical Theatre	Warwick, Rhode Island	1955–99
Washington Square Players	Cooperstown, New York	1930s
Watergate Amphitheatre	Washington, D.C.	1950s
Waterside Playhouse	Manteo (Roanoke Island), North Carolina	1950s
Wawasee Playhouse	Syracuse, Indiana	1950s
Wayside Theatre	Middletown, Virginia	1960s
Weathervane Playhouse	Newark, Ohio	1968–
Weathervane Theatre	Whitefield, New Hampshire	1965–
Wellesley Summer Theatre	Wellesley, Massachusetts	1940s
Wellfleet Harbor Actors Theater	Wellfleet, Massachusetts	1985–
Wellworth Players	Hurleyville, New York	1930s
Wentworth-by-the-Sea Summer Theatre	Portsmouth, New Hampshire	1950s
West Newbury Summer Theatre	West Newbury, Massachusetts	1940s, '50s
West Suburban Playhouse	Glen Ellyn, Illinois	1950s
West Virginia Public Theatre	Morgantown, West Virginia	1985–
Westbury Music Fair	Westbury, Long Island, New York	1956–
Westchester Country Playhouse	Mt. Kisco, New York	1930s–'50s
Westchester Dinner Theatre	Yonkers, New York	1960s
Western Michigan's Cherry County Playhouse	Muskegon, Michigan	1954–
Western Stage	Salinas, California	1973–
Westhampton Playhouse	Westhampton Beach, Long Island, New York	1950s
Weston Playhouse	Weston, Vermont	1937–
Westport Country Playhouse	Westport, Connecticut	1931–
Wharf Theatre	Provincetown, Massachusetts	1920s–'30s
White Barn Playhouse	Westport, Connecticut	1950s–
White Barn Theatre	Irwin, Pennsylvania	1950s,'60s
Wildwood Players, Wildwood Amusement Park	Cleveland, Ohio	1930s
Will Geer Theatricum Botanicum	Topanga, California	1979–
William & Mary College Summer Theatre	Williamsburg, Virginia	1950s
Williamstown Playhouse	Williamstown, Massachusetts	1930s
Williamstown Theatre Festival	Williamstown, Massachusetts	1955–
Will-O-Way Playhouse	Bloomfield Hills, Michigan	1950s

Windermere Summer Theatre	Seal Harbor, Maine	1950s
Windham Playhouse	Windham, New Hampshire	1950s–'60s
Wingspread Theatre	Colon, Michigan	1950s
Woodstock Playhouse	Woodstock, New York	1940s–'60s
Woodstock Theatre	Woodstock, Illinois	1930s
Yardley Summer Playhouse	Yardley, Pennsylvania	1940s, '50s
Young Playhouse	Centerville, Massachusetts	1930s
Young's Gap Players	Parksville, New York	1930s

Notes

Preface

1. Samuel Marx, "By Samuel Marx," *Variety*, 20 September 1939.
2. "Grant Made for History on Summer Theater," *New York Times*, 8 November 1969.

Introduction

1. *Summer Stock*, dir. Charles Walters, with Judy Garland and Gene Kelly, Metro-Goldwyn-Mayer, 1950.
2. Eugene Burr, "The Drama in the Dell," *Theatre Time* I, 2 (1949): 52.
3. Foster Rhea Dulles, *A History of Recreation: America Learns to Play*, 2nd ed. (New York: Appleton-Century-Crofts, 1965), 387.
4. Cindy S. Aron, *Working at Play: A History of Vacations in the United States* (New York: Oxford University Press, 1999), 249.
5. Dulles, *History of Recreation*, 397.
6. Aron, *Working at Play*, 46–7.
7. "The Summer Exodus," *Century Magazine* 28 (July 1889): 47–8, quoted in Aron, *Working at Play*, 53.
8. Aron, *Working at Play*, 223.
9. Peter J. Schmitt, *Back to Nature: The Arcadian Myth in Urban America* (New York: Oxford University Press, 1969), 4.
10. Liberty Hyde Bailey, "What This Magazine Stands For," *Country Life in America*, I (November 1901): 24, quoted in Schmitt, *Back to Nature*, 4.
11. Richard Hofstadter, *The Age of Reform: From Bryan to F.D.R.* (New York: Alfred A. Knopf, 1956), 24.
12. *Proceedings*, National Conference on Outdoor Recreation (Washington: Government Printing Office, 1924), 12; *Proceedings* (1926): 164; Henry S. Canby, "Back to Nature," *Yale Review*, n.s. 6 (July 1917): 756, quoted in Schmitt, *Back to Nature*, 184–5.
13. Schmitt, *Back to Nature*, 16.
14. Ibid., 172.
15. Earl Pomeroy, *In Search of the Golden West: The Tourist in Western America* (New York: Alfred A. Knopf, 1957), 117.

16. Aron, *Working at Play*, 2–3, 254–7.
17. Stephen Langley, *Theatre Management and Production in America*, rev. ed. (New York: Theatre Arts, 1990), 125.
18. Ibid.
19. Dulles, *History of Recreation*, 391–2.
20. Ibid., 397.

Chapter 1

1. Christopher St. John, ed., *Ellen Terry and Bernard Shaw, A Correspondence* (New York: G.P. Putnam's Sons, 1932), author's preface, xviii.
2. John Frick, "A Changing Theatre," in *The Cambridge History of American Theatre, Vol. II, 1870–1945*, ed. Don B. Wilmeth and Christopher Bigsby (New York: Cambridge University Press, 1999), 201.
3. Brooks McNamara, "Popular Entertainment," in *The Cambridge History of American Theatre, Vol. II, 1870–1945*, eds. Don B. Wilmeth and Christopher Bigsby (New York: Cambridge University Press, 1999), 401–2.
4. Edwin Lewis Levy, "Elitch's Gardens, Denver, Colorado: A History of the Oldest Summer Theatre in the United States (1890–1941)," Ph.D. diss., Columbia University, 1960, 38, 175–6.
5. Caroline Dier, *The Lady of the Gardens* (Hollywood: Hollycroters, 1932), 22, cited in Levy, "Elitch's Gardens," 176.
6. Levy, "Elitch's Gardens," 37–8.
7. Ibid., 53.
8. *Rocky Mountain News* (Denver, CO), 2 May 1890, 6, cited in Levy, "Elitch's Gardens," 42–3.
9. Program in the files of the State Historical Society, Denver, n.d., cited in Levy, "Elitch's Gardens," 40.
10. Levy, "Elitch's Gardens," 46–7.
11. Ibid., 49.
12. Ibid., 192.
13. Ibid., 57–8.
14. Ibid., 58–9.
15. *Denver Post*, 27 July 1902, 7, quoted in Levy, "Elitch's Gardens," 190.
16. Levy, "Elitch's Gardens," 54, 376.
17. *Denver Post*, 8 June 1913, Sec. III, 1, quoted in Levy, "Elitch's Gardens," 171.
18. Willi Burke, interview with the author, 15 May 1996.
19. Levy, "Elitch's Gardens," 172.
20. Ibid., 67–8.
21. John B. Oblak, *Bringing Broadway to Maine: The History of Lakewood, Lakewood, Maine* (Terre-Haute, IN: Moore-Langen, 1971), 11.
22. Ibid., 15–28.

23. Herbert Swett, "Who Built Lakewood," quoted in Oblak, *Bringing Broadway*, 18.
24. Ibid., 35.
25. Program copy, 22 June 1918, quoted in Oblak, *Bringing Broadway*, 35.
26. Oblak, *Bringing Broadway*, 30.
27. "Lakewood Musical Comedy Company Opens" (program copy), Saturday, 24 June 1916, quoted in Oblak, *Bringing Broadway*, 30.
28. Dorothy Stickney, *Openings and Closings* (Garden City, NY: Doubleday, 1979), 62.
29. Oblak, *Bringing Broadway*, 74–86, 154–9.
30. "Broadway Shows in Maine Woods," *Boston Sunday Globe*, 11 June 1927, quoted in Oblak, *Bringing Broadway*, 78.
31. Herbert L. Swett, "A Musical Milestone," Program Copy, 31 August 1936, in Oblak, 100.
32. "Broadway in Maine: Lakewood Theatre Is Summer Workshop for Theatrical Celebrities," *Boston Sunday Herald*, 9 August 1926, quoted in Oblak, *Bringing Broadway*, 67–8.
33. Interview with Mrs. Elizabeth Swett Mills, 1967, quoted in Oblak, *Bringing Broadway*, 117.
34. Oblak, *Bringing Broadway*, 115–19.
35. Ibid., 66–7.
36. Sheldon Cheney, *The New Movement in the Theatre* (New York: Mitchell Kennerley, 1914), 178.
37. Ibid., 178–9.
38. Ibid., 179–80.
39. Constance D'Arcy Mackay, *The Little Theatre in the United States* (New York: Henry Holt, 1917), 25.
40. "The Huguenot Players of New Rochelle," pamphlet, Walter Hartwig clips file, Billy Rose Theatre Collection, New York Public Library for the Performing Arts at Lincoln Center.
41. Ibid.
42. Lawrence Langner, *The Magic Curtain* (New York: E. P. Dutton, 1951), 67–72, 90–5.
43. Hutchins Hapgood, *A Victorian in the Modern World* (New York: Harcourt, Brace, 1939), 391, 392–3, quoted in Robert Sarlós, *Jig Cook and the Provincetown Players* (Amherst: University of Massachusetts Press, 1982), 46.
44. Hapgood, *Victorian*, 394, quoted in Sarlós, *Jig Cook*, 46.
45. Sarlós, *Jig Cook*, 6.
46. This legendary tale about Jones is strongly refuted by Sarlós in *Jig Cook and the Provincetown Players*, which is, by far, the most scholarly and detailed examination of the theatrical group's history. He argues that there is no evidence to support the story and that the one extant photograph seems to refute it.
47. Sarlós, *Jig Cook*, 18, and Helen Deutsch and Stella Hanau, *The Provincetown: A Story of the Theatre* (New York: Farrar & Rinehart, 1931), 8–9.

48. Susan Glaspell, *The Road to the Temple* (New York: Frederick A. Stokes, 1927), 251.

49. Ibid., 253–4.

50. Sarlós, *Jig Cook*, 26.

51. Glaspell, *Road to the Temple*, 255–6.

52. Ibid.

53. Cook cited in Deutsch and Hanau, *Provincetown*, 26.

54. In my review of the "Andy Hardy" filmography, I have yet to hear that actual line uttered. The film that most approximates that spirit, however, is *Babes in Arms* (MGM, 1939) which is about a group of kids, all with entertainer parents down on their luck, who decide to mount a show to make money and save the day.

55. Mary Heaton Vorse, *Time and the Town: A Provincetown Chronicle* (New York: Dial Press, 1942), 116–17.

56. Ibid., 118.

57. John Mason Brown, "The Four Georges: G. P. Baker at Work," *Theatre Arts Monthly*, July 1933, 546, 551.

58. Cheney, *New Movement*, 192–3.

Chapter 2

1. Alice Keating Cheney, "The Beginning of the Jitney Players," *Madison's Unique Contribution to Summer Theater in America*, pamphlet accompanying exhibition, Madison Historical Society, Madison, CT, July 31–August 1, 1970, 7.

2. Ibid., 8.

3. George MacAdam, "The Strolling Player Returns by Jitney," *New York Times Book Review and Magazine*, 8 July 1923, n.p.

4. Ibid.

5. Cheney, "Beginning," 7.

6. Constance Smith, "New England: The Jitney Players," *Theatre Arts Monthly*, August 1929, 589, and MacAdam, "Strolling Player," n.p.

7. MacAdam, "Strolling Player," n.p.

8. Ibid.

9. Smith, "New England," 589.

10. Ibid., 590.

11. Richard Aldrich, "150 Broadways in the Hills," *New York Times Magazine*, 1953, Aldrich clipping file, Billy Rose Theatre Collection, New York Public Library for the Performing Arts, New York City. In this article, Aldrich claims that the weekly salary was $25, which, given the period and the financial straits of the players, would have been unusually generous.

12. Robert Lewis Taylor, "The Level Head-1," *New Yorker* (Profile), 30 July 1955, 38, 40.

13. Norris Houghton, *But Not Forgotten: The Adventure of the University Players* (New York: William Sloane, 1951), 31–2.

14. Ibid., 39.

15. It is noteworthy that upper Cape Cod theatres still enjoy the support of patrons from the Woods Hole Marine Biology Laboratory. Perhaps their tastes have turned to more serious fare in the intervening years, however: the artistic director of the Cape Cod Theater Project of Woods Hole recently heralded the "rare, profound, insightful questions" of the local scientists for helping his company develop new scripts (Robert Simonson, "A New Vigor for Theater on the Cape," Arts & Leisure sec., *Sunday New York Times*, 4 August 2002, 24).

16. Houghton, *But Not Forgotten*, 127.

17. Ibid., 108.

18. Ibid., 338.

19. Ibid., 336.

20. Ibid., 336.

21. Ibid., 202.

22. Ibid., 32.

23. Ibid., 268.

24. Mariarden brochure, clip file, Billy Rose Theatre Collection, New York Public Library for the Performing Arts.

25. Ibid.

26. "Denishawn Schools, New York and Mariarden (Peterborough, NH), 1923," Denishawn Collection, Dance Division, New York Public Library for the Performing Arts.

27. Mariarden brochure, 1923.

28. Manhattan Little Theatre Club, incorporation papers, Walter Hartwig scrapbooks, Ogunquit Playhouse archives, Ogunquit, Maine.

29. Manhattan Theatre Camp, 1927 brochure, clippings file, Billy Rose Theatre Collection, New York Public Library for the Performing Arts.

30. *Adam* broadside, Mariarden clip file, Billy Rose Theatre Collection.

31. W. G. K., "*Loose Moments*, A Summer Try-Out Comes to the Vanderbilt," *New York Sun*, 5 February 1935.

32. Samuel Marx, "By Samuel Marx (Story Editor, Columbia Pictures)," *Variety*, 20 September 1939, 91.

33. Manhattan Theatre Colony brochure, 1946, clip file, Billy Rose Theatre Collection.

34. "Shutters on Playhouse, Mean 'End of Summer,' Walter Hartwig Closes a Highly Successful Season with a Prophecy for an Even Better One in 1940. Growth of Ogunquit Playhouse is Spectacular," *Wells-Ogunquit Compass*, 8 September 1939, clipping, Ogunquit Playhouse archive, Ogunquit, Maine.

35. Elliot Norton, "New Theatre Showman's Dream," *Boston Sunday Post*, 4 July 1937.

36. "Shutters on Playhouse, Mean 'End of Summer,' " Ogunquit Playhouse archive.
37. *Pittsfield Sun*, 20 October 1887, quoted in Susie Kaufman, "Berkshire Playhouse Finding Aid History," Stockbridge Public Library, Stockbridge, Massachusetts.
38. Kaufman, "Berkshire Playhouse Finding Aid History," 3–5.
39. Unidentified clipping, Berkshire Playhouse/Theatre Festival Archive, Stockbridge Library.
40. Ibid.
41. Ibid.
42. Mary Heaton Vorse, *Time and the Town: A Provincetown Chronicle* (New York: Dial Press, 1942), 197.
43. Ibid., 200.
44. Ibid., 201.
45. Raymond Moore, "The Cape Playhouse" prospectus, Spring 1927, Cape Playhouse Archives, Dennis, Massachusetts.
46. Raymond Moore, letter to the patrons of the Cape Playhouse, 11 August 1928, Richard Myers Papers, Box 28, Cape Cod Playhouse, Wisconsin Center for Film and Theatre Research, Madison, Wisconsin.
47. Marcia J. Monbleau, *The Cape Playhouse* (South Yarmouth, MA: Allen D. Bragdon Publishers, 1991), 11–13.

Chapter 3

1. Charlotte Harmon and Rosemary Taylor, *Broadway in a Barn* (New York: Thomas Crowell, 1957), frontispiece.
2. John K. Hutchens, "Far from Broadway, Footlights Glow," *New York Times Magazine*, 3 July 1938, 10.
3. Eric Arthur and Dudley Witney, *The Barn: A Vanishing Landmark in North America* (New York: Arrowood, 1972), 11.
4. Eric Sloane, *An Age of Barns* (New York: Dodd, Mead, 1985), 9.
5. Dean Hughes, "The Barn," in Eric Arthur and Dudley Witney, *The Barn: A Vanishing Landmark in North America* (New York: Arrowood, 1972), 24.
6. Arthur and Witney, *The Barn*, 20.
7. Allen G. Noble and Richard K. Cleek, *The Old Barn Book* (New Brunswick, NJ: Rutgers University Press, 1996), 26.
8. Thomas Visser, *Field Guide to New England Barns and Farm Buildings* (Hanover, NH: University Press of New England, 1997), 15–16.
9. Elric Endersby, Alexander Greenwood, and David Larkin, *Barn: The Art of a Working Building* (Boston: Houghton Mifflin, 1992), 64.
10. Ibid., 65.
11. Richard Babcock, telephone conversation with author, 10 July 1995. Mr. Babcock is a noted barn restorer and historian whose many accomplishments include the barn theatre complex at the Wolf Trap Foundation for the Performing Arts Center, Vienna, Virginia.

12. Visser, *Field Guide*, 22–3.

13. Ibid.

14. Noble and Cleek, *Old Barn Book*, 49–50.

15. Arthur and Witney, *The Barn*, 234–5.

16. Noble and Cleek, *Old Barn Book*, 3.

17. Babcock, telephone conversation.

18. Unidentified clipping, *Literary Review*, 24 December 1920, Madison Playbarn file, Charlotte L. Evarts Memorial Archives, Madison Town Hall, Madison, Connecticut.

19. Constance Wilcox Pignatelli, typescript, Box 381, Evarts Archives.

20. Mary Heaton Vorse, *Time and the Town: A Provincetown Chronicle* (New York: The Dial Press, 1942), 197–200.

21. Ibid., 201.

22. "Dorset Playhouse, First of Kind in Vermont," unidentified newspaper, Albany, New York, 5 January 1930, Dorset Town Archive, Dorset, Vermont.

23. Warren E. Murray, "The History of the Dorset Players," unpublished typescript, Dorset Town Archive, Dorset, Vermont.

24. "History of the Barn . . .," playbill, New London Barn Playhouse, August 1955, New London Barn Playhouse Archives, New London, New Hampshire.

25. Robert Coleman, unattributed review, *New York Dramatic Mirror*, quoted in "Old Barn Is Now Theatre/New London Atmosphere Really Rural," *Manchester Union Leader*, 10 August 1948, Charles Jobes scrapbook, New London Barn Playhouse archives, New London, New Hampshire.

26. "New London Barn Playhouse Sixtieth Anniversary Issue," supplement to the *Argus-Champion* and *Eagle Times*, 9 June 1993, 2–4, New London Barn Playhouse archives, New London, New Hampshire.

27. "Good News," playbill, New London Barn Playhouse, 1987, New London Barn Playhouse archives, New London, New Hampshire.

28. Jim Seavor, "That's Entertainment in Matunuck," *Sunday Journal Magazine*, Providence, Rhode Island, 5 June 1983, 5.

29. "How to Build a Little Theater—First Find the Right Barn," *PM*, 23 June 1947, in clip file, Forestburgh Summer Theater, Billy Rose Theatre Collection, New York Public Library for the Performing Arts.

30. Ibid.

31. *Boston Evening Transcript*, June 1937, Box #2, Boothbay Playhouse archives, Boothbay Region Historical Society, Boothbay Harbor, Maine.

32. Playbill, The Barnstormers, Tamworth, New Hampshire, 1935 season, in clip file, The Barnstormers, Harvard Theatre Collection, Cambridge, Massachusetts.

33. Donald J. Walker, *Local Barn Makes Good or a True Historie of the Coming of the Thespians*, unpublished typescript, Humanities and Social Sciences Division, Library of Congress, Washington, D.C.

34. Helen F. Price, "The Mountain Playhouse," *Johnstown (Pa.) Democrat*, clip in 1939 scrapbook, Mountain Playhouse archive, Jennerstown, Pennsylvania.

35. Lawrence Langner, *The Magic Curtain* (New York: E. P. Dutton, 1951), 297.

36. Ibid., 296.

37. Raymond Moore, program note, playbill, June 1929, Cape Playhouse archive, Dennis, Massachusetts.

38. The Cape Playhouse Souvenir Book, 1946 season, Cape Playhouse archive.

39. Herbert Muschamp, "Broadway's Real Hits are its Antique Theaters," *New York Times*, Arts and Leisure section, 30 July 1995, 1, 32.

40. Susan Bennett, *Theatre Audiences: A Theory of Production and Reception* (London: Routledge, 1990), 76, quoting Wilfried Passow, "The Analysis of Theatrical Performance: The State of the Art," *Poetics Today*, 2, 3 (1981): 240.

41. Michael Hays, *The Public and Performance: Essays in the History of French and German Theatre 1871–1900* (Ann Arbor: University of Michigan Press, 1981), 3, quoted in Bennett, *Theatre Audiences*, 137.

42. Bennett, *Theatre Audiences*, 137.

43. Lillian Ross, "Every Little Touch Helps," Onward and Upward with the Arts, *New Yorker*, 20 August 1949, 49.

44. "Summer Resorts," *Architectural Forum*, March 1948, 110.

45. Ross, "Every Little Touch Helps," 49.

46. Richard Beckhard and John Effrat, "Richard Aldrich Answers Some Questions on Summer Theatre," *Blueprint for Summer Theatre*, 1949 Supplement, ed. Richard Beckhard and John Effrat (New York: John Richard Press, 1949), 3.

47. Harold L. Wise, "Over the Hill to the Playhouse," *Blueprint for Summer Theatre, 1950 Supplement*, ed. Richard Beckhard and John Efrat (New York: John Richard Press, 1950), 7.

48. Richard Beckhard and John Effrat, "Meet the People," *Blueprint for Summer Theatre*, ed. Richard Beckhard and John Effrat (New York: John Richard Press, 1948), 7.

49. Ibid., 1948, 8.

50. Noble and Cleek, *Old Barn Book*, 14.

51. Martha S. LoMonaco, *Every Week, a Broadway Revue: The Tamiment Playhouse, 1921–1960* (Westport, CT: Greenwood, 1992), 92.

52. Hutchens, "Far From Broadway," 10.

53. Ibid.

Chapter 4

1. Zelda Fichandler, "Institution-as-Artwork," *Theatre Profiles*, 7 (New York: Theatre Communications Group, 1986), 11.

2. Ibid.

3. Robert Karoly Sarlós, *Jig Cook and the Provincetown Players: Theatre in Ferment* (Amherst: University of Massachusetts Press, 1982), 34.

4. Susan Glaspell, *The Road to the Temple* (New York: Frederick A. Stokes, 1927), 257–8.

5. Sarlós, *Jig Cook*, 51.

6. Ibid.

7. Glaspell, *Road to the Temple*, 258.

8. Mike Gold quoted in Sarlós, *Jig Cook*, 52, and in Helen Deutsch and Stella Hanau, *The Provincetown, A Story of the Theatre* (New York: Farrar & Rinehart, 1931), 41–2.

9. The quality of "Horse Sense" was attributed to Robert Porterfield by Peter Cullen, quoted in Mark Dawidziak, *The Barter Theatre Story: Love Made Visible* (Boone, NC: Appalachian Consortium Press, 1982), 87, but it is applicable to all three founders.

10. Francis Grover Cleveland, interview with the author, 13 August 1993.

11. Ibid.

12. Martha Leavitt, "From College to Stage Career, VI—Francis G. Cleveland," *New York Herald Tribune*, 29 December 1935, Francis Grover Cleveland file, Harvard Theatre Collection, Cambridge, Massachusetts.

13. D. Quincy Whitney, "An Actor's Seven Decades on the Stage," *Boston Sunday Globe*, New Hampshire Weekly Arts and People, 30 May 1993, 16.

14. Francis Grover Cleveland, *At Random: A Small Compendium of Ill-Considered Remarks and Inaccuracies Which Appeared in the 1980 Programs on the Occasion of the Fiftieth Anniversary of New Hampshire's Oldest Summer Theatre* (Tamworth, NH: The Barnstormers, 1980), 8.

15. Cleveland, interview.

16. Elizabeth Steele, interview with the author, 13 August 1993.

17. Cleveland, *At Random*, 9.

18. Ibid., 10.

19. Cleveland, interview.

20. Cleveland, *At Random*, 8–9.

21. "The Tamworth Theatre," playbill, 1935 season, the Barnstormers file, Harvard Theatre Collection.

22. Whitney, "An Actor's Seven Decades," 16.

23. Craig Wilson, "Barnstormers Taking Bows for 62 Years," *USA Today*, 13 August 1992, D2.

24. Ibid.

25. Steele, interview.

26. Wilson, "Barnstormers," D2.

27. Cleveland, interview.

28. Francis G. Cleveland, letter to patrons, 4 May 1979, the Barnstormers archive, Tamworth, New Hampshire.

29. Wilson, sidebar, D1.

30. Ellen M. Dinerstein, interview with the author, 26 August 1993.

31. Tim Clark, "Reflections and Dreams: An Incomplete History of the Peterborough Players," 60th anniversary program, the Peterborough Players business office, Peterborough, New Hampshire, 1.

32. Playbill, scrapbook 1, the Peterborough Players archive, Peterborough Historical Society, Peterborough, New Hampshire.

33. Alfred Kreymbourg to EBS, no date, scrapbook 1, the Peterborough Players archive.

34. *Peterboro Transcript*, 1934, scrapbook 1, the Peterborough Players archive.

35. Martin C. Powers, "Prominent Artists See Poem Plays at Peterboro Playhouse," *Keene Sentinel*, 2 August 1933, scrapbook 1, The Peterborough Players archive; "Hadley Barn to Be Studio," *Peterboro Transcript*, scrapbook 1, the Peterborough Players archive.

36. *Peterboro Transcript*, 1934, scrapbook 1, the Peterborough Players archive.

37. "Hadley Barn to be Studio."

38. Powers, "Prominent Artists."

39. Ibid.

40. Mary Young to Sally Stearns [Brown], 1933, scrapbook 1, the Peterborough Players archive.

41. Robert A. Wilkin, "Peterborough Hops to Curtain Call," *Christian Science Monitor*, 3 September 1958, Peterborough Players file, Harvard Theatre Collection.

42. Alfred Kreymbourg to EBS, 11 August 1933, scrapbook 1, the Peterborough Players archive.

43. J. Wesley Ziegler, "A Short History of the Peterborough Players," 1963 playbill, Peterborough Players file, Harvard Theatre Collection.

44. Rosanna Cox, interview with the author, 28 January 2003, and quoted in Clark, "Reflections and Dreams," 2.

45. Ziegler, "A Short History."

46. Cox, interview.

47. Dinerstein, interview.

48. Ibid.

49. Ibid.

50. Fritz Weaver, quoted in Dawidziak, *Barter Theatre*, 67.

51. Rex Partington, interview with the author, 23 August 1994.

52. Ibid.

53. Richard Rose, interview with the author, 24 August 1994.

54. Mary Dudley Porterfield, interview with the author, 24 August 1994.

55. Dawidziak, *Barter Theatre*, 8–10, 89.

56. Ibid., 9.

57. Robert Porterfield and Robert Breen, "Toward a National Theatre," *Theatre Arts*, October 1945, 599–602.

58. Partington, interview.

59. "Agreement between Barter and Commonwealth of Virginia," co-signed by Robert H. Porterfield, president of the Barter Theatre of Virginia, and William A. Wright, chairman, Virginia Conservation Commission, 3 April 1946, the Barter Theatre archive, Abingdon, Virginia.

60. Rose, interview.
61. Pearl Hayter, interview with the author, 24 August 1994.
62. Ibid.
63. Fritz Weaver quoted in Dawidziak, *Barter Theatre*, 43.
64. "A Code of Ethics for People in the Theatre" (pamphlet), Barter Theatre archive, Abingdon, Virginia, in Dawidziak, *Barter Theatre*, 117.

Chapter 5

1. Morton Eustis, "The Summer Theatres," *Theatre Arts Monthly*, June 1933, 429–30.
2. Ibid., 430.
3. Lawrence Langner, *The Magic Curtain* (New York: E. P. Dutton, 1951), 296.
4. "New Tops for Summer Co.'s," *Variety*, 1 July 1936.
5. Alfred Harding, "Equity's Summer Theatre Policy is Working," *Equity*, July 1936, 5.
6. *The New York Dramatic Mirror* 42 (10 June 1899): 12, quoted in Alfred Bernheim, *The Business of the Theatre* (New York: Benjamin Blom, 1932), 93.
7. Bernheim, *Business of Theatre*, 93–4.
8. Langner, *Magic Curtain*, 296–7.
9. Dorothy Stickney, *Openings and Closings* (Garden City, NY: Doubleday, 1979), 62.
10. Bernheim, *Business of Theatre*, 95.
11. Alfred Harding, "The Summer Theatre Has Grown Up," *Equity*, September 1941, 9.
12. Jack Poggi, *Theater in America: The Impact of Economic Forces 1870–1967* (Ithaca, NY: Cornell University Press, 1968), 145.
13. Ibid.
14. Stage directors and choreographers were employed under Actors' Equity contracts until forming their own professional association, the Society of Stage Directors and Choreographers, in 1959.
15. For a detailed history of the founding and early years of Actors' Equity, consult Alfred Harding's *The Revolt of the Actors* (New York: William Morrow, 1929).
16. Alfred Harding, "Summer Theatre: Boon or Bane?" *Equity*, September 1934, 9.
17. Alfred Harding, "More Light on the Summer Theatre," *Equity*, October 1934, 9, 12.
18. Alfred Harding, "Not Enough on Summer Theatre as Yet," *Equity*, November 1934, 10.
19. Ibid.
20. Alfred Harding, "Editorial—Regulation for the Summer Theatres," *Equity*, April 1935, 3.
21. Ibid.
22. Alfred Harding, "Summer Stock Contract and Conditions," *Equity*, April 1936, 6.
23. Ibid.

24. A senior member of Actors' Equity had more than two years' stage experience while a junior member had less than two years' experience. A jobber was defined as a nonprofessional resident of the community in which the theatre was located or any nonprofessional actor employed by the company. Jobbers were restricted to two consecutive weeks of employment but could be retained longer if they agreed to join Equity.

25. Equity undoubtedly was eager to increase its membership. According to statistics compiled by Paul Ackerman for *The Billboard* magazine in July 1937 and reprinted in *Equity* that same month, the union's membership had dropped significantly in the 1930s. In 1937, Equity had 4,600 members as compared to 10,000 during the boom years between 1920 and 1930. Employment, not surprisingly, was also down. Seventy-five hundred actors were regularly employed in the 1920s, but during the 1934–35 season, the last year for which Ackerman had complete statistics, only 2,703 actors, excluding chorus members, had jobs.

26. "Equity Tightening Straw Hat Reins; Fewer Tryouts and Troupes Seen," *Variety*, 15 April 1936.

27. "New Tops for Summer Co.'s."

28. Lewis Nichols, "Broadway Moves Out Along the Highway," *New York Times*, 2 August 1936, 15.

29. Harding, "Equity's Summer Theatre Policy," 5.

30. Harry J. Lane, "Where Are You Going to Spend the Summer?" *Equity*, May 1938, 7.

31. "Summer Theatre Inspection," *Equity*, June 1938, 23.

32. "Keith Volunteers for Summer Stock Check," *Equity*, May 1939, 4.

33. Robert Keith, letter, 13 June 1939, published in "Robert Keith Resigns Summer Stock Job," *Equity*, July 1939, 10.

34. "Special Notification to All Equity Members, Equity Agents, Stock Managers Containing Equity Rules, Regulations, Contracts Covering Summer Stock Employment," *Equity*, June 1938, 11.

35. Wilella Waldorf, "Two on the Aisle, Summer Stock Managers Going Ahead After First Convention," *New York Post*, 18 April 1942.

36. Ibid.

37. Ibid.

38. John Huntington, "For Love and Money," in *Blueprint for Summer Theatre 1951 Supplement*, ed. Richard Beckhard and John Effrat (New York: John Richard Press, 1951), 17.

39. Eugene Burr, "The Drama in the Dell," *Theatre Time*, Summer 1949, 53.

40. "Curbs on Summer Stock," *New York Herald-Tribune*, 9 March 1943.

41. Summer Stock files, GC48.30, Actors' Equity Association Archive, Performing Arts Collection, Robert F. Wagner Labor Archives, Elmer Holmes Bobst Library, New York University, New York, hereafter cited as Equity Archive.

42. Summer Stock files, GC49.93, Equity Archive.

43. Burr, "Drama in the Dell," 55.

44. Paul Barry, "In Defense of the Apprentice System, *Equity*, April 1965, 28.

45. Louisette Roser, "Apprenticitis," *Blueprint for Summer Theatre 1952 Supplement*, ed. John Effrat (New York: John Richard Press, 1952), 30–2.

46. Harding, "Summer Theatre Has Grown Up," 9.

47. "The Best Summer Season Yet," *Equity*, September 1946, 3; "Annual Meeting Report," *Equity*, May 1947, 10.

48. "1953 Summer Theatres," *Blueprint for Summer Theatre 1953 Supplement*, ed. John Effrat (New York: John Richard Press, 1953), 91.

49. Review, *Blueprint for Summer Theatre, Equity*, April 1948, 22.

50. Elliot Norton, "There is Some Pleasure and Some Pain—Second Thoughts of a First-Nighter," *Boston Post*, 23 June 1940.

51. Ibid.

52. Ibid.

53. Vernon Rice, "Summer Theatre '29 and '49," *Blueprint for Summer Theatre 1949 Supplement*, ed. Richard Beckhard and John Effrat (New York: John Richard Press, 1949), 1, 4.

Chapter 6

1. John Anderson, "Mr. Anderson Laments 'Straw Hat' Failure," *New York Journal-American*, 11 August 1940.

2. Helen Ormsbee, "Guest Stars Are the Rage Again, 1939 Restoring an 1880 System," *New York Herald Tribune*, 2 July 1939.

3. Burns Mantle, "Summer Theatres to Revive Star System as an Experiment," *New York Daily News*, 11 June 1940.

4. Melville Burke, "Danger Sign Sighted on the Rustic Trail," *New York Times*, 18 September 1949.

5. *New York Mirror, and Ladies Literary Gazette* 2 February 1828, quoted in Alfred L. Bernheim, *The Business of the Theatre: An Economic History of the American Theatre, 1750–1932* (New York: Benjamin Blom, 1932), 27.

6. Letter from C. A. Logan to Sol Smith, 1848, quoted in *Theatre in the United States: A Documentary History, Volume I: 1750–1915*, ed. Barry B. Witham (New York: Cambridge, 1996), 90.

7. Newspaper article, *Spirit of the Times*, 4 May 1850, quoted in Witham, *Theatre in the United States*, 93.

8. Bernheim, *Business of the Theatre*, 31.

9. Ibid., 26–33.

10. Lewis Nichols, "Broadway Moves Out Along the Highway," *New York Times*, 2 August 1936.

11. Robert Lewis Taylor, "Profiles: The Level Head—1," *New Yorker*, 30 July 1955, 31.

12. John O'Shaughnessy, quoted in "The Star System??? A Good Force or a Bad Force in Summer Theatre??? Commentaries by Stars, Directors, Producers, Actors," *Blueprint for Summer Theatre 1951 Supplement*, ed. Richard Beckhard and John Effrat (New York: John Richard Press, 1951), 25, hereafter cited as "The Star System???"

13. Richard Highley, "Stars in Your Aisles," *Blueprint for Summer Theatre 1953 Supplement*, ed. John Effrat (New York: John Richard Press, 1953), 45.

14. Raymond Bramley, letter to Summer Theatre Committee, Actors' Equity Association, 5 October 1948, Summer Stock files, GC48.30, Equity Archive.

15. E. J. Dias, "A Look at the Arts" *(New Bedford, Mass.) Sunday Standard-Times*, 25 July 1948, Summer Stock files, GC48.30, Equity Archive.

16. Ibid.

17. Clarence Derwent, "Summer Stock Progress?" *Blueprint for Summer Theatre 1952 Supplement*, ed. John Effrat (New York: John Richard Press, 1952), 27.

18. "Two-for-Oneing 'Henry,' " *Variety*, 20 September 1938.

19. Mantle, "Summer Theatres."

20. Jeanne Stein, "Edward Everett Horton," *Focus on Film #1*, 1970, clip file, Edward Everett Horton, Billy Rose Theatre Collection, New York Public Library for the Performing Arts.

21. William Miles, " 'Straw Hat'—How It Grew," *Christian Science Monitor*, 21 August 1957.

22. Ormsbee, "Guest Stars."

23. "Dramatic Asides," *White Plains Reporter*, 25 May 1940.

24. William Miles, "Money in Summer: A Silo Circuit Veteran Tells How to Combine Art with Some Profit," *Boston Evening Transcript*, 3 June 1939.

25. Edward O. Lutz, interview with the author, 4 May 1993.

26. Stephen Langley, interview with the author, 11 May 1993.

27. Ibid.

28. John B. Oblak, *Bringing Broadway to Maine* (Terre-Haute, IN: Moore-Langen, 1971), 132–3.

29. Ibid., 133–4.

30. Elinor Hughes, "The Summer Playhouses as Offshoots of Broadway," *Boston Herald*, 6 July 1941.

31. Charlotte Harmon with Rosemary Taylor, *Broadway in a Barn* (New York: Thomas Crowell, 1957), 134.

32. Richard Aldrich, "Straw Hat Stars," *New York Times*, 2 July 1950.

33. Herman E. Krawitz, "Stock Theatres Can Be Successful," *Blueprint for Summer Theatre 1953 Supplement*, ed. John Effrat (New York: John Richard Press, 1953), 54.

34. Aldrich, *New York Times*, 2 July 1950.

35. Bill Ross, quoted in "The Star System???," 25.

36. Ibid.

37. Diana Herbert, quoted in "The Star System???," 22.

38. Sidney B. Whipple, "Summer Theater," *New York World-Telegram*, 21 August 1940.

39. Donald Cook, quoted in "The Star System???," 20.

40. Jeff Morrow, quoted in "The Star System???," 21.

41. Cook, quoted in "The Star System???," 21.

42. Lewis Harmon, quoted in "The Star System ???," 21.

43. Charlotte Harmon, *Broadway in a Barn*, 133.

44. Lewis Harmon, 21.

45. Theron Bamberger, "The Drama Goes Rustic," *Theatre Time* 3, no. 3 (Summer 1951): 27.

46. Arthur Sircom, letter to Actors' Equity Association, 28 August 1948, Equity Archive, Summer Stock file, GC48.30.

47. Lillian Ross, "Every Little Touch Helps," Onward and Upward with the Arts, *New Yorker*, 20 August 1949, 44.

48. Paula Laurence, quoted in "The Star System???," 23.

49. Ben Irving, "The Corn Is Greener," *Blueprint for Summer Theatre 1950 Supplement*, ed. Richard Beckhard and John Effrat (New York: John Richard Press, 1950), 9.

50. Ibid.

51. Henry Morgan, interview with author, 29 January 1993.

52. John Carradine, quoted in "The Star System???," 20.

53. Ross, "Every Little Touch Helps," 3.

54. Robert Perry, quoted in "The Star System???," 25.

55. Laurence, 23.

56. Charlotte Harmon, *Broadway in a Barn*, 92–4.

57. Ross, "Every Little Touch Helps," 7.

58. Harold J. Kennedy, *No Pickle, No Performance* (Garden City, NY: Doubleday, 1978), 67.

59. Ibid., 68–9.

60. Lawrence Langner, *The Magic Curtain* (New York: Dutton, 1951), 310.

61. Ross, "Every Little Touch Helps," 2.

62. Alan Hewitt, "Why Be An Actor? A Survey of Employment in the Theatre," *Equity*, September 1949, 5.

63. "The New Look for Summer Stock," *Equity*, March 1948, 7–8.

64. "Actors' Equity Association and Chorus Equity Association New Rules for 1953 Stock," *Blueprint for Summer Theatre 1953 Supplement*, ed. John Effrat (New York: John Richard Press, 1953), 56.

65. Rotary stock, according to Equity definition, consists of small circuits of theatres, usually located in cities, through which stock companies tour each week. There are the same number of companies as theatres, and they all open and close simultaneously, thus rotating a single production from one house to the next along the

circuit. Ideally, each of the host theatres has produced one of the productions with its own resident company. Both of the rotary tours on the 1952 summer circuit, however, were organized by individual producers who rehearsed and sent the companies to designated roadhouses.

66. Paul G. Jones, "Equity (U.S.A.) Stock," *Blueprint for Summer Theatre 1953 Supplement*, ed. John Effrat (New York: John Richard Press, 1953), 27.

67. Charlotte Harmon, *Broadway in a Barn*, 232.

Chapter 7

1. Robert Coleman, "Lambertville Is Offering More Than a Good Show," *New York Daily Mirror*, 4 July 1952.

2. Herman E. Krawitz, interview with author, 21 July 1993.

3. Donald J. Walker, "Local Barn Makes Good or 'A True Historie of the Coming of the Thespians.'" Unpublished typescript. Humanities and Social Sciences Division. Library of Congress, Washington, D.C.: 2–3.

4. Ibid., 13–14.

5. Lester Trauch, "Appendix 2: Memories of the Early Bucks County Playhouse," in *The Genius Belt: The Story of the Arts in Bucks County, Pennsylvania*, ed. George S. Bush (Doylestown, PA: James A. Michener Art Museum, 1996), 164.

6. Ibid.

7. Walker, "Local Barn," 15.

8. Ibid.

9. Gilda Morigi, *The Difference Began at the Footlights: A Story of Bucks County Playhouse* (Stockton, NJ: Carolingian Press, 1973), 46.

10. Sidney Fields, "Only Human," *New York Daily Mirror*, 3 July 1953.

11. Gail Hillson, quoted in "The Star System???," in *Blueprint for Summer Theatre 1951 Supplement*, ed. Richard Beckhard and John Effrat (New York: John Richard Press, 1951), 22.

12. Steve Slane, "Why a Music Tent?" *Blueprint for Summer Theatre 1954 Supplement*, ed. John Effrat (New York: John Richard Press, 1954), 66.

13. Frank Aston, "Terrell Predicts Arenas All Over," *New York World-Telegram and Sun*, 6 June 1961.

14. "Music Tents: It's an Old Tradition," *Life*, 11 August 1958.

15. Margo Jones, *Theatre-in-the-Round* (Westport, CT: Greenwood, 1951), 55.

16. "Summer Stock's Icumen In, Don't Be a Cuckoo!" *Equity*, June 1951, 6.

17. Walter Terry, "Music Circus and Mime Theatre," *New York Herald Tribune*, 30 August 1953.

18. David Mitchell, "Call Him 'Sinjun,'" *New York Herald Tribune*, 8 July 1953.

19. "Public Flocks to Tent Theater, Gold Mine for Young Producer," *Boston Sunday Herald*, 13 July 1952.

20. Robert H. Bishop III, letter to the editor, *Wall Street Journal*, 29 August 1956, B13, F5, St. John Terrell Papers, 1949–1964, Archives Division, State Historical

Society of Wisconsin, Wisconsin Center for Film and Theater Research, Madison, Wisconsin, hereafter cited as Terrell papers.

21. William Miles, "Summer Theater as a Business," *Christian Science Monitor*, 22 August 1957.

22. Edward Lutz, interview with the author, 4 May 1993.

23. "Music Tents: It's an Old Tradition."

24. Mitchell, "Call Him 'Sinjun.' "

25. "Pubic Flocks to Tent Theater."

26. John Keating, "Summer Theatre: Terrell's Still Mining Gold in Old Musicals," *Cue*, 28 August 1954.

27. Coleman, "Lambertville."

28. Press release, 1952, B1, F6, Terrell papers.

29. Press release, 1955, B1, F6, Terrell papers.

30. Correspondence, n.d., B1, F6, Terrell papers.

31. Publicity notes, 1955 season, B1, F4, Terrell papers.

32. "Lambertville Music Circus Started New Theater Trend," *Trenton Sunday Times-Advertiser*, 2 August 1959.

33. Ibid.

34. Correspondence, St. John Terrell to Vernon Duke, April 1959, B15, F19-1, Terrell papers.

35. Prototype Memo of Understanding, B2, F2-3, Terrell papers.

36. Ibid.

37. Ibid.

38. Production Costs—Weekly Fixed Costs, 1949, B2, F2-15, Terrell papers.

39. Investment Profile, 1949, B2, F2-13, Terrell papers.

40. William Miles, "Money in Summer," *Boston Evening Transcript*, 3 June 1939.

41. Krawitz, interview.

42. Ibid.

43. Cornelius P. Cotter, letter to Justin Golenbock, 14 August 1951, B7, F1-1, Terrell papers.

44. Ibid.

45. Wayne Robinson, "Music Circus Gets Wheels; Motorized Show to Go South," *(Philadelphia) Sunday Bulletin*, 24 August 1952.

46. Motor Music Circus File, B13, F4, Terrell papers.

47. Lutz, interview.

48. Danton Walker, "Broadway," *New York Daily News*, 31 May 1958.

49. Ibid.

50. Slane, "Why a Music Tent?" 66–7, 78.

51. Donald D. Ryan, "Tent Show Earns Big-Business Tag: An Idea as Old as the Acropolis," *Christian Science Monitor*, 17 November 1958.

52. Aston, "Terrell Predicts."

53. Bishop letter, B13, F5-10, Terrell papers.

54. Miles, "Summer Theater as a Business."

55. Gerald Bordman, *American Musical Theatre: A Chronicle* (New York: Oxford, 1978), 636.
56. David Richards, "A Magic to Drive Out the Blahs," *Washington (D.C.) Star-News*, 19 August 1973.
57. Ibid.
58. Harry Harris, "Valley Forge Music Fair's Anni Marks the 30-Year Partnership of Guber and Gross in Showbiz," *Variety*, 24 July 1985.
59. "Guber and Gross, 30 Years on . . .," *Variety*, 4 June 1986.
60. "Major Improvement in Store for Sacramento's Music Circus," *Sacramento Stage and Theatre*. Available at <http://www.sacnews.net/sacstage/major.html>
61. Curt Yeske, "Showman Terrell Dies at 81," *The Times of Trenton (N.J.)*, 20 October 1998.
62. Robert McG. Thomas Jr., "St. John Terrell, 81, a Re-Enactor of History," *New York Times*, 20 October 1998.

Chapter 8

1. Moss Hart and George S. Kaufman, *George Washington Slept Here* (New York: Random House, 1940), 66–7.
2. Thomas Gale Moore, *The Economics of the American Theater* (Durham, NC: Duke University Press, 1968), xiv.
3. Hart and Kaufman, *George Washington Slept Here*, 147.
4. Gilda Morigi, *The Difference Began at the Footlights: A Story of Bucks County Playhouse* (Stockton, NJ: Carolingian Press, 1973), 80–8.
5. Ned Armstrong, " 'Children's Hour' and 'Candide' Final Bills at Bucks County Playhouse for 1958 Season: New Definition of Small Summer Barn Seen," press release, September 1958, clip file, Bucks County Playhouse, Billy Rose Theatre Collection, New York Public Library for the Performing Arts.
6. "John Kenley's Ohio Operation: Names, Low Scale, High B.O.," *Variety*, 20 March 1974.
7. John Kenley, interview with the author, 26 August 1992.
8. Moore, *Economics of American Theater*, 140.
9. Ibid., 109.
10. The cultural transformation of America in the mid-twentieth century has been extensively documented in numerous sources. As it specifically relates to the theatre, I strongly recommend reading volume 3 of *The Cambridge History of American Theatre* (Cambridge: Cambridge University Press, 2000), and in particular, Christopher Bigsby's brief introduction to the volume which cites works by such seminal writers as Daniel Bell, Erich Fromm, Paul Goodman, Kenneth Keniston, and others, whose insights help to explain the societal ferment that transformed American theatre in the 1950s and '60s.
11. Moore, *Economics of American Theater*, 108–9.

12. Albert W. Niemi Jr., *U.S. Economic History/A Survey of the Major Issues* (Chicago: Rand McNally, 1975), 291.

13. Fred A. Cotton to Eleanor E. Walton, correspondence, GC57.87, Equity archive.

14. "Pension Now Included in New Stock Contracts," *Equity*, June/July 1963, 13.

15. Thomas G. Ratcliffe Jr., "Summer Theatre at the Crossroads," *Blueprint for Summer Theatre, 1954 Supplement*, ed. John Effrat (New York: John Richard Press, 1954), 33–4.

16. Robert Coleman, "Critics to Give Strawhat a Kicking Around," *New York Sunday Mirror*, 13 September 1953.

17. Eleanor E. Walton, letter to Fred A. Cotton, GC57.87, Equity Archive.

18. Bob Brooks and Willi Burke, interview with the author, 15 May 1996.

19. Lee Falk, "What's Wrong With Summer Stock or Three Wolves and a Copper Goose," *Equity*, April 1959, 13.

20. Ibid., 13–14.

21. William Blake, "Eternity," "Poems from MSS., c. 1793," "Poems and Fragments," *The Complete Poetry and Selected Prose of John Donne & The Complete Poetry of William Blake*, ed. Geoffrey Keynes, Nonesuch Edition (New York: Random House, 1941), 579.

22. Franklyn Lenthall and James Wilmot, interview with the author, 11 August 1993.

23. Sherwood Keith, letter to patrons, fall 1951, Box #1, Boothbay Playhouse Archives, Boothbay Region Historical Society, Boothbay Harbor, Maine.

24. Ken Crotty, "Boothbay Experiment; Mr. Jory Hoodwinked," *Boston Post*, 21 June 1953.

25. Harold L. Cail, "Two on the Aisle," *Portland (Maine) Evening Express*, 12 March 1954.

26. Robert Coleman, "Music Circuses Strong Barn Competition," *New York Daily Mirror*, 16 April 1955.

27. Coleman, "Critics to Give Strawhat a Kicking Around."

28. Lenthal and Wilmot, interview.

29. Ibid.

30. Burt Farnham, "It Takes All Kinds," *Boothbay (Maine) Register*, 2 August 1962.

31. "Theater," listings, *Time*, 30 July 1965.

32. Eliot Norton, "Five U.S. Premieres Booked for Boothbay, Me., Playhouse," *Boston Record American*, 3 July 1968.

33. Franklin Wright, "Thoughts and Things," *Portland (Maine) Evening Express*, September 1965.

34. "Playhouse Interest Group Formed," *Boothbay (Maine) Register*, 5 September 1974.

35. Lenthal and Wilmot, interview.

36. Kenley, interview.

37. Ibid.

38. Ibid.

39. Ibid.

40. Kay L. Coughenour, "An Investigation of the Philosophies and Practices of John Kenley (Theatrical Producer and Manager): A Guide to Producer/Management Factors for Success in a Summer Theatre," Ph.D. diss., Kent State University, 1977, 99.

41. John Kenley, "Who Killed Summer Stock (Not John Kenley)," typescript, author's collection, 4.

42. Ibid.

43. Hubert Meeker, "Nothing Straw Hat About His Theatre!" *Journal Herald* (Dayton, Ohio), 18 June 1966, quoted in Coughenour, "Investigation of the Philosophies," 6–7.

44. Kenley, "Who Killed Summer Stock," 1.

45. Coughenour, "Investigation of the Philosophies," 100–1, 152–5.

46. Kenley, interview.

47. Norman Leger, interview with the author, 25 August 1993.

48. Ibid.

49. Edgar J. Driscoll Jr., "Informality Enlivens N.H. Barn Players," *Boston Globe*, 19 July 1972.

50. Leger, interview.

51. Norman Leger, "There's More Than a Name to a Title . . . or How *Do* the Barn Players Select Their Shows???," *Mame*, playbill, New London Barn Playhouse, 1986 summer season, New London Barn Playhouse archive, New London, NH.

52. Ibid.

53. Leger, interview.

54. Ibid.

55. Nan Robertson, "Actors Hone Their Craft on Williamstown Stage," *New York Times*, 30 June 1985.

56. Ibid.

57. Tom Buckley, "Footlights at Williamstown Lure Pros and Starry-Eyed," *New York Times*, 28 July 1972.

58. Andre L. Speyer, "Williamstown Theatre: A Casual Remark Started It All 25 Years Ago," *Transcript* (Williamstown, Mass.), 18 November 1978.

59. Robertson, "Actors Hone Their Craft."

60. Speyer, "Williamstown Theatre."

61. Steve Lawson, "The Legacy of Nikos," *New York Times*, 29 January 1989.

62. Hilary De Vries, "At Williamstown, a Search for a Vision," *New York Times*, 18 June 1989.

63. Julie Michaels, "Nikos—Williamstown's Guru," *Berkshire (Pittsfield, Mass.) Sampler*, 23 July 1978.

64. Ibid.

Chapter 9

1. Alison Harris and Anne Keefe, interview with the author, Westport Country Playhouse, 13 December 2002.
2. Joanne Woodward, interview with the author, 8 January 2001.
3. Keefe, interview.
4. James B. McKenzie, interview with the author, 21 September 1992.
5. Harris and Keefe, interview.
6. Woodward, interview.
7. "New Century Campaign Proposed Renovation," information card, Westport Country Playhouse, Development Office, Westport, Connecticut, 2001.
8. Harris and Keefe, interview.
9. McKenzie, interview.
10. Harris and Keefe, interview.
11. Ibid.
12. Carl Schurr and Wil Love, interview with the author, 26 July 2001.
13. "The Totem Pole Playhouse Story," 1960 playbill, Totem Pole Playhouse Archive, business office, Fayetteville, Pennsylvania.
14. John Putch, *This Is My Father: A Documentary About William H. Putch*, 60 min., PutchFilms, 1998.
15. Wil Love, interviewed in Putch film.
16. Lois Armstrong, "After Her Husband's Death Jean Stapleton and Her Kids Try to Keep His Theatre Alive," *People*, 22 June 1984, 44.
17. Jean Stapleton, interviewed in Putch film.
18. Bill Putch, "30 Years Over the Rainbow," 30th anniversary playbill, Totem Pole Playhouse Archive.
19. Paul Mills Holmes, interviewed in Putch film.
20. Schurr and Love, interview.
21. Sue McMurtray, interview with the author, 27 July 2001.
22. Schurr and Love, interview.
23. Ibid.
24. Paul Mills Holmes, interview with the author, 27 July 2001.
25. Jason Rubin, interview with the author, 26 July 2001.
26. McMurtray, interview.
27. Schurr and Love, interview.
28. Adrienne Wilson Grant, telephone interview with the author, 2 April 2002.
29. Ibid.
30. Ibid.
31. Adrienne Wilson Grant and Susan Jones, assistant to the producer, onsite interview with the author, 18 July 2002.
32. Greg Titherington, "If You (Re)Build It, They Will Come," *Cast & Crew* (April 1998), 1.

33. Ibid.
34. Roger Cole, quoted in Jack Beaudoin, "A Star Is Barn," *Portland (Maine) Press Herald*, 12 November 1997.
35. Susan Jones, interview with the author, 18 July 2002.
36. Adrienne Wilson Grant, telephone interview with the author, 10 April 2003.
37. Ibid.
38. Foster Rhea Dulles, *A History of Recreation: America Learns to Play*, 2nd ed. (New York: Appleton-Century-Crofts, 1965), 397.
39. Holly Butler, "Jim McKenzie—a Man for All *Summer* Seasons," *Westport (Connecticut) News*, 15 June 1988.
40. Harris and Keefe, interview.
41. Putch interview in *This Is My Father*.
42. Lawrence Langner, *The Magic Curtain* (New York: E. P. Dutton, 1951), 309.
43. Megan Bell, interview with the author, 6 May 2003.
44. Elizabeth Capinera, interview with the author, 6 May 2003.
45. Michele Fields, interview with the author, 6 May 2003.
46. Kristy Farrell, interview with the author, 6 May 2003.
47. Capinera, interview.
48. Holmes, interview.
49. Woodward, interview.
50. Ibid.
51. Robert H. Nutt, letter to the author, 12 October 1992.
52. Holmes, interview.
53. Morton Eustis, "The Summer Theatres," *Theatre Arts Monthly*, June 1933, 429–30.

Bibliography

Actors' Equity Association Archive. Summer Stock files, letters, news clippings. Performing Arts Collection, Robert F. Wagner Labor Archives. Elmer Holmes Bobst Library, New York University, New York City.

"Actors' Equity Association and Chorus Equity Association New Rules for 1953 Stock." In *Blueprint for Summer Theatre 1953 Supplement*, edited by John Effrat. New York: John Richard Press, 1953, 56.

"Agreement between Barter and Commonwealth of Virginia," co-signed by Robert H. Porterfield, president of the Barter Theatre of Virginia, and William A. Wright, chairman, Virginia Conservation Commission, 3 April 1946. Barter Theatre archive. Abingdon, Virginia.

Aldrich, Richard. *Gertrude Lawrence as Mrs. A*. New York: Greystone Press, 1954.

——. "150 Broadways in the Hills." *New York Times Magazine*, 1953. Aldrich clip file. Billy Rose Theatre Collection. New York Public Library for the Performing Arts at Lincoln Center.

——. "Straw Hat Stars." *New York Times*, 2 July 1950.

Anderson, John. "Mr. Anderson Laments 'Straw Hat' Failure." *New York Journal-American*, 11 August 1940.

"Annual Meeting Report." *Equity*, May 1947.

Armstrong, Lois. "After Her Husband's Death Jean Stapleton and Her Kids Try to Keep His Theatre Alive." *People*, 22 June 1984.

Armstrong, Ned. " 'Children's Hour' and 'Candide' Final Bills at Bucks County Playhouse for 1958 Season: New Definition of Small Summer Barn Seen." Press release, September 1958. Clip file, Bucks County Playhouse. Billy Rose Theatre Collection. New York Public Library for the Performing Arts at Lincoln Center.

Aron, Cindy S. *Working at Play: A History of Vacations in the United States*. New York: Oxford University Press, 1999.

Arthur, Eric, and Dudley Witney. *The Barn: A Vanishing Landmark in North America*. New York: Arrowood, 1972.

Aston, Frank. "Terrell Predicts Arenas All Over." *New York World-Telegram and Sun*, 6 June 1961.

Bamberger, Theron. "The Drama Goes Rustic." *Theatre Time*, 3, no. 3 (Summer 1951).

Barnstormers. Playbills, press releases. Barnstormers' file, Harvard Theatre Collection. Cambridge: Cambridge, Massachusetts.

Barry, Paul. "In Defense of the Apprentice System." *Equity*, April 1965.

Beaudoin, Jack. "A Star Is Barn." *Portland (Maine) Press Herald*, 12 November 1997.

Beckhard, Richard, and John Effrat. "Meet the People." *Blueprint for Summer Theatre*, edited by Richard Beckhard and John Effrat. New York: John Richard Press, 1948.

——. "Richard Aldrich Answers Some Questions on Summer Theatre." In *Blueprint for Summer Theatre, 1949 Supplement*, edited by Richard Beckhard and John Effrat. New York: John Richard Press, 1949.

Bennett, Susan. *Theatre Audiences: A Theory of Production and Reception*. London: Routledge, 1990.

Berkshire Playhouse/Theatre Festival Archive. News clips, playbills. Stockbridge Public Library, Stockbridge, Massachusetts.

Bernheim, Alfred. *The Business of the Theatre*. New York: Benjamin Blom, 1932.

"Best Summer Season Yet." *Equity*, September 1946.

Blake, William. "Eternity," "Poems from MSS., c. 1793," "Poems and Fragments." *The Complete Poetry and Selected Prose of John Donne and The Complete Poetry of William Blake*, edited by Geoffrey Keynes. Nonesuch Edition. New York: Random House, 1941.

Boothbay Playhouse Archive, Box #2. News clippings, Boothbay Region Historical Society. Boothbay Harbor, Maine.

Bordman, Gerald. *American Musical Theatre: A Chronicle*. New York: Oxford University Press, 1978.

Brown, John Mason. "The Four Georges: G. P. Baker At Work." *Theatre Arts Monthly*, July 1933.

Buckley, Tom. "Footlights at Williamstown Lure Pros and Starry-Eyed." *New York Times*, 28 July 1972.

Burke, Melville. "Danger Sign Sighted on the Rustic Trail." *New York Times*, 18 September 1949.

Burr, Eugene. "The Drama in the Dell," *Theatre Time*, 1, no. 2 (May 1949).

Butler, Holly. "Jim McKenzie—A Man for All *Summer* Seasons." *Westport* (Com.) *News*, 15 June 1988.

Cail, Harold L. "Two on the Aisle." *Portland (Maine) Evening Express*, 12 March 1954.

Cape Playhouse. Playbills, letters, business documents. Cape Playhouse archive, Dennis, Massachusetts.

Cheney, Alice Keating. "The Beginning of the Jitney Players." *Madison's Unique Contribution to Summer Theater in America*. Pamphlet accompanying exhibition, July 31–August 1, 1970. Madison Historical Society, Madison, Connecticut.

Cheney, Sheldon. *The New Movement in the Theatre*. New York: Mitchell Kennerley, 1914.

Clark, Tim. "Reflections and Dreams: An Incomplete History of the Peterborough Players." 60th anniversary program. Peterborough Players Business Office, Peterborough, New Hampshire.

Cleveland, Francis Grover. *At Random: A Small Compendium of Ill-Considered Remarks and Inaccuracies Which Appeared in the 1980 Programs on the*

Occasion of the Fiftieth Anniversary of New Hampshire's Oldest Summer Theatre. Tamworth, NH: Barnstormers, 1980.

——. Letter to patrons, 4 May 1979. Barnstormers archive, Tamworth, New Hampshire.

"Code of Ethics for People in the Theatre." Barter Theatre archive. Abingdon, Virginia.

Coleman, Robert. "Critics to Give Strawhat a Kicking Around." *New York Sunday Mirror*, 13 September 1953.

——. "Lambertville Is Offering More Than a Good Show." *New York Daily Mirror*, 4 July 1952.

——. "Music Circuses Strong Barn Competition." *New York Daily Mirror*, 16 April 1955.

Coughenour, Kay L. "An Investigation of the Philosophies and Practices of John Kenley Theatrical Producer and Manager: A Guide to Producer/Management Factors for Success in a Summer Theatre." Ph.D. diss., Kent State University, 1977.

Crotty, Ken. "Boothbay Experiment; Mr. Jory Hoodwinked." *Boston Post*, 21 June 1953.

"Curbs on Summer Stock." *New York Herald-Tribune*, 9 March 1943.

Dawidziak, Mark. *The Barter Theatre Story: Love Made Visible.* Boone, NC: Appalachian Consortium Press, 1982.

De Vries, Hilary. "At Williamstown, a Search for a Vision." *New York Times*, 18 June 1989.

"Denishawn Schools, New York and Mariarden Peterborough, NH, 1923." Denishawn Collection, Dance Division. New York Public Library for the Performing Arts at Lincoln Center.

Derwent, Clarence. "Summer Stock Progress?" In *Blueprint for Summer Theatre 1952 Supplement*, edited by John Effrat. New York: John Richard Press, 1952, 27.

Deutsch, Helen, and Stella Hanau. *The Provincetown: A Story of the Theatre.* New York: Farrar & Rinehart, 1931.

Dias, E. J. "A Look at the Arts" *(New Bedford, Mass.) Sunday Standard-Times*, New Bedford, Massachusetts, 25 July 1948. Summer stock files, GC48.30. Actors' Equity Association Archive, Performing Arts Collection, Robert F. Wagner Labor Archives, Elmer Holmes Bobst Library, New York University, New York.

"Dorset Playhouse, First of Kind in Vermont." Unidentified newspaper clip, Albany, New York, 5 January 1930. Dorset Town Archive, Dorset, Vermont.

Driscoll, Edgar J., Jr. "Informality Enlivens N.H. Barn Players." *Boston Globe*, 19 July 1972.

"Dramatic Asides." *White Plains Reporter*, 25 May 1940.

Dulles, Foster Rhea. *A History of Recreation: America Learns to Play.* 2nd ed. New York: Appleton-Century-Crofts, 1965.

Endersby, Elric, Alexander Greenwood, and David Larkin. *Barn: The Art of a Working Building*. Boston: Houghton Mifflin, 1992.

"Equity Tightening Straw Hat Reins; Fewer Tryouts and Troupes Seen." *Variety*, 15 April 1936.

"Equity's Summer Theatre Policy Is Working." *Equity*, July 1936.

Eustis, Morton. "The Summer Theatres." *Theatre Arts Monthly*, June 1933.

Falk, Lee. "What's Wrong with Summer Stock or Three Wolves and a Copper Goose." *Equity*, April 1959.

Farnham, Burt. "It Takes All Kinds." *Boothbay (Maine) Register*, 2 August 1962.

Fichandler, Zelda. "Institution-as-Artwork." *Theatre Profiles 7*. New York: Theatre Communications Group, 1986.

Fields, Sidney. "Only Human." *New York Daily Mirror*, 3 July 1953.

Frick, John. "A Changing Theatre." In *The Cambridge History of American Theatre, Vol. II, 1870–1945*, edited by Don B. Wilmeth and Christopher Bigsby. New York: Cambridge University Press, 1999.

Gerard, Jeremy. "The Changing Face of Summer Theater." *New York Times*, 16 June 1985.

Glaspell, Susan. *The Road to the Temple*. New York: Frederick A. Stokes, 1927.

"Good News." Playbill. New London Barn Playhouse, 1987. New London Barn Playhouse archive. New London, New Hampshire.

Goodrich, Anne. *Enjoying the Summer Theatres of New England: A Guide*. Guilford, Connecticut: Pequot Press, 1954.

"Grant Made for History on Summer Theater." *New York Times*, 8 November 1969.

"Guber and Gross, 30 Years On . . ." *Variety*, 4 June 1986.

"Hadley Barn to Be Studio," *Peterboro Transcript*. Scrapbook 1, Peterborough Players archive. Peterborough Historical Society, Peterborough, New Hampshire.

Harding, Alfred. "Editorial—Regulation for the Summer Theatres." *Equity*, April 1935.

——. "Equity's Summer Theatre Policy Is Working." *Equity*, July 1936.

——. "More Light on the Summer Theatre." *Equity*, October 1934.

——. "Not Enough on Summer Theatre as Yet." *Equity*, November 1934.

——. "Summer Stock Contract and Conditions." *Equity*, April 1936.

——. "Summer Theatre: Boon or Bane?" *Equity*, September 1934.

——. "The Summer Theatre Has Grown Up." *Equity*, September 1941.

Harmon, Charlotte and Rosemary Taylor. *Broadway in a Barn*. New York: Thomas Crowell, 1957.

Harris, Harry. "Valley Forge Music Fair's Anni Marks the 30-Year Partnership of Guber and Gross in Showbiz." *Variety*, 24 July 1985.

Hart, Moss, and George S. Kaufman. *George Washington Slept Here*. New York: Random House, 1940.

Hartwig, Walter. Scrapbooks. Papers. Ogunquit Playhouse Archive. Ogunquit, Maine.

——. Clip File. Billy Rose Theatre Collection. New York Public Library for the Performing Arts at Lincoln Center.

Henderson, Mary. *Theater in America, 200 Years of Plays, Players, and Productions.* New York: Harry N. Abrams, 1986.

Hewitt, Alan. "Why Be an Actor? A Survey of Employment in the Theatre." *Equity,* September 1949.

Hewitt, Barnard. *Theatre U.S.A. 1665–1957.* New York: McGraw-Hill, 1959.

Highley, Richard. "Stars in Your Aisles." In *Blueprint for Summer Theatre 1953 Supplement,* edited by John Effrat. New York: John Richard Press, 1953, 45.

"History of the Barn . . ." Playbill. New London Barn Playhouse, August 1955. New London Barn Playhouse archives, New London, New Hampshire.

Hofstadter, Richard. *The Age of Reform: From Bryan to F.D.R.* New York: Alfred A. Knopf, 1956.

Houghton, Norris. *But Not Forgotten: The Adventure of the University Players.* New York: William Sloane, 1951.

"How to Build a Little Theater—First Find the Right Barn," *PM,* 23 June 1947. Clip file, Forestburgh Summer Theater. Billy Rose Theatre Collection. New York Public Library for the Performing Arts at Lincoln Center.

Hughes, Elinor. "The Summer Playhouses as Offshoots of Broadway." *Boston Herald,* 6 July 1941.

Huguenot Players of New Rochelle. Pamphlet. Walter Hartwig clip file. Billy Rose Theatre Collection. New York Public Library for the Performing Arts at Lincoln Center.

Huntington, John. "For Love and Money." In *Blueprint for Summer Theatre 1951 Supplement,* edited by Richard Beckhard and John Effrat. New York: John Richard Press, 1951.

Hutchens, John K. "Far from Broadway, Footlights Glow." *New York Times Magazine,* 3 July 1938.

Irving, Ben. "The Corn Is Greener." In *Blueprint for Summer Theatre 1950 Supplement,* edited by Richard Beckhard and John Effrat. New York: John Richard Press, 1950.

"John Kenley's Ohio Operation: Names, Low Scale, High B.O." *Variety,* 20 March 1974.

Jones, Margo. *Theatre-in-the-Round.* Westport, CT: Greenwood, 1951.

Jones, Paul G. "Equity U.S.A. Stock." In *Blueprint for Summer Theatre 1953 Supplement,* edited by John Effrat. New York: John Richard Press, 1953.

Kaufman, Susie. "Berkshire Playhouse Finding Aid History." Stockbridge Public Library, Stockbridge, Massachusetts.

Keating, John. "Summer Theatre: Terrell's Still Mining Gold in Old Musicals." *Cue,* 28 August 1954.

"Keith Volunteers for Summer Stock Check." *Equity,* May 1939.

Keith, Sherwood. Letter to patrons, fall 1951. Box #1. Boothbay Playhouse Archives. Boothbay Region Historical Society, Boothbay Harbor, Maine.

Kennedy, Harold J. *No Pickle, No Performance.* Garden City, NY: Doubleday, 1978.

Krawitz, Herman E. "Stock Theatres Can Be Successful." In *Blueprint for Summer Theatre 1953 Supplement*, edited by John Effrat. New York: John Richard Press, 1953.

"Lambertville Music Circus Started New Theater Trend." *Trenton Sunday Times-Advertiser*, 2 August 1959.

Lane, Harry J. "Where Are You Going to Spend the Summer?" *Equity*, May 1938.

Langley, Stephen. *Theatre Management and Production in America*. Rev. ed. New York: Theatre Arts, 1990.

Langner, Lawrence. *The Magic Curtain*. New York: E.P. Dutton, 1951.

Lawson, Evelyn. *Theater on Cape Cod*. Yarmouth Port, MA: Parnassus Imprints, 1969.

Lawson, Steve. "The Legacy of Nikos." *New York Times*, 29 January 1989.

Leavitt, Martha. "From College to Stage Career, VI—Francis G. Cleveland." *New York Herald Tribune*, 29 December 1935. Francis Grover Cleveland file. Harvard Theatre Collection, Cambridge, Massachusetts.

Leger, Norman. "There's More Than a Name to a Title . . . or How *Do* the Barn Players Select Their Shows???" *Mame* playbill, New London Barn Playhouse, 1986 summer season. New London Barn Playhouse archive, New London, New Hampshire.

Levy, Edwin Lewis. "Elitch's Gardens, Denver, Colorado: A History of the Oldest Summer Theatre in the United States 1890–1941." Ph.D. diss., Columbia University, 1960.

LoMonaco, Martha S. *Every Week, A Broadway Revue: The Tamiment Playhouse, 1921–1960*. Westport, CT: Greenwood, 1992.

MacAdam, George. "The Strolling Player Returns by Jitney." *New York Times Book Review and Magazine*, 8 July 1923.

Mackay, Constance D'Arcy. *The Little Theatre in the United States*. New York: Henry Holt, 1917.

"Major Improvement in Store for Sacramento's Music Circus," *Sacramento Stage and Theatre*. Website: http://www.sacnews.net/sacstage/major.html.

Mantle, Burns. "Summer Theatres to Revive Star System as an Experiment." *New York Daily News*, 11 June 1940.

Mariarden. Clip file. News clippings, brochures, business documents. Billy Rose Theatre Collection. New York Public Library for the Performing Arts at Lincoln Center.

Marx, Samuel. "By Samuel Marx, Story Editor, Columbia Pictures." *Variety*, 20 September 1939.

McNamara, Brooks. "Popular Entertainment." In *The Cambridge History of American Theatre, Vol. II, 1870–1945*, edited by Don B. Wilmeth and Christopher Bigsby. New York: Cambridge Univrsity Press, 1999.

Michaels, Julie. "Nikos—Williamstown's Guru" *(Pittsfield, Mass.) Berkshire Sampler*, 23 July 1978.

Miles, William. "Money in Summer, a Silo Circuit Veteran Tells how to Combine Art with Some Profit." *Boston Evening Transcript*, 3 June 1939.

——. "Summer Theater as a Business." *Christian Science Monitor*, 22 August 1957.

——. " 'Straw Hat'—How It Grew." *Christian Science Monitor*, 21 August 1957.

Mitchell, David. "Call Him 'Sinjun.' " *New York Herald Tribune*, 8 July 1953.

Monbleau, Marcia J. *The Cape Playhouse*. South Yarmouth, MA: Allen D. Bragdon Publishers, 1991.

Moore, Raymond. "The Cape Playhouse" prospectus. Spring 1927. Cape Playhouse Archives, Dennis, Massachusetts.

——. Letter to the patrons of the Cape Playhouse, 11 August 1928. Richard Myers Papers, Box 28, Cape Cod Playhouse file. Archives Division. State Historical Society of Wisconsin. Wisconsin Center for Film and Theatre Research, Madison, Wisconsin.

Moore, Thomas Gale. *The Economics of the American Theater*. Durham, NC: Duke University Press, 1968.

Morigi, Gilda. *The Difference Began at the Footlights: A Story of Bucks County Playhouse*. Stockton, NJ: Carolingian Press, 1973.

Murray, Warren E. "The History of the Dorset Players." Unpublished typescript. Dorset Town Archive, Dorset, Vermont.

Muschamp, Herbert. "Broadway's Real Hits Are Its Antique Theaters." *New York Times*, Arts and Leisure, 30 July 1995.

"Music Tents: It's an Old Tradition." *Life*, 11 August 1958.

"New Century Campaign Proposed Renovation." Information card, 2001. Westport Country Playhouse, Development Office. Westport, Connecticut.

"New London Barn Playhouse Sixtieth Anniversary Issue." Supplement to the *Argus-Champion* and *Eagle Times*, 9 June 1993. New London Barn Playhouse archive, New London, New Hampshire.

"New Look for Summer Stock." *Equity*, March 1948, 7–8.

"New Tops for Summer Co.'s." *Variety*, 1 July 1936.

Nichols, Lewis. "Broadway Moves Out along the Highway." *New York Times*, August 2 1936.

Niemi, Albert W., Jr. *U.S. Economic History/A Survey of the Major Issues*. Chicago: Rand McNally, 1975.

"1953 Summer Theatres." In *Blueprint for Summer Theatre 1953 Supplement*, edited by John Effrat. New York: John Richard Press, 1953.

Noble, Allen G., and Richard K. Cleek. *The Old Barn Book*. New Brunswick, NJ: Rutgers University Press, 1996.

Norton, Eliot. "Five U.S. Premieres Booked for Boothbay, Me., Playhouse." *Boston Record American*, 3 July 1968.

——. "New Theatre Showman's Dream." *Boston Sunday Post*, 4 July 1937.

——. "There Is Some Pleasure and Some Pain—Second Thoughts of a First-Nighter." *Boston Post*, 23 June 1940.

Oblak, John B. *Bringing Broadway to Maine: The History of Lakewood, Lakewood, Maine*. Terre-Haute, IN: Moore-Langen, 1971.

"Old Barn Is Now Theatre/New London Atmosphere Really Rural." *Manchester Union Leader*, 10 August 1948. Charles Jobes scrapbook. New London Barn Playhouse archives, New London, New Hampshire.

Ormsbee, Helen. "Guest Stars Are the Rage Again, 1939 Restoring an 1880 System." *New York Herald Tribune*, 2 July 1939.

"Pension Now Included in New Stock Contracts." *Equity*, June/July 1963.

Peterborough Players archive. Scrapbooks, letters, news clippings, business documents. Peterborough Historical Society. Peterborough, New Hampshire.

Pignatelli, Constance Wilcox. Typescript. Box 381, Charlotte L. Evarts Memorial Archives. Madison Town Hall, Madison, Connecticut.

"Playhouse Interest Group Formed," *Boothbay* (Maine) *Register*, 5 September 1974.

Poggi, Jack. *Theater in America: The Impact of Economic Forces 1870–1967*. Ithaca, NY: Cornell University Press, 1968.

Pomeroy, Earl. *In Search of the Golden West: The Tourist in Western America*. New York: Alfred A. Knopf, 1957.

Porterfield, Robert, and Robert Breen. "Toward a National Theatre." *Theatre Arts*, October 1945.

Powers, Martin C. "Prominent Artists See Poem Plays at Peterboro Playhouse." *Keene Sentinel*, 2 August 1933. Scrapbook 1, Peterborough Players archive. Peterborough Historical Society, Peterborough, New Hampshire.

Price, Helen F. "The Mountain Playhouse." *Johnstown* (Pa.) *Democrat*. Clip in 1939 scrapbook. Mountain Playhouse archive, Jennerstown, Pennsylvania.

Proceedings. National Conference on Outdoor Recreation. Washington, D.C.: Government Printing Office, 1924, 1926.

"Public Flocks to Tent Theater, Gold Mine for Young Producer." *Boston Sunday Herald*, 13 July 1952.

Putch, Bill. "30 Years over the Rainbow," 30th anniversary playbill. Totem Pole Playhouse Archive, theatre business office. Fayetteville, Pennsylvania.

Putch, John. *This Is My Father: A Documentary about William H. Putch*, 60 min. PutchFilms, 1998.

Ratcliffe, Thomas G., Jr. "Summer Theatre at the Crossroads." In *Blueprint for Summer Theatre 1954 Supplement*, edited by John Effrat. New York: John Richard Press, 1954.

Review of *Blueprint for Summer Theatre*. *Equity*, April 1948.

Rice, Vernon. "Summer Theatre '29 and '49." *Blueprint for Summer Theatre 1949 Supplement*, edited by Richard Beckhard and John Effrat. New York: John Richard Press, 1949.

Richards, David. "A Magic to Drive Out the Blahs." *Washington* (D.C.) *Star-News*, 19 August 1973.

"Robert Keith Resigns Summer Stock Job." *Equity*, July 1939.

Robertson, Nan. "Actors Hone Their Craft on Williamstown Stage." *New York Times*, 30 June 1985.

Robinson, Wayne. "Music Circus Gets Wheels; Motorized Show to Go South." *(Philadelphia) Sunday Bulletin*, 24 August 1952.

Roser, Louisette. "Apprenticitis." In *Blueprint For Summer Theatre 1952 Supplement*, edited by John Effrat. New York: John Richard Press, 1952.

Ross, Lillian. "Every Little Touch Helps," Onward and Upward with the Arts. *New Yorker*, 20 August 1949.

Ryan, Donald D. "Tent Show Earns Big-Business Tag: An Idea as Old as the Acropolis." *Christian Science Monitor*, 17 November 1958.

Sarlós, Robert Karoly. *Jig Cook and the Provincetown Players: Theatre in Ferment*. Amherst: University of Massachusetts Press, 1982.

Schmitt, Peter J. *Back to Nature: The Arcadian Myth in Urban America*. New York: Oxford University Press, 1969.

Seavor, Jim. "That's Entertainment in Matunuck" (Providence, RI) *Sunday Journal Magazine*, 5 June 1983.

"Shutters on Playhouse Mean 'End of Summer,' Walter Hartwig Closes a Highly Successful Season with a Prophecy for an Even Better One in 1940. Growth of Ogunquit Playhouse Is Spectacular." *Wells-Ogunquit Compass*, 8 September 1939. Clipping, Ogunquit Playhouse archive, Ogunquit, Maine.

Slane, Steve. "Why a Music Tent?" *Blueprint for Summer Theatre 1954 Supplement*, edited by John Effrat. New York: John Richard Press, 1954.

Sloane, Eric. *An Age of Barns*. New York: Dodd, Mead, 1985.

Smith, Constance. "New England: The Jitney Players." *Theatre Arts Monthly*, August 1929.

"Special Notification to All Equity Members, Equity Agents, Stock Managers Containing Equity Rules, Regulations, Contracts Covering Summer Stock Employment." *Equity*, June 1938.

Speyer, Andre L. "Williamstown Theatre: A Casual Remark Started It All 25 Years Ago" *(Williamstown, Mass.) Transcript*, 18 November 1978.

St. John, Christopher, editor. *Ellen Terry and Bernard Shaw, A Correspondence*. New York: G. P. Putnam's Sons, 1932.

"Star System ??? A Good Force or a Bad Force in Summer Theatre ??? Commentaries by Stars, Directors, Producers, Actors." In *Blueprint for Summer Theatre 1951 Supplement*, edited by Richard Beckhard and John Effrat. New York: John Richard Press, 1951.

Stein, Jeanne. "Edward Everett Horton." *Focus on Film #1*, 1970. Clip file, Edward Everett Horton. Billy Rose Theatre Collection, New York Public Library for the Performing Arts at Lincoln Center.

Stickney, Dorothy. *Openings and Closings*. Garden City, NY: Doubleday, 1979.

"Summer Resorts." *Architectural Forum*, March 1948.

"Summer Stock's Icumen In, Don't Be a Cuckoo!" *Equity*, June 1951.

Summer Stock. Film directed by Charles Walters, with Judy Garland and Gene Kelly. Metro-Goldwyn-Mayer, 1950.

"Summer Theatre Inspection." *Equity*, June 1938.

Taubman, Howard. *The Making of the American Theatre*. Rev. ed. New York: Coward-McCann, 1967.

Taylor, Robert Lewis. "The Level Head-1." *New Yorker*, 30 July 1955.

———. "The Level Head-2." *New Yorker*, 6 August 1955.

Terrell, St. John. Papers, 1949–64. Correspondence, press releases, business documents. Archives Division. State Historical Society of Wisconsin. Wisconsin Center for Film and Theater Research, Madison, Wisconsin.

Terry, Walter. "Music Circus and Mime Theatre." *New York Herald Tribune*, 30 August 1953.

Thomas, Robert McG., Jr. "St. John Terrell, 81, a Re-Enactor of History." *New York Times*, 20 October 1998.

Titherington, Greg. "If You (Re)Build It, They Will Come." *Cast & Crew*, no. 41 (April 1998).

"Totem Pole Playhouse Story." 1960 playbill. Totem Pole Playhouse Archive, theatre business office. Fayetteville, Pennsylvania.

Trauch, Lester. "Appendix 2: Memories of the Early Bucks County Playhouse." In *The Genius Belt: The Story of the Arts in Bucks County, Pennsylvania*. edited by George S. Bush. Doylestown, PA: James A. Michener Art Museum, 1996.

"Two-for-Oneing 'Henry.' " *Variety*, 20 September 1938.

Visser, Thomas. *Field Guide to New England Barns and Farm Buildings*. Hanover, NH: University Press of New England, 1997.

Vorse, Mary Heaton. *Time and the Town: A Provincetown Chronicle*. New York: Dial Press, 1942.

W. G. K. "*Loose Moments*, A Summer Try-Out Comes to the Vanderbilt." *New York Sun*, 5 February 1935.

Waldorf, Wilella. "Two on the Aisle, Summer Stock Managers Going Ahead after First Convention." *New York Post*, 18 April 1942.

Walker, Danton. "Broadway." *New York Daily News*, 31 May 1958.

Walker, Donald J. "Local Barn Makes Good or a True Historie of the Coming of the Thespians." Unpublished typescript. Humanities and Social Sciences Division. Library of Congress, Washington, D.C.

Whipple, Sidney B. "Summer Theater." *New York World-Telegram*, 21 August 1940.

Whitney, D. Quincy. "An Actor's 7 Decades on the Stage." New Hampshire Weekly Arts and People, *Boston Sunday Globe*, 30 May 1993.

Wilkin, Robert A. "Peterborough Hops to Curtain Call." *Christian Science Monitor*, 3 September 1958. Peterborough Players file. Harvard Theatre Collection, Cambridge, Massachusetts.

Wilmeth, Don B. and Christopher Bigsby, eds. *The Cambridge History of American Theatre*, 3 vols. New York: Cambridge University Press, 1998–2000.

Wilmeth, Don B. and Tice L. Miller, eds. *Cambridge Guide to American Theatre.* New York: Cambridge University Press, 1993.

Wilson, Craig. "Barnstormers Taking Bows for 62 Years." *USA Today,* 13 August 1992.

Wise, Harold L. "Over the Hill to the Playhouse." In *Blueprint for Summer Theatre 1950 Supplement,* edited by Richard Beckhard and John Effrat. New York: John Richard Press, 1950.

Witham, Barry B., ed. *Theatre in the United States: A Documentary History, Volume I: 1750–1915.* New York: Cambridge, 1996.

Wright, Franklin. "Thoughts and Things." *Portland* (Maine) *Evening Express,* September 1965.

Yeske, Curt. "Showman Terrell dies at 81." *Times of Trenton* (N.J.), 20 October 1998.

Ziegler, J. Wesley. "A Short History of the Peterborough Players." 1963 playbill. Peterborough Players file. Harvard Theatre Collection, Cambridge, Massachusetts.

Interviews Conducted by the Author

Although I have not quoted directly from all of these interviews in the book, all of these people helped me better understand the history and artistry of American summer stock theatre.

Adams, Margaret. 27 July 1993.
Aupperlee, Wm. John. 10 August 1994.
Austin, Ray. 5 August 1994.
Babcock, Richard. 10 July 1995.
Beckhard, Richard. 17 March 1993.
Bell, Megan. 6 May 2003.
Brent, Tommy. 16 June 1994.
Brooks, Bob and Willi Burke. 15 May 1996.
Bruskin, Perry. 18 June 1986.
Capinera, Elizabeth. 6 May 2003.
Carmichael, Pat and Fred. 10 August 1994.
Cleveland, Francis Grover. 13 August 1993.
Cocuzza, Ginnine. 28 June 1995.
Conrys, Kathleen. 31 July 1995.
Cox, Rosanna. 28 January 2003.
Craig, Colin. 26 August 1993.
Davis, Carleton. 27 July 1993.
Dinerstein, Ellen M. 26 August 1993.
Dunlap, Richard. 9 August 1994.
Duttweiler, Norman. 31 July 1995.
Ericson, Richard, Laura Harris, and Renny Serre. 13 July 1994.
Farrell, Kristy. 6 May 2003.
Fields, Michele. 6 May 2003.
Gipson, Joan. 10 July 1993.
Grant, Adrienne Wilson. 2 April 2002, 18 July 2002, and 10 April 2003.
Harris, Alison and Anne Keefe. 13 December 2002.
Hart, Bunny (Frederica D.). 10 August 1993.
Hayter, Pearl. 24 August 1994.

Holmes, Paul Mills. 27 July 2001.
Hubert, Marcie. 25 August 1994.
James, David. 16 December 1992.
Jones, Susan. 18 July 2002.
Kenley, John. 26 August 1992.
Kimbell, Jon. 16 December 1992.
Krawitz, Herman E. 21 July 1993.
Kuchenbecker, Sharon. 16 December 1992.
Labelle, Joan. 13 July 1994.
Lane, John. 10 August 1993.
Langley, Stephen. 11 May 1993.
Leger, Norman. 25 August 1993.
Lenthall, Franklyn and James Wilmot. 11 August 1993.
Lloyd, Sam and Barbara. 4 August 1994.
Lutz, Edward O. 4 May 1993.
Marafino, Teresa Stoughton. 10 July 1993.
Maust, James. 10 July 1993.
McPherson, Fillmore. 25 August 1994.
McKenzie, James B. 21 September 1992.
McMurtray, Sue. 27 July 2001.
Morgan, Henry. 29 January 1993.
Nassivera, John. 11 August 1994.
Partington, Rex. 23 August 1994.
Paterson, William. 25 November 1994.
Polese, James K. 16 December 1992.
Pond, Helen and Herbert Senn. 27 July 1993.
Porterfield, Mary Dudley. 24 August 1994.
Quirin, Peg and Ed. 14 July 1994.
Rose, Richard. 24 August 1994.
Ross, William. 23 October 1992.
Rubin, Jason. 26 July 2001.
Schurr, Carl and Wil Love. 26 July 2001.
Shepard, Joan and Evan Thompson. 19 February 1993.
Steele, Elizabeth. 13 August 1993.
Stettler, Steve. 5 August 1994.
Swann, William. 10 August 1994.
Wethers, Lulu Brown. 26 August 1993.
Wilson, Jim. 14 July 1994.
Woodward, Joanne. 8 January 2001.

Index